THE VOTE
WOMEN'S
FIERCE FIGHT

Cover Image: Rose Bower, a suffragist and musician from the Black Hills of South Dakota, played the trumpet and cornet and whistled, invaluable skills for announcing open-air meetings and raising money.

Credit: "Miss Rose Bower of North Dakota [sic]"; Photograph; PR068 Subject File; Box 10; New York Heritage Digital Collection, 49695, New York Historical Society

Cover Design and formatting: www.goodlifeguide.com/publishing

PGM Press

Englewood, NJ 07631

To the past and present fierce fighters for justice and equality,
and to the next generation, including my cherished
grandchildren: Sophie, Natalie, Will, Francesca, Fergus, Zinn,
Quinn, Balan, Gray, Archer, and Granger.

Epigraph

"It was a continuous, seemingly endless chain of activity. Young suffragists who helped forge the last links of that chain had not been born when it began. Old suffragists who forged the first link were dead when it ended."[1]

—Carrie Chapman Catt
President, National American Woman Suffrage
Association

"Unless women are prepared to fight politically they must be content to be ignored politically."[2]

—Alice Paul
Chair, National Woman's Party

"If we do not use the franchise we shall give our enemies a stick with which to break our heads, and we shall not be able to live down the reproach of our indifference for one hundred years."[3]

—Mary Church Terrell
First President of the National Association of Colored
Women

CONTENTS

AUTHOR'S NOTE

PART I: 1648–1900 1

Chapter 1 Unsettle the Status Quo: 1648–1865 1
Chapter 2 Confront Great Odds: 1866–1877 17
Chapter 3 Gain Momentum: 1878–1900 33

PART II: 1900–1910 52

Chapter 4 Persevere: 1900–1906 52
Chapter 5 Stir Things Up: 1907–1909 67
Chapter 6 Radical Changes: 1909–1910 78

PART III: 1911–1913 94

Chapter 7 A Whirlwind: 1911 94
Chapter 8 Right is Might: 1912 106
Chapter 9 Breakthrough: 1913 123

PART IV: 1914–1916 144

Chapter 10 Hard-Fought Campaigns: 1914....................144
Chapter 11 Undauntable Suffragists: 1915 159
Chapter 12 Battle Cry: 1916..181

PART V: 1917 .... **202**

    Chapter 13 Silent Sentinels: January–April 1917 202
    Chapter 14 Tireless Struggles: January–April 1917 216
    Chapter 15 Arrests!: Spring–September 1917....................226
    Chapter 16 Night of Terror: September–December 1917......245

PART VI: 1918–1919 .... **267**

    Chapter 17 Fiery Tactic: January–October 1918 267
    Chapter 18 Assault on Congress: October–December 1918....279
    Chapter 19 Escalation: January–March 1919 289
    Chapter 20 On the Brink: March–June 1919 303

PART VII: 1919–1920 .... **310**

    Chapter 21 Up to the States: June–December 1919.........310
    Chapter 22 Unite Again: January–July 1920....................322
    Chapter 23 Justice Bell: August–September 1920 333

Epilogue...344
Acknowledgments 355
Select Bibliography...357
Notes 364
Index..402

Author's Note

Women's fierce fight for the right to vote is one of the great dramatic stories in American history. Yet, it has been a forgotten story. There is no national holiday commemorating even one of its many leaders: Susan B. Anthony, Elizabeth Cady Stanton, Lucy Stone, Sojourner Truth, Abigail Scott Duniway, Anna Howard Shaw, Carrie Chapman Catt, Mary Church Terrell, Lucy Burns, and Alice Paul. There have been no bestselling books by popular authors of American history or epic movies depicting the struggle replete with vivid personalities, political intrigues and betrayals, pageantry and parades, pickets and protests. There is no widespread knowledge among Americans that women were denied the vote until 1920. No general awareness that throughout the fight, women were ridiculed and harassed. No wholesale outrage that on the evening and into the night of November 14-15, 1917, now known as the "Night of Terror," more than 30 women who had been arrested and imprisoned for picketing the White House were beaten by prison guards. No honoring of the women who protested their imprisonment by going on hunger strikes and were brutally force-fed. Little recognition that, in the end, the victory was won by two votes, one cast by a legislator who decided to do what his mother told him to do.

Why is the woman suffrage movement, the unyielding fight for the right to vote, an unheralded story in American history? It is not because of a lack of information. In fact, there is a massive amount of material in archives throughout the United States and online. Perhaps the story of the long fight for woman suffrage is minimized, even ignored, in America's historical narrative because it undermines the popular myth that American democracy was perfect from its beginnings. It refutes the rhetoric that historic women were concerned only about domestic matters. It reveals the powerful resistance against women's entry into American politics. It topples the tenet that men are the most important and interesting historic figures. It debunks the belief that women were satisfied with the status quo.

I trace my interest in this stirring story back to my mother, Maritza Leskovar Morgan. She was born in 1920, two years after the birth of Czechoslovakia (now the Czech Republic) as a democratic republic in 1918. As a child, I knew that her heroes were Tomáš Masaryk and Edvard Beneš, revolutionary leaders who became the first and second presidents of Czechoslovakia.

My mother was Czech through her father's ancestry. Although her father and stepmother immigrated to New York City, she spent much of her childhood with relatives in Czechoslovakia, in Koryčany, a small village, and graduated from a high school in Brno, a nearby city. She left Czechoslovakia in 1938 shortly before Adolf Hitler's forces occupied the Sudetenland region of her country. A serious student of history, my mother was aware of the role that the vote had played in Hitler's rise to power. In the 1932 presidential election in Germany, Adolf Hitler ran against Paul von Hindenburg, the current president. Hindenburg won, but Hitler's strong showing (more than 13 million votes, or 36%) resulted in Hindenburg appointing him the Chancellor of Germany. Upon Hindenburg's death in 1934, a referendum, or direct vote by the electorate, was held to merge the post of president and chancellor. It was overwhelming approved. Hitler had complete control of the country.

That experience taught my mother a political truth that she passed on to me—voting matters. Generations of brave and determined American women believed that too. That is why they tenaciously engaged in the fight for the right to vote, which culminated when the Nineteenth Amendment was added to the United States Constitution in 1920—144 years after the Declaration of Independence and 131 years after the Constitution was adopted and after twenty-six other countries had granted woman suffrage.

"It was a continuous, seemingly endless chain of activity. Young suffragists who helped forge the last links of that chain had not been born when it began. Old suffragists who forged the first link were dead when it ended," noted Carrie Chapman Catt, a leader of the final fight for victory.[1]

The Vote: Women's Fierce Fight is a chronological, multipronged narrative of the American woman suffrage movement that interweaves multiple themes: the reordering of women's roles and rights; suffragists' resilience, persistence, inventiveness, conflicts, strategies, and tactics; opponents' duplicity, trickery, betrayal, and brutality; international connections, race, immigration, and class. It is a huge story with a long timeline in which I interrelate the state and federal campaigns, and the campaigns of the two national organizations: the National American Woman Suffrage Association and the National Woman's Party. There are numerous locations, unique characters, and spectacular events with contemporary resonance for key issues, such as voter suppression, women's activism, and gender equality.

My research for *The Vote: Women's Fierce Fight* has taken place over many years as I traveled to libraries, historic places, and archives to study petitions, resolutions, reports, letters, telegrams, newspaper and magazine articles, songs, poems, cartoons, photographs, diaries, first-hand accounts, artifacts, and scholarly books and articles. At what is now the Belmont-Paul Women's Equality National Monument, I surveyed suffrage banners, flags, and exhibits. Kenneth Florey and Coline Jenkins, the great-great granddaughter of Elizabeth Cady Stanton, showed me their large collections of suffrage memorabilia.

Over the past thirty years, I have taken road trips to learn from and photograph historic sites and landmarks. In 1993, I went to Seneca Falls, New York, for the dedication of the Women's Rights National Historical Park, where, attached to the side of Wesleyan Chapel, there is a plaque honoring the resolution proposed by Elizabeth Cady Stanton, seconded by Frederick Douglass, and passed by participants in the 1848 Women's Rights Convention: "That it is the duty of the women of this country to secure to themselves their sacred right to the elective franchise."[2]

Haunted by the harsh treatment meted out to suffrage pickets who were incarcerated in Occoquan Workhouse, near Lorton, Virginia, I went to see the buildings that remained. Standing in that desolate place, I read the historic marker dedicated in 1982: "Their courage and dedication . . . aroused the nation to hasten passage and ratification of the 19th Amendment in 1920." In Rochester, New York, I found the bronze statue, depicting Susan B. Anthony and Frederick Douglass having tea together, located near the Susan B. Anthony Museum and House. A bronze sculpture of a locked ballot box marks the location of the polling place where Susan B. Anthony voted in 1872, an act for which she was arrested. In Canandaigua, New York, a bust of Anthony is located outside of the courtroom where she was tried and found guilty for voting as a woman.

In Lafayette, Oregon, I photographed the illustrated historic marker to Abigail Scott Duniway, known as the "Mother of Suffrage in the Northwest." In Denver, Colorado, my quest led me to Fairmount Cemetery to visit the grave of J. Warner Mills, a lawyer and member of the Colorado Legislature. His epitaph starts with "Champion of the Minority," followed by a list of his accomplishments, including: "Author of Equal Suffrage Bill Granting Colorado Women Right to Vote in 1893." A road trip in southeastern Pennsylvania included Valley Forge and the National Patriots Bell Tower to see the iconic suffrage symbol— the "Justice Bell." Commissioned by suffragist Katherine Wentworth Ruschenberger, the Justice Bell is a one-ton replica of the Liberty Bell, but without the crack and with the words "establish justice" added to the inscription. During the suffrage battle, the bronze clapper was chained to prevent the bell from ringing until victory.

My passion to learn more and more about women's fight for the vote led to illuminating experiences. In 1995, I went to Washington, D.C. to celebrate the seventy-fifth anniversary of the Nineteenth Amendment where I noted that the largest group of co-celebrants was Delta Sigma Theta, an African American sorority. The founding members, college students at Howard University, had marched in the grand suffrage parade in Washington, D.C. on March 3, 1913, the day before the inauguration of Woodrow Wilson. In 2013, my nine-year-old granddaughter Sophie and I marched in the centennial parade celebrating that historic march.

In conjunction with a television special about my photography of women's graves, *Honoring American Heroines* the magnificent Belmont [illegible] in Woodlawn Cemetery in [illegible] a Belmont's [illegible] Belmont had mightily [illegible] a prominent [illegible], in the fight for the [illegible] to newspaper accounts [illegible] er elaborate funeral, [illegible] along with a purple, white, and gold banner of the National Woman's Party. I stood by as one of the heavy doors was unlocked and strenuously shoved until it opened. And there it was, attached to a long pole at the head of Alva Belmont's marble catafalque---a large faded and frayed purple, white, and gold banner!

My intent is to present an expansive story of women's fierce fight for the vote. To underscore the fact that women's fight for the vote was a national news story, I have included headlines and quotes from newspapers across America. As a measure of the magnitude of the struggle and suffragists' persistence, I presented accounts of state woman suffrage amendment referenda campaigns. Aspects of the British suffrage movement and its influence on the American movement are highlighted. To honor the women who fought the fight, I named many women who are not well known. I covered the crucial campaign for ratification that followed Congress's passage of the Nineteenth Amendment.

This arduous and costly fifteen-month ordeal is typically left out of the telling of the woman suffrage story, or told only through the final nail-biting campaign in Tennessee.

I wrote this book during a tumultuous time in America—the 2016 presidential campaign and election and the following two years. It was unnerving to juxtapose the pervasive resistance to enfranchising women with the blatant misogyny that surfaced during this time. In the end, however, the women I wrote about sustained me and provided a model for persistence. And they still do. I think of Alice Paul, Rose Winslow, Dora Lewis, and others who endured jail and force-feeding, steadfastly pioneering nonviolent civil protest. I learn from suffrage lobbyists, including Maud Wood Park and Maud Younger who adroitly dealt with political trickery and hostile politicians. I am inspired by Sojourner Truth and Ida B. Wells-Barnett (now commonly known as Ida B. Wells), African American suffragists who defied racism. I remember Carrie Chapman Catt's comment after conducting a grueling campaign that ended in one more painful defeat, the 1915 defeat of a woman suffrage referendum in New York. At campaign headquarters in New York City, when it was clear that male voters had refused to enfranchise women, Anna Howard Shaw, then president of the National American Woman Suffrage Association, asked Carrie Chapman Catt, then head of the Empire State Campaign Committee:

> How long will it delay your fight, Carrie?

> Only until we can get a little sleep. Our campaign will be on again tomorrow morning—and forever until we get the vote, Catt replied.[3]

PART I

Chapter 1

Unsettle the Status Quo: 1648-1865

Vote . . . and Voyce. —Mistress Margaret Brent

Women's fight for the vote in America is typically said to have lasted seventy-two years, a figure that is arrived at by subtracting two dates —1848 from 1920. The first date, 1848, is when the first women's rights convention met in Seneca Falls, New York, and Elizabeth Cady Stanton, the sharp-minded, upbeat, thirty-two-year-old mother who had spearheaded the convention, moved this resolution: "That it is the duty of the women of this country to secure to themselves their sacred right to the elective franchise."[1] The latter date is when the Nineteenth Amendment was ratified and added to the United States Constitution: "The right of citizens of the United States to vote shall not be denied or abridged by the United States or by any State on account of sex."[2] That seventy-two year period, however, is just a slice of the story.

The whole story begins two hundred years earlier on a bluff overlooking the St. Mary's River. There, a group of English setters, who had arrived in 1634 on board two ships, the *Ark* and the *Dove,* had purchased land from the Yaocomico Indians and founded St. Mary's City, the first capital of the Maryland colony. Today St. Mary's City is an outdoor living history museum known as Historic St. Mary's City. On the grounds, are a reconstructed State House of 1676; a working colonial farm; a Woodland Indian Hamlet; a replica of a square-rigged ship; and a

1

gazebo surrounded by a garden, a landmark to the beginnings of women's fight for the vote.

Large black letters on the gazebo inform visitors that they are at the Margaret Brent Garden. I have twice visited that landmark honoring Margaret Brent, the first woman known to have demanded the vote, a touchstone fact for suffragists. It is an elegant structure with a spectacular view of the St. Mary's River that is so wide at this point it looks like a large lake. In the gazebo is a square brick pedestal, measuring about four feet by four feet, with two side-by-side bronze tablets inscribed with information about Margaret Brent.

On top of the pedestal sits a bronze bas-relief depicting a meeting room of the legislative assembly, the ruling body of the colony. Nine assemblymen are shown, some seated, others standing at a table covered with a cloth. In the center is a statue of Margaret Brent, standing with her back to the table, her billowing sleeves and the hem of her floor-length dress swirling back as if she is in motion, confidently striding toward the men. One of whom, the new Governor Thomas Green, is posed as if he was going to rise and greet her. As well he should have, because Margaret Brent, who was about thirty-seven years old when she arrived in St. Mary's City with her brothers Giles and Fulke and sister Mary, was a formidable woman, a prominent landowner who quite successfully managed her own financial and legal affairs, including going to court to settle disputes and collect monies owed her. The caption under the bas-relief reads: "In 1648 Margaret Brent Asks for Vote . . . and Voyce."

Margaret Brent's historic demand inscribed on the bas-relief in the Margaret Brent Garden Gazebo in Historic St. Mary's City, Maryland. (Penny Colman Collection)

The story behind the scene goes like this: Cecil Calvert, Lord Baltimore and proprietor of the colony, had appointed his brother Leonard as the governor and as his attorney to represent him there. Shortly before his death in 1647, Leonard Calvert had named Margaret Brent the executor of his estate and instructed her to "take all and pay all."[3] Upon his death, the Provincial Court also appointed Margaret Brent as Lord Baltimore's attorney in colonial affairs.

We do not know the reasons for these unprecedented decisions—appointing a woman as an executor of a governor's estate and as attorney for the proprietor of the colony—but surely Margaret Brent's reputation as a successful businesswoman was a factor, as well as her successful courtroom experience and reputation for diplomacy. All of which were needed; the colony was in crisis. A raid by a ship captain and his crew had destabilized colonial life. Buildings were damaged. Some settlers had fled to nearby Virginia. Food was in short supply. The soldiers Calvert had hired to restore order had not been paid; destitute, angry, and hungry, they were threatening mutiny.

Understandably, given the dire situation and empowered by the authority vested in her, Margaret Brent wanted a vote and voice in the official decision-making body of the colony. On January 21, 1648, she appeared before the assembly and demanded not just one vote but two—one for herself and one as Lord Baltimore's attorney, "hoping that with her influence," speculates historian Bernard Bailyn, "the Assembly would vote the soldiers' pay." But Margaret Brent's daring demand was summarily denied by Governor Thomas Green. There were, writes Bailyn, "impassible limits . . . to women's public roles."[4]

Margaret Brent "protested against all the proceedings." Then she set about to faithfully execute her responsibilities, including paying the soldiers by selling some of Lord Baltimore's cattle, an act that pacified the soldiers but infuriated Lord Baltimore. Attempting to set him straight, the assemblymen wrote to Lord Baltimore informing him that Margaret Brent had saved his colony: "As for Mistress Brent's undertaking and meddling with your Lordship's estate here . . . she rather deserved favour and thanks from your Honour" rather than "all those bitter invectives you have been pleased to Express against her."[5]

Lord Baltimore never did calm down; eventually, Margaret Brent relocated to Virginia and lived on her plantation named "Peace" until her death in about 1671.

Margaret Brent could audaciously live the life she did because she never married; thus she had the legal status under coverture of a *feme sole,* meaning that she retained her individual rights to manage her own affairs. As a married woman, she would have become a *feme covert* and been subsumed into her husband's legal identity and lost control of her property, earnings, children, even her own body. She could not have entered into contracts or sued or been sued. Coverture was part of the legal system known as English Common Law that the colonists brought with them from England along with a patriarchal system of organizing society that privileged men over women.

The roots of the patriarchal system are ancient and embedded with traditional beliefs and practices that are germane to the story of women's fight for the vote. "That politics was considered a male domain, that women were not political beings is an understanding as old as Western civilization," write historians Linda K. Kerber and Jane Sherron De Hart.[6] Viewed as inferior to men, women were expected to be deferential, chaste, pious, and unquestioning. Key men during the 1700s subscribed to this worldview.

During a stint as envoy to France, Thomas Jefferson, the main author of the Declaration of Independence, was appalled to meet French women who engaged in serious discussion with men and met with politicians, a phenomenon he decried as a "desperate state." American women, he wrote (undoubtedly with a sigh of relief) who "have the good sense to value domestic happiness above all other . . . . have been too wise to wrinkle their foreheads with politics. They are contented to soothe and calm the minds of their husbands returning from political debate."[7] When he was third President of the United States, Jefferson wrote to Albert Gallatin, the Secretary of the Treasury: "The appointment of a woman to office is an innovation for which the public is not prepared, nor I."[8]

When John Adams was a delegate to the Continental Congress, his wife Abigail wrote him a now famous letter, dated March 31, 1776: "In the new Code of Laws which I suppose will be necessary for you to make I desire you would Remember the Ladies, and be more generous and favourable to them than your ancestors." To which John Adams replied, "As to your extraordinary Code of Laws, I cannot but laugh . . . depend upon it. We know better than to repeal our Masculine systems." Abigail Adams pointedly responded, "I can not say that I think you very generous to the Ladies, for whilst you are proclaiming peace and good will to men, Emancipating all Nations, you insist upon retaining an absolute power over Wives."[9]

Shortly after his exchange with Abigail, John received a letter from James Sullivan, a member of the provincial congress of Massachusetts, regarding altering voter qualifications, a pertinent issue because severing ties with Great Britain meant each colony had to write a state constitution. A hodgepodge of restrictions existed throughout the thirteen colonies. All voters had to own property or pay taxes, a status commonly believed to denote independent-mindedness. But the amount of property or taxes varied. Religious restrictions limited voting: Catholics were barred from the vote in some colonies; Jews in some; Baptists in others. Residence and age requirements varied. Here and there, the names of property-owning, tax-paying single women and widows appeared on lists of voters. In Uxbridge, Massachusetts, after the sudden death of her very wealthy husband, Lydia Taft was allowed to vote in 1756, and again in 1758 and 1765.

In his reply to James Sullivan about altering voting qualifications, John Adams ruled out non-property-owning men as voters, because they were "dependent on others" and therefore would be influenced by the people on whom they depended. As for women, Adams wrote, "their Delicacy renders them unfit for Practice and Experience, in the great Business of Life, and the hardy Enterprizes of War, as well as the arduous Cares of State. Besides, their attention is So much engaged with the necessary Nurture of their Children, that Nature has made them fittest for domestic Cares." He vehemently warned Sullivan: "Depend upon it, sir, it is dangerous to open So fruitfull a Source of Controversy and Altercation, as would be opened by attempting to alter the Qualifications of Voters. There will be no End of it. New Claims will arise. Women will demand a Vote."[10]

As the first vice president and second president of the United States, John Adams was a highly influential and powerful man. There is no reason to assume that he changed or even modified the warning about women and the vote he gave Sullivan. As for the now-familiar repartee between Abigail and John, it has been typically interpreted as lighthearted banter. But I wonder: Abigail Adams, a serious-minded woman who managed their children and farm while John was frequently away, clearly expressed displeasure with John's response in a letter to her friend Mercy Otis Warren, a political playwright and poet who would later write a three-volume history of the American Revolution: "He is very saucy to me in return for a List of Female Grievances which I transmitted to him. I requested that our Legislators would consider our case . . . In return he tells me he cannot but Laugh at my extraordinary Code of Law."[11]

After the Revolutionary War, twelve of the thirteen new state constitutions limited voting rights to propertied men only. The exception was New Jersey, where under its new state constitution approved in 1776, "all inhabitants of this Colony, of full age, who are worth fifty pounds" were enfranchised, a dramatic change from New Jersey's colonial charter that limited the vote to "male freeholders."[12]

As many as 10,000 "widowed or unmarried women, some black men, and at least one black woman" voted in local elections in New Jersey.[13] With the emergence of political parties in 1790,

6

women voters were courted by politicians. "How respectfully attentive each young Federalist and Republican has been to the fair elector!" wrote one observer. "How ready to offer them his horses, his carriages, to drag them in triumph to the election ground!"[13] After an election, however, losing candidates frequently scapegoated women.

In 1807, possibly feeling threatened by needing to woo increasing numbers of women voters and after a hotly contested election, the New Jersey Legislature passed a bill restricting the vote to "free white male citizens," without any property requirement. John Condict who had almost lost an election, perhaps because of women voters, introduced the bill under the guise of election reform. The change was "highly necessary," read the New Jersey statute, "to the safety, quiet, good order and dignity of the state."[14]

This pattern of enfranchising and disenfranchising women was repeated across America throughout women's fight for the vote. In 1838, Kentucky, the first state legislature to grant partial-suffrage to women, gave widows who paid taxes and had school-age children the right to vote in school board elections. That right was repealed in 1902 and restored in 1912. In the Territory of Washington, women won and lost the right to vote twice: In 1883, the legislature approved a woman suffrage bill; in 1887, the Territory Supreme Court ruled that the bill was unconstitutional; in 1888 the legislature passed another woman suffrage bill in January only to have it declared unconstitutional in August. The right to vote on certain matters at school meetings was granted to women in rural New Jersey in 1887. The types of matters were whittled down in 1895, "leaving a fraction of New Jersey women with a fraction of suffrage," writes historian Delight Dodyk.[15]

From May to September 1787, fifty-five white men, meeting secretly in Philadelphia, Pennsylvania, wrote the framework for governing the new nation: the United States Constitution. Today, the iconic first three words of the preamble, "We the People . . ." are emblazoned in huge shiny letters on the front of the National Constitution Center in Philadelphia.[16] Many visitors undoubtedly read the "We" as inclusive of women. At the time, notes historian Jean H. Baker, "The authors of the Constitution never envisioned any explicit consideration of women."[17] The old English law of coverture under which a wife's legal status was subsumed by her husband's was "left virtually intact," writes historian Linda Kerber.[18] Determining voter qualifications was left to individual states.

The Constitution was ratified in 1789; two years later, ten amendments, known as the Bill of Rights, were added. The First Amendment protects certain rights, including the "right of the people . . . to petition the Government for a redress of grievances," a right imported from England that dates back centuries.[19] That right to petition was exercised repeatedly throughout women's fight for the vote. Countless petitions were signed by legions of advocates, only to be ignored by legislators.

In the 1790s, groundbreaking writers asserted bold ideas about women's nature, ability, rights, and roles. The essayist, poet, and playwright Judith Sargent Murray, who avidly read books from history to theology in her family's library, boldly proclaimed the idea of female equality: "The idea of the incapability of women, is . . . totally inadmissible."[20] The English philosopher and writer Mary Wollstonecraft passionately advocated educating women, writing: "I wish to persuade women to endeavor to acquire strength, both of mind and body."[21] Her classic book, *A Vindication of the Rights of Woman,* was widely read in America.

Other "strong-minded" women challenged the status quo. On July 4, 1828, Frances "Fanny" Wright, a tall, elegant, articulate Scottish immigrant, gave the first public speech on political subjects by a woman in America to a promiscuous audience (both women and men). In a voice described as "rich and thrilling," she denounced slavery, the church, greed, and restrictions on women.[22] Heralded as "a person of extraordinary powers of mind," Fanny Wright advocated for education and legal and voting rights for women; improvements for workers;

8

and "clear-headed thinking, free of prejudice and stereotypes."[23] Critics attacked, accusing her of being a harlot and "a crazy atheistical woman."[24] *Harper's Weekly*, a widely read magazine, published a cartoon depicting her with the head of a goose with a large bill half open to display a fat, pointed tongue, and the caption: "A DOWNRIGHT GABBLER, a goose that deserves to be hissed."[25]

Catharine Beecher, a widely read proponent of "separate spheres, an ideology that designated the domestic sphere as women's domain and the public as men's, wrote scathingly: "Who can look without disgust and abhorrence upon such a one as Fanny Wright, with her great masculine person, her loud voice . . . mingling with men in stormy debate . . . attacking the safeguards of all that is pure and lovely in domestic virtue."[26] For later fighters for women's rights, Fanny Wright was an inspiring role model.

During the 1830s, other women steadily claimed the right to speak out in public, despite being scorned and slandered, threatened and assaulted by crowds that threw everything from rotten eggs to manure to brickbats. In 1832 and 1833, a free black woman, Maria Stewart, the first known American-born woman to give public lectures to audiences of mixed gender and race, gave four speeches denouncing slavery and advocating equal rights for black women before a backlash prompted her to retire.

Freethinker and feminist Ernestine Rose was born Ernestine Louise Potowska in Poland. Acclaimed as "a person of extraordinary powers of mind," Ernestine Rose gave anti-slavery, pro-women's rights, and freedom-of-religion lectures to large crowds.[27] In 1836, she submitted what was likely the first petition supporting women's property rights to the New York Legislature. "Agitate! Agitate! Ought to be the motto of every reformer," she declared.[28]

Sarah and Angelina Grimké, two stern-faced sisters from South Carolina, set off a firestorm when William Lloyd Garrison, the founder of the American Anti-Slavery Society, hired them as the first woman agents, or public anti-slavery speakers. Appalled by what they saw growing up in a prominent slave-owning family in Charleston, the Grimkés published powerful tracts and letters, and spoke passionately about the horrors of slavery before mixed audiences. In 1838, Angelina Grimké addressed a legislative committee (and a crammed-in crowd of onlookers) when she spoke at the Massachusetts State House. Well aware of her historic role, Angelina Grimké later wrote to a friend: "We Abolitionist Women are Turning the world upside down."[29]

She was unfazed by Catharine Beecher's broadside admonishing her that: "IN ALL CASES. . . . Men are the proper persons to make appeals to the rulers."[30] Firing back, Angelina Grimké replied: "Whatever it is morally right for a man to do, it is morally right for woman to do. . . . It is woman's right to have a voice in all the laws and regulations by which she is to be governed."[31] Sarah Grimké proclaimed: "I surrender not our claim to equality."[32]

After a few tumultuous years, Angelina Grimké retired from public speaking and married the abolitionist Theodore Weld. Sarah Grimké retired too and lived with them. Their radical actions and writings, however, inspired others. "What a trio! For me to love!" wrote newly married Elizabeth Cady Stanton, after her husband Henry Stanton, Theodore's best friend and fellow abolitionist, had taken her to meet them.[33] Shortly after their visit, Elizabeth and Henry left for London where Henry, who was a delegate, would attend the first meeting of the World's Anti-Slavery Convention.

Thanks to the Internet, we can examine a painting of that gathering online, enlarge it, zoom in, and click on some of the figures to get their identity. The painting, *The Anti-Slavery Society Convention,* 1840, painted in 1841 by Benjamin Robert Haydon, depicts the audience of more than 500 seated delegates, clad in black, listening to a gray-haired man at a rostrum in the forward-leaning stance of an orator. In the background, behind a long

10

waist-high barrier draped with cloaks, is a crowd of featureless spectators, many wearing bonnets.

Checking the identity of some of the figures, we learn that the orator is Thomas Clarkson, a pioneering British abolitionist. Henry Stanton is seated in the front row. But no amount of zooming and peering will help us find the delegation of eight American women, including the much-admired reformer and Quaker preacher Lucretia Coffin Mott. We must imagine them among the faceless figures seated behind the spectators' barrier, where they were relegated after the male delegates voted to refuse to seat them.

A slightly built, lissome woman with deep-set eyes and a high forehead, Lucretia Mott was forty-three years old and a seasoned activist when twenty-four-year-old Elizabeth Cady Stanton met her in London. According to Stanton, she "embraced every opportunity to talk" with Lucretia Mott. She later wrote that they "resolved to hold a convention as soon as we returned home, and form a society to advocate the rights of women."[34]

The convention happened eight years later in Seneca Falls, New York. In July 1848, Jane Hunt held a tea party at her house in Waterloo, New York, a village near Auburn where Lucretia Mott was visiting her sister Martha Coffin Wright, and near Seneca Falls where Elizabeth Cady Stanton lived. Joining them was Mary Ann M'Clintock, who also lived in Waterloo. Together the women wrote a call for "a convention to discuss the social, civil, and religious condition and rights of women" to be held in Wesleyan Chapel at Seneca Falls on July 19 and 20.[35] Stanton, the principal author of the foundational document of the convention, the Declaration of Sentiments and Resolutions, modeled it after the Declaration of Independence, famously adding "and women" to the familiar five words, "all men are created equal."

The Declaration of Sentiments included eighteen grievances ranging from legal discrimination to lack of education and employment to the destruction of woman's "self-respect." All of the resolutions passed unanimously, except the one Elizabeth Cady Stanton had insisted on: *Resolved, That it is the duty of the women of this country to secure to themselves their sacred right to the elective franchise."*[36] Elizabeth's husband Henry had threatened to leave town if she proposed it. (Henry left town.)

With the stalwart support of Frederick Douglass, the former slave, eminent abolitionist orator, and newspaper publisher, the resolution passed. "In due time," Stanton recalled, "Douglass and I carried the whole convention."[37] They had first met around 1840 at an abolition event, when, as he later recalled, she "did me the honor to sit by my side and by the logic of which she is master, successfully endeavored to convince me of the wisdom & truth of the then new gospel of woman's rights."[38]

As Elizabeth Cady Stanton had predicted, the Seneca Falls Women's Rights Convention sparked "no small amount of misconception, misrepresentation, and ridicule."[39] It was derided in newspapers as "a most insane and ludicrous farce." The resolutions were denounced as "a monstrous injury to all mankind."[40] Unwavering activists held a second women's rights convention two weeks later in nearby Rochester, New York. A third convention was held in 1850 in Salem, Ohio.

Anti-slavery lecturer and teacher Betsy Mix Cowles, known as a woman of "uncommon intellect" and a "playful disposition," was elected president of the Salem convention.[41] Her attributes undoubtedly helped her manage the men in attendance who were officially allowed no role except as silent observers. Even many years later, the proceedings are inspiring and informative, including fervent letters from Lucretia Mott and Elizabeth Cady Stanton that were read aloud. The twenty-two resolutions, seeking to improve every aspect of women's lives, from their self-esteem to their finances, still resonate today.

The Salem convention had been strategically scheduled several weeks before state legislators met to revise the Ohio state constitution. A petition adopted by the delegates, lest any legislator remain uninformed, documented the "unjust" legal status of women and demanded that in the "New Constitution . . . Women shall be secured not only the Right of Suffrage, but all the political and legal rights that are guaranteed to men."[42] The petition with 8,000 signatures was sent to the constitutional convention. It is unknown whether delegates read it. What we do know is that, despite the women's thorough efforts, the new state constitution granted no rights to women.

Meanwhile, while attending an anti-slavery convention in Boston, the mild-appearing, strong-willed Lucy Stone proposed the idea of holding a national woman's rights convention. A committee was formed and a call sent to all the major newspapers that read: "The signs are encouraging: the time opportune. Come then, to this Convention. It is your duty, if you are worthy of your age and country."[43]

Lucy Stone had become an anti-slavery lecturer soon after she graduated from Oberlin College in 1847. Early in her public speaking career, she saw *The Greek Slave,* a marble statue by Hiram Powers, of a full-size nude female figure, standing with chains around both wrists and tangled across a leg: "Hot tears came to my eyes at the thought of the millions of women who must be freed." That night she infused women's rights in her anti-slavery lecture. An official of the Massachusetts Anti-Slavery Society chastised her, saying, "people came to hear anti-slavery, and not woman's rights."

"I was a woman before I was an abolitionist. I must speak for women," she replied and offered to resign.[44] But she was too effective to lose. Thousands of people attended her lectures, captivated by her "hypnotic power" and "voice of an angel."[45] The official agreed to a deal: She was paid $4 a week to give anti-slavery lectures on weekends, when crowds were the largest. On weekdays, covering her own expenses, she gave woman's rights lectures with titles, such as "Legal and Political Disabilities of Women."

Almost a thousand people from eleven states, including California, assembled in Brinley Hall, Worcester, Massachusetts, to attend the first National Woman's Rights Convention on October 23–24, 1850. Lucretia Mott, Frederick Douglass, and Ernestine Rose were there. Elizabeth Cady Stanton, who was pregnant with her fourth child (she would eventually have seven) sent a letter to be read.

Paulina Wright Davis, a pioneer in lecturing about women's anatomy who would later found the New England Woman Suffrage Association, gave the opening address. Davis, writes historian Joelle Million, "wanted to set the movement's tone as one of charitable understanding and forbearance." Whereas Lucretia Mott, Million writes, "disagreed." She believed that men "should be held responsible for" the wrongs done to women. Contrary to the view "that women should *ask* that their rights be *given* to them," Mott insisted that women "*demand* their rights be *yielded* to them on the ground of common humanity."[46] News of the convention appeared in newspapers across the country and in Europe, some of it fair-minded and some mean-spirited such as an article in a New York City newspaper that dismissed the convention as a "motley gathering of fanatical radicals, of old grannies, male and female, of fugitive slaves and fugitive lunatics."[47]

Well aware that they were closely scrutinized for signs of unconventional dress and behavior, especially anything that could be considered masculine, activist women consciously projected an aura of respectability, order, and seriousness. Their conventions were well organized and smoothly run, despite the inevitable hecklers and hooligans. The agenda was full of speeches, reports, appeals, petitions, resolutions dealing with suffrage, property rights, access to education, opportunities for employment, and equality with men.

At the 1852 National Women's Rights Convention in Syracuse, New York, two women who would become leaders gave their first women's rights speeches. Matilda Joslyn Gage was a twenty-five-year old freethinker, writer, and a friend and neighbor of Native Americans in Western New York. Impressed by the equality of Iroquois women, Gage thought that "Native Americans should be the inspiration for women in the suffrage movement," writes historian Sally Roesch Wagner.[48]

Thirty-one-year old Susan B. Anthony had recently retired after teaching for fifteen years, at half the pay of a man. The year before, Anthony, who grew up in a Quaker household, had met Elizabeth Cady Stanton. At the time, Susan B. Anthony was a leader in the temperance movement, or the crusade to limit, even prohibit, the use of alcohol. When a group of men, supported by many women, took over a temperance organization that she had founded, she committed her indefatigable energy and superb organizing skills to the emergent women's rights movement. (Susan B. Anthony and Elizabeth Cady Stanton would be coadjutors for fifty-one years. In the 1880s, Stanton, Anthony, and Gage would produce the first three volumes of the *History of Woman Suffrage*.)

Harriet Forten Purvis and her sister Margarette, prominent African American abolitionists and suffragists, organized the Fifth National Woman's Rights Convention in Philadelphia. Ernestine Rose, who presided over the convention, boldly stated and asked, "Our claims are based on that great and immutable truth, the rights of all humanity. . . . Tell us, ye men of the nation . . . whether woman is not included in that great Declaration of Independence?"[49]

On the second day of the convention, October 20, 1854, a newspaper in Athens, Tennessee, published a contrived scenario reflecting the deep-seated fear expressed throughout the struggle that a "triumph of woman's rights" would unsex women and men: "A strong minded woman in Pennsylvania offers for sale—a good husband, warranted sound and kind in any kind of harness. He is of handsome figure and can trot his babies an hour easily, . . . never snuffs at his dish-cloth. . . . The present owner being about to emigrate to California, the above property must be sold without delay."[50]

With the onset of the Civil War in 1861, abolitionist men implored women to suspend their campaign for woman's rights and focus solely on aiding the war effort. Believing that they would be rewarded with suffrage after the war was won, Elizabeth Cady Stanton and other leaders, with the exception of Susan B. Anthony, agreed to suspend their efforts for women's rights. Women aided in every aspect of the war. They were factory workers, farmers, nurses, spies, fundraisers, and, in male disguise, fought as soldiers. Women gathered in groups to knit and sew, send food and medical supplies, raise money, tend to wounded soldiers and help their families. In 1863, Elizabeth Cady Stanton and Susan B. Anthony organized the Women's Loyal National League and spearheaded a campaign that collected nearly three hundred thousand signatures on a petition that significantly influenced the passage and ratification of the Thirteenth Amendment that abolished slavery.

On January 9, 1866, nine months after the end of the Civil War, this headline appeared in a Staunton, Virginia newspaper: WOMEN ON THE RAMPAGE. The women were "Mesdames E. Cady Stanton, Lucy Stone, and Susan B. Anthony, all of them ardent advocates of women's rights." Their "rampage" was their Petition for Universal Suffrage, asking Congress to pass "an amendment of the Constitution of the United States that shall prohibit the several States from disfranchising any of their citizens on the ground of sex."[51]

The fight for women's rights had recommenced. A call was issued for the Eleventh National Women's Rights Convention to meet in May.

Chapter 2

Confront Great Odds: 1866-1877

First, because I felt it was a duty, and second out of curiosity.
—Portia Gage

WOMAN'S RIGHTS: ELEVENTH NATIONAL CONVENTION OF THE STRONG MINDED FEMALES, was the headline of a New York City newspaper's coverage of the first gathering after the Civil War.[1] At the meeting in May 1866, activists agreed to re-form into the American Equal Rights Association (AERA)—a new organization "to secure Equal Rights to all American citizens, especially the right of suffrage, irrespective or race, color or sex."[2]

Wendell Phillips, the president of the American Anti-Slavery Society (AASS), supported the vision, but, for now, just for black men: "I hope some day to be bold enough to add 'sex,'" he had said in a speech to the AASS. "However, my friends we must take up but one question at a time, and this hour belongs exclusively to the negro."

"Do you believe the African race is composed entirely of males?" his longtime friend and ally Elizabeth Cady Stanton fired back.[3]

In July, Congress adopted the Fourteenth Amendment. The first section granted citizenship rights and equal protection of the laws to "all persons born or naturalized in the United States," including former slaves. In the second section pertaining to voting rights, suffragists were stunned that the word *male*, a word that had not previously appeared in the United States Constitution, was used three times in reference to the word *citizen*.[4]

Alarmed, outraged, and feeling betrayed, Elizabeth Cady Stanton and Susan B. Anthony launched an intense but ultimately futile campaign to block ratification of the Fourteenth Amendment. In frustration, they turned their attention to Kansas where the first referendum on a woman suffrage amendment to a state constitution would be held on November 5, 1867. The amendment that had been approved by the Kansas Legislature would eliminate the word *male* from the clause in the state constitution that defined voter qualifications. Another measure on the ballot would eliminate the word *white*. Lucy Stone and her husband Henry Blackwell had campaigned for several weeks in the spring. Stanton and Anthony arrived in September.

Kansas was frontier country where federal troops were subjugating Native Americans. Settlers lived in primitive cabins, food was scarce, roads were mere tracks across the prairies, and chinch bugs were everywhere. "This morning I think we picked a few thousand out of the ruffles of our dresses," reported Susan B. Anthony in a letter to her family.[5] In November, the all-white male electorate rejected both referenda. Out of thirty thousand ballots, the 9,070 votes cast to remove the word *male* were anointed by Susan B. Anthony as the "first ever cast in the United States for the enfranchisement of women."[6]

The Kansas campaign marked the introduction of suffrage ribbons, and the use of a color to symbolize suffrage—yellow, the color of sunflowers. The Hutchinson Family Singers, a popular singing group from New Hampshire, campaigned with Stanton and Anthony. "I got to know those noble women well," John Hutchinson recalled. The "Kansas Suffrage Song" was sung to a familiar tune, "Old Dan Tucker," with lyrics, co-written by John Hutchinson that were both bold and reassuring: "We're bound to win our voting rights . . . Fear not, we'll darn each worthy stocking, Duly keep the cradle rocking."[7]

That same year, 1867, suffragists had no better luck in New York testifying at a constitutional convention that was considering changes to the state constitution. Stanton and

Anthony appeared before the committee chaired by the abolitionist and newspaper publisher Horace Greeley. Attempting to counter Greeley's belief that women did not want to vote, they had secretly asked Greeley's wife to sign a pro-suffrage petition. A sympathetic member on Greeley's committee agreed to present it. "Mr. Chairman," he said, "I hold in my hand a petition signed by Mrs. Horace Greeley . . . asking that the word 'male' be stricken from the constitution."[8]

Their tactic backfired. Greeley, humiliated and furious, made sure that black men were enfranchised, but not women. "We are satisfied that public sentiment does not demand and would not sustain an innovation so revolutionary and sweeping, so openly at war with a distribution of duties and functions between the sexes," he wrote in the official report.[9]

Despite the setbacks with the insertion of *male* in the United States Constitution and the defeats in Kansas and New York, suffragists across the country continued agitating. In Arkansas, on March 5, 1868, at a constitutional convention, Miles L. Langley attempted to ensure that women were enfranchised in the revised state constitution, but "alas," he wrote in a letter to Susan B. Anthony, he was met with "ridicule, sarcasm and insult."[10] That same month in Vineland, New Jersey, Portia Gage accompanied her husband John when he went to vote in a municipal election. She later wrote that she went "first, because I felt it as a duty, and second, out of curiosity." Like most women, she had been told that polling places were "dangerous . . . where it would not be *safe* for a woman." Instead, she discovered that she felt "stronger, wiser and better for having come in contact with the political influence." The men "were quiet and well behaved" and she was "not 'jostled' or molested." Her only discomfort was feeling "embarrassed" that she was the only woman.[11]

For the 1868 federal election in November, Portia and John took their places on the platform where the election officials sat. Others joined them, including Margaret Pryor who had attended the 1848 Women's Rights Convention in Seneca Falls and signed the Declaration of Sentiments. Next to them was a 12-by-6-inch box used for picking grapes where, by the end of the day, 172 black and white women had cast their ballots. Women also voted or tried to vote in Kansas, Michigan, Maine, and Massachusetts.

Early in 1869, the Fifteenth Amendment had been proposed in Congress that prohibited disenfranchisement "on account of race, color, or previous condition of servitude," but not sex.[12] The omission of the word *sex* enflamed the debate over "the Negro's hour" versus universal suffrage. Dissension among friends, allies, even family members erupted at the 1869 AERA Annual Meeting where Stanton argued with Frederick Douglass, who supported the Fourteenth and Fifteenth Amendments, as did Lucretia Mott's son-in-law, while Mott supported universal suffrage.

Charles Remond, an abolitionist orator who was born a free black man, declared: "All I ask for myself I claim for my wife and sister."[13] The abolitionist and poet Frances Ellen Watkins Harper, a free black woman, "would not have Black women put a single straw in the way" of the enfranchisement of black men.[14] Lucy Stone believed "that the safety of the government would be more promoted by the admission of woman as an element of restoration and harmony." Nevertheless, she now said: "I thank God for that XV Amendment, and hope it will be adopted in every State."[15]

Sojourner Truth, a former slave and a preeminent abolitionist and women's rights orator, said: "I feel that I have the right to have just as much as a man. There is a great stir about colored men getting their rights, but not a word about the colored women; and if colored men get their rights, and not colored women theirs, you see the colored men will be masters over the women, and it will be just as bad as it was before. So I am for keeping the thing going while things are stirring; because if we wait till it is still, it will take a great while to get it going again."[16]

Anthony vowed to work against the amendment because it "put two million more men in position of tyrants."[17] Stanton spewed racist and xenophobic diatribes, name-calling and denigrating "ignorant" immigrant men and demonizing black men. Frederick Douglass warned her that she was alienating black women and supportive black men with the "flings at the negro . . . as an ignorant monster possessing the ballot."[18] (According to historian Leigh Fought, Douglass and Stanton "over the years appeared able to discuss the issue and negotiate their way back to friendship.")[19]

The contentious AERA meeting added to the buildup of resentment that Stanton and Anthony had engendered during the Kansas campaign when they teamed up with George Francis Train, a wealthy, flamboyant entrepreneur, and pro-woman suffrage speaker, but also a rabid racist. He was "a lunatic, wild and ranting," declared Lucy Stone.[20] Although Stanton acknowledged that Train was a "charlatan," she and Anthony accepted money from him to fund an extensive pro-suffrage lecture tour and *The Revolution*, their weekly newspaper "charged to the muzzle with literary nitro-glycerine."[21]

On May 15, 1869, after the fractious AERA meeting, Stanton and Anthony met with a group of like-minded women and founded a new organization: the National Woman Suffrage Association (NWSA). Six months later, Lucy Stone and her husband Henry Blackwell formed the American Woman Suffrage Association (AWSA). The two organizations differed in goals and tactics.

The NWSA embraced a broad range of radical causes, such as equal working conditions, divorce law reform, women's right to serve on juries, equal education, ending the death penalty, eliminating the double standard of sexual behavior, and passing a woman suffrage amendment to the United States Constitution. Men could be members but not officers. The AWSA eschewed radical causes and focused on conducting suffrage campaigns to amend voter qualifications in state constitutions. Men could be members and officers. Stone and Blackwell founded the *Woman's Journal*, a weekly newspaper that was published without the provocative tone of *The Revolution*. The AERA with its goal of universal suffrage ceased to meet.

Lucretia Mott pleaded with both groups to "merge their interest in one common cause."[22] Stanton offered to resign as the NWSA's president if that would reunite them. Frederick Douglass signed a document seeking reconciliation. "Whether what ought to be, will be, in this case, is quite open to debate," he wrote in a Washington, D.C. newspaper. "There cannot, however be any harm in making the endeavor."[23]

That same year in South Carolina, Louisa Rollin, a socially prominent black woman and one of five sisters who were heralded for their refinement and intelligence, had advocated for universal suffrage on the floor of the South Carolina House of Representatives. Her sister Charlotte "Lottie" Rollin was elected secretary at the founding meeting of the South Carolina Woman's Suffrage Association (SCWSA).

Addressing the integrated audience, Lottie Rollin said: "It had been so universally the custom to treat the idea of woman suffrage with ridicule and merriment that it becomes necessary . . . [to] assure the gentlemen present that our claim is made honestly and seriously. We ask suffrage not as a favor, nor as a privilege, but as a right based on the ground that we are human beings and as such, entitled to all human rights."[24]

In Missouri, Virginia Minor, president of the Woman Suffrage Association of Missouri, was known for being "sweet and retiring-looking," with "ladylike manners," and an "old-fashioned" charm. At the October 1869 convention in St. Louis, she set the audience abuzz, boldly proclaiming: "The Constitution of the United States gives me every right and privilege to which every other citizen is entitled." Her claim was based on Section 1 of the Fourteenth Amendment. Women were enfranchised, she and her husband Francis, a lawyer, argued, because women were citizens and one of the "privileges or immunities of citizens" was the right to vote.[25] Resolutions supporting that interpretation were approved at the Missouri convention and widely distributed in a pamphlet. Francis Minor sent the resolutions to Stanton and Anthony to publish in *The Revolution.* In a letter, he wrote: "We no longer beat the air—no longer assume merely the attitude of petitioners. We claim a right based on citizenship."[26]

Two months later, on December 10, 1869, Governor John A. Campbell signed a bill passed by the Legislature of the Territory of Wyoming enfranchising women over the age of twenty-one. As a teenager in Salem, Ohio, Campbell had attended the 1850 Women's Rights Convention, and he had been impressed by the women's competence. When legislators attempted to rescind woman suffrage, he turned down a large bribe and vetoed their bill. "It is simple justice," he wrote, "to say that the women entering for the first time in the history of the country, upon these new and untried duties, have conducted themselves in every respect with as much tact, sound judgment, and good sense, as men."[27]

A towering bronze statue commemorating that historic event stands before the capitol in Cheyenne, Wyoming. The statue represents Esther Morris, who became known as the "Mother of Woman Suffrage." Depicted standing on a mound with a sage bush at her right side, Morris is clad in a long-sleeved, ankle-length dress with a wide ruffle from her chin to her belt and a windblown skirt, her hair short and curly, her strong-featured face with her eyes gazing straight ahead, and her right knee raised in mid-stride. Pointed-toed shoes are on her feet. A long bouquet is cradled in her left arm and her right arm, extended down and behind her, is holding an unfurled scroll.

Six-foot-tall Esther Hobart Morris, who had been an orphan, a widow, a successful businesswoman, and the mother of three sons, lived in a small log cabin with a sod roof in South Pass City, a town that grew up around a gold mine. Her exalted role in the suffrage victory stems from a widely disseminated story that she held a tea party and convinced William Bright, a South Pass City saloonkeeper and a member of the first Wyoming Territorial Legislature, to support woman suffrage. There is no evidence Morris held a tea party, but Bright did later credit her and his wife Julie as influencing him to introduce the first successful woman suffrage bill. Morris, however, can claim credit as the first woman justice of the peace in the United States.

On February 12, 1870, acting governor S. A. Mann of the Territory of Utah, signed a bill enfranchising women. (Utah had been settled by members of The Church of Jesus Christ of Latter-day Saints, commonly called Mormons, who practiced polygamy. Seventeen years later, the United States Congress passed legislation banning polygamy and disenfranchising Utah's women.) Newspapers across the country reported that Wyoming and Utah had adopted woman suffrage. The cause that had been "ridiculed, scorned and scoffed at" was inexorably gaining credibility.[27] Opponents noticed and they were stirring. A pro-suffrage newspaper in Bellows Falls, Vermont, reported yielding to pressure to publish anti-suffrage views: THE COMBAT DEEPENS! read the headline."[29]

Steadfast suffragists held local, state, and national meetings; wrote articles, petitions, letters to the editor; and refused to pay taxes. Two elderly sisters, Julia and Abby Smith, had seven of their cows —Jessie, Daisy, Proxy, Minnie, Bessie, Whitey, and Lily— confiscated when they withheld their taxes. By the time they won a lawsuit against the tax collector, they were down to two cows: Taxey and Votey. Other suffragists protested by going to the polls.

Mary Olney Brown, known as "a woman of more than ordinary intellectual endowments, and . . . a firm advocate of equality of race and sex before the law," had followed the Oregon Trail from Chautauqua County in New York to the Territory of Washington.[30] On Election Day in 1869, she and her daughter had gone to the polling place in Olympia, the capital, accompanied by their husbands. Officials refused to accept the women's ballots. Mary Olney Brown wrote letters urging women to vote. She was dubbed a "fanatic" for promoting such an "absurdity."

On Election Day in 1870, her sister, Charlotte Olney French, "a woman of energy and influence" who lived in Grand Mound, enlisted a group of women to host a picnic dinner at a schoolhouse where the election was held. After the dinner and drinks, which left everyone, including the election judges, "in good humor," Charlotte Olney French, "being a good talker," reassuringly handled all the questions and concerns about women voting. Then, "as if they had always been accustomed to voting," the women, French going first, handed in their ballots. One elderly woman, Mrs. Sargent, thanked the Lord "that He had let her live until she could vote."

Women in nearby Black River had promised to try to vote if the Grand Mound women were successful. A rider on a fast horse had been stationed in Grand Mound to observe what happened, then ride to Black River with the news. Spying the women depositing their ballots, he rode off at a gallop to Black River, where he "swung his hat, and screeched at the top of his voice, 'They're voting! They're voting!'"[31]

Many women voted in Black River and in Grand Mound. In Olympia, Mary Olney Brown and two other women were refused the right to vote. Sixteen years later, Mary Olney Brown died. Today, the top half of her gravestone is missing but the bottom half still stands, inscribed with these words: "She was a faithful advocate of Equal Suffrage for women."[32]

In 1871, Victoria Claflin Woodhull, whose friend Senator Benjamin Butler had arranged for her appearance, testified in Washington, D.C., before a congressional committee that not only the Fourteenth Amendment, but also the Fifteenth Amendment, enfranchised women because "women, black and white, belong to races."[33]

A full-page engraving in Frank Leslie's Illustrated Newspaper, *February 4, 1871, of Victoria Woodhull's address to a congressional committee. A "deputation of female suffragists" accompanied her. (Library of Congress)*

A newcomer to the fight for woman suffrage, Victoria Woodhull was known for her beauty and unconventional life. Born in Homer, Ohio, she grew up surrounded by quackery. Her father hawked bogus medicines. Her mother offered séances and palm readings to gullible customers. Married at fifteen to an alcoholic, drug-abusing quack doctor, Victoria had two children. After divorcing and remarrying, she moved to New York City where she and her sister Tennessee (Tennie) met Cornelius Vanderbilt, a fabulously wealthy man for whom they performed a "magnetic healing." In turn, Vanderbilt helped them open a brokerage firm where they made a fortune as the first women stockbrokers. He also financed their newspaper *Woodhull & Claflin Weekly* that covered radical causes including free love, an inflammatory issue that opponents of women's rights had charged was on the suffragists' agenda.

Susan B. Anthony was in the audience when Victoria Woodhull testified. Impressed by her eloquence and persuasiveness, Anthony invited her to speak to the National Woman's Rights Convention that was meeting in Washington, D.C., later in the day. Soon, however, their growing alliance proved to be a serious liability. The Victoria Woodhull who calmly spoke in Washington morphed into a flame-throwing speaker at NWSA's convention in New York City, threatening "treason" and "plotting revolution" and caused many NWSA members to drop their membership.[34]

Woodhull connived to get NWSA's endorsement for her self-declared candidacy for president of the United States, prompting Horace Greeley to use the pages of his newspaper to castigate NWSA and its association with Woodhull and free love. "Yes, I am a Free Lover," she had unabashedly proclaimed, "I have an inalienable, constitutional and natural right to love whom I may, to love as long or as short a period as I can; to change that love every day if I please, and with the right neither you nor any law you can frame have any right to interfere."[35]

Henry Beecher, a prominent preacher in New York City and former president of AWSA, echoed Greeley's attacks. In retaliation, Woodhull charged Beecher with hypocrisy and published an exposé in the *Woodhull & Claflin Weekly* of Henry Beecher's affair with Elizabeth "Lib" Tilton, a member of his church. What became known as the Beecher-Tilton Affair embroiled suffragists in the scandal. Stanton, it soon became known, was Woodhull's source: Lib had confided in Anthony, who confided in Stanton, who told Woodhull. Theodore Tilton—Lib's husband, a suffragist, and a friend of Stanton and Anthony—sued Beecher.

The sensational trial involving prominent suffragists and sex and free love heaped bad national publicity on the cause. "This Beecher-Tilton affair is playing the deuce with woman suffrage in Michigan," Henry Blackwell, who was there campaigning for a woman suffrage amendment referendum, wrote to his wife Lucy Stone. "No chance of success this year I fancy!"[36] (Beecher's trial ended in a hung jury. Male voters in Michigan overwhelmingly defeated the woman suffrage amendment.)

Virginia and Francis Minor's and Victoria Woodhull's interpretation of the Fourteenth and Fifteenth Amendments evolved into a strategy known as the "New Departure." If Congress agreed with the interpretation, it could pass a declaratory act that would enable women to vote. Anthony was upbeat: She felt "new life" with the prospect that "our battle is to be short, sharp & decisive under this 14th & 15th amendment claim." But, a joint congressional judiciary committee soon blocked that path to enfranchisement, issuing a report declaring that women were not citizens, they were only "members of the state."[37]

Nevertheless, women across the country continued to go to polling places. The elderly Angelina Grimké Weld and Sarah Grimké, and about fifty other women in Massachusetts, marched to the polls in a snowstorm to cast their ballots in a separate box. Sojourner Truth attempted to vote in Michigan. Marilla Ricker attempted to vote in New Hampshire. In North Carolina, 200 black women dressed in men's clothing registered and voted.

In St. Louis, Virginia Minor's attempt to register was rebuffed by the registrar Reese Happersett. She and her husband filed a lawsuit, *Minor v. Happersett* (as a married woman she could not file it on her own), that would slowly work its way through the Missouri court system and finally to the United States Supreme Court.

Susan B. Anthony and fourteen other women went to the polling place in Rochester, New York, where she convinced an election inspector that they had a constitutional right to vote. "Well I have been & gone & done it!! Positively voted," she triumphantly wrote to Elizabeth Cady Stanton.[38] A nationally known figure, Anthony garnered a lot of press coverage and prompted national attention to the woman suffrage issue.

Perhaps fearing a growing movement, officials decided to arrest Susan B. Anthony for voting without "the legal right to vote" because she was "a person of the female sex."[39] She was tried in June 1873 and convicted when the judge preempted the jurors' role by ordering them to "find a verdict of guilty."[40] It was,

Anthony recorded in her diary—"The greatest judicial outrage history has ever recorded."[41]

Charges were also filed against the other women and the election inspectors who accepted the women's ballots. Eventually, the charges were dropped. A group of women in Rochester gathered to protest in a room where they hung three American flags union down and draped in black. (Union down is an official sign of distress.) Later that year, a registrar refused to register Mathilde C. Weil in New York City because, he said, "It cannot be done, since Miss Anthony tried it."[42]

On March 29, 1875, the United States Supreme Court ruled in *Minor v. Happersett* that "the Constitution of the United States does not confer the right of suffrage upon any one."[43] That signaled the death knell for the New Departure; now woman suffrage could only be won state-by-state or by an amendment to the United States Constitution. The results from the labor-intensive, costly state-by-state referenda campaigns were dismal: "With the best campaign possible for us to make," Susan B. Anthony pointed out, "we obtained a vote of only one-third. One man out of every three voted for the enfranchisement of the women of his household, while two out of every three voted against it."[44]

Nine months later, all day and into the night of December 31, 1875, "gay and joyous" flag-waving people dressed in their finery rode in their carriages draped with red, white, and blue bunting, sang patriotic songs, blew horns, clanged bells, ignited Roman candles, and watched soldiers parade through the streets. There were concerts, parties, pageants, and speeches galore. At midnight, houses and public buildings "burst into a blaze of light that rivaled the noon-day sun, while screaming whistles, booming cannons, pealing bells, joyous music and brilliant fire-works made the midnight which ushered in the centennial year 1876, a never-to-be-forgotten hour."[45]

The country's first World's Fair, the Centennial International Exhibition, would open on May 10, 1876, and run until November in Philadelphia, where the Declaration of Independence had been signed in 1776. Exhibits from many states and eleven foreign countries would fill two hundred buildings in Fairmount Park, located on the banks of the Schuylkill River. Dazzling items would be displayed: telephone, typewriter, mechanical calculator, and Heinz ketchup. President Ulysses S. Grant and Emperor Pedro II of Brazil would switch on the powerful Corliss Centennial Engine that would power all the other machines on display. The massive forearm with the hand holding the torch for the unfinished Statue of Liberty was shipped from France, a fundraising gambit. For 50 cents, adventurous visitors could climb a ladder and stand on the balcony, just below the bronze flame.

Denied the right to vote, many women were not inclined to join in the hoopla. Instead, it was suggested, women "draped in black, should march in solemn procession, bells slowly tolling, bearing banners with the inscription: 'Taxation without representation is tyranny,' 'No just government can be formed without the consent of the governed,' 'They who have no voice in the laws and rules are in a condition of slavery.'"

The Toledo Woman Suffrage Association in Ohio refused an invitation to participate in a citywide centennial planning committee because women "have no centennial to celebrate, as the government still holds them in a condition of political serfdom, denying them the greatest rights of citizenship—representation."[46] A barrage of criticism in the local newspapers did not change their minds. They hung a banner—"Woman Suffrage and Equal Rights"—across the main street in Toledo.

In Philadelphia, a wealthy society woman, Elizabeth Duane Gillespie, the great-granddaughter of Benjamin Franklin, eschewed activists of the ilk of Susan B. Anthony as too extreme. Most women of her elite class, living at a time in America dubbed the Gilded Age, were content to leave politics to their husbands, believing they could exert their influence through them. In

30

nonpolitical realms, however, Elizabeth Gillespie was an activist. She organized an all-woman committee that raised a significant amount of money for the Centennial Exhibition. When told that there would not be a women's exhibition in the Main Exhibition Hall, Gillespie redirected her committee's efforts and raised the money to build a Women's Pavilion.

Only exhibits by women were allowed in the majestic Women's Pavilion, topped by an observatory with a cupola. Everything from inventions to needlework and painting and sculpture were on display. Emma Allison, a *"genuine lady engineer,"* operated a flower-trimmed six-horsepower Baxter steam engine that powered several looms, a printing press, and other machinery, all of which were operated by women. Visitors, wrote one reporter, gazed at Allison, "with feelings half of amazement and half admiration."[47]

On July 4, 1876, an oppressively hot day, Susan B. Anthony—with a furled document, the "Declaration of Rights for Women of the United States," concealed in her handbag—and four other women took their seats at the main event with tickets they had surreptitiously obtained. Immediately after the reading of the Declaration of Independence, Anthony audaciously interrupted the proceedings and walked to the platform and presented a speechless Vice President Thomas Ferry with a copy of the Declaration that ended with the words: "We ask justice, we ask equality, we ask that all the civil and political rights that belong to citizens of the United States, be guaranteed to us and our daughters forever."[48]

They exited, handing out copies of the Declaration to the aroused and curious audience. At a platform in front of Independence Hall, Matilda Joslyn Gage held an umbrella to block the broiling sun as Anthony read the rousing document. Triumphantly, they then arrived at a nearby church, where eighty-four-year old Lucretia Mott presided over the National Woman Suffrage Association (NWSA) convention.

For five hours, distinguished women and men spoke. Elizabeth Cady Stanton read the 1848 Declaration of Sentiments. The Hutchinson Family Singers performed protest songs, such as "A Hundred Years Hence" by Frances Dana Gage with the words:

Then woman, man's partner, man's equal shall stand.

While beauty and harmony govern the land;

To think for oneself will be no offense,

The world will be thinking, a hundred years hence.[49]

Chapter 3

Gain Momentum: 1878-1900

We take our stand on the solidarity of humanity. —Anna Julia Cooper

"This is the first time in my life that I have trod these halls, and what has brought me here? I say oppression—oppression of women by men," declared eighty-three-year-old Julia Smith, whose cows had been confiscated when she and her sister Abby refused to pay their taxes as a protest against their disenfranchisement.[1]

She was testifying before the United States Senate Committee on Privileges and Elections. The Committee was considering a Sixteenth Amendment to enfranchise women. First introduced by Representative George Washington Julian of Indiana in 1868, the amendment was revised and introduced on January 10, 1878, by Senator Aaron Augustus Sargent of California. So many spectators showed up that the Committee had to move to a larger room, but even then, crowds packed the hallways. Elizabeth Cady Stanton spoke while the chairman rudely read newspapers, cut his nails, yawned, jumped up to close and open a door or a window. "It was with difficulty," she later reported, "that I restrained the impulse more than once to hurl my manuscript at his head."[2]

Fueling the widespread claim that women did not want to vote, Madeleine Vinton Dahlgren, the prominent widow of a Civil War hero, submitted a letter insisting that enfranchising women would disrupt the "distinct duties" ordained by God that women perform as "mothers, wives, sisters, daughters."[3] Her signature, along with that of Ellen Ewing Sherman, the wife of General William Tecumseh Sherman, headed a list of one thousand signatures on an anti-woman suffrage petition. Not surprisingly, the Senate Committee issued a negative report.

Year after year, suffragists testified before congressional committees, only to be rebuffed. Finally, nine years later, in 1887, on the second day of the annual NWSA Convention in Washington, D.C., the United States Senate held the first debate and vote on the Sixteenth Amendment. NWSA delegates filled the gallery. Anti-suffrage senators spoke: Joseph E. Brown of Georgia and George G. Vest of Missouri insisted that the "Creator intended spheres of men and women to be different . . . women are too emotional to vote . . . we must not unsex our mothers and wives."[4] Pro-suffrage Henry A. Blair of New Hampshire heralded women's contributions and proclaimed, "The independence, equality and dignity of all human souls is the fundamental assertion of those who believe in what we call human freedom."[5] Joseph N. Dolph of Oregon said, "I do not think a single objection which is made to woman suffrage is tenable."[6]

The final vote was 16 yeas, 34 nays, 26 absent. Defeated but optimistically determined, NWSA delegates passed a resolution: "That we rejoice in this evidence that our demand is forcing itself upon the attention and action of Congress, and that when a new Congress shall have assembled, with new men and new ideas, we may hope to change this minority into a majority."[7] Victory, they appeared to believe, was attainable for their generation.

The next year, 1888, was the fortieth anniversary of the Seneca Falls Woman's Rights Convention. To mark it, NWSA issued a call for the first meeting of the International Council of Women (ICW), where "Women of the Old World and the New . . . should in the spirit of universal sisterhood unite in harmonious effort to destroy this worst form of aristocracy—cast in sex."[8] For eight days, women and men from every state and territory of the United States and from eight countries—Iceland, India, England,

Finland, Denmark, France, Norway, and Canada—met in a "splendid agitation."[9]

On the platform adorned with fragrant flowers stood a large portrait of Lucretia Mott, who had died in 1880. Anthony, Stanton, and other dignitaries sat on plush sofas and chairs. Soft music played in the hall as delegates took their seats. The "entire audience arose with clapping of hands and waving handkerchiefs" when Susan B. Anthony introduced Elizabeth Cady Stanton. "Long ago in America," Stanton said, "we heard the deep yearnings of the souls of women in foreign lands for freedom responsive to our own."[10]

American and international activists had been long connected through visits, letters, books, magazine articles, and newspapers. Mary Wollstonecraft's book *A Vindication of the Rights of Women* was Lucretia Mott's "pet book" that she shared with others.[11] Harriet Martineau, the English pioneer in sociology, had visited Lucretia Mott in 1834. They continued exchanging views on radical issues through letters. Frederika Bremer, the Swedish writer and women's rights activist, "was guided and sustained" by her contact with American women leaders during her 1849–1851 tour of America.[12] International progress was reported at NWSA conventions, even about "the tiny island of Pitcairn, in the Southern Pacific" where women "have the same suffrage as men" and "the Cape of Good Hope" where "women have a limited vote."[13]

News of the 1850 National Woman's Rights Convention, published in the international edition of the *New York Tribune,* motivated a group of women in Sheffield, England to petition the House of Lords for the right to vote. Mary Muller, an activist in New Zealand writing under the pseudonym Femmina in *An Appeal to the Men of New Zealand,* cited "America" as having "shown us the advantages of things the English mind feared to attempt."[14]

French socialist and feminist activists Jeanne Deroin and Pauline Roland, who were serving prison terms for their activism in the Prison of St. Lazare in Paris, wrote a letter that was read at the 1851 NWSA National Convention: "DEAR SISTERS: Your courageous declaration of Woman's Rights has resounded even to our prison, and has filled our souls with inexpressible joy . . . from the depths of the jail which still imprisons our bodies without reaching our hearts, we cry to you, Faith, Love, Hope, and send to you our sisterly salutations."[15]

In their fierce fight for the vote, American women were part of an international phenomenon in which women around the world remained connected—informing, inspiring, and energizing each other in their struggle.

Efforts had been underway for several years to reunite the two suffrage associations: NWSA and AWSA. The new organization—the National American Woman Suffrage Association (NAWSA)—held its first convention in February 1890 in Washington, D.C. Stanton, who would soon leave for an extended visit abroad, was elected president. Anthony, or "Saint Anthony, as her followers love to call her," was elected the vice-president.[16] Stone, who was unable to attend, was elected chair of the executive committee. WOMEN ASSOCIATIONS CONSOLIDATE, read the newspaper headline in Maysville, Kentucky.[17] A Los Angeles newspaper proclaimed: UNITED SUFFRAGISTS.[18] Stanton, with her "handsome, kindly face, framed by its wealth of snow-white hair," gave a long and spirited speech.[19] Within less than ten years, she predicted, women would be voting in every state in the country! (One can only wonder if her optimism was real or a strategy to keep suffragists engaged.)

That same year, Wyoming applied for statehood with woman suffrage in its constitution, setting off a conflagration in Congress. "I am unalterably opposed to female suffrage in any form," thundered Representative Joseph E. Washington of Tennessee. Representative William C. Oates of Alabama confessed, "I like a woman who is a woman and appreciates the sphere to which God and the Bible have assigned her. I do not like a man-woman."[20]

Woman suffrage, predicted Senator John Reagon of Texas, will make "men of women" and "women of men." That would mean, he warned: "We are to have women for public officers, women to do military duty . . . and men to wash the dishes, men to nurse the children, men to stay home while the ladies go out and make stump speeches." Admitting Wyoming with woman suffrage, declared Senator George G. Vest of Missouri, "would be not only a calamity but an absolute crime."[21]

Hearing about the brouhaha, Wyoming legislators declared in a telegram that they would "remain out of the Union a hundred years rather than come in without woman suffrage."[22] Given that ultimatum, Congress voted to admit Wyoming. Thus, Wyoming became the forty-fourth state and the first equal-suffrage state. When the news reached Elizabeth Cady Stanton in London, she wrote in her diary: "I cannot express the joy that this victory has brought to my soul."[23] Susan B. Anthony was campaigning in South Dakota when she received a telegram with the news. A crowd of supporters cheered when she announced that Wyoming had been added to the "suffrage column."

Although her "hopes" had been "dashed to the earth" in other state woman suffrage referenda campaigns, Anthony had responded to requests that she campaign in South Dakota because "I shall not be cast down, even if voted down."[24] A newcomer to the fight for the vote was also campaigning in South Dakota: Carrie Chapman Catt, a handsome woman with wide-set eyes, a forward thrusting jaw, and, as she herself described it—"a voice like a foghorn" that "can be heard in out of door meetings."[25]

Part of the new generation of activists, Catt was born Carrie Lane in Wisconsin in 1859, and grew up in Iowa. She was thirteen years old when President Ulysses S. Grant ran for reelection against Horace Greeley. Her family supported Greeley. Seeing that her father and the hired farmhand had changed clothes to go to town to vote, but not her mother, Carrie asked why her mother had not gotten ready to go. Her mother replied that she was not going. "Then how are you going to vote for Greeley?"

Carrie asked, prompting her family to laugh at her. Later, an unsuspecting neighbor boy stopped by. He laughed when Carrie said: "I think it's very unfair that women can't vote, don't you?"

"What's so funny about women voting?" she demanded to know.

"Well, naturally they can't vote," he replied.

An indignant Carrie Lane rebuked him, sending him scurrying away. Years later she said: "I never forgot that rank injustice done to my mother. I verily believe I was born a suffragist."[26]

The only woman in her graduating class at Iowa State Agricultural College (now Iowa State University), Carrie Lane had a series of jobs before devoting herself full time to the fight for the vote: law clerk, teacher, first female superintendent of schools in Mason City, Iowa, a journalist, and a public speaker. She was married twice to men who supported woman suffrage: Leo Chapman, a journalist, who died four years after their wedding, and George Catt, a civil engineer, who supported her suffrage work by providing financial resources and the freedom to spend extensive time working for suffrage away from home.

In 1885, she had attended her first all-women gathering, a convention of the American Association of University Women, a newly founded professional organization for college graduates. The women, enthused Catt, were "the strongest, best-educated, most earnest, broad-minded and philosophical women in the United States."[27] Soon active in the Iowa Woman Suffrage Association, Catt organized, spoke, and canvassed house-to-house for signatures on woman suffrage petitions. In 1890, she and George moved to Boston, Massachusetts, home of the veteran activist Lucy Stone, whom Catt often visited, learning all she could from her.

Between 1890 and 1894, suffragists conducted woman suffrage referenda campaigns in South Dakota, Colorado, Kansas, and New York.

"Under God the People Rule" was South Dakota's motto when it entered the Union in 1889. For the 1890 campaign, suffragists added "Women Are People" and printed the modified motto on their banners: "Under God the People Rule. Women Are People." It was a grueling campaign through the "hottest and driest summer on record." Susan B. Anthony endured long rides in stagecoaches that creaked, swayed, and jounced passengers with every turn of the wheel over deeply rutted dirt roads; nights in primitive sod houses, where people shared beds and ate meager rations, such as "sour bread, muddy coffee and stewed green grapes"; and unpredictable weather: "Droughts, hot winds, hail storms, lightning"; and, as always "chinch bugs."[28]

Two spectacular rallies were held. Speakers came from as far away as Massachusetts, 400 local clubs were organized, and literature was distributed, including 50,000 copies of a pro-suffrage speech. But the odds were against them: Anthony had raised $8,000 for the campaign; representatives of the brewery and liquor industry, fearing that women would vote to prohibit the sale of alcohol, had raised $500,000. A delegation of Russian immigrants to the state Democratic convention were bribed to wear "great yellow badges lettered 'Against Woman Suffrage and Susan B. Anthony.'"

Carrie Chapman Catt was depressingly pessimistic: "We have not a ghost of a show for success. . . . The Lutherans, both German and Scandinavian, and the Catholics are bitterly opposed. . . .We are converting women to 'want to vote' by the hundreds, but we are not having any appreciable effect upon the men. . . . Ours is a cold, lonesome little movement."

Male voters soundly defeated the South Dakota Woman's Suffrage Referendum by a majority 22,710: 22,972 yeas, 45,682 nays.

A measure enfranchising Native American men, who had gained citizenship by relinquishing rights to their land, was approved. That meant, Catt pointed out: "Only idiots, insane persons, traitors, Chinese, and women are now disfranchised" in South Dakota.[29]

(In a referendum, the wording of the measure on the ballot could be tricky, causing confusion, or leading voters to skip voting on the measure. In South Dakota the measure read: "Shall the word 'male' be stricken from Section one of Article seven, of the constitution? Yes. No. All electors desiring to vote in favor of striking out the word 'male' must erase the word 'no.' All voters desiring to vote against striking out the word 'male' must erase the word 'yes.'"[30] Suffragists soon realized that they had to educate male voters on how to approve a woman suffrage measure, adding another task to a campaign.)

Carrie Chapman Catt's second campaign was in Colorado in 1893. A woman suffrage referendum had been defeated in 1877. Undeterred, Colorado suffragists carried on, organizing and educating. Caroline Nichols Churchill, an outspoken writer and editor, founded the *Queen Bee,* the state's first women's rights newspaper. In 1890, with only $25 to defray expenses, a small group of women got together, including Ellis Meredith who was dubbed "the Susan B. Anthony of Colorado," her mother Emily R. Meredith, and Elizabeth Piper Ensley, a black woman who had lived in Boston and Washington, D.C., where she had belonged to women's clubs and suffrage organizations. A widow with two children, Ensley had moved to Denver in the 1880s.

Enlisting the help of J. Warner Mills, a sympathetic lawyer and politician, suffragists managed to get a suffrage bill through the legislature and signed by the governor, putting the measure on the ballot in a referendum. (They had strategically gotten a provision in the 1876 constitution that allowed woman suffrage to become a state law through a simple majority vote in a referendum, rather than through a constitutional amendment that required a two-thirds majority.)

Carrie Chapman Catt arrived in September after raising the money to cover her expenses. In Denver, the capital, Catt implemented the "society plan," an innovative organizing strategy to enlist wealthy and influential women and men. She traveled widely, speaking several times a day in far-flung communities, including mining camps where she garnered a great deal of support.

On one occasion, Catt needed to get down a mountain for her next speaking engagement, but she missed the only train. A mule team would not get her there in time, so she accepted a train worker's offer to take her down on a handcar, a forty-five minute ride. She lost her hat, her hairpins, and braced for death as the car "swung around a sharp curve and balanced on two wheels for an appreciable space of time." Finally she arrived on time, "hair flying, gasping and shaken to the marrow."[31]

Male voters approved equal suffrage for women in Colorado on November 7, 1893, by a majority of 6,347: 35,798 yeas, 29,451 nays. Three women were soon elected to the Colorado House of Representatives. (The first bill one of the women legislators introduced was to raise the age of consent at which a girl is declared capable of agreeing to engage in sex from 16 to 18. It had been raised from 10 to 16 in 1891).

The following year, 1894, was a redo of the unsuccessful campaigns of 1867: a constitutional convention in New York and a referendum in Kansas. Suffragists in both states ceaselessly worked in ultimately futile campaigns. In New York, suffragists vigorously canvassed, wrote appeals and letters, lobbied delegates, gave speeches, and signed petitions, one with 600,000 signatures. Large numbers of vocal anti-suffragists appeared, including a bishop with a petition with 15,000 signatures. Known as "Remonstrants" and "Antis," their claims included the usual litany that women do not want to vote. That they do not serve in the military. And that a woman is "unfitted for the ballot because she was influenced by pity, passion and prejudice rather than by judgment."[32]

Despite suffragists' intensive efforts, delegates at the constitutional convention in New York refused to approve a woman suffrage referendum. "It is very humiliating for women . . .

to have their sacred rights at the mercy of a masculine oligarchy," wrote Elizabeth Cady Stanton."[33]

In Kansas, suffrage workers were optimistic about winning. After all, women had been voting for years in municipal and school elections. Local suffragist Annie Diggs, a gentle-looking poet, temperance worker, journalist, and president of the Kansas Equal Suffrage Association, and Laura M. Johns, a peripatetic suffrage organizer and president of the Kansas State Suffrage Association, were also prominent in the two main political parties: the Republican and the recently formed People's Party, commonly known as the Populist Party. Diggs, Johns, and hundreds of women ceaselessly worked to win the support of the political parties and to convert male voters to the cause. But their efforts were futile.

Male voters defeated the woman suffrage referendum by a majority of 34,837: 95,302 yeas, 130,139 nays. In a report to NAWSA, Annie Diggs wrote: "The grief and disappointment of the Kansas women were indescribable."[34]

By the late 1890s, NAWSA was redoubling its efforts to make inroads in Southern states where white supremacy was commonly accepted and entrenched and enforced by laws and statutes, as well as by threats and violence. Equal suffrage was widely perceived as a threat to the status quo. In 1887, no Southern senators had voted for the Sixteenth Amendment to enfranchise women. The amendment was blocked from being voted on in the House of Representatives by Southerners on the House Judiciary Committee.

In 1895, NAWSA held its annual convention in Atlanta, Georgia. Tactics appealing to racism were employed in an attempt to assure Southerners that the historic connection between abolition and women's rights had been severed. Susan B. Anthony asked Frederick Douglass, always an honored guest at NAWSA conventions, not to attend. Anthony's African American friend and suffragist, Ida B. Wells-Barnett, a prominent investigative journalist, confronted Anthony. "Knowing the feelings of the South with regard to Negro participation on equality with whites," Anthony explained that she "did not want to subject" Douglass "to humiliation" or "get in the way of bringing southern women into our suffrage association."[35] While Anthony may have recruited Southern women to the cause, Wells-Barnett replied, she "had also confirmed white women in their attitude of segregation."[36]

Furthermore, at this convention, Henry B. Blackwell gave a speech titled "Woman Suffrage a Solution of the Negro Problem." He "urged the South to adopt woman suffrage" and require an "educational qualification," or a literacy qualification for voters. "Apply it to your own State of Georgia," he pointed out, "where there are 149,895 white women who can read and write, and 143,471 negro voters, of whom 116,516 are illiterates."[37] These tactics are searing examples of the perniciousness of the issue of race in the efforts to secure support for the enfranchisement of women.

Several weeks later, Frederick Douglass died, just hours after attending the National Council of Women's triennial convention in Washington, D.C., where he sat on the platform beside Susan B. Anthony. At his funeral, Anthony gave an emotional eulogy and read a tribute from Elizabeth Cady Stanton. Carrie Chapman Catt, who was determinedly wooing Southern women into NAWSA, complained that Anthony's participation in Douglass's funeral "has completely taken the wind out of our sails." She wrote to a friend: "You should see some of the clippings I have from the Southern Press and some of the letters. They were a little suspicious of us all along, but now they know we are abolitionists."[38]

On January 23, 1896, Susan B. Anthony gave the opening remarks at NAWSA's Twenty-Eighth Annual Convention in Washington, D.C. Pointing to the seating section for the delegates, she noted that the large American flag had three extra stars. The big one was for Wyoming "because it stood alone for a quarter of a century as the only place where women had full suffrage." A small star was for Colorado, where men, for the first time, "voted to grant women equal rights."[39]

The other small star was for Utah where women had been enfranchised by the territorial legislature in 1870, only to be deprived of their right by the United States Congress in 1887. Having recently approved a new state constitution that banned polygamy, Utah had been admitted to the United States. The new constitution also enfranchised women, a victory spearheaded by Emmeline B. Wells. A Mormon and the seventh wife of Daniel H. Wells, with whom she had three daughters, Emmeline Wells was the longtime editor of the *Women's Exponent* and a close friend of Stanton and Anthony. "I believe in women," Wells once wrote, "especially thinking women."[40]

In 1896, woman suffrage amendment referenda were on the ballot in two states: Idaho and California. Suffragists came from far and wide to help. In Idaho, sixty-two-year old Abigail Scott Duniway from Oregon gave 140 lectures, traveling 12,000 miles through rugged country "by river, rail, stage and buckboard and canvassed many a mile on foot."[41] Duniway, known for being cantankerous, had been fighting for the vote since 1871 when she founded a women's rights newspaper, *The New Northwest,* and accompanied Susan B. Anthony on a two-month, two-thousand-mile lecture tour through the Territories of Oregon, Washington, and British Columbia in Canada. The mother of six children and sole supporter of her family after her husband was disabled by a team of runaway horses, Duniway had a "wondrous deep contralto voice." Her lectures were said to be "logical, sarcastic, witty, poetic, and often eloquent."[42]

Carrie Chapman Catt arrived in Idaho in August. Mary Bradford from Colorado arrived in September. For six weeks, she "traveled over sandhills, mountains, valleys and sage plains" to organize suffrage clubs and gain converts for the cause. On Election Day, November 3, 1896, intrepid suffragists "stood all day in ankle-deep snow" and gave each male voter a flier reading:

44

"Vote for the woman suffrage amendment."[43] Male voters approved the Idaho Women's Right to Suffrage Amendment, known as Senate Joint Resolution 2, by a majority of 5,844: 12,126 yeas, 6,282 nays.

As they would throughout women's fight for enfranchisement, opponents tried to overturn the victory. In this case, they filed a lawsuit. The issue was that more voters voted on candidates than they did on the amendment. Opponents claimed that the amendment had to win by a majority of the total number of voters. Newspapers around the country reported that the amendment had been defeated. Suffragists spent weeks of waiting and worrying until December 16 when the Idaho Supreme Court unanimously ruled that the amendment had carried. OUR WOMEN CAN VOTE! proclaimed a Lewiston, Idaho newspaper.[44] The *Woman's Journal* cheered: "Welcome, Idaho! State No. 4 has wheeled into line!"[45]

In California at the start of the legislative session in January 1895, a multitude of prominent and formidable women arrived *en masse* in Sacramento to lobby and testify for equal suffrage, including Laura de Force Gordon, who had given the first suffrage speech in California shortly after she settled there in 1868; Ellen Clark Sargent, president of the California Equal Suffrage Association; Clara Shortridge Foltz, a pioneering lawyer who would achieve significant legal reforms; and Naomi Bowman Talbert Anderson, a poet and lecturer, who was born to free black parents. In March, a bill was passed and signed by the governor authorizing a referendum on a woman suffrage resolution in 1896.

Seventy-six-year-old Susan B. Anthony devoted eight months to the campaign. Suffrage workers canvassed voters and circularized tons of literature. Leaflets were on display in streetcars; left in hotels, libraries, theaters, and post offices; and slipped into packages and grocery parcels. Hundreds of precinct meetings were held. Children were enlisted—"Every boy and girl who could sing, play, declaim, write an essay or in any other way entertain was enlisted for oratorical debates, prize essays and public meetings."[46] Members of the Colored Woman's Club, led by Mary T. Longley, successfully convinced many black male voters to support the amendment.

Just days before the election, the Liquor Dealers' League launched a scare campaign and unleashed a "vituperative frenzy of hostility," paying for scurrilous material that appeared in the pages of the major newspaper.[47] In a letter to "saloon-keepers, hotel proprietors, druggists, and grocers throughout the state," the League warned: "It is to your interest and ours to vote against this amendment."[48] Male voters defeated the California Women's Suffrage Amendment by a majority of 26,744: 110,355 yeas, 137,099 nays.

The following year, Susan B. Anthony celebrated both the win and the defeat at NAWSA's Twenty-Ninth Annual Convention held in Des Moines, Iowa, despite blizzard conditions: "I rejoice exceedingly over Idaho. I also rejoice exceedingly over the grand work done in California."[49] Reading her optimistic words, we might surmise that Susan B. Anthony believed that the fight would be won soon. But it was not to be. Congress would ignore the proposed Sixteenth Amendment. Suffragists would slog through years of strenuous efforts state-by-state, yielding no equal suffrage victories, just defeats. Only miniscule hard-won progress was made in gaining partial suffrage.

"I am so dead tired and heart-sore that I almost wish I were lying quiet in my grave," wrote seventy-three-year-old Caroline Elizabeth Merrick after testifying before the Suffrage Committee of the 1898 Louisiana Constitutional Convention: "God help all women, young and old! They are a man-neglected, God-forgotten lot, here in Louisiana, when they ask simply for a reasonable recognition, and justice under the Constitution now being constructed, and under which they must be governed and pay taxes. . . . Oh, Lord, how long!"[50]

As for many women, a discriminatory incident had prompted Caroline Merrick to fight for women's rights. It had happened in

1878, when she was on the board of St. Ann's Asylum, a home for destitute women and children. A will in which a woman had left St. Ann's a thousand dollars was declared invalid because it had been witnessed by women including Caroline Merrick. "The bequest went to the State—and the women went to thinking and agitating," wrote Merrick.

The next year, Merrick and Elizabeth Lyle Saxon, president of the Ladies Physiological Association dedicated to the study of female anatomy—a scandalous, even taboo topic—obtained signatures from four hundred people on a petition that listed grievances such as "excluded from holding office . . . debarred from being witnesses in wills or notarial acts." As for the vote, the petition read: "As a question of civilization, we look upon the enfranchisement of woman as an all important one." They presented the petition at the 1879 constitutional convention.

When asked if she would testify, Saxon replied: "I would, I would lay my life down for the cause, if necessary, to insure its success." She told Merrick who considered having her son-in-law speak for her because her voice was not very strong: "Represent yourself now, if you only stand up and move your lips." The convention granted women a tidbit—the ability to hold some school offices.[51] Now, nineteen years later at the 1898 constitutional convention, Merrick reported that tax-paying women were granted the right to vote on tax matters—"a mere crumb—but a prophetic crumb." Prophetic because the following year, a coalition of suffragists and civic-minded residents of New Orleans organized 10,000 tax-paying women to approve a measure raising taxes to improve the antiquated sewer and drainage system, thus ending the cycle of floods and epidemics. "The battle was won," Merrick wrote, "as was universally conceded, by the energy of the woman's vote." To "womanly sweetness," she proclaimed, was added "*power*—a power which could not only be felt but which would have to be counted."[52]

Notwithstanding Merrick's optimism, many suffragists came to think that the fight for the vote was in "the doldrums."[53] In fact, according to historian Sara Hunter Graham, it was undergoing a "suffrage renaissance . . . to become the movement of the masses . . . packaged in a form more attractive to a wider audience."[54] The transformation was spearheaded by grassroots suffragists and national leaders such as Carrie Chapman Catt, who declared that a defeat was merely a "victory deferred."[55] A new three-year course of study in politics was created for local suffrage clubs to prepare women to be informed voters. Efforts were made to inject women's history in library collections and school textbooks to counterbalance the glut of "fathers" in history books: "Pilgrim Fathers, Plymouth Fathers, Forefathers, Revolutionary Fathers, City Fathers, Church Fathers . . . but, no mothers!"[56]

The "Society Plan" to recruit wealthy, socially prominent women and men was implemented on a national level. Parlor meetings, or small-group gatherings in a private home, were held to recruit conservative women who thought it was improper for women to attend public events like mass meetings. Many of these women belonged to women's clubs that were affiliated with the General Federation of Women's Clubs, founded by Jane Cunningham Croly, an influential journalist who wrote under the name "Jennie June." Women's clubs, historian Elna C. Green writes, "provided a forum for discussing women's issues and a training ground for honing the skills necessary to address those issues," thus preparing new recruits for the suffrage cause.[57]

NAWSA sought alliances with members of other organizations that had proliferated to address various issues such as the Women's Christian Temperance Union (WCTU). Originally established "as a non-violent protest against the dangers of alcohol," WCTU had broadened its agenda under the leadership by Frances Willard, a dynamic, charismatic woman, with a broad vision of social reform from temperance to improved municipal sanitation to strong anti-rape laws. A friend of Susan B. Anthony, Willard, whose motto was "do everything," advocated for woman suffrage as a tool women could use to secure reforms.[58]

No alliances, however, were made with organizations of black women who steadfastly fought for the right to vote. Black women from Rhode Island to Louisiana to North Dakota organized local suffrage clubs across the country, some named after early activists, including Sojourner Truth and Frances Ellen Watkins Harper. The philanthropist known as the "Mother of Clubs," Mary McCoy, who had been born in an Underground Railroad station, and Lucinda Thurman, a prominent community organizer, founded the Michigan State Association of Colored Women's Clubs. Other black women organized and spoke out on the national level, such as Mary Ann Shadd Cary, a pioneering journalist and lawyer, with "determination shining from her sharp eyes."[59] The preeminent educator, writer, and orator Anna Julia Cooper, who had been born the daughter of a slave and her white owner, declared at the World's Congress of Representative Women in 1893: "We take our stand on the solidarity of humanity."[60]

The journalist and activist Josephine St. Pierre Ruffin, who had worked with Lucy Stone and Julia Ward Howe for woman suffrage in Massachusetts in the 1870s, founded the *Woman's Era*, the first newspaper solely written and published for black women. When Ruffin's newspaper printed a call to form a national organization, hundreds of black women responded, gathering in Boston on July 29–31, 1895, for the first meeting of the National Federation of Afro-American Women. In her opening speech, Ruffin declared that it was time "to stand forth and declare ourselves and our principles, to teach an ignorant and suspicious world that our aims and interests are identical with those of all good, aspiring women."[61]

The Thirtieth NAWSA convention, in 1898, marked the fiftieth anniversary of the Seneca Falls Woman's Rights Convention. Elizabeth Cady Stanton, now eighty-two years old and limited by failing eyesight, sent a paper to be read aloud in which she exhorted delegates to "with active, aggressive warfare, take possession."[62] Mary Church Terrell, president of the National

Association of Colored Women's Clubs, addressed the convention: "In spite of the obstacles encountered, the progress made by colored women along many lines appears like a veritable miracle of modern times. . . . Seeking no favors because of their color, nor charity because of their needs they knock on the door of Justice and ask for an equal chance."[63]

The Colored American: National Negro Newspaper, *February 17, 1900, published this sketch of Mary Church Terrell after her second address to the National American Woman Suffrage Association (NAWSA). The caption noted: "Her address on 'Woman Suffrage' the Hit of the Recent Gathering of America's Brainiest Women." (Library of Congress)*

The horrific news in the spring of 1892 that her close friend Robert Moss had been lynched by a white mob in Memphis, Tennessee, had spurred Terrell to join forces with other black women to organize the Colored Women's League of Washington "to promote the best interest of the colored people in any direction that suggests itself."[64] In her autobiography, Mary Church Terrell wrote that from a very early age she believed in "woman suffrage with all my heart . . . . . I am glad I always believed in this great cause, not only because it gives me satisfaction to know that I was on the right side of the question when it was most unpopular to advocate it, but because it was the means of bringing me into direct, personal contact with some of the brainiest and finest women in the country."[65]

A large audience of women and men, some "white-haired and wrinkled," others "in the prime and vigor of life" attended NAWSA's Thirty-Second Annual Convention in February 1900. They listened with "a moist eye and tightened throat" as Susan B. Anthony spoke in her "fine voice with its rich alto vibrations." Eighty years old and "clad as usual in soft black satin with duchesse lace in the neck and sleeves and the lovely red crepe shawl falling gracefully from her shoulders," Susan B. Anthony announced her resignation as NAWSA's president.[66] She had anointed Carrie Chapman Catt to succeed her. Anna Howard Shaw remained the vice president. "I am not retiring now," Anthony informed the audience, "because I feel unable, mentally or physically, to do the necessary work. . . . I want to see you all at work, while I am alive, so I can scold if you do not do it well."[67]

PART II

Chapter 4

Persevere: 1900-1906

Work, each of you, with all your heart. —Charlotte Perkins Gilman

"College women should realize their debt to the pioneers," concluded Maud Wood Park, a smart, socially astute woman known for her commitment to the fight for the vote. A recent graduate of Radcliffe College, she had been astonished when one of her professors asked who supported woman suffrage. Out of 72 students, only Park and another student raised their hands. At the 1900 NAWSA convention, the first one she had attended, Park was struck by the fact that she was by far the youngest person there. Deeply moved by hearing Susan B. Anthony speak, Maud Wood Park realized "the heroism of her service not for herself but for the sex, and so for the whole human race."[1] That same year, she recruited her closest friend at Radcliffe, Inez Haynes Irwin, to cofound the College Equal Suffrage League (CESL). Park personally organized CESL branches in thirty states that coalesced into a national organization of energetic young college-educated suffragists, and affiliated with NAWSA.

Dramatic floral displays and multicolored flags of thirty nations flanked the speakers' platform at the 1902 NAWSA Annual Convention. (The flags were on loan from suffragist Clara Barton, founder of the American Red Cross, who had received them as gifts for her work in providing relief abroad.) Above the platform hung the resplendent suffrage flag with its regal blue background and four golden stars for the states where women were fully enfranchised: Wyoming, Colorado, Utah, and Idaho. Telegrams and letters from well-wishers were read aloud. John Hutchinson, the ninety-year-old sole survivor of the Hutchinson Family Singers, with a white beard to the middle of his chest, a bushy mustache, shaggy eyebrows, and long hair down to his shoulders, led the huge crowd in singing "The Battle Hymn of the Republic," the stirring Civil War song written by suffragist Julia Ward Howe.

More than a thousand people attended the weeklong event held in February in Washington, D.C., a joint event with the first meeting of the International Woman Suffrage Conference. Clara Bewick Colby, founder of the influential suffrage publication the *Women's Tribune*, extended greetings from Elizabeth Cady Stanton and read her paper on "Educated Suffrage." All voters, Stanton wrote, must be able to "read and write the English language." She called for Congress to enact a law for "educated suffrage" because, she pointed out: "As women are governed by a 'male aristocracy' we are doubly interested in having our rulers able at least to read and write."[2] Susan B. Anthony vehemently disagreed. "As women," she declared, "we cannot ask that any one be disenfranchised."[3]

Mass immigration in the late 1800s had prompted a resurgence of American xenophobia that fueled support for a literacy requirement for voters. An informal vote at the next NAWSA convention revealed "a great deal of sentiment" for "educated suffrage," undoubtedly because some delegates had participated in campaigns where they had observed opponents bribing non-English-speaking immigrant men to vote against enfranchising women. (Immigrant men with their "first papers," or papers stating their intention to become a citizen, could vote. A few states, such as South Dakota, allowed immigrant men to vote even without "first papers.")

Some Southern delegates embraced "educated suffrage" as a way to maintain white supremacy; among them was Belle

Kearney, whose speech at the convention was titled "Woman Suffrage to Insure White Supremacy." NAWSA's leaders, however, affirmed that their official policy "continued to be to ask and work only for the removal of the sex qualification."[4]

Elizabeth Cady Stanton died on October 24, 1902, two weeks before her eighty-seventh birthday, and fifty-four years after she read aloud the Declaration of Sentiments with its sweeping demands at the 1848 Seneca Falls convention. Much had been accomplished in various domains, such as legal rights, opportunities for education and employment, and personal freedom. Piece by piece, *feme covert* (legal rights and obligations of a married woman are subsumed by her husband) was being very slowly dismantled. As for the fight for the vote, the record was dismal.

Partial suffrage had been won in twenty-seven of the forty-five states, but these gains were often challenged in the courts and legislatures. Women in some partial-rights states reported being barred from the polling places. Legislators in Kentucky had recently repealed women's right to vote in school board elections. Suffragists differed as to the value of partial suffrage. "Although our speakers liked to enumerate these scraps of suffrage as signs of progress, in Massachusetts," explained Maud Wood Park, "the fact that only a small minority of eligible women usually voted in school elections was used at legislative hearings, year after year, by anti-suffragists seeking to prove that most women did not want to vote."[5]

Women in only four sparsely settled Western states had gained equal suffrage, and not for lack of effort on the part of suffragists, who challenged the accepted norms of feminine behaviors and persistently canvassed, campaigned, organized, strategized, orated, published, petitioned, and lobbied. "On average, in every year between 1870 and 1890, 4.4 states considered legislation giving women the vote," writes historian Lee Ann Banaszak.[6] Virtually all of it, however, was either buried by a committee or defeated by legislators in a floor vote, leaving many suffragists "exhausted and despairing for a number of years," their scant resources depleted.[7] The 1898 equal suffrage campaign in Washington spearheaded by Laura E. Peters exemplifies the chicanery of the legislative opposition.

Peters, a "radical, aggressive, progressive" woman with "a beautiful singing voice," had moved to the Territory of Washington in 1864 and voted during 1883–1887, the period when women were enfranchised by the Territorial Legislature before being disenfranchised by the Territorial Supreme Court.[8] "I was paralyzed when I saw . . . that the rights had been taken from us, and I have hardly got over my paralytic shock yet." Peters said. "I believe we should go into the war and fight against the war on women."[9]

A politically active woman, Laura Peters was elected a delegate to the People's Party (also known as the Populist Party) state convention in 1896. As a member of the platform committee, she forced that convention to pledge for woman suffrage. When fusion forces, an alliance of Populists and other progressive parties, won a majority in the legislature, Peters went to the capitol in Olympia to ensure that the newly elected legislators passed a bill submitting a woman suffrage amendment to voters in a referendum.

That they did, and the bill was sent to the governor's office for his signature, or so supporters thought. But, when "by the merest accident," Peters's friend, Senator Thomas Miller, checked on the bill: "Lo and behold! He discovered that the true bill had been stolen during a short recess and an absolutely worthless bill embossed and signed."

Exposing the "fraud," Miller managed to get a "true bill" passed, but not until the last day the legislature was in session. Peters urgently requested that she be appointed a "special messenger" to personally deliver the bill to the governor for his signature, pointing out that "the bill had been delayed, deformed, pigeon-holed and stolen," and that she "would not feel safe until it was made law by the governor's signature." Her request was approved, and "duly sworn" she "very proudly carried the bill to the office where Gov. John R. Rogers affixed his signature to it."[10] Her success was short lived: Male voters overwhelmingly defeated the Washington Women's Right to Vote, Amendment to Article VI, Sec. 9 by a majority of 17,864:15,986 yeas, 33,850 nays, a loss Peters said that "cut her sorely."

Laura E. Peters died in 1902. Interestingly, the story of the stolen bill and her role as a "special messenger" was reported in her obituary, undoubtedly in admiration, and perhaps as a cautionary note to suffragists to remain vigilant, a stance they would need to adopt over and over in their fight for the vote.[11]

Shortly before Elizabeth Cady Stanton died, her daughter Harriot Stanton Blatch, along with her husband and daughter Nora (her other child, Helen, died at the age of five), returned to the United States, having lived in England for twenty years. During her years in England, Blatch had embraced the "great socialistic questions of the day—capital and labor, woman suffrage and race prejudice." A prominent member of the Women's Franchise League, founded in 1889 by Emmeline and Richard Pankhurst, she was honored as one of thirty British women for her work "toward women's freedom or freedom generally."[12]

In 1903, forty-five-year-old Emmeline Pankhurst, now a widow, and her daughters Christabel, Sylvia, and Adela, who ranged in age from twenty-three to eighteen, founded the Women's Social and Political Union (WSPU), a militant suffrage organization that would reverberate in America. "Deeds, Not Words" was the WSPU's call to arms. In an article trivializing and ridiculing members of the WSPU, a British newspaper coined the word suffragette, a moniker the WSPU boldly appropriated. The phrase—"Votes for Women"—first appeared on a WSPU banner made from a small piece of white calico with the words painted in black furniture stain. Pankhurst and Harriot Stanton Blatch would remain allies in the fight for the vote.

Forthright and politically astute, Harriot Stanton Blatch returned to America during a period now known as the Progressive Era. Many Americans embraced activism in response to the massive economic and social problems resulting from post–Civil War rapid industrialization and urbanization fueled by an influx of immigrants, a powerless labor force trapped in exploitative jobs and overcrowded tenements. Journalists (dubbed "muckrakers"), writers, photographers, artists, academics, and reform-minded citizens—especially middle-class women—tackled many issues: corporate corruption, poverty, slums, factory conditions, child labor, political bosses and their machines, schools, temperance, and public health.

Settlement houses, an idea that originated in England, were established in urban areas populated by working-class, impoverished immigrants. Professional women and wealthy and middle-class volunteer women lived in the settlement houses with the purpose of building a community with their immigrant working-class neighbors, both to learn from them and provide services, including education, cultural events, health care, child care, legal aid, and recreation. Hull House, the most famous settlement house in America, was established in 1889 in Chicago by the much-admired reformer Jane Addams, who would become the first American woman to be awarded the Nobel Peace Prize.

Addams, a suffragist and leader in NAWSA, stressed the practicality of voting: Women needed the vote—an "implement for self-government," she called it—in order to ameliorate their living and working conditions, thus protecting their homes, children, and communities. It was women's responsibility, indeed their "duty," to become conscientious citizens who voted for reform-minded politicians.[13] This argument, writes historian Victoria Bissell Brown, "converted" many "reform-minded women" to the fight for the vote "out of frustration when politicians failed to take their lobbying seriously and/or opposed the reforms they supported."[14]

The fight for the vote during the nineteenth century had not been high on working women's agenda; more immediate was the fight for fair and equal wages, safe working and living conditions, and a shorter working day. That dynamic changed by the end of the 1880s. Wage-earning women like Mary Kenney, a skilled bookbinder who organized trade unions, joined women's fight for the vote. The daughter of Irish working-class immigrants, Kenney moved from Hannibal, Missouri, to Chicago in 1882. There she lived in Hull House and became a close friend of Jane Addams and Florence Kelley. Kelley, a fiery, influential socialist and reformer, had deep roots in the fight for women's rights. Her great-aunt Sara Pugh had been a member of the female delegation, along with Lucretia Mott, that was refused a seat at the 1840 World Anti-Slavery Convention. Her father, William Kelley, was a friend of Anthony and Stanton and a long-serving member of Congress who advocated for woman suffrage.

The experience of living with passionate activists, Mary Kenney once said, "gave my life new meaning and hope."[15] At Hull House, she created the "Jane Club," a cooperative with six apartments for low-income women. In 1894, she married John O'Sullivan and moved to Boston, where they lived in a settlement house. Bucking the norm that, once married, a woman left the paid workforce, she continued organizing workers and trade unions. Also upending the norm, her husband, a labor editor for the *Boston Globe*, shared in caring for their three children until his death in an accident in 1902.

A year later, Mary Kenney O'Sullivan founded the Women's Trade Union League (WTUL), a pioneering organization run by wage-earning women that brought together a diverse group of people: wage-earning women; trade unionists; and professional women, including lawyers, and social reformers. WTUL's purpose was to organize wage-earning women into trade unions, promote labor-friendly legislation, and fight for woman suffrage.

A few years later, O'Sullivan spoke before NAWSA and testified before congressional committees (an annual tradition begun in 1869 by Anthony and Stanton). Standing before members of the House Judiciary Committee, she bluntly told the representatives: "Right here in Washington, in your big bindery of the Government, a trade to which I gave the larger part of my life, the women who do equal work with the men do not receive equal pay. The Government more than any other employer has taken advantage of women of my class because they do not have the vote."[16]

The fight for the vote entered the twentieth century with new recruits joining forces with battle-worn veterans, including women dubbed the "New Woman." Young and energetic, these women were typically single, well-educated professionals who embraced feminism and self-fulfillment. New organizations joined the fight, including labor unions and the Men's League for Woman Suffrage. The Socialist Party of America, organized in 1901, included a woman suffrage plank in its party platform, although not all socialists were suffragists. The issue was not about equality, but about which struggle should come first—votes for women or freeing the working class from the tyranny of capitalism. An exchange between Eugene V. Debs, a renowned labor leader, and Susan B. Anthony illustrates this divide.

They had first met in 1879, when twenty-four-year-old Debs escorted fifty-nine-year-old Susan B. Anthony to her hotel when she arrived by train to speak in Terre Haute, Indiana, over the objections of local officials. "As we walked along the street," Debs recalled, "I was painfully aware that Miss Anthony was an object of derision and contempt."[17] Many years later, Debs went to Anthony's home in Rochester, New York, to pay his respects. As the story goes, Anthony was surprised that Debs remembered her.

"Remember you! How could anyone ever forget Susan B. Anthony," Debs told her. During their amicable conversation, Anthony said: "Give us suffrage and we'll give you socialism." To which Debs replied: "Give us socialism and we'll give you the vote."[18] Charlotte Perkins Gilman, a longtime suffragist as well as a prominent intellectual, feminist, poet, and author of the influential *Women in Economics*, weighed in on the issue by writing a poem "The Socialist and the Suffragist" with six stanzas contrasting the different perspectives and concluding:

Work, each of you, with all your heart—

Just get into the game![19]

Women's fight for the vote, while not yet a juggernaut, was a widely recognized and active movement. More states were considering suffrage bills, and suffragists were less likely to be ridiculed. When Carrie Chapman Catt, NAWSA's president, testified at a constitutional convention in Virginia, a reporter described her as "a fine looking woman" whose "speech was an eloquent and scholarly appeal for the incorporation of a woman's suffrage clause into the new Constitution of Virginia."[20] Victories, however, were elusive. Instead of woman suffrage, racist and classist provisions to restrict suffrage were added to the new Virginia state constitution.

In New Hampshire in 1903, suffragists campaigned throughout a bitterly cold winter. Carrie Chapman Catt came and debated the Reverend Lyman Abbott, the anti-suffragists' front man. She reported that at a crowded meeting she "laid him out . . . as flat as dishwater."[21] But no matter; male voters defeated the New Hampshire Voting Rights for Women Amendment by a majority of 7,626: 14,162 yeas, 21,788 nays. Legislators in only four states had granted women partial-suffrage rights on school matters or tax issues. Congressional committees "utterly ignored" the question of enfranchising women, their members "stone deaf" to activists' "pleadings and arguments."[22]

Worn down by years of intensely organizing and campaigning, in addition to caring for her mother and husband, both of whom were terminally ill, Carrie Chapman Catt resigned as president at the 1904 NAWSA convention. Anna Howard Shaw, who had given up careers as an ordained minister and as a medical doctor to fight for the vote, was elected president, with Catt agreeing to serve as vice president.

A statue of Anna Howard Shaw, located in Anna Howard Shaw Memorial Park, Big Rapids, Michigan, is inscribed with her words: "Nothing bigger can come to a human being than to love a great cause more than life itself." (Penny Colman Collection)

A close friend of Susan B. Anthony and the life companion of Anthony's niece Lucy Anthony, Anna Howard Shaw was a heralded orator, skilled at using irreverence and humor to deflate self-righteous opponents. Speaking to a large audience of women in Utah, she related her encounter with a man who believed that "a girl should be born with a burning desire to wash dishes." Laughter and applause erupted when Shaw advised the audience to tell such men "to go soak their heads in water til [sic] they were blessed with a little sense."[23] As president, she refused to endorse policies that "advocated the exclusion of any race or class from the right of suffrage."[24]

In June, Shaw, Carrie Chapman Catt, eighty-four-year-old Susan B. Anthony, Mary Church Terrell, and Charlotte Perkins Gilman were among the American delegates who went to Berlin, Germany, for the first meeting of the International Woman

Suffrage Alliance (IWSA), formerly the International Woman Suffrage Conference. Catt, who had long been interested in international suffrage movements, was elected president. Apparently worried that she would overshadow them, some German activists asked Susan B. Anthony not to attend a mass public meeting. Anthony complied and remained in her hotel room.

The presiding officer, however, opened the meeting by asking: "Where is Susan B. Anthony?" At that, reported Anna Howard Shaw, "The entire audience rose, men jumped on their chairs, and the cheering continued without a break for ten minutes." Later, while Shaw eagerly told Anthony about the crowd's exuberant response to the "mere mention" of her name, she unexpectedly noticed that Anthony's "lips quivered and her brave old eyes filled with tears." The tribute meant so much, Shaw realized, because "what the world called stoicism in Susan B. Anthony throughout the years of her long struggle had been, instead, the splendid courage of an indomitable soul—while all the time the woman's heart had longed for affection and recognition."[25]

The four days of meetings included many speeches given in German, French, or English, and then translated into the other two. This unprecedented event was widely covered in the press; perhaps because they had never seen such a gathering of activist women (or because of their inherent assumptions about women's abilities), male reporters were entranced by the delegates' intelligence, self-assurance, and sophistication.

Following the IWSA event, the International Council of Women (ICW) held its convention. Although founded by Elizabeth Cady Stanton and Susan B. Anthony in 1888, ICW was reluctant to support woman suffrage, for fear of alienating its conservative members. Nevertheless many suffragists attended the ICW convention, including the American delegates, several of whom spoke. Mary Church Terrell gave a speech that needed no translator; fluent in several languages, she first gave her speech in English, and then repeated her speech in German and in French, dazzling the audience. Demand was so great to hear Charlotte Perkins Gilman talk about her provocative book *Women and Economics* that she gave it twice, delighting some and infuriating others with her provocative ideas, including that women's unpaid work in housekeeping and child rearing was a form of oppression.

A year later, in June 1905, Anna Howard Shaw and Carrie Chapman Catt, along with delegates from the East Coast and Midwest, were on their way to Portland, Oregon, site of NAWSA's Thirty-Seventh Annual Convention, the first to be held on the West Coast. Traveling by train, Shaw and Catt, their journey well publicized in newspapers, were greeted with flowers, and gave speeches from the rear platform at stops along the way.

Two cities had vied for the honor of hosting NAWSA's 1905 convention: Buffalo, New York, and Portland, Oregon. The two-fold lures of Portland, a thriving port city built on the banks of the Willamette River, with spectacular mountains nearby, won out. First was the Lewis and Clark Exposition, which would include the dedication of Alice Cooper's seven-foot bronze statue of Sacajawea with her infant, Jean-Baptiste, strapped to her back. A Lemhi Shoshone woman, Sacajawea helped guide Captain Meriwether Lewis and Second Lieutenant William Clark on their perilous westward expedition.

The second lure was that a woman suffrage amendment referendum would be on the ballot in Oregon in 1906. Having suffered defeats in 1884 and 1900 referenda, the moribund Oregon Equal Suffrage Association needed the boost of hosting a national convention with its roster of leaders, who by now were nationally renowned: Susan B. Anthony, Anna Howard Shaw, and Carrie Chapman Catt. A show of force would also belie the age-old argument that women did not want the vote.

Suffragists from around the country traveled to Portland to attend the ten-day convention, which ran from the end of June through the Fourth of July. They met at the First Congregational Church, where there were large letters made of flowers spelling the word "progress" in front of the pulpit. Elegant vases filled with white lilies, red roses, and sundry other flowers were on the speakers' platform. Banners, buntings, and flags hung throughout the church. Delegates wearing yellow badges greeted Susan B. Anthony with a "wild ovation" and threw flowers onto the platform. "Well, this is rather different from the receptions I used to get fifty years ago," she said, eyeing the heap of flowers. "They threw things at me then—but they were not roses."[26]

Eight months later, in February 1906, Susan B. Anthony, suffering from a bad cold, missed many sessions at the NAWSA Annual Convention held in Baltimore, Maryland. Appearing pale and weak, she attended a fundraiser for the Oregon campaign, with the vote just four months away. Donating a small bag with seventeen five-dollar gold pieces, a birthday gift from friends, she said, "I suppose they wanted me to do as I liked with the money and I wish to send it to Oregon."

On one of the last days of the convention, Anthony again summoned the strength to address the delegates. Appearing so "frail as to seem almost spiritual," she invoked the foremothers: "Mary Wollstonecraft, Lucretia Mott, the Grimké sisters, Elizabeth Cady Stanton, Lucy Stone—a long galaxy of great women." She issued a call to arms: "The fight must not cease; you must see that it does not stop."[27] Several days later in Washington, D.C., at a gala birthday party for her, a weakened Susan B. Anthony was reported to have said: "There have been others just as true and devoted to the cause—I wish I could name every one—but with such women consecrating their lives— failure is impossible!"[28]

Four weeks later, on March 13, 1906, Susan B. Anthony died at her home in Rochester, New York. SUSAN B. ANTHONY DIES PEACEFULLY, announced the front-page headline in a Los Angeles, California newspaper.[29] Two days later, her funeral was held. Thousands of people—ten thousand by some estimates—braved a fierce storm of icy wind and swirling snow to file past her coffin, above which hung the silk suffrage flag, still with only four gold stars, despite decades of steadfast efforts, oftentimes under unfathomably difficult conditions.

In the eulogy, Anna Howard Shaw proclaimed, "The ages to come will revere her name."[30] A "beautiful and impressive" memorial service was held at the next NAWSA Annual Convention. Frances "Fannie" Barrier Williams, who helped found the National Association of Colored Women, was asked to speak "in behalf of colored people." Subtly but pointedly acknowledging NAWSA's resistance to aligning with black women suffragists, Williams began, "My presence on this platform shows that the gracious spirit of Miss Anthony still survives in her followers." She continued by reminding the delegates of their heritage—"When Miss Anthony took up the cause of women she did not know them by their color, nationality, creed or birth, she stood only for the emancipation of women from the thralldom of sex. . . . She saw no substitute for liberty."[31]

Heeding Anthony's command that the "fight must not cease," suffragists hastened to help the Oregon referendum campaign, with the vote less than three months away. Shortly before the election, the Brewers' and Wholesale Liquor Dealers' Association secretly informed 2,000 liquor retailers: "It will take 50,000 votes to defeat woman suffrage." Figuring that twenty-five times 2,000 equals 50,000, each retailer was instructed to round up twenty-five additional voters. Twenty-five sample, pre-marked ballots and a return postal card indicating their participation were enclosed with instructions: "You need not sign the card. Every card has a number and we will know who sent it in. Let us all pull together. . . . Let us each get 25 votes."[32]

Male voters defeated the Oregon Suffrage for Women Amendment, known as Measure 2, by a majority of 10,173: 36,902 yeas, 47,075 nays. Women who had served as poll watchers were convinced they had been cheated. Young men were seen handing out anti-suffrage cards at the polling places, each one promised an extra dollar if woman suffrage was defeated.

Women poll watchers were blocked from watching judges count the ballots.

Shortly before Susan B. Anthony died she had told Anna Howard Shaw, "Think of it! I have struggled for sixty years for a little bit of justice and die without securing it."[33] With her death, the question remained: How many more years of struggle would be needed? Suffragists carried on, bolstering their resolve by highlighting progress, even in defeats. Anna Howard Shaw heralded the Oregon men who cast "yea" votes: "Their descendants will not be ashamed of their fathers' act."[34] Celebrating the news that women in Finland won full suffrage in 1906, Shaw underscored global solidarity—"Wherever freedom comes to any woman that is our victory."[35]

Chapter 5

Stir Things Up: 1907-1909

The time has come. —Rose Schneiderman

"The American men are in for it," warned a newspaper in Toledo, Oregon.[1] The alarming news was that Harriot Stanton Blatch had founded the Equality League of Self-Supporting Women, an organization made up of "any woman who earns her own living, from a cook to a mining engineer" whether union or non-union, industrial or professional.[2] Blatch, who thought the suffrage movement was "in a rut," had set out to stir things up.[3] She paid the expenses for women workers to testify for the first time before New York legislators in Albany. Clara Silver, a garment industry organizer, told the men: "Bosses think and women come to think of themselves that they don't count for so much as men" because women are denied suffrage."[4]

Blatch also invited Anne Cobden-Sanderson, an English suffragette to give lectures in America. Cobden-Sanderson, a prominent, affluent, middle-aged woman, undertook militant action when she realized that the public was indifferent, even approving, when young, working-class suffragettes were sent to jail. Seeking to attract public attention, she had participated in an attempt by WSPU members to enter the House of Commons to advocate for woman suffrage. Blocked by a line of police, then charged by police on horseback, the band of unarmed, battered, and bloodied suffragettes struggled onward. Some made it inside, where they were arrested, including Anne Cobden-Sanderson. "We have talked so much for the Cause now let us suffer for it," she said in court.[5] "I am a law breaker because I want to be a law maker," she declared, repeating the words of John Burns, a labor activist during his trial for incitement in the 1880s.[6]

Cobden-Sanderson refused to pay a fine and was sentenced to two months of hard labor in the notorious Holloway Prison. Her imprisonment precipitated an outcry. "One of the nicest women in England suffering from the coarsest indignity and the most injurious form of ill-treatment," protested her friend, the eminent playwright George Bernard Shaw, in a letter to a London newspaper that was reprinted in a New York City newspaper.[7]

Newspapers from New York to San Francisco to Pensacola, Florida, covered Cobden-Sanderson's three-month lecture tour. Reporters described her as a "persuasive talker" with "gray hair worn in a fluffy-coiffure held by a band of broad lavender ribbon." Enthusiastic crowds gathered to hear her lecture, "Why I Went to Prison." In Washington, D.C., she met with suffragist Belva Lockwood, the audacious lawyer who won the right for women lawyers to practice before the United States Supreme Court. A newspaper published an account, "English Suffragette Hits American Suffragists," with this exchange:

"What impressed me so much in this country," mused Mrs. Sanderson, "is the indifference, the timidity of your women. They seem afraid to go ahead, to do anything for fear of offending some one, is it, or because they think it is not proper to take a hand in politics?. . . ."

"Well, we may appear not to be doing much," said Mrs. Lockwood, seriously, but we are, just the same."[8]

In New York City, Maud Malone was doing a great deal. A tall, slender librarian about twenty-six years old with wavy brown hair and bespectacled eyes "with a glint of humor in them," Maud Malone grew up in a family of political agitators who publicly supported radical issues, such as Ireland's fight for independence from England.[9] She embraced women's fight for the vote. Unafraid of any consequences, Malone initiated new tactics— setting up polling places for women, holding open-air meetings, organizing parades, heckling politicians, and going to jail.

Traditionally, suffragists held small parlor meetings in private homes or raised money to rent a hall. Realizing that the few people who came were already supporters, Maud Malone "decided that if we wanted the vote we had to go to the people and ask for it." In a letter to the editor published in a New York City newspaper, she had announced the start "of a series of open-air meetings." The "active public agitation carried on in England and other countries," she wrote, "has proved of immense educational value by directing public thought to this great question." She specifically invited "women of any nationality" to participate, an explicit counterpoint to the nativism that was then prevalent.[10]

Maud Malone held her first open-air meeting at a corner of Madison Square Park, at the intersection of Fifth Avenue and Broadway at Twenty-Third Street, on January 1, 1908. Braving an icy-cold wind, Malone and a handful of "blue-cheeked, pinked-nosed women" gave speeches, passed out literature, got signatures on a petition, and sold yellow "Votes for Women" buttons for a nickel.[11] Within a year, she was holding open-air meetings four and five nights a week from the Lower East Side to Harlem.

Crowds varied in size and ranged in attitude, from rowdy and rude to occasionally attentive and willing to shout—"Votes for Women!" Troublesome spectators threw stuff, shoved, pushed, heckled, and booed. At an open-air event on Wall Street in February, a raucous mob drowned out the speakers. Men in the buildings on both sides of the street pelted the speakers with wet sponges, ticker tape in long strings, hard rolls, and apple cores. At another event, Harriot Stanton Blatch and Bettina Borrmann Wells, a young English suffragette, were kicked and knocked down. (In London, Emmeline Pankhurst made speeches "under the blistering fire of dried peas" launched by "small boys with pea-shooters.")[12]

Maud Malone was arrested for speaking without a license, although she had been told she did not need a license. With her "head erect . . . like a modern Joan of Arc," she marched to the police station, followed by a "turbulent mob." Defiantly, she appeared before the magistrate who let her go, saying, "I trust you won't do it again."[13] But, of course, she did. Each arrest garnered bold headlines, keeping the issue of woman suffrage before the public: MAUD MALONE ARRESTED; ARREST MAUD MALONE AGAIN; MAUD MALONE, MARTYR; SAD FOR SUFFRAGETTE: MAUD MALONE WARNED BLACKWELL'S ISLAND FOR HER IF SHE KEEPS TALKING.[14] (Blackwell's Island was a notorious prison.

Maud Malone at an open-air meeting in New York City. Her hat, with decorations atop a broad brim, was known as a picture hat. A woman, to the right of Malone, appears to be speaking to and casting a critical eye on the man beside her. (Library of Congress)

The idea of open-air meetings, also called street meetings, spread. Standing on a wooden box beside a "Votes for Women" banner or on the backseat of a car displaying suffrage placards, streamers, pennants, and flags, intrepid suffragists gave speeches wherever a crowd gathered: street corners, parks, parties, fairs, farm shows, carnivals, concert intermissions, between innings at baseball games, movie theaters, the beach, factory gates, church and school events. Adele Clark, a Virginia suffragist, said she "couldn't see a fireplug without beginning 'Ladies and Gentlemen.'"[15] An artist,

Clark would set up her easel and get out her paints to lure a crowd.

In Massachusetts, suffragists flew a mammoth kite, big enough to carry a huge "Votes for Women" banner, to signal the start of a meeting. Suffragists who were told they could not speak on the beach in Nantasket waded into the water and spoke to the audience gathered on the beach. After suffragists drove their car covered with "Votes for Women" signs in a circus procession, the ringmaster invited them to give a speech and pass out literature.

Many conservative, mainstream suffragists, however, strenuously disapproved. Women's "power is in their womanliness . . . [suffrage] will come as a sort of a 'by-product' if women go quietly on their way with whatever work is set before them," said Gabrielle Steward Mulliner.[16] "Shall our women be degraded by talking on the street corners?" Josephine Reuter indignantly asked. "I personally object to our women appearing in public," echoed Belle Grey Taylor.

The controversy over the propriety of open-air meetings exemplified a longstanding issue for women—decorum. Historically suffragists, with their prim parlor meetings and elegant, orderly conventions, had carefully operated within the confines of conventional female behavior. Now, however, a new generation of suffragists was pushing the limits. Not because they were "wishing to attract notoriety," said Bettina Borrmann Wells. "Would you be willing to have cats and rats, bad eggs and cabbages . . . thrown at you for anything but a strong conviction?"[17]

Shortly after the first open-air meeting in January, Maud Malone and Bettina Wells had defied the police who refused to give them a permit, and held a suffrage parade in New York City on February 16, 1908, perhaps the first one in America. (Suffrage parades were held later that same year in Boone, Iowa, and in Oakland, California.) "We are trying to wake up public sentiment in favor of our demands," Malone said.[18]

A reporter counted "between 1,000 and 1,200 male onlookers, and twenty-eight women marchers wearing yellow 'Votes for Women' buttons." Listing the names of the leaders, the reporter included military titles: "Miss Maud Malone, the American General . . . Lydia K. Commander, Brigadier General . . . Miss Lieut. [Lieutenant] Marcella Malone . . . Miss Roddie Miner and Mrs. Julia Goldzier, Corporals of the Guards."[19] Did the reporter add the military titles, mocking the suffragists? Or did the suffragists proudly adopt them?

We do not know. But, we do know that suffragists commonly used martial language: Elizabeth Cady Stanton wrote about "councils of war" and the "mode of attack"; "ammunition" and "bullets"; "combat" and the "enemy"; "weapons" and "revolution"; Susan B. Anthony evoked a "grand army of women." Anna Howard Shaw declared, "We shall win the war."[20] Carrie Chapman Catt exhorted suffragists to "Let the bugle blow again and yet again . . . the final battle is on." The *History of Woman Suffrage* is replete with military images including "rebellion of women" and "battles in this war for justice"[21]

Although parades were commonplace, the novelty of a woman suffrage parade, even a very small one, garnered considerable press coverage. Accounts appeared in newspapers across America. In Honolulu, Hawaii, a newspaper headline read: PROMINENT LADIES WHO WERE IN PARADE OF AGITATORS FOR EQUAL SUFFRAGE.[22] Sketches of Malone and Wells and other suffragists illustrated the article.

In the spring, Maud Malone teamed up with Harriot Stanton Blatch to conduct a tour of open-air meetings in upstate New York. Traveling by trolley, they started the tour in Seneca Falls, Blatch's hometown and site of the women's rights convention organized by her mother in 1848. Vassar College, Blatch's alma mater, in Poughkeepsie, New York, was their last stop.

Vassar's anti-suffrage president banned suffrage events. Not to be deterred, Inez Milholland, an activist student, proposed meeting in the Roman Catholic cemetery that bordered the north side of the campus. A tall, spirited, smart, and athletic woman, Inez Milholland grew up in a socially engaged, wealthy family. She had spent the previous summer participating with suffragettes in London.

A good-sized group of students, alumnae, and local suffragists showed up at the cemetery, some climbing over the fence, others using a gate. It was a pleasant day in early June, so they sat in a circle on the grass. Instead of a yellow "Votes for Women" banner, Blatch displayed one inscribed: "Come, let us reason together" (perhaps in case the president showed up). Rose Schneiderman, a prominent member of Blatch's Equality League, came from New York City to speak, arriving late, having missed the "fast mail train." She discussed trade unionism and "got fully twice as much applause as any of the rest."[23]

A Jewish Polish immigrant, Rose Schneiderman was less than five feet tall with wavy red hair. She started working at the age of thirteen to support her widowed mother and siblings. In time, she became a skilled caps and hats lining-maker and an officer in the United Cloth Hat and Cap Makers Union. An electrifying orator, she fiercely advocated trade unionism, vividly evoked working women's lives of hardship and exploitation, and persuasively connected the vote with the power to improve working conditions. At a convention of women trade unionists, Schneiderman declared: "The time has come when working women of the State of New York must be enfranchised and so secure political power to shape their own labor conditions."[24]

In New York City on Election Day, November 3, 1908, the weather forecast was for rain, not that rain would deter Maud Malone from once again setting up an authentic polling place for women. In bold, black letters on a large yellow poster, she printed an invitation to women to come vote, pinned it to the front of her demure ankle-length outfit, and marched up Seventh Avenue, unfazed by spectators' taunts and "accompanying clang of cowbells, whistles, horns and calls."[25]

She had opened her first "woman's poll" in the Harlem Casino in 1905. A replica of an official all-male polling place, Malone's poll included election inspectors, polling clerks, ballot clerks, and canvas-covered voting booths with a pencil tied to a little shelf for marking the ballot. Twenty-five young women, trained by Malone, were on hand to help the novice voters. Five hundred forty women showed up and voted—"Blushing maidens to white-haired old women . . . pretty girls and homely girls . . . and middle-aged women, deeply interested in affairs political, economic, and social."[26]

More than a thousand women voted at Maud Malone's polls in 1908 including Carrie Chapman Catt. Harriot Stanton Blatch drove a touring car to the polls with a delegation from the League of Self-Supporting Women. The event received extensive coverage in a New York City newspaper, illustrated with four photographs, including one of nine fashionably dressed women seated in and standing around Blatch's large touring car replete with "Votes for Women" posters and a large banner. Once again, Maud Malone demonstrated her ability to keep a spotlight on the cause, thus educating public opinion and garnering support.

At NAWSA's Fortieth Annual Convention in Buffalo, New York, delegates passed a resolution signaling their intent to actively seek a federal woman suffrage amendment to the United States Constitution (aka the Susan B. Anthony Amendment), a strategic addition to their arduous and costly state-by-state campaigns. The plan was to bombard Congress with resolutions, letters of support, and testimonials from legislatures, unions, organizations, clubs, dignitaries, and international leaders. Carrie Chapman Catt was put in charge of a nationwide campaign to obtain signatures on a "Great Petition," demanding a federal suffrage amendment that would be delivered to Congress in 1910. That same year, four states were holding woman suffrage amendment referenda: for the first time in Oklahoma, the fourth time in South Dakota, the fifth time in Oregon, and for the second time Washington.

Washington suffragists had persuaded NAWSA to hold its annual convention in Seattle to coincide with the Alaska-Yukon-Pacific Exposition (AYP), a world's fair that would draw huge crowds. Seizing the opportunity to energize public support, suffragists launched a publicity campaign and planned events to be held at the fair. But, would that be enough to convert Washington's male voters who had overwhelmingly defeated the 1898 referendum? Determined to end the fourteen-year drought since women were enfranchised in Utah and Idaho in 1896, suffragists were cautiously confident.

OH THE WOMEN! THEY ARE COMING TO SEATTLE BY THE TRAIN LOAD THIS WEEK, read the peppy headline in a Seattle newspaper, announcing the arrival of delegates to NAWSA's 1909 annual convention.[27] The eye-catching black-and-white illustration depicted a three-quarters view of a steam locomotive, so vividly rendered that readers might imagine it chugging off the left side of the page. The tender, or coal car, and a line of passenger cars stretched across the page, disappearing into the horizon at the right side. The train was bedecked with sketches of suffragists, all youthful-looking women wearing ankle-length dresses: two standing on the cow catcher, seven standing on the front and side of the locomotive, three seated on top, and many more seated and standing along the top of the cars. Oval frames with headshots of illustrious national leaders were scattered to the right of the train.

The train had traveled from Chicago, Illinois, to Spokane, Washington, picking up suffragists along the way. "Suffrage is surely becoming popular," enthused a reporter, the "progress of delegates across the country is rather like a triumphant march."[28] During an eighteen-hour layover in Spokane, they were welcomed by Emma Smith DeVoe and May Arkwright Hutton, the president and vice president of the Washington Equal Suffrage Association, who had arranged a series of events: tours of Spokane, a chance to swim at a local club, and a performance by a chorus of 1,000 women and men, accompanied by a pipe organ, singing the international suffrage battle hymn. It had been recently adopted at the International Woman Suffrage Alliance (IWSA) meeting in London with the lines: "Bondage is behind you / Freedom is before."[29] (There were many suffrage songs. In 1909 Henry W. Roby published *The Suffrage Song Book: Original Songs, Parodies and Paraphrases.* Roby, a prominent physician in Kansas, adapted the lyrics to popular melodies such as "Three Blind Mice" that began: "Three blind men, . . . They each ran off with a woman's right."[30])

The festivities in Spokane culminated with a six-course banquet in an ornate ballroom. Nelson S. Pratt, the mayor of Spokane, presented Anna Howard Shaw with a gavel made from wood grown in Wyoming, Colorado, Utah, and Idaho, the four full suffrage states. When President Shaw uses it to call "to order the national convention in Seattle," proclaimed Pratt, "it will echo and reecho a movement which in importance and results will equal the shot heard 'round the world at the beginning of the American revolution."

The suffragists left for Seattle aboard another Northern Pacific train arranged for by DeVoe. It made four stops, where "some of the most prominent women in the country" gave speeches from the rear platform of the passenger car. Banner-waving women and children wearing white outfits greeted them with cheers, songs, and baskets of roses, cherries, and apples. "The reason we are here," said Anna Howard Shaw in Tacoma, "is due to the fact that the men of Washington are making a desperate effort to be just."[31]

On July 1, 1909, with a sharp crack of her gavel, President Anna Howard Shaw opened the weeklong convention. Reporters enthusiastically covered the gala affair. A dirigible with a "Votes for Women" banner hovered over the crowds at the Alaska-Yukon-Pacific Exposition. Suffragists distributed buttons, thousands of leaflets, and sold balloons stamped with "Votes for Women" during Suffrage Day at the fair. A group of suffragists climbed to the top of Mount Rainier and planted a "Votes for

Women" flag, creating more publicity for public consumption. Whether all this hoopla for woman suffrage would produce a victory remained to be seen.

In New York City, the mayoral campaign was underway. Escalating her tactics, Maud Malone went boldly politicking. Standing up in her seat at campaign events, invariably surrounded by men, she called out to the candidate, "I demand to know how you stand on the question of the right of women to vote." Unfazed by booing, hissing, and cries of "Put her out!" Malone stood her ground until the police ejected her. Once again, she garnered national publicity. A newspaper in Marion, Ohio, dubbed her "a regular Mrs. Parkhurst [*sic*] of martyrdom."[32]

Coincidentally, Emmeline Pankhurst, herself, arrived in New York City in late October 1909 for a six-week speaking tour. News of Emmeline Pankhurst's visit had aroused anxieties among some Americans about the importation of militancy, SUFFRAGETTE IS HEADED THIS WAY, a newspaper in Walla Walla, Washington warned its readers, and advised "mere men" to "take to the woods until storm is past."[33]

Chapter 6

Radical Changes: 1909-1910

I was exalted. —Alva Belmont

"American women should be allowed suffrage," Emmeline Pankhurst proclaimed to great applause at a grand reception in New York City. "They are just as fit for the franchise as are the American men."[1] A thousand people crowded in to greet her: "Every type of suffragette, ranging from the real dyed-in-the-wool militant English kind to the less aggressive 'Maud Maloners' as followers of the young woman who breaks up political gatherings are called, down to the timid specimens who applaud the movement from the security of her home," wrote a reporter. On October 25, 1909, she spoke in Carnegie Hall. The British fight "may be violent," she told the audience, "but where did men get anything but by violence? Where would this republic be if your fathers had not thrown the tea into Boston harbor?"

Five hundred women were seated on a stage bordered with flags and banners. An article in a New York City newspaper enumerated some of their professions. The data was provided by NAWSA's new National Press Bureau, funded by Alva Belmont. (Belmont had acquired great wealth by defying social norms and divorcing her philandering first husband William Vanderbilt.) The list underscored women's increasingly empowered lives, an incongruous juxtaposition with their political disenfranchisement: "79 teachers, 57 physicians, 6 dentists, 49 social workers, 38 trained nurses, 120 trade unionists; 8 actresses . . . 10 musicians . . . mountain climber, 4 civil engineers, 46 business women; 16 authors . . . 3 sculptors, 1 architect; 4 journalists . . . 16 civil service women, 25 lawyers, and representatives of 13 trades."[2]

Belmont was listed in the program as Mrs. O. H. P. Belmont, O. H. P. being the three initials of her recently deceased, wealthy, second husband's name, Oliver Hazard Perry Belmont. She observed the proceeding from her perch in a box seat facing the stage. Blunt-speaking and used to getting her own way, Belmont had joined NAWSA after a dinner conversation with Anna Howard Shaw that lasted almost until breakfast.

Six months before Pankhurst's Carnegie Hall speech, Alva Belmont was in London as NAWSA's delegate to the IWSA's fourth annual meeting. London was astir, jittery as waves of suffragettes demonstrated and hundreds served time in Holloway Prison, some of them for the second or third time. IWSA's president, Carrie Chapman Catt (former NAWSA president), opposed militancy. Such tactics, she firmly believed, would alienate American men—legislators and voters—who were needed to approve woman suffrage. The political system in Britain, she pointed out, only required the backing of one man, the prime minister, who controlled the government. "We have to get rid of the oldest and hardest prejudice in all history: your fight is against one man, ours against a majority of men; yours is a battle, ours an evolution; yours is picturesque and very tragic, ours is commonplace but sure," she told her British counterparts.[3]

Impatient with Catt's conservative leadership, and "curious to hear these women whom all the public—men, press, and 'society' abused," Alva Belmont went to a WSPU event in Royal Albert Hall where Emmeline Pankhurst and six other women who had just been released from prison were awarded the Holloway Prison Medal, a silver brooch designed by Pankhurst's daughter Sylvia. "Such electric fervor I had never seen nor felt in all my experience," Belmont later wrote. "I was exalted."[4]

Invigorated and determined to enliven the fight for the vote, Alva Belmont hosted two fundraising events in late August at Marble House, her mansion in Newport, Rhode Island. In Salem, Oregon, a front-page newspaper headline read: SUFFRAGE BREAKS OUT AT NEWPORT.[5] The public could wander through the lush gardens for $1. For $5, they could tour her opulent home, over which flew the suffrage flag with still only four stars. An orchestra played in the gardens. Prominent women, including ninety-year-old Julia Ward Howe, gave speeches in a white tent.

The events scandalized the members of high society who summered there. "Woman suffrage has usurped as topic of talk the place of piffle and pink teas," observed a local reporter. An article in the *World Today*, concluded that Alva Belmont's suffrage fundraiser "caused gossip . . . throughout the country. That this gossip will have an excellent effect no one who is interested in the great question has any doubt."[6]

In November, Alva Belmont directed her energy at the other end of the economic spectrum. On November 22, 1909, at a mass meeting at Cooper Union Hall in New York City, organized by WTUL and the Shirt-Waist Makers' Union, Local 25, labor leaders gave speeches in support of garment workers' grievances: abysmal wages, dangerous conditions, harassment, and punitive rules. Finally, Clara Lemlich, a young immigrant garment worker from Ukraine, leapt to her feet, demanding to speak. Known for her bold leadership and bravery in previous strikes, including one in which she was arrested seventeen times and suffered six broken ribs, Lemlich, a tiny woman, was lifted to the speaker's platform. "I have no further patience for talk," she shouted. "I make a motion that we go out in a general strike." Thrusting her arm upward, Lemlich challenged the crowd to swear to an ancient oath: "If I turn traitor to the cause I now pledge, may this hand wither from the arm I now raise."[7]

Between 20,000 and 40,000 thousand workers, mostly young Jewish women, went on strike, now known as the "Uprising of 20,000." Alva Belmont set up fundraising events with society women where young pickets told how they were manhandled, beaten with billy clubs, iron pipes, and sticks by the police and thugs hired by the company. She rented the New York Hippodrome, a recently built, ornate, 5,300-seat theater, for a

80

rally that she kicked off by leading a parade of strikers. "Votes for Women" flags hung on the walls of the building that had a stage big enough to hold a circus. Huge banners printed with slogans hung from the ceiling: "We Demand Equal Pay for Equal Work" and "Give Women the Protection of the Vote."

"The constant proselytizing of suffrage zealot Alva Belmont, who often bailed strikers out of jail, got young workers talking about the vote," writes historian Annelise Orleck.[8] The strike ended with many gains for workers who were rehired, except for Clara Lemlich who was blacklisted. She accepted a job politicizing working women and cofounded the Wage Earners' Suffrage League. Belmont's firsthand experience with working women convinced her: "We must have radical changes." That, she believed, required that "women are recognized on an equal footing with men."[9]

Set on raising NAWSA's visibility, Alva Belmont financed the relocation of its headquarters from the home of Harriet Taylor Upton, NAWSA's treasurer, in Warren, Ohio, to the seventeenth floor of a building in New York City. Her lavish office had red silk on the walls of the anteroom, chairs made of French walnut and carved ebony, and a green velvet carpet. On the ground floor, she opened an affordable self-service lunchroom for working women, complete with free suffrage buttons and literature. She founded the Political Equality Association (PEA), with branch offices in various locations where working women could attend lectures.

Wanting to include black women in PEA, Alva Belmont met with Sarah J. S. Garnet of the Colored Women's Equal Suffrage League of Brooklyn, and Irene L. Moorman, president of the Negro Women's Business League. They arranged a meeting at the Mount Olivet Baptist Church. Newspapers around the country noted the event. INVITES NEGROES TO JOIN, read the headline in a Topeka, Kansas newspaper. Belmont told the gathering, "I feel that unless this cause means freedom and equal rights to all women, of every race, of every creed, rich or poor, its doctrines are worthless, and it must fail."[10] She invited both women and men to join PEA. Over a hundred "colored" people did just that, making Belmont even more notorious among conservative suffragists, earning her the reputation as "an evil influence."[11]

Alice Paul had gone to England in 1907 to continue her education, having already graduated from college and graduate school. A slender woman with a mass of dark hair, Alice Paul had dramatic eyes—"big and quiet; dark—like moss agates,"[12] wrote Inez Haynes Irwin. Others described her eyes as blue-green or blue-violet or dark violet. Everyone agreed that Paul's gaze was irresistible.

Alice Paul, head of the nonviolent, militant National Woman's Party (NWP), was an innovative, savvy strategist and fearless, charismatic leader in the final decade of the fierce fight for the vote. (Library of Congress)

Born in Mt. Laurel, New Jersey, Alice Paul grew up a Quaker; in her world, everyone supported woman suffrage. She had not met any opponents, until the night she heard Christabel Pankhurst, Emmeline's daughter, speak at the University of Birmingham, in England. She was "quite entrancing," Alice Paul later recalled, but Christabel Pankhurst was "shouted down" by rowdy, hostile students. Shocked by the rancor and antagonism, Paul "became from that moment very anxious to help in this movement." When word of the "unforgivable spectacle" reached Lord Oliver Lodge, head of the university, he arranged for Christabel Pankhurst to return to speak. This time the offending students sat in silence. Alice Paul was transformed, becoming a "heart and soul convert."[13] She joined the WSPU and engaged in militant tactics in England and Scotland.

On November 9, 1909, Alice Paul and Amelia Brown, intent on disrupting a speech by Henry Asquith, the notably anti-woman-suffrage prime minister, disguised themselves as scrubwomen and walked with the morning cleaning crew into Guildhall, a medieval building with towers and huge rooms with high-arched ceilings and stained glass windows. Once inside, they dodged police on the lookout for troublemakers, especially suffragettes. One officer got so close that Alice Paul, crouched in a dark place, felt his cloak brush against her face. Finally, safely hidden in a gallery overlooking the banquet hall, they waited until evening.

"It was a weary vigil," Paul later told a reporter, who described her as "a delicate slip of a girl." The prime minister, Paul said, "made a most eloquent speech." They listened, "waiting for a chance to break in. At last, there came a pause. So their voices could be heard, Amelia Brown quickly took off a shoe and broke a small stained glass window. One, she said "that could be easily replaced." Together, they shouted—"How about votes for women?"

"You would have thought," Alice Paul told the reporter, that they had "thrown a bomb . . . Mr. Asquith was the most startled of all. You see the hall was guarded by a cadre of police, and he felt safe from interruption."[14] They were both arrested and sentenced to one month of hard labor in Holloway Prison where they demanded the right to be treated as political prisoners, not criminals, and refused to eat. (The WSPU had officially endorsed hunger strikes, along with the right to be treated as political prisoners. In September, the British government had ordered prison doctors to start force-feeding hunger-striking suffragettes, a policy that other doctors would condemn as potentially life threatening.)

On December 9, Alice Paul and Amelia Brown were released from Holloway. They had been repeatedly force-fed by a doctor who poured a mixture of milk and raw egg in a tube that he had pushed through a nostril into their stomach. In a greatly weakened condition, Alice Paul was taken to a friend's house, where a sympathetic doctor tended to her. Amelia Brown suffered from severe gastritis after she returned to her home. Emmeline Pankhurst, who had recently returned from America, presented them with the hunger striker medal, engraved with their name and the slogan "For Valor" and "Fed by Force."

Alice Paul returned to Philadelphia on January 20, 1910, nine days after she turned twenty-five years old. Her mother and brother met her and took her to their family home in New Jersey. A reporter who interviewed Paul described her as "full of enthusiasm for the cause." She talked "with pride about her friend Miss Lucy Burns," another American overseas student turned suffragette, who was in charge of the WSPU's operation in Scotland. Her answer to the question of "whether she intended to introduce militant tactics in America on her return" was more a sidestep than a definitive "yes," or "no."[15] For now, she said, she planned to continue her education. (Paul would eventually earn a Ph.D. and three law degrees.)

In England, in early February, Emmeline Pankhurst declared a truce in response to the creation of the Conciliation Committee for Woman's Suffrage, an effort to provide some women with the right to vote in Parliamentary elections. It appeared, Pankhurst

84

wrote, "that the tide had turned in our favour . . . the Government was weary of our opposition."[16] The chairman was Lord Lytton, a member of the House of Lords and the brother of Lady Constance Lytton.

Lady Lytton, a "tall and excessively spare and slender" woman with "refined and sensitive" features and "an expression of gentle melancholy," had joined the WSPU in January 1909, shortly after her fortieth birthday.[17] A longtime advocate for prison reform, she embraced woman suffrage after talking with Annie Kenney, who had gone to jail with Christabel Pankhurst in 1905. A mill worker from the age of ten, Kenney had had a finger torn off by a whirling bobbin. She had challenged Lady Lytton's belief that class prejudice was "more injurious" than sex barriers. "Well I can only tell you," Annie Kenney told her, "that I, who am a working-class woman, have never known class distinction and class prejudice to stand in the way of my advancement, whereas the sex barrier meets me at every turn."[18]

Shortly before the truce began, Lady Lytton was incensed by news of brutal treatment of two working-class suffragettes imprisoned in Walton Gaol in Liverpool. When she had been arrested and imprisoned in London, a doctor had examined her, discovered a heart condition, and ordered her early release. Convinced that she had received special treatment because of her upper-class status, Lady Lytton set out to discover how she would be treated if prison officials did not recognize her. Adopting the name Jane Warton, Lytton cut her hair short and put on a tweed hat, long green cloth coat, woolen scarf and gloves, and a pair of pince-nez glasses.

She got herself arrested in Liverpool by breaking a window at a demonstration outside the prison. As Jane Warton, Lady Lytton was sentenced to fourteen days in Walton Gaol where she refused food. Using a slate pencil and ink made from soap mixed with the dirt from the floor, she wrote "Votes for Women," sayings from Henry David Thoreau's *Duty of Civil Disobedience*, and Bible verses such as "Only be thou strong and very courageous" on her cell wall. At night, she "dreamt of fruits, melons, peaches, and nectarines, and of a moonlit balcony that was hung with the sweetest-smelling flowers, honeysuckle and Jessamine, apple-blossom and sweet scented verbena."

On her fourth day in prison, at six o'clock in the evening, a doctor appeared with five wardresses and the feeding apparatus. As Lady Lytton, Constance Lytton had not been force-fed. As Jane Warton, she would be force-fed eight times before her identity was discovered. On one occasion, as the doctor left her cell, he slapped her face. Later that night, she heard the ghastly sounds of forced-feeding in the cell next to her. She was sure it was suffragette Elsie Howey. When the sound ceased, she tapped on the wall and called out, "No surrender," with what little voice she had left. "No surrender," Elsie Howey replied.[19]

Her family finally tracked her down and she was released on orders from a senior official in the government. Although greatly weakened, Lady Constance Lytton gave speeches and wrote articles about her ordeal as Jane Warton. Despite official denials, her exposé ignited public indignation and helped reform the treatment of prisoners. She never fully recovered from her ordeal. Lady Constance Lytton's gambit was reported in newspapers across America.

In April 1910, NAWSA held its Forty-Second Annual Convention in Washington, D.C. Alice Paul was invited to report on what she called "the storm-center of our movement, the English suffrage movement." She assured delegates, "It is not a war of women against men, for the men are helping loyally, but a war of men and women together against the politicians . . . who because of their own political interests seem afraid to enfranchise women."[20]

What was dubbed the "hiss" incident happened at this convention. The sound was allegedly heard when the first president to address a convention, William Howard Taft, appeared to associate some women with "Hottentots or any other uneducated, altogether unintelligent class" of voters. Mortified by the hiss, "a most unwise and ungracious act," Anna Howard Shaw, NAWSA's president, sent Taft an abjectly apologetic letter. Delegates passed a resolution "assuring" him of women's "patriotism and public spirit."[21] This incident exemplifies NAWSA's efforts to portray suffragists as unthreatening, loyal, and deferential, all in an effort, it appeared, to prove that women voters would not upend the existing social and political status quo.

By 1910 in America, the issue of woman suffrage was inexorably before the public. That year, in Missouri, the suffrage movement that had been "smoldering . . . burst into flame," sparked by accounts of the British movement. Five young women in St. Louis formed the St. Louis Equal Suffrage League, and invited Ethel Arnold, an English suffragist on a lecture tour in America, to come to St. Louis. Arnold's "charm, culture and cogent reasoning" wooed new members and disarmed opponents.[22]

In New Mexico, a sparsely settled, rugged region, women organized a State Federation of Women's Clubs. The Federation's Legislative Department took a "bold stand for woman suffrage and better laws for women and children." Women "began searching the statutes and questioning their attorneys and husbands regarding laws."[23] Suffrage became a popular topic of conversation. Adelina "Nina" Otero-Warren, the first woman from New Mexico and first Latina to run for national office, would soon emerge as a leader in the fight of the vote.

In Washington, D. C., enthusiastic crowds lined a parade route of fifty automobiles—Rambler touring cars, Buick Model 10 Roadsters, and Ford Model-T town cars. Each car was packed with piles of petitions and suffragists wearing "Votes for Women" sashes and waving flags. In a ceremony at the capitol, suffragists delivered petitions, collectively dubbed the "Great Petition," from every state, with a total of more than 400,000 signatures, to a group of supportive senators and representatives.

In New York City, Harriot Stanton Blatch organized the first large-scale suffrage parade. "Flying their banners and wearing yellow 'Votes for Women' sashes, the greatest suffrage parade and demonstration ever seen in New York moved on Union Square thousands strong this afternoon," gushed a reporter.[24] Two women trumpeters led a band. Women drove sixty-three automobiles, bedecked with banners. College women wearing their caps and gowns marched. Working women marched. As did middle-class women, many of whom braved their husbands' disapproval as they transgressed the limits of ladylike behavior. (Blatch insisted that women march in a disciplined militaristic fashion to project courage and discipline. To ensure that they did, she required participants to attend marching classes.)

On November 8, 1910, male voters in four states would cast their ballot for or against a woman suffrage referendum to amend the state constitutions, for the first time in Oklahoma, the fourth time in South Dakota, the fifth time in Oregon, and the second time in Washington.

In Oklahoma, suffragists in the WCTU had been at work since it was organized as a territory in 1890, asking legislators to enfranchise every citizen. Instead, men were granted full suffrage and women received school suffrage. In 1895, Laura Gregg, a field organizer from Kansas, had been sent by NAWSA to lecture and organize suffrage clubs in towns along the Rock Island and Santa Fe Railroad line. (A field organizer was a paid position, a source of employment for suffragists.) A year later, Julie B. Nelson, a field organizer from Minnesota, spent three months organizing suffrage clubs in twenty-three more towns.

In 1898, a suffrage bill had been defeated when a key senator who had promised to support the bill accepted a bribe from the Saloonkeepers League and killed the bill. "A crime robbed us of it," reported suffragists who knew "how to bear defeats with fortitude . . . but a defeat by the defection of a friend is a new thing in the history of our movement."[25]

Oklahoma had become the forty-sixth state in 1907. In 1909, suffragists used the newly adopted process of initiative and referendum, a means through which citizens could take the initiative to draft legislation, or a constitutional amendment, and secure signatures on a petition proposing the measure. After the predetermined number of signatures were obtained, the measure was placed on the ballot to be voted on in a referendum. Suffragists had determinedly undertaken the arduous initiative and referendum process because it had allowed them to bypass the obstinate legislature and get a woman suffrage amendment measure on the ballot.

NAWSA sent money and organizers. Speakers lectured throughout the state. Adelia Stephens and Mary Barber went to the "most hostile parts," working through "the heat and dust" of the scorching summer. Standing on boxes and wagon seats, they addressed "large, unsympathetic crowds." Their "endurance and loyalty" was tested "almost to the breaking point." Labor unions pledged support, as did many other groups, including socialists who, it was reported, "were always helpful but they were intensely disliked and sometimes their friendship only made the way more difficult." (When they worked for suffrage, temperance workers' advocacy of prohibition and socialists' critique of capitalism often stirred up antagonism.)

Male voters defeated the Oklahoma Women's Suffrage Amendment by a majority of 40,120: 88,808 yeas, 128,928 nays. For suffragists, the "disappointment was intense."[26]

In South Dakota, local suffragists had requested help. NAWSA sent organizers and money. Alva Belmont had paid $600 a month to help fund the campaign. For the fifth time, male voters defeated the South Dakota Women's Suffrage Amendment by a majority of 22,419: 35,290 yeas, 57,709 nays. Eager to persevere, suffragists held a post-election convention. Several hours were spent discussing "the newly introduced slogan 'Votes for Women,' brought over from England." Was it "dignified" or "unladylike?"[27] Could they adopt it and not be considered militant?

In Oregon, Abigail Scott Duniway, president of the Oregon Equal Suffrage Association, used the initiative and referendum process to get an amendment on the ballot that would enfranchise only tax-paying women and men. Offended that the measure would exclude most members of the working class, many suffragists refused to support it. The Oregon Suffrage for Women Taxpayers Amendment was defeated by a majority 23,795: 35,270 yeas, 59,065 nays.

The campaign in Washington lasted twenty months, from February 1909, when the legislature approved the referendum, to November 8, 1910. The massive Cascade Mountain range bisects the state of Washington, with majestic volcanic mountains like Mount Rainier and Mount St. Helens. Likewise, the leadership of the woman suffrage campaign was divided between May Arkwright Hutton, based in Spokane, on the eastern side of the range and Emma Smith DeVoe, based in Seattle, on the western side. (A fortuitous geographical solution, since they vehemently disagreed about strategy.)

Emma Smith DeVoe was a genial, refined, fashionable woman with a beautiful singing voice. A paid organizer for NAWSA since the mid-1890s, she had lobbied in twenty-eight states and territories, including Idaho, where she had met suffragist May Arkwright Hutton. Hutton, a formidable woman with a large-sized body, owned a boarding house in Kellogg, Idaho. At the age of 10, she was sent to live with her blind paternal grandfather. She cooked and cleaned for him and took him to political meetings. After one meeting, a young lawyer who would become president of the United States, William McKinley, spent the night at their house. Hutton long remembered McKinley, "patting my head," and saying, "I believe when this lassie grows up she will be a voter."[28] (That she did with the 1896 victory in Idaho, but lost the right to vote when she moved to Spokane.)

Occasionally May Arkwright Hutton donned overalls and worked in a mine that she and her husband Al had a stake in. The day a lode of silver and lead was discovered, May and Al Hutton suddenly became very, very rich. Other wealthy women shunned her. She dressed too flamboyantly, looked too bulky, was too outspoken, and associated with the wrong kind of people: "the laundry girl, the shop girl, the stenographer, the teacher, the working woman of every type, whose home and fireside and bread are earned by their own efforts."

Educating herself by reading books, newspapers, journals, and joining the local Shakespeare Club, May Hutton became an incisive writer and speaker. In 1904, she ran for election as a representative to the state legislature, "just like any man. I gave away cigars—and hustled."[29] She lost by only eighty votes. Knowing her to be staunchly pro-miners and unions, mine owners contributed $20,000 to defeat her.

In 1906, May and Al Hutton moved to Washington. At first, DeVoe and Hutton worked well together, organizing a suffrage club in Spokane and publishing a book of suffragists' recipes, the *Washington Women's Cook Book*, that was sold to raise money and to reinforce a domestic image of suffragists. (Hattie A. Burr of Boston edited and published *The Woman Suffrage Cook Book* in 1886, the first of its kind.) But their collaboration turned competitive over their divergent ideas about how to run the 1910 woman suffrage referendum campaign.

May Arkwright Hutton organized a low-key campaign: "Our campaign in Washington is an appeal, not a fight." She persuaded the WCTU to keep a low profile, so as to not activate the "whiskey" lobby. Emma Smith DeVoe's campaign blended traditional methods with new ones, reflecting the burgeoning consumer culture: advertisements; billboards; loads of literature; and multiple buttons, pins, and pennants. Posters were plastered everywhere, a practice Hutton criticized: "In my opinion these posters in the face of the people . . . only arouses [sic] antagonism which we particularly desire to avoid."[30] DeVoe's campaign, writes historian Rebecca Mead, was "a hybrid of older, conservative educational tactics and newer modern ideas."[31]

Suffragists compiled poll lists, hand-writing thousands of names of voters to be contacted; spoke at countless meetings, clubs, unions, and civic organizations; set up a suffrage booth at fairs; and engaged in woman suffrage conversations with people, from family members to the man who collected their garbage. A man was hired to visit lumber camps, hang out in hotel lobbies, and ride on trains and boats for the purpose of having casual woman suffrage conversations with men. A suffrage play was widely performed, including at the State House.

Male voters approved the Washington Women's Right to Vote Amendment by a majority 22,623: 52,299 yeas, 29,676 nays—equal-suffrage state number five! A Wenatchee newspaper celebrated with a banner headline across the top of its front page: WOMAN SUFFRAGE SWEEPS THE STATE.[32] Suffragists across America celebrated the first victory in fourteen years. "In point of wealth, population, and political influence, Washington is the most important state yet won," Carrie Chapman Catt said at a celebration in Washington, D.C.[33]

The outcome of the 1910 constitutional convention in New Mexico, however, reminded suffragists of the obstacles they faced: The suffrage clause in the new constitution that enfranchised all men, could now *only* be amended by a vote by three fourths of the legislature and a two-thirds majority of the highest number voting in every county. That virtually unachievable vote count, suffragists reported, was "expressly designed to prevent woman suffrage and it destroyed all possibility of it."[34] In addition, although women were granted limited school suffrage, a majority of voters could petition to have that right suspended.

Shortly after the Washington victory, Prime Minister Asquith dissolved Parliament, with no promise of any action on the Conciliation Bill. In an attempt to confront Asquith, Emmeline Pankhurst led a deputation of women to the House of Commons. They were met and were brutally attacked by a cordon of police. It was a "wild turmoil" according to Henry Nevison, who marched beside Pankhurst that day, a day that would be forever known as "Black Friday."[35]

Mary Jane Clarke, Emmeline Pankhurst's sister, was one of the women the police assaulted on Black Friday. Several days later, she was arrested for throwing a stone and sentenced to a month in Holloway, where she was force-fed. Shortly after her release, on Christmas Day 1910, Mary Jane Clarke died of a burst blood vessel in her brain. A Bridgeport, Connecticut newspaper reported her death: SUFFRAGETTE DIES ON LEAVING PRISON.[36]

PART III

Chapter 7

A Whirlwind: 1911

From shore to shore let rights be flashed. —Madame Nordica

It was a bitterly cold day. Massive chunks of ice floated in the harbor the day Sylvia Pankhurst, on board the steamship *St. Paul,* arrived in New York Harbor. The jagged skyline—buildings of varying heights topped with differently shaped roofs, from flat to tapered to spires—reminded her of a "ruined castle on the horizon." Harriot Stanton Blatch met her, along with a swarm of reporters. "I had arrived at the height of the interest and sympathy felt by America in the English movement," she later wrote.[1]

For three and a half months, Sylvia Pankhurst spent most of her nights traveling by train across America—Baltimore, Pittsburgh, Cleveland and Cincinnati; Nashville, Chicago, Minneapolis, and St. Louis; Topeka, Los Angeles, Oakland, and San Francisco. MISS PANKHURST ARRIVES LIKE LAMB, NOT LIKE LION, read the headline in a St. Louis, Missouri newspaper.[2] She lectured several times a day in widely varying venues, from the back seat of automobiles at outdoor meetings to huge halls. She spoke at universities and private homes.

In Des Moines, Iowa, local suffragists arranged for her to address the legislature where a woman suffrage bill was pending— the second woman to do that, after Susan B. Anthony forty years earlier. "The Speaker bowed low and led me to the dais; the legislators were cordial. The women assured me I had helped them," Sylvia Pankhurst recalled.[3] She addressed the Michigan Legislature and legislative committees in Illinois, New York, and New Hampshire. Her appearances perhaps swayed some legislators, but not enough to result in even a partial-suffrage victory.

Audiences listened intently as she described her own prison ordeal, starting with riding in "Black Maria," the prison van where each prisoner was "locked in the stuffy darkness of the little compartments, each just large enough to contain a seated person, bumping against the wooden sides as the springless vehicle jolted" over the road paved with cobblestones.[4]

When asked why English suffragettes were militantly smashing windows, Pankhurst explained: "Our mothers and grandmothers were suffragists. They held their meetings and sent their petitions by postage. But no one had heard much about them." History books, she pointed out, show that men have always created "a great disorder" to gain freedom.

Suffragettes would win the vote, she predicted, within the next year, promising—"We are prepared to die if we must."[5] (Within two years, suffragettes' militant tactics included cutting telegraph wires and nationwide bombing and arson campaigns.)

Perplexed that American suffragists were so timid, Sylvia Pankhurst mused, "They have so little faith in themselves."[6] She harshly criticized women who indulged in what she dismissively considered frivolous activities: "Bridge, balls, dinners—I think the women who give their lives to such things as that ought to be swept off the face of the earth."[7]

Shortly before Sylvia Pankhurst returned to England, a fire on March 25, 1911, in New York City, killed 146 garment workers, mostly immigrant girls and women. Known as the Triangle Shirtwaist Factory fire, the catastrophe dramatically exposed unsafe sweatshop conditions: workers crammed into poorly ventilated spaces crowded with long workbenches; large machines, flimsy fire escapes, unreliable elevators; locked exit doors; and only a few buckets of water to extinguish a fire before it raged out of control. Horse-drawn fire engines quickly arrived, but firefighters' ladders were too short to reach the factory located on the eighth, ninth, and tenth floors of the Asch Building.

The horrific event prompted calls for reforms and underscored the connection between workers' rights and suffrage. "It is enough to silence forever the selfish addleheaded drivel of the anti-suffragist who recently said at a legislative hearing that working women can safely trust their welfare to their 'natural protectors.' . . . We claim in no uncertain voice that the time has come when women should have the one efficient tool with which to make for themselves decent and safe working conditions—the ballot," wrote Mary Ware Dennett, a divorced suffragist who had recently gone to work for NAWSA to support herself and two young sons.[8] (After a few years Dennett resigned and did pioneering work in sex education and birth control.)

Sylvia Pankhurst boarded a steamship on April 11 to return to England. Her lecture tour had garnered extensive publicity and softened the image of militancy; inspired mainstream American suffragists, even emboldened some of them; educated the public; and earned perhaps as much as several thousand dollars for the English movement. Several weeks later, on May 6, 70,000 spectators lined Fifth Avenue to watch the suffrage parade, organized by Harriot Stanton Blatch, the largest ever held in America.

Three young women led the parade, including Inez Milholland, who had graduated from Vassar College and was attending New York University School of Law. (Harvard University, Yale University, and Cambridge University had refused to admit her because she was a woman.) They wore long, white, flowing dresses and a purple, white, and gold "Votes for Women" sash across their chest. Inez Milholland held a long pole with one end inserted in a flagpole-carrying belt and the other end attached to a large banner trimmed with yellow fringe along the bottom. Alberta Hill and Sarah McPike walked on either side, holding a long cord attached to the bottom of the banner to keep it flat so that spectators could read the words on the banner:

FORWARD, OUT OF ERROR,
LEAVE BEHIND THE NIGHT;
FORWARD THROUGH THE DARKNESS,
FORWARD INTO LIGHT.

Next came the fife and drum band and bagpipers. Then row after row of women, between two and three thousand from every segment of society, marched four abreast in orderly lines, carrying banners: "Women Need Votes to End Sweat Shops"; "Suffrage Pioneers Gained for Married Working Women the Right to Their Wages"; "New York State Denies the Vote to Criminals, Idiots, and Women." There were jewelers, milliners, dressmakers, factory workers, society women, writers, artists, musicians, explorers, physicians, lawyers, and farmers. College students and professors marched, dressed in academic regalia. Shirtwaist workers marched, carrying a red banner draped with black in memory of the victims of the Triangle Shirtwaist Factory Fire. There were bands and floats. Women participated who had once objected to parades as unladylike. So did women who had been too timid, or who had heeded the objections of their husband or fiancé or parents.

The spectators who lined Fifth Avenue were respectful, until the men's division with an estimated one- to two-hundred men marched by, eliciting a few jeers, boos, a taunt—"Hold up your skirts, girls!—echoing the age-old canard that woman's rights "unsexed" men.[9] The men marched on. A photograph of the men's division appeared on the front pages of newspapers as far away as Illinois and North Dakota. The parade was flawlessly executed. It ended in Union Square, where there were 10,000 people, mostly men, their heads covered with a hat, some flat caps but mostly a black derby, crowded shoulder to shoulder. Suffragists sang, "Women's Political March," a song composed for the march by Elsa Gregori. They distributed literature. They lectured from a carriage seat or automobiles, even atop a pile of bricks.

Over 3,000 women marched in military precision in the 1911 suffrage parade in New York City, as did a contingent of men—unfazed by spectators' taunts. (Library of Congress)

The beautifully organized and executed parade surely agitated the editors of a *The New York Times*. An anti-suffrage editorial published the morning of the parade read: "If the parade turns out as well as its promoters expect, doubtless many thousands of persons in New York, who have never given much thought to the matter, will feel to-night that woman suffrage is nearer at hand. . . . We sincerely hope, for their own sakes and the sake of the State, that they will fail."[10]

In California, the campaign was underway to convince male voters to vote "yes" for the California Women's Suffrage Proposition, Proposition 4 to remove the word "male" from voter qualifications in the California Constitution. A special election was scheduled for October 10, 1911.

California suffragists faced well-financed enemies. It would take a "whirlwind campaign" to win, declared Elizabeth Lowe Watson, the eloquent pastor of the First Spiritualist Union of San Francisco and president of the California Equal Suffrage Association. Veterans of the losing 1896 campaign and new recruits seized their task with "unbounded enthusiasm."[11] By the time the 1911 campaign ended, it had become "a veritable cyclone."[12]

Anti-suffragist businessmen and their lawyers and lobbyists feared that women would vote for all or some of the following: prohibition, regulations governing business practices, and legislation benefiting workers. In Los Angeles, anti-suffrage men formed the Committee of Fifty. Anti-suffrage women, who feared upsetting the status quo, joined the Women's Association Opposed to Woman Suffrage. Selina Solomons, president of the Votes for Women Club of San Francisco, had "numberless hand-to-hand encounters" with anti-suffragists, whom she wrote, held "ante-diluvian arguments and theories . . . a product of a certain wobbly structure of the brain cells, which neither logic nor fact could remedy."[13] (A full-length photograph shows Solomons looking authoritative—left hand in a fist on her hip and a no-nonsense expression.)

Selina Solomons, whose sister was one of the first American woman psychiatrists and her brother was a distinguished explorer, had organized the Votes for Women Club to recruit working women to the fight for the vote. Located in a loft with walls covered with suffrage posters and banners, the club served nutritious lunches for a nickel. A typical menu included: four kinds of soup, five kinds of salad, and creamed codfish. Afternoon tea was served in a "Rest and Reading Room." Piles of suffrage reading material were placed everywhere. A haven for low-wage-earning girls and women, the club soon attracted affluent shoppers, who occasionally ate lunch with a shop girl from whom they had recently bought something.

Anti-suffragists distributed excerpts from "Arguments Against Women's Suffrage, 1911," a speech by Senator J. B.

Sanford: "Let the manly man and the womanly woman defeat this amendment and keep woman where she belongs in order that she may retain the respect of all mankind."[14] Anti-suffrage placards urged a "no" vote because "Home-Loving Women Do Not Want the Ballot." A full-page anti-suffrage advertisement with quotes by Carrie Chapman Catt and Harriot Stanton Blatch, distorted to make them inflammatory, appeared in major newspapers. Small advertisements appeared claiming that woman suffrage was a failure in Colorado. On September 22, an anti-suffrage Los Angeles newspaper editorialized:

> The working man—whether he be a Republican, a Democrat or a Socialist—who walks along Broadway or Spring Street on Saturday afternoon and sees thousands of fashionably-attired girls and women of mature age parading in autos and making woman-suffrage speeches says to himself: "Are these butterflies to be entrusted with the task of making laws for men?"[15]

Apart from avowed enemies, suffragists had to convince the general public that appeared to be "amused, indifferent, and incredulous" to approve the amendment.[16] That they did by "incorporating modern methods of advertising publicity, mass merchandising, and mass entertainment in their fight for the vote," writes historian Margaret Finnegan.[17]

Suffragists from around the country pitched in to help the campaign, including Alma Lafferty from Colorado, where she was a member of the state legislature. Individuals and organizations donated money. Skillful speakers intrepidly traversed the vast state: city streets, village squares, mining camps, granite quarries, farms, fairs, fiestas, teas, garden fêtes, ferry boats, theaters, halls, churches, factories, schools, and stadiums. A society woman rode her fine horse for three days through the hills and mountains campaigning for woman suffrage, speaking from atop her horse. Brass bands, short speeches, singing and dancing, as well as some amusing monologues and fireworks were advertised to lure crowds to mass meetings.

Members of the College Equal Suffrage League (CESL) toured the state in the "Blue Liner," a 1910 seven-seat, four-cylinder Packard touring car owned by Frances Baker Patterson who went by the name Frank. She had driven the "Blue Liner" during the 1910 suffrage campaign in Washington, where the elegant car had attracted the attention of men and garnered newspaper articles with catchy headlines: AUTO PARTIES WILL WHOOP UP VOTES FOR WOMEN, appeared in a San Francisco newspaper.[18]

When the CESL bought $75 worth of tickets, a traveling troupe from Australia, "The Australian Boys," put woman suffrage in a show in the Valencia Theater, adorned with huge yellow banners inscribed "Our Mothers Vote, Why Don't Yours." Fourteen boys performed a suffrage song-and-dance, each with a huge yellow letter pinned on his chest that spelled "Votes for Women" when they lined up. The manager gave a speech about the benefits of woman suffrage in Australia. At the finale, yellow balloons with a suffrage leaflet as a tail floated down.

Suffragists ascended in a hot air balloon and dropped suffrage leaflets. For the Labor Day parade, a float pulled by a team of six black horses carried children holding a sign: "Give Our Mother a Vote." Earning the distinction as the first woman float driver, Maud Younger drove a team of six white horses pulling a float for the Wage Earners' Suffrage League (WESL). Younger, who grew up in a wealthy San Francisco family, had spent five years working in a New York City settlement house. Returning to San Francisco, she became a waitress, organized the first waitress union (she was nicknamed the "Millionaire Waitress"), and founded the WESL.

A blizzard of literature blanketed the state, some published in different languages—Spanish, Yiddish, and German—while other pieces were tailored to particular groups, including one titled, "Opinions of Eminent Local Catholic Clergy." Thousands of pro-suffrage articles and letters to the editor appeared in newspapers. An article in a San Francisco newspaper by Julia Hochheimer, illustrated with her full-length picture, debunked the "old and puerile" argument that voting would "unsex women."[19] Advertisements were placed in foreign-language newspapers: French, Italian, Swiss, and Portuguese. Suffrage propaganda appeared on thousands of buttons, pennants, banners, badges, pins, flags, ribbons, stickers, stationery, and circulars. Posters were hung in streetcars. "Snipe" posters, a single sentence printed on narrow strips of stiff paper that would last outdoors, were securely tacked on barns, and fences. A suffrage shop opened in San Francisco to sell suffrage materials.

On "Postcard Day," 15,000 postcards were sold by suffragists, each with a yellow chrysanthemum in a buttonhole and a basket of postcards on her arm. Merchants put suffrage propaganda, featuring many shades of gold and yellow, in their window displays. Electric street signs illuminating suffrage messages were used for the first time. Billboards appeared throughout San Francisco, printed with enormous letters reading: JUSTICE TO CALIFORNIA WOMEN; VOTE YES TO AMENDMENT FOUR. Different mottoes appeared in smaller print, including one reading: "Give your girl the same chance as your boy." Original material was written: poems, limericks, parodies, skits, plays, and leaflets. There were essay and poster contests, one with a prize of $500. Suffrage campaign songs were composed. Ida Diserenz created a popular stereopticon presentation comprised of forty-one slides depicting various aspects of women's lives.

At noon, on October 9, the day before the election, suffragists were galvanized by the news that the famous American opera singer Madame Lillian Nordica, who was in San Francisco to sing at the groundbreaking for the Panama Celebration, would appear in support of woman suffrage that night in Union Square. Horse-drawn advertising wagons with oversized advertising sails spread the news. By seven o'clock, thousands of people filled the square and jammed the streets. A band played. Suffragists gave speeches, standing in automobiles stationed around the square. Madame Nordica arrived at nine o'clock, riding in the "Blue Liner" decorated with garlands of oak leaves, giant yellow chrysanthemums, "Votes for Women" pennants, and a white blanket embroidered in yellow draped over the front.

An elegant, gracious woman, Madame Nordica stood and gave a short speech: "Ladies and gentlemen—or may I say 'fellow citizens' for after tomorrow I hope we may be regarded as fellow citizens and not nonentities, municipally speaking. . . . Let the word be flashed from the Pacific to the Atlantic: 'For men and women equal rights.'"

"Sing for us," people shouted. Accompanied by the band, Madame Nordica sang "America the Beautiful," changing a phrase to: "From shore to shore let rights be flashed." Then, unaccompanied, she sang "The Star-Spangled Banner," asking the crowd to sing with her.

The next day, Election Day, October 10, a large photograph and an article headlined: DIVA SINGS FOR SUFFRAGE, appeared on the front page of a morning newspaper.[20] Suffragists around the state were up at dawn. More than a thousand would serve as poll watchers in San Francisco, some standing for twelve hours. In Oakland, the Colored Women's Suffrage League monitored two precincts. When Mary Coolidge, a white woman in charge of Oakland poll watchers, offered to have "her husband protect them," a young member of the League replied "quite calmly that they could take care of themselves."[21] Pinkerton men were hired to watch the vault in San Francisco where ballots were placed.

Young suffragists drove the "Blue Liner" to the Relief Home, the residence of "old men, men on crutches, men who could not see very 'good.'" Men who had listened to suffrage speakers and whose "old hearts had warmed to the thought of casting a lame man's or a blind man's, or a dying man's perfectly sound vote 'for the women.'" And so, reported Louise Herrick Wall, the "Blue Liner," still covered with garlands "plied back and forth with her crippled loads, until the last old voter" had voted for the woman suffrage amendment. "We fellows that are on the scrap-heap ain't afraid of women," one man told her.[22]

By nightfall, it appeared that city voters had defeated the woman suffrage amendment. Selina Solomons watched the count at election committee headquarters where "all was gloom."[23] Newspapers across the country reported the defeat. Only *The San Francisco Call* held out hope, predicting that the amendment would pass by 4,000 votes. Slowly, positive returns came in from small towns, villages, mining communities, and ranches. HOPES OF CALIFORNIA WOMEN MOUNT WITH THE RISING TIDE OF SUFFRAGETTE VOTES, reported a newspaper in Phoenix, Arizona.[24]

Male voters approved the California Women's Suffrage Proposition by a majority 3,587: 125,037 yeas, 121,450 nays—equal-suffrage state number six!

"We had kept back our womanish tears," Solomons later recalled. "Now we gave free rein to our emotions, in both manly and womanly fashion, with handshaking and back-slapping, as well as hugging and kissing one another."[25] The news reached Boston late at night, sending a reporter rushing to a suffragist's apartment to get her reaction. Standing outside her door, he called out, "I want to know what you think of the California victory." "Think!" she replied. "I'm standing on my head with joy."[26]

NAWSA held its Forty-Third Annual Convention in Louisville, Kentucky in October. Delegates, exuberant from victories in Washington and California, arrived with votes-for-women tags and butterfly stickers on their luggage. Yellow badges and six-star buttons were pinned on their dresses and coats, giving onlookers the impression that they were "victors and conquerors." For suffragists eager for new ideas, Mary Ware Dennett had set up a display of items and materials that she had solicited from California suffragists: small "snipe" posters, big street posters, advertisements, promotional material for events. Emmeline Pankhurst, who was on her second speaking tour in America, addressed the convention delegates. A letter was read from Carrie

Chapman Catt who was on an around-the-world-trip "to organize the whole world for Woman Suffrage."[27]

Before Emmeline Pankhurst returned to London in November, she, along with Harriot Stanton Blatch and Alva Belmont, attempted to address a crowd on Wall Street in New York City. A large crowd shouting catcalls and insults forced them to retreat. A New York City newspaper headlined the unseemly spectacle: WALL STREET HOWLS AT SUFFRAGETTES.[28] The clamorous crowd reflected the fact that woman suffrage was no longer a marginalized issue. Anti-suffrage anxieties had been heightened by the victories in Washington and California. Josephine Jewell Dodge had recently founded the National Association Opposed to Woman Suffrage (NAOWS). A philanthropist who sponsored a nursery that provided day care and education for the children of immigrant working mothers, Dodge believed "that women can be more useful to the community without the ballot than if affiliated with and influenced by party politics." A pamphlet published by the NAOWS listed six reasons to "Vote NO on Woman Suffrage":

BECAUSE 90% of the women either do not want it, or *do not care.*

BECAUSE it means *competition* of women with men instead of *co-operation.*

BECAUSE 80% of the women eligible to vote are married and can only double or annul their husband's votes.

BECAUSE it can be of no benefit commensurate with the additional expense involved.

BECAUSE in some States more voting women than voting men will place the Government under petticoat rule.

BECAUSE it is unwise to risk the good we already have for the evil which may occur.[29]

Chapter 8

Right is Might: 1912

I will never get cold in a cause like this. —Inez Milholland

"How about the women?" Maud Malone called out, interrupting Theodore Roosevelt, who was speaking to a large crowd the night before the Republican Party presidential primary in New York. Men threatened her, yelling: "'Sit down or you'll be put out,' Miss Malone dared them to do it. No one did," wrote a reporter.[1] Pandemonium ensued. Men howled, hissed, and threw their programs and other missiles. Roosevelt tried to calm the crowd. The band played, adding to the confusion. A policeman approached her. Maud Malone stood her ground. Grabbing her, the policeman carried her out of the hall. Newspapers across America reported the incident. The front-page headline in a Palatka, Florida newspaper read: MILITANT WOMAN BESTS ROOSEVELT.[2]

Three candidates were on the presidential primary ballot: the current president, William Howard Taft, who was running for reelection; Roosevelt, a former president who had selected Taft to succeed him but had become disillusioned with him; and Robert La Follette, a progressive senator from Wisconsin. Taft opposed woman suffrage. Roosevelt sidestepped the issue, saying women should decide. La Follette was an ardent supporter.

Taft won the New York primary and became the Republican Party's candidate for president. Theodore Roosevelt founded a new political party, the Progressive Party. Now, he strongly supported woman suffrage, perhaps because of his run-in with Maud Malone, or perhaps because large numbers of newly enfranchised women would vote in 1912. Thus, the Progressive Party became the first major party to endorse woman suffrage.

106

Jane Addams became the first woman to give a seconding speech at a major party convention when she nominated Roosevelt for president. In doing so, she violated NAWSA's policy of nonpartisanship, a breach that NAWSA overlooked because of her prominence.

Woodrow Wilson, then governor of New Jersey, was the Democratic Party's candidate. Born in Virginia, Wilson spent his formative years in Georgia and South Carolina. If elected president, he would be the first Southerner to win the office since Zachary Taylor in 1848. After earning a law degree and a Ph.D. in political science, Wilson taught at several colleges and served as president of Princeton University before entering politics. A conventional man with traditional views of women, Wilson believed that: "Suffrage for women will make absolutely no change in politics—it is the home that will be disastrously affected. Somebody has to make the home and who is going to do it if the women don't."[3]

In the spring of 1912, Harriot Stanton Blatch, president of the Women's Political Union (WPU), the renamed Equality League of Self-Supporting Women, started recruiting marchers for another suffrage parade in New York City, even more impressive than previous parades. "The enemy must be converted through his eyes," Blatch insisted. "He must see uniformity of dress. . . . The enemy must see women marching in increasing numbers year by year out on the public avenues, holding high their banner, 'Votes for Women.'"[4]

The weather was perfect for the parade on May 4, 1912, sunshine with a light breeze. It started at five o'clock so that working women could march. The number of marchers, as many as 20,000, and an estimated 500,000 spectators, was more than double from the previous year. Fifty-four women riding superb horses led the parade. Fourteen-year-old Phyllis Muller and Mabel Ping-Hua Lee, a student from China who was studying at Barnard College, were among the horsewomen. Inez Milholland skillfully handled her horse when it reared, adding excitement for the crowd.

Many divisions, representing every segment of society, were lined up at cross streets, waiting to fall in line in the parade. At the east side of Ninth Street, there were doctors, lawyers, investigators, nurses, writers, artists, musicians, actresses, craftsmen, and social workers. On the west side, there were industrial workers, millinery, shirtwaist, laundry, and domestic workers. The Men's League for Woman Suffrage was at the east side of Thirteenth Street. Rabbi Stephen S. Wise marched with his ten-year-old son, James. "We had to laugh nearly all the way on account of the things that were shouted at us . . . 'Who's taking care of the baby . . . Oh, Flossy dear, aren't they cute,'" he wrote in his diary.[5] Uptown a division of black suffragists waited to fall in line. Pioneer suffragists marched, as did socialists. Annie Smith Peck, the celebrated mountain climber, carried the "Votes for Women" banner like the one she had planted in honor of the Joan of Arc Suffrage League at the top of Coropuna, a 21,000 foot-high dormant volcano in the Peruvian Andes. The parade lasted more than two hours.

The success of the parade alarmed the editors at *The New York Times*, prompting them to publish an anti-suffrage editorial: "The situation is dangerous . . . women will get the vote . . . and play havoc with it for themselves and society, if the men are not firm and wise enough and, it may as well be said, masculine enough to prevent them."[6] A week later, another harangue appeared in the newspaper: "The agitation for woman suffrage is no joke . . . it is a real activity, a source of danger to the Republic. . . . The movement must be quelled."[7]

Did the anti-suffrage editorials in *The New York Times* impede the fight for the vote? They certainly did not help, given that *The New York Times* was a highly regarded, influential newspaper with a national circulation.

On November 5, 1912, Woodrow Wilson was elected the twenty-eighth President of the United States. During the campaign, Maud Malone had been arrested for confronting him during his appearance at the Brooklyn Academy of Music. Seated in the first balcony, she rose up and shouted her question—"How about votes for women?"

"Put her out!" the crowd bellowed.

Wilson quieted them and asked: "What is it, Madame?"

"Mr. Wilson you just said you were trying to destroy a monopoly and I ask you what about woman suffrage. The men have the monopoly," Malone replied.

"Woman suffrage, Madame, is not a question that is dealt with by the National Government at all. I am here only as the representative of the National party."

"I am speaking to you as an American, Mr. Wilson."

"I hope you will not consider it a discourtesy if I decline to answer on this occasion."

"Why do you decline?"

"Put her out! Put her out! Put her out!" the crowd chanted. A man grabbed her arm. She wrenched herself free. She ignored Judge Otto Kempner, who was in the audience and bellowed, "I am a Judge, and if you don't behave yourself I will have you placed under arrest."[8] Accompanied by cheers, Captain Bernard Hayes, a large police officer, walked up the aisle followed by other officers. Grabbing her from the front and behind, the officers wrestled Maud Malone out of her seat and hustled her out the nearest exit, a fire escape.

Arrested for "willful disturbance of a public meeting," she refused her brother Sylvester's offer to bail her out. Instead, Maud Malone spent the night in jail, becoming the first American suffragist to go to jail for the cause. The next day, she was paroled to the custody of Sylvester. Three days later, she appeared before Judge Kempner, who ordered her to stand trial. He denounced her as a "scatter-brained, loose-tongued, ill-mannered . . .

malicious disturber and lawbreaker. . . . Persons of your type only retard the day of women's enfranchisement just as the stone throwers and window smashers in England are setting back instead of advancing their cause in that country."[9]

Accompanied by Sylvester, Maud Malone appeared at her trial with a "Votes for Women" badge and a celluloid button with an image of Elizabeth Cady Stanton pinned on her coat. Half a dozen suffragists sat in the courtroom. Three justices considered the charge against her. The issue was not that she asked a question, one of them said, but that she did not sit down when Wilson declined to answer her question, thus agitating the audience. Malone agreed that her action had provoked the crowd. "There is no telling about these foolish men," she said. "They go around and around like windmills when a woman's voice is heard in one of their meetings."[10]

A celluloid pin-back button with Elizabeth Cady Stanton's image was produced by Maud Malone's Harlem Equal Rights League. Malone wore one pinned to her coat during her trial in 1912. (The Suffrage Collection of Dr. Kenneth Florey)

The justices issued their guilty verdict, and then, a reporter noted, they "settled back in their seats to enjoy a good laugh about it." Maud Malone insisted on being given a sentence, or a fine, so that she could appeal the decision. Fined $5, she instructed her lawyer, James P. Kohler, to draw up papers for an appeal. (Susan B. Anthony had planned to take the same course of action, but was thwarted when her lawyer paid her fine.) In Bismarck, North Dakota, a newspaper published her picture on the front page with the caption: "Miss Maud Malone Convicted for Her Heckling of Wilson."[11]

The Appellate Division, Supreme Court, State of New York, upheld Maud Malone's conviction for heckling Woodrow Wilson, now the President of the United States. The decision was heralded in an article reprinted in newspapers from Pennsylvania to Utah. Headlined—HOW LAWLESS SUFFRAGETTES WOULD SOON BE SUPPRESSED IN AMERICA, the article was illustrated with three images: Maud Malone holding a large poster inscribed "Women Vote in Colorado, Idaho, Wyoming, Utah / Why Not New York?"; a prostrate suffragette in Holloway Prison being force-fed; and several items with the caption "used by the 'Wild Women'—the Militant Suffragettes of England—in their Outrages Against Property, . . . a Pile of Oil-Soaked Kindling for Burning Down Houses, Saws, Drills, a Jack and 'Jimmies' for Breaking into Places to be Destroyed."[12] The sensational warning was clear, lest American suffragists adopt the militant and increasingly destructive and violent tactics of British suffragettes.

In 1912, woman suffrage referenda were on the ballot in six states: Ohio, Arizona, and Wisconsin for the first time; Michigan for the second time; Kansas, the third time; Oregon, the sixth time. The referenda had been secured by three different methods: an initiative petition in Arizona and Oregon; legislative authorization of referenda in Kansas, Wisconsin, and Michigan; and a constitutional convention referral in Ohio.

Year after year in Ohio, suffragists got various woman suffrage bills before the legislature, only to have them repeatedly stalled in a committee, or defeated in a floor vote. In 1894, women were granted school suffrage. In 1904 and 1905, a full suffrage bill languished in committees. In 1908, the measure was favorably voted out of committee, but not voted upon on the floor. In 1910, the legislators defeated a woman suffrage bill.

At the 1912 Ohio Constitutional Convention, a woman suffrage clause to remove the words "white male" from the current constitution was favorably reported out of committee. For three weeks, pro-suffrage legislators and suffragists battled "interests, vicious and commercial" who opposed the suffrage amendment "from every possible angle."[13] Finally on March 7, convention delegates approved the Ohio Women's Suffrage Amendment that would be submitted to the male voters in a referendum. A special election was set for September 3, 1912.

Suffragists campaigned vigorously for three months, led by NAWSA's former treasurer, the politically savvy Harriet Taylor Upton, who was the recently elected president of the Ohio Woman Suffrage Association. More than fifty suffragists hurried to Ohio. Some stayed for a few days. Others remained for months. Rosalie Gardiner Jones and Elisabeth Freeman came from New York with their yellow "Votes for Women" wagon drawn by a horse named "Suffraget." They slept in their wagon and mostly ate their meals sitting on the ground beside their wagon. "We could have driven in an automobile but then we wouldn't have to stop so often" and talk to people along the way, Jones explained.

Twenty-nine-year-old Rosalie Jones had grown up in a wealthy, socially prominent family. Her mother and sister belonged to the New York State Anti-Suffrage Association. Outspoken and independent-minded, Rosalie Jones was dubbed "the Maverick" by a niece. She would soon be known in the fight for the vote as "General Jones."[14]

Thirty-six-year-old Elisabeth Freeman was born in England, grew up in poverty in America and then returned to England. In London, she was arrested after intervening with a policeman who was beating a woman. Freeman and the woman, who turned out to be a suffragette, were arrested and imprisoned. Radicalized by the experience, Freeman enlisted in the British fight for the vote. Quirky and highly skilled at public speaking, attracting recruits, and garnering publicity, Freeman, who frequently wore a gypsy costume, had returned to America shortly before joining up with Rosalie Jones.

Ohio suffragists spent about $40,000 on their campaign. The German-American Alliance and the Personal Liberty League that represented the liquor interest spent over $600,000. A group of wealthy women organized an anti-suffrage group, arguing that women didn't want the vote, and that enfranchising women would put more power "into the hands of woman agitators, women Socialists, and undesirables."[15] Male voters defeated the Ohio Women's Suffrage Amendment by a majority 87,455: 249,420 yeas, 336,875 nays. WOMAN'S SUFFRAGE ONLY AMENDMENT LOST BY OHIO VOTE, reported a Washington, D.C. newspaper.[16] There were forty-two amendments on the ballot!

On February 14, 1912, the Arizona Territory, where pioneer suffragists' attempts to win the right to vote had been repeatedly thwarted, entered the Union as the state of Arizona. At the first session of the state legislature, Frances "Fannie" Willard Munds, head of the Arizona Women Suffrage Organization, presented a woman suffrage bill that the legislators refused to even consider. "So, Frances Willard Munds," her daughter later wrote, "went to work in real earnest."[17]

Throughout the summer, Fannie Munds spearheaded the efforts that obtained enough signatures on an initiative petition to authorize a woman suffrage referendum. The petition, writes historian Heidi Osselaer, included the signatures of "a significant number of Mexican American, African American, and Chinese American voters."[18] With just two months before the election, Fannie Munds, who lived in Prescott, opened a suffrage headquarters in the Adams Hotel in Phoenix. Suffragists secured the support of labor unions, political party leaders, and newspaper editors. NAWSA sent an experienced organizer, Laura Gregg from Kansas. Alice Park came from California at her own expense and supervised the distribution of literature. It was a low-key campaign, with no parades or demonstrations to alert the opposition.

On Election Day, suffragists were at the polls, handing out cards with voting instructions. "What are you going to be when you get the vote?" a very tall policeman asked Fannie Munds, who was about five feet tall. "I'm going to be a policeman," she replied, causing the assembled voters to laugh. "She's all right boys," the policeman said. "She would make a real dangerous and courageous policeman."[19] The Suffrage and Right to Hold Office for Women Amendment was approved by a majority of 7,240: 13,442 yeas, 6,202 nays—equal-suffrage state number seven! (In 1913, Frances Willard Munds would represent Arizona at the IWSA Convention in Budapest, Hungary. In 1914, she was elected a state senator.)

Since the 1850s, women in Wisconsin had argued for woman's rights. Mathilde Franszriska Anneke, a well-educated, radical, free-thinking woman, who had fled Germany after the uprising in 1848, published one of the first feminist journals in America, the *Deutsche Frauen-Zeitung*, "dedicated to the complete emancipation of women." (German was commonly spoken at this time in America.) In 1853, she traveled from Milwaukee to New York City to attend the women's rights convention, dubbed the "mob convention" because of disruptive thugs. Anneke spoke in German, with Ernestine Rose as her translator: "My voice was overwhelmed by the sounds of sneers, scoffs, and hisses—the eloquence of tyranny."[20]

In 1886, a referendum granting women school suffrage, using separate ballots and separate boxes, was finally approved by male voters. A key leader in that victory was Olympia Brown, the first woman to graduate from an established theological school. Brown, who gave 300 speeches in the 1867 Kansas campaign, had moved to Wisconsin from Connecticut with her husband and two children to be the minister of a Universalist church in Racine. In 1887, she resigned to devote herself full time to the fight for the vote. Although she was a riveting speaker and experienced organizer, her domineering personality caused tensions with other suffragists, in particular, her tactical decision to "avoid publicity as much as possible, while working quietly to create a public sentiment in favor" of woman suffrage.[21]

Younger suffragists took the lead in the 1912 campaign in Wisconsin. Ada L. James, who had attended suffrage meetings with her mother and grandmother, joined forces with Theodora Winton Youmans. Youmans, a journalist and editor, wrote that the campaign "was as lively as we—some trained, some untrained, in suffrage campaigns—could make it."[22] From his airship, celebrity pilot Lincoln Beachey scattered suffrage leaflets over a crowd at the state fair. Aboard the *Mary E*, a little launch, suffragists cruised fifty miles up the scenic Wolf River, stopping at every landing to speak and hand out literature.

The anti-suffrage forces counter-campaigned, aided by the State Retail Liquor Dealers' Protective Association that published a slew of articles, verses, and pictures in their magazine depicting woman suffrage as foolish and dangerous. Male voters defeated Wisconsin Women's Suffrage Referendum, Question 4, by a majority of 91,318: 135,736 yeas, 227,054 nays.

In 1866, Michigan legislators had defeated a woman suffrage bill by one vote. The next year, in 1867, they granted women taxpayers limited school suffrage. Seven years later, in an 1874 referendum, male voters defeated the Michigan Woman Suffrage Amendment, Proposal 1, by a majority of 95,880: 40,077 yeas, 135,957 nays. Demoralized suffragists disbanded.

Ten years elapsed before Michigan suffragists rallied, held a convention, organized the Michigan Equal Suffrage Association, and focused on a municipal suffrage bill. For a vote on the bill in 1889, suffragists descended on the capitol, including a large delegation from Detroit who arrived on a special train. Tipped off by a friendly journalist, they removed an anti-suffrage circular that had been placed on legislators' desks. The bill was defeated by one vote.

In 1893, the municipal suffrage bill finally passed and was signed into law by the governor. But, only after a qualification was added that women had to be able to read the state constitution in the English language. The opposition challenged the law in court and the Michigan Supreme Court declared the law unconstitutional. Two years later George Waldo, a representative who had promised his mother and wife that he would support woman suffrage, introduced a woman suffrage amendment resolution that was defeated by one vote. In the aftermath of the defeats, suffragists in Michigan had ceased their efforts to obtain suffrage, instead they focused on educating the public and politicians.

Unexpectedly, in March 1912, Governor Chase Osborn, a woman suffrage supporter, called a special session of the Michigan Legislature that authorized a woman suffrage amendment referendum in November. Suffragists scrambled to get organized and in June launched an intensive education campaign. On November 5, the first returns were overwhelmingly in favor of the measure. Newspapers were announcing another suffrage victory. Suffragists were heralding another victory. However, it would be many weeks before all the remaining precincts (especially those where the political machine was controlled by the liquor industry) reported their returns and the result was official. For now, suffragists counted Michigan as a victory.

In Kansas, in the summer of 1912, anti-suffragist C. F. Tibbles, known as "Clarence, the Untrue," was poised to do his dirty deed, distributing *Business Versus Woman Suffrage*, an official-looking book of anti-suffrage letters "cunningly devised to arouse the prejudice of every kind of businessman or reform worker." Tibbles would surreptitiously leave copies of the book on the seats in trains and streetcars and send them to newspaper offices. He had shown up in previous campaigns in Oregon and Ohio. Forewarned of his imminent arrival, Kansas suffragists stayed up all night sending letters to newspapers and the Associated Press, exposing his plan. Thus, "'Clarence the Untrue' was effectively bound and gagged."[23]

Lucy Browne Johnston, the lively president of the Kansas Equal Suffrage Association, who supported traveling libraries and woman suffrage, led the campaign. It was a toilsome campaign that lasted through "the hottest summer and the coldest,

116

stormiest winter . . . workers learned what it meant to travel across country with the mercury ranging from 110 in the shade to 22 degrees below zero."[24]

Ice cream festivals were held to raise money. Women sold eggs and butter. Pansy Clark raised $500 selling large orange balloons printed with "Votes for Women," or "Votes for Mother." Donations came from other states, including Nebraska and Florida. From Washington, Emma Smith DeVoe sent copies of their suffrage cookbook. An army of suffragists, more than 2,000 women and men, canvassed house-to-house; toured by horseback, automobile, and train; distributed tons of literature; and spoke everywhere and anywhere people gathered.

On November 5, 1912, male voters in Kansas approved the Equal Suffrage Amendment by a majority of 16,049, the largest to date: 175,246 yeas; 159,197 nays—equal-suffrage state number eight! Kansas had been a prohibition state for years, noted Lucy Johnston: "Our people, both men and women, having had 32 years' experience in keeping the brewers and distillers out of our state, knew how to meet them in this battle, and to circumvent their activities."[25]

A silent film, *Votes for Women*, produced in 1912 by NAWSA, had been used as a fundraiser. The film, a parable in which two suffragists recruit a senator by persuading his fiancée to join them, included footage from an actual suffrage parade and cameo appearances by Jane Addams, Anna Howard Shaw, and Inez Milholland. The following year, Harriot Stanton Blatch and Emmeline Pankhurst appeared in *What 80 Million Women Want*, featuring a suffragist who clears her betrothed's reputation by exposing a crooked political boss.

An anti-suffrage silent film, *Lively Affair*, produced by an unknown production company, featured unattractive, mannish-looking, bloomer-clad women. One woman leaves her baby with her namby-pamby husband, another hands her baby to a young passer-by, another steals a bicycle to attend a suffrage meeting, where they end up gambling and fighting. Another film, *A Busy Day*, stars a young Charlie Chaplin in drag portraying a jealous, crude suffragist who repeatedly slugs and kicks her husband and the police, who respond in kind. She ends up being thrown off a pier and left to drown. We can only speculate about the effect of the anti-suffrage films. But depictions of virulent disrespect and abuse of suffragists surely goaded others to do the same.

In Oregon, a woman suffrage amendment was on the ballot for the sixth time. Suffragists differed as to what type of campaign to conduct: the low-key "still hunt" fiercely advocated by Abigail Scott Duniway, longtime president of the Oregon Equal Suffrage Association (OESA); or a grassroots, coalition-building, stunt-enhanced, publicity-savvy active campaign. Duniway refused to budge, immobilizing the state organization. In December 1911, Anna Howard Shaw had sent a letter to OESA members "severely criticizing their apathy and lack of preparation."[26]

In mid-February, Abigail Scott Duniway became seriously ill. The acting president of the OESA, Viola Coe, spearheaded an active campaign that was joined by a cross-section of workers, such as Marie Equi, a well-known lesbian and iconoclastic physician, who defied the laws and provided birth control information and abortions. Esther Pohl Lovejoy, who was born in a lumber camp and became a physician, organized Everybody's Equal Suffrage League, aimed at wage-earning women. Harriet "Hattie" Redmond, the daughter of emancipated slaves, was the president of the Colored Women Equal Suffrage League.

It was widely anticipated that women would be enfranchised in the Republic of China that had been established on January 1, 1912, ending 4,000 years of imperial rule. A Seattle newspaper reported: SUFFRAGE HAS WON. Suffragists celebrated the momentous event. The Woman's Club Campaign Committee sent a telegram to the Chinese Consul in Portland: "Greetings and congratulations to the great republic of China . . . it has made the republic a government of all the people, and not a government of half the people, as we have in Oregon."

On April 12, 1912, a newspaper reported that "Side by side with their Caucasian sisters, seven Portland Chinese women sat at a banquet." The headline read: CHINESE WOMEN DINE WITH WHITE. Dr. S. K. Chan, a physician and president of a local equal suffrage society for Chinese women, and two of her daughters Bertie and Fannie were there. Bertie Chan translated her mother's remarks: "Oregon is now bounded on four sides by states that have recognized the rights of women. On the north there is Washington, on the east there is Idaho, on the south there is California, and far away, across the waters on the west, there is China. I hope the time is not far off when Oregon herself will take her place among them."[27]

The time came on November 5. After five defeats, male voters approved the Oregon Suffrage for Women Amendment by a majority of 4,161: 61,265 yeas, 57,104 nays—equal-suffrage state nine! As was true in other states, not all women were enfranchised. Native American women could not become citizens unless they were married to white men. First-generation women and men who emigrated from Asia were ineligible for United States citizenship. (In China, the Chinese Assembly unexpectedly postponed the promised equal suffrage. Chinese women finally won the right to vote in 1949.)

Governor Oswald West asked seventy-eight-year-old Abigail Scott Duniway to write and sign the Equal Suffrage Proclamation. When she went to register to vote, the first woman to do so in Multnomah County, the registrar asked whether she should be listed as "retired."

"No," Duniway replied, "I am not retired yet . . . I am still working to the best of my ability to help bring equal suffrage to every part of the United States."[28]

Throughout the country, suffragists celebrated the record-setting victories—four new equal-suffrage states, although the count in Michigan was not yet official. In New York City, on November 9, 1912, "a river of fire" dazzled the 400,000 spectators at the nighttime parade celebrating the four new stars on the suffrage flag. On a chilly Saturday night, 20,000 women and girls and several thousand men and boys marched up Fifth Avenue.

The "river of fire" was created by a novelty imported from Paris, France, that hung from a pole—an orange pumpkin-shaped lantern with a single light bulb inside. The light bulb was attached to a battery that a marcher carried in a pocket. Women trumpeters marched, playing the triumphal march from the opera *Aida*. A chorus of 200 women and men along with a brass band marched while singing "Our Right is Might," a song composed for the parade by Minnie C. E. Walsh. Ten charioteers, including Inez Milholland, drove snow-white horses that pulled a chariot, one for each of the ten full-suffrage states. When a reporter asked Milholland, an eloquent and tireless suffragist, whether her flimsy charioteer costume kept her warm enough, she replied, "I will never get cold in a cause such as this."[29]

On November 13, suffragists filled Carnegie Hall for a "Celebration of Citizenship." Ten stars on the suffrage flag were lighted up "in a burst of electricity."[30] A week later, another celebration at Carnegie Hall was held to welcome Carrie Chapman Catt, who had returned from her twenty-month trip "suffrage proselytizing" around the world.[31] Suffragists' penchant for pageantry was again on display: Representatives of fourteen countries presented her with a flag, the suffrage chorus performed, and the ten suffrage states were represented by women wearing white robes and carrying shields and banners. Meanwhile, anti-suffragists held a luncheon at which a speaker said: "It is a woman's duty to be delightful, ornamental, and useful and she could not be more so with the vote. . . . Where the ballot is placed in the hands of those unfit to use it there follows ruin, rapine, and terror."[32]

Two days later, delegates gathered in Philadelphia for NAWSA's Forty-Fourth Annual Convention. Two suffragists from Michigan reported that it appeared that the amendment would be defeated by "fraudulent returns."[33] Ballot boxes had been lost and ballots burned. Precincts were withholding their count, suffragists believed, until it was known how many votes would be needed to defeat the amendment. Governor Osborn denounced the trickery. Finally, on December 29, 1912, the final returns were announced: Male voters in Michigan had defeated the Michigan Woman Suffrage Amendment by 762 votes: 247,373 yeas, 248,135 nays. Four months later, a special election for another referendum on woman suffrage was held in Michigan. The opposition unleashed open warfare and the amendment was soundly defeated. Instead of ten there were nine equal-suffrage states on the suffrage map, representing approximately two million women voters: Wyoming, Colorado, Utah, Idaho, Washington, California, Arizona, Kansas, and Oregon. Inez Haynes Irwin pointed out that "one-fifth of the Senate, one-seventh of the House and one-sixth of the electoral vote came from Suffrage States."[34] Slowly suffragists were gaining voting power that could be used as leverage in the fight for a federal woman suffrage amendment.

Relentless suffragists across America continued their fierce fight for the vote. General Rosalie Gardiner Jones introduced a new tactic—the suffrage pilgrimage, perhaps imitating a recent suffrage hike undertaken by British suffragettes who had hiked from Edinburgh to London. In the middle of winter in New York, Jones led an "Army of the Hudson" on a thirteen-day, 150-mile hike from New York City to Albany. The goal was to present a suffrage petition to Governor-elect William Sulzer, while distributing literature and speaking along the way.

Wearing ankle-length, dark brown cloaks with oversized hoods, tricorn hats, backpacks printed with "Votes for Women," and carrying tall birch staffs, about 200 pilgrims, as they called themselves, set off on December 16. Newspaper reporters, dubbed "war correspondents," covered Jones and her army. Journalist Emma Bugbee hiked with the pilgrims, phoning in her story every night. General Jones was assisted by Colonel Ida Craft, the main speaker; Captain Jessie Hardy Stubbs, who was also an ardent peace advocate; and Surgeon-General Lavinia

Dock, a pioneering nurse who had helped found a group that became the National League for Nursing. Once, when Jones felt too weary to continue walking Lavinia Dock told her about a soldier who gave his feet names and urged them forward as if they were horses. Naming her feet after friends, "Percy" and "Meredith," Jones found that the suggestion worked!

Slogging through mud and slushy snow, enduring rain, fog, and wind, a bedraggled remnant of pilgrims entered Albany late on the afternoon of December 28. GENERAL JONES AND ARMY REACH CAPITAL, announced the front-page headline in a Boise, Idaho newspaper.[35] "We have left a trail of thought and suggestions behind us. . . . The process of awakening the public mind to the need of votes for women is very slow, but we feel that this pilgrimage has brought the matter before the public in a manner that would have been possible no other way," said General Rosalie Jones.[36] Very slow, indeed.

Chapter 9

Breakthrough: 1913

Girls, get out your hatpins, they are going to rush us. —Suffrage Marcher

Grace Wilbur Trout of Oak Park, Illinois, a writer, wife, and mother, whose notable physical feature was thick, curly, dark hair that tumbled above her ears and down her forehead, had been elected president of the Chicago Political Equality League in 1910, and greatly increased the membership. That same year, she conducted the first Suffrage Automobile Tour in Illinois, a whirlwind weeklong trip in a seven-passenger automobile, driven by a chauffeur over many rutted dirt roads, with stops in sixteen towns. In the town square or at a street corner, the chauffeur would put the car's top down, and she would stand on the back seat and make the opening speech. Three women who accompanied her spoke next: Catharine Waugh McCulloch, a lawyer who explained suffrage from the legal standpoint; S. Grace Nicholes, a settlement worker who presented a working woman's viewpoint; and Ella S. Stewart, president of the Illinois Equal Suffrage Association (IESA), who discussed the international perspective. Two reporters accompanied them, providing daily newspaper coverage. After the last stop in Wheaton, a reporter wrote: "Suffragists tour ends in triumph. . . .With mud-bespattered 'Votes of Women' still flying."[1] Grace Trout was also on the board of the IESA. By 1912, she was tired and "desired above all things to retire to private life." But, in October, she agreed to serve as the president of the IESA.

She agreed because of the urgings of her twenty-one-year-old son who had been in California during the 1911 suffrage campaign. "He had seen every vicious interest lined up against the women and had become convinced of the righteousness of the cause," Trout later explained. "He said to me: 'Mother, ... you can do a work that no one else can do.' He had that blind faith that sons always have in their mothers—and I listened to his advice." Then, shortly after her election, her son suddenly died. "So our work," she later reflected, "sometimes comes toward us out of the sunshine of life, sometimes it comes toward us out of life's shadows, and all that we do is not only for those who are here, and those who are coming after us, but is in memory of those who have gone on before."[2]

Like many suffragists, Catherine Waugh McCulloch worked to secure other rights for women, including equal guardianship with their husbands over their children and raising the age of consent for girls. (State suffrage associations had committees for a variety issues, from laws and legislative actions to education.) After graduating from law school in 1886, she became the eighteenth woman permitted to practice law in Illinois. Married to a fellow law student, Catherine McCulloch formed a legal business with him—McCulloch and McCulloch—and had four children. HUSBAND AND WIFE PARTNERS IN BUSINESS AND HOUSEWORK, read a newspaper headline in Tacoma, Washington.[3] During the Wisconsin campaign, she and her husband and four children spent their vacation there campaigning.

The first woman elected as a Justice of the Peace in Evanston, Illinois, McCulloch made news from coast to coast when she announced that she would drop the stipulation in the marriage vows that a wife promised to "obey" her husband. A newspaper in Astoria, Oregon, reported that she "promises that neither party will be obliged to make any pledges that the other party is not bound by."[4]

In 1891, McCulloch, who was known for her "good judgment and fair methods," had written an equal-suffrage amendment for the state constitution that was presented to the legislature.[5] It passed in the House, although not by the required constitutional majority. The Senate refused to consider it. Instead, in the last days of the legislative session, legislators passed a slipshod School Suffrage Bill that would take four decisions by the Illinois Supreme Court to clarify. The court's decisions affirmed women's right to vote for candidates for some school offices. Most important, the court affirmed that the state legislature had the power to pass suffrage bills directly, thus circumventing the requirement to amend the state constitution through a referendum. An astutely strategic Catharine McCulloch seized the opportunity to write a presidential and municipal suffrage bill that would allow women to vote for presidential electors and municipal positions, such as mayors and aldermen. It was introduced in 1893, but not voted on.

Every year thereafter, the IESA, the WCTU, clubwomen, and labor organizations were among the many groups that continued the ceaseless efforts. In 1911, Grace Wilbur Trout accompanied Catharine McCulloch to a session of the legislature. "I was indignant at the way the suffrage committee was treated," Trout later recalled. Upon her election as the IESA's president in 1912, she planned a new strategy with the newly elected head of the IESA's Legislative Committee, Elizabeth K. Booth. Their low-key campaign would be "without special trains, special hearings, or spectacular activities of any kind at Springfield," the capital. It would be a "quiet, educational campaign." Knowing that they would have to win over legislators who opposed suffrage, they decided not to "attack or criticize" them.[6]

Elizabeth Booth, a mild-appearing wife and mother, spent February 1913 in Springfield closely observing legislators, learning their names, politics, family members, habits, hobbies, daily schedule, favorite food and drink, quirks, garnering every detail. She recorded the information and pasted a photograph of each man in a card index system she created. About one third of legislators were pro-suffrage, one third were bitter enemies, leaving a pool of about fifty men they needed to convert to make up the majority necessary to pass the suffrage bill.

On Friday evenings during the legislative session, Elizabeth Booth rode the train from Springfield to Chicago, socializing with legislators who were returning home for the weekend. She asked about their families. She showed interest in their activities, including breeding pigs. Grace Trout thoroughly canvassed the state, soliciting support. Booth and Trout exemplified the ingenuity, resourcefulness, and diligence that suffragists across the country employed as they devised their strategies and tactics, always tailoring their methods to their particular situation.

Their sometimes seemingly hopeless low-key campaign finally converted enough previously doubtful senators and secured the governor's support for the Presidential and Municipal Suffrage Bill. The Illinois Senate passed the bill on May 7, 1913, by a majority of 14: 29 yeas, 15 nays. But, the House was another matter: "Every one knew that the House would kill it," wrote Gertrude Foster Brown, a tall, energetic pianist and teacher, who grew up in Illinois and had come from New York City to lobby.[7] (Brown titled her autobiography, *Suffrage and Music: My First Eighty Years*.)

Representative Charles L. Scott introduced the bill in the House. Trout and Booth enlisted help: Antoinette Funk, an "attractive, impetuous, eloquent and persuasive" Chicago lawyer, arrived on May 13.[8] A week later they were joined by Ruth Hanna McCormick, who had recently moved to Springfield with her infant daughter and husband state senator Medill McCormick. A seasoned lobbyist, McCormick was the daughter of the legendary politician Mark Hanna. (She would later be elected to the U.S. House of Representatives.)

Grace Trout went to the precincts of representatives marked "doubtful" on Elizabeth Booth's card index to hold mass meetings, generating popular support among their constituents. Booth, Funk, and McCormick lobbied legislators and monitored the progress of the bill in the House. It was sent to the wrong committee, but the mistake had seemed unintentional. However, when Grace Trout returned, she happened to be on an elevator with two legislative opponents, one of whom glanced at her and facetiously remarked to his companion: "How surprised some folks will be later on." On alert, Trout and loyal legislators worked late into the night to rectify the "mistake."[9] In the morning, the suffrage bill was ordered to a friendly committee, foiling their enemies.

Each step of the way through the legislative process, the first reading and the second reading, opponents tried to kill the bill. The head of the United Liquor Dealers Association arrived in Springfield. Detectives shadowed Booth, Trout, Funk, and McCormick. Ever vigilant in public, they never discussed their plans or the names of legislators who had privately promised to vote for the bill. When the bill survived intact to the third and final reading before a vote, opponents put enormous pressure on William McKinley, the young Speaker of the House, to kill the bill. Haggard and worn-looking, McKinley told Grace Trout that hundreds of opponents were calling him, day and night. They threatened to ruin his political career. How much pro-suffrage sentiment was there, he asked her; he had to know. Suffragists around the state were eager to storm the capital. Trout and Booth held them off, reinforced by advice from a supportive legislator who said: "Don't let them come. You'll never be able to hold your men if a crowd of women come down here."

Trout mobilized Harriette Taylor Treadwell, an elementary school principal, who innovated a telephone brigade. At fifteen-minute intervals, prominent pro-suffrage men and women called McKinley's home and office from Saturday morning to Monday evening. Margaret Dobyne, head of the IESA's press committee, put out a call for telegrams and letters. Thousands of letters and telegrams greeted McKinley when he arrived in Springfield. He scheduled the final vote for June 11.

On that day, Elizabeth Booth and Ruth Hanna McCormick sat in the gallery keeping track of the votes. Antoinette Funk served as a messenger between them and Grace Trout, who was stationed at the door to the House to keep an eye on the regular doorkeeper, an opponent who could not be trusted to keep lobbyists from illegally entering the House during a session, and to prevent any friendly legislators who might have second thoughts from trying to sneak out.

All morning and into the afternoon, the opposition used one delay tactic after another. Late in the afternoon, the voting started. After two roll calls, the bill had not passed. Confident that they had the votes, Elizabeth Booth wrote the names of representatives who had promised to support the measure on a piece of paper, reached over the gallery railing, and dropped the paper into the hands of a powerful representative who staunchly opposed the bill. She had quietly befriended him, asking only for "fair play." He had agreed. The note read: "Please see that these men vote."[10] True to his promise, he complied. The men voted and the measure passed by a majority of 25: 83 yeas, 58 nays. From inside the House chamber, Grace Trout heard a "deafening roar and several men rushed out and exclaimed—'We have won. The bill has passed.'" Turning her face to the wall, she shed a few tears. Turning around she saw "about ten men who were all surreptitiously wiping their eyes."[11]

Governor Edward Dunne, who was under great pressure to veto the measure, signed the Presidential and Municipal Suffrage Act into law. PARTIAL SUFFRAGE FOR ILLINOIS WOMEN, announced a headline in a Salt Lake City, Utah newspaper.[12] The enemies of the measure would eventually fail in their efforts to have the Illinois Supreme Court declare it unconstitutional.

Telegrams announcing the victory were sent. Flags raised. The IESA held a splendid banquet and invited all the legislators, even their opponents and their wives. Fifty thousand people watched two thousand women march down Michigan Avenue in Chicago. A platoon of mounted police led the parade awash in yellow pennants, balloons, and banners. Catherine Waugh McCulloch, Grace Trout, Elizabeth Booth, Antoinette Funk, and Ruth Hanna McCormick—dubbed the "Big Five"—rode in a car trailing yellow streamers. Then Illinois suffragists did what suffragists did whenever and wherever women were enfranchised, even if only partially: They stayed intensely engaged, registering women, running civic education classes, campaigning in other states, and working for a federal amendment.

It was an outstanding victory. A non-western state, a state east of the Mississippi River, had granted more than a sliver of voting rights to women. The right to vote for presidential electors gave Illinois women voting power on a national level, thus "bringing an incalculable influence and power into the arena of national politics."[13] Suffragists across the country added what became known as "The Illinois Bill" to their arsenal of tactics in the fight for the vote.

Three months before the Illinois victory, suffragists had commanded the nation's attention with a grand parade, the Woman Suffrage Procession in Washington, D.C. on March 3, 1913, the day before President Wilson's inauguration. The idea originated with Alice Paul, who had a unique ability to envision and precisely execute visual and emotionally evocative events.

Paul knew that NAWSA's state-by-state strategy, requiring untold amounts of money and dedicated suffragists' ceaseless efforts, reaped far more defeats than victories. She knew that the well-financed enemies of woman suffrage aggressively sought to undo state gains in the courts or in the legislatures. That some states had constitutions that were difficult, if not impossible, to amend. It was time, Alice Paul unequivocally concluded, to concentrate solely on winning the federal woman suffrage amendment that had been introduced in Congress in 1878, as the Sixteenth Amendment to the Constitution.

In 1912, she had visited her friend Lucy Burns. A fearless, eloquent, thirty-three-year-old tall and muscular woman with a pile of bright red hair, Burns had just returned from England. They both had worked closely with Emmeline Pankhurst, who trained them in WSPU's militant methods. Now, reunited in America, Alice Paul and Lucy Burns wholly committed themselves to revitalizing the campaign for a federal woman suffrage amendment. Neither Burns nor Paul would "hesitate for a moment to suffer torture, to die" for the cause of woman suffrage.[14]

The heart of their strategy was the policy adopted by the Pankhursts' WSPU to hold whichever political party held the most power responsible for the failure to pass a federal woman suffrage amendment. This meant that suffragists, especially the millions of women voters in the nine equal-suffrage states, would work to defeat elected officials in that party, even if they were pro-suffrage. The point was to motivate pro-suffrage politicians to convert anti-suffrage or uncommitted members of their party. Paul and Burns also planned to stage large-scale events to put a national spotlight on the issue of woman suffrage, demanding the attention of President Wilson and Congress.

Wanting to affiliate with NAWSA, Paul and Burns sought Jane Addams's advice. Given NAWSA's nonpartisan policy, Addams told them, the executive board would absolutely reject their plan to hold the party in power responsible. But she liked the idea of a grand parade and pageant. With Addams's backing, board members appointed Alice Paul the new chair of NAWSA's Congressional Committee, Lucy Burns the vice chair, and approved the plan for a grand parade and pageant, a "Woman Suffrage Procession, on March 3, 1913, the day large crowds would be gathering in Washington, D.C., for the inauguration of Woodrow Wilson as President of the United States on March 4.

The first meeting of the Congressional Committee's Executive Committee was held on January 2, 1913, in their new headquarters, a basement room at 1420 F Street, Washington, D.C. Alice Paul and Lucy Burns were there along with the lawyer Crystal Eastman, a feminist and socialist like her brother Max, with whom she lived in New York City's Greenwich Village; Mary Ritter Beard, a historian and a member of the WTUL; and Dora Kelly Lewis, a wealthy member of a prominent family, who had become a widow with three small children at the age of twenty-eight. A tall woman with a kindly face that belied steely courage and fortitude, Dora Lewis, now fifty-one years old, was

130

involved in worker's rights, prison reform, and woman suffrage. A member of NAWSA, she had met Alice Paul at an open-air meeting. Their quest for women's right to vote transcended their almost twenty-five-year difference in age and very different life experiences.

Soon other women joined forces with Alice Paul and Lucy Burns, including Elizabeth Thacher Kent, the previous head of the Congressional Committee. As the wife of William Kent, a congressman from California, she had political connections that she used to advance the cause. The mother of seven children, Elizabeth Kent was an early conservationist and good friends with another supporter of woman suffrage, the famous naturalist John Muir. With just two months before the grand parade and pageant, committee members enthusiastically went to work.

The head of the press committee was Helen Hamilton Gardener, an author and rationalist orator, who in 1888 had debunked the view that women's intellectual capacity was less than men's because women's brains weighed less. A diminutive, delicate-appearing woman, Gardener, who was born Alice Chenoweth, wrote press releases and distributed photographs that garnered national publicity. A photograph of an elegantly posed Inez Milholland appeared in a Washington, D.C. newspaper with the caption "Most Beautiful Suffragist to be Pageant Herald."[15] The headline in a Tulsa, Oklahoma newspaper read: SUFFRAGETTES PLAN BIG UNIQUE PARADE.[16] ("Suffragette," the term for English militants, was occasionally used in American publications, perhaps intentionally stigmatizing the American women. "Suffs" was also used, perhaps to belittle the cause.)

Suffragists across America gathered to march in Washington, D. C. Grace Trout was the head of the Illinois delegation that included Ida B. Wells-Barnett, the African America journalist, who had recently founded, along with her white co-activists Belle Squire and Virginia Brooks, the Alpha Suffrage Club, the first black woman suffrage club in Chicago.

Ida Bell Wells-Barnett, pioneering journalist and civil rights activist, was a co-founder of the bi-racial National Association for the Advancement of Colored People. She is honored today in many ways, including the renamed Congress Parkway to Ida B. Wells Drive in Chicago. (Library of Congress)

On the morning of the grand parade, the Illinois delegation was practicing in the drill hall at the parade headquarters. Holding a pennant printed with Illinois and nine stars, each woman wore a white turban with nine stars tilted at a military angle, and a long white stole printed with "Illinois" over an ankle-length dress. Suddenly, Grace Trout, who had been at a planning meeting, appeared and made an announcement that startled the delegates, leaving some embarrassed and a few indignant: "Many of the eastern and southern women have greatly resented the fact that there are to be colored women in the delegations . . . the national association has decided it is unwise to include the colored women, I think we should abide by its decision."

Schuyler Coe Brandt chimed in, "You are right; it will prejudice southern people against suffrage if we take the colored women in our ranks."

"But this is entirely undemocratic," interjected Virginia Brooks, known as the "Joan of Arc" of West Hammond, Illinois. "If the women of other states lack moral courage, we should show them that we are not afraid of public opinion. We should stand on our principles. If we do not the parade will be a farce." Then Ida Wells-Barnett, "her cheeks stained with tears and voice quavering," told the group: "The southern women have tried to evade the [race] question time and again by giving some excuse or other every time it has been brought up. If the Illinois women do not take a stand now in this great democratic parade then the colored women are lost."

Clearly moved, Grace Trout replied: "It is time for Illinois to recognize the colored woman as a political equal and you shall march with the delegation." When it appeared that Trout had made a principled decision, instead of an expedient one, someone pulled her aside, prompting her to say she had to consult with Genevieve Stone, chair of the Illinois delegation and wife of the Illinois congressman. Upon her return, Grace Trout again told Ida Wells-Barnett, "I am afraid that we shall not be able to have you march with us. . . . I shall have to ask you to march with the colored delegation. I am sorry, but I felt that is the right thing to do."[17]

Ida Wells-Barnett refused to abide by the decision. She would either march with the Illinois delegation or not at all. Virginia Brooks and Belle Squire, president of the No Vote, No Tax League, offered to march with her in the colored delegation that would march at the end of the parade. Wells-Barnett appeared to agree. But, she and Squire and Brooks had devised another plan. About halfway along the parade route, Ida Wells-Barnett, wearing her white turban and stole and holding an Illinois pennant, waited in the crowd. When the Illinois delegation appeared, she slipped out of the crowd and took her place in line beside Belle Squire and Virginia Brooks. In perfect step, the three women defiantly marched.

General Rosalie Gardner Jones and her suffrage army, dubbed pilgrims, hiked 230 miles from New York City to Washington, D.C., to participate in the grand parade.

General Rosalie Jones, in her trademark hooded brown cloak, leading her "Army of the Hudson" through Newark, New Jersey, on their way to Washington, D. C., to join the grand Woman Suffrage Procession. (Library of Congress)

From Wilmington, Delaware, they tramped south into Maryland. COOL GREETINGS IN SOUTH, read the headline in a Chicago newspaper. "The army's reception cooled off rapidly from the minute it crossed the Mason and Dixon line . . . The question of whether the agitation for enfranchising women means giving negro women the vote menaces them closely," wrote a war correspondent.[18] Two businessmen who claimed to represent "many thousands of Southern men" approached Jones. They demanded to know "how the army stood upon the question of suffrage for negro women." That question was a matter for "certain States," and they should "solve their own problems," she had replied. "General," said the men, "if you advocate votes for negro women you will indeed find that your way to Washington lies through the enemy's country."[19]

On February 26, the pilgrims left Baltimore headed for Laurel, a twenty-two mile hike. For the first time, they were "hissed and followed by a hostile crowd, and throughout the day . . . met with rebuffs and coldness"; most probably a response to the fact that a group of black women holding a yellow banner lettered with "Votes for Negro Women" had greeted the hikers.[20] In addition, rumors were afloat that black women who lived in Buzzard Glory, the segregated settlement in Laurel, planned to march with the army into Washington, D. C. Clearly, in the eyes of local residents the suffrage hikers were stirring up trouble. In one hamlet, a crowd of boys accosted them, and "screaming a resemblance of the famous 'rebel yell,' bombarded the scattered pilgrims with stones, paper wads, sticks and a few rotten eggs."[21] HOOTS, INSULTS, CLUBS AND ROCKS FOR HIKING ARMY," read the vivid headline in a Richmond, Virginia newspaper.[21]

As Jones and her army entered Laurel, "three carriage loads of colored women, who wore 'votes for women' pins" followed them. But, then drove off. The incidents roiled the hikers, some said they would disband before allowing black women to march. Others were unfazed: "Let them come," said Elisabeth Freeman. "We cannot with dignity force them to stay out if they desire to follow us . . . ," General Jones told a war correspondent.[22] The black suffragists' intervention, the attacks on the pilgrims, and their internal dissension underscored the intractability of race issues in the fight for the vote. And the determination of black women to advocate for themselves.

For seventeen days, Jones and her army, often bedraggled and beset with aches, pains, and blisters, had tramped through ankle-deep mud, slush, snow, braved windy blasts and torrential rain, and endured taunts from college students. They also basked in cheers and goodwill from people like the woman who gave them hardboiled eggs that were still hot, telling them to warm their hands, then eat the eggs. Newspapers across America had covered the unprecedented hike, awakening public interest in the cause and the upcoming grand march.

Five miles outside Washington, a troop of twenty women dressed in white astride white horses met General Jones and her intrepid suffrage army, augmented by people who had hiked part way (fourteen hikers completed the entire journey), and led them into Washington, D.C. JONES ARMY MAKES GOAL; FOLKS SHOUT, cheered a newspaper headline in Rock Island, Illinois.[23] Tens of thousands of onlookers enthusiastically cheered and applauded as they triumphantly marched down Pennsylvania Avenue.

On March 3, 1913, an estimated 5,000 to 8,000 women from every state and many countries marched in what was called "the greatest parade of women . . . an astonishing demonstration."[24] It was a beautiful sunny day. The Great Demand Banner was posted on the sides of a wagon pulled by two white horses:

WE DEMAND AN AMENDMENT TO THE CONSTITUTION OF THE UNITED STATES ENFRANCHISING THE WOMEN OF THIS COUNTRY

Inez Milholland mounted on Gray Dawn, a white charger, prepared to lead the 1913 grand "Woman Suffrage Procession." (Library of Congress)

Inez Milholland, astride Gray Dawn, a magnificent horse, was dramatically dressed in a white suit, long white boots and gloves, and a pale-blue cloak with a golden Maltese cross. She wore a single star tiara atop her long, dark, thick, curly hair that was gathered at her neck and cascaded down her back.

Holding a banner inscribed with "World-Wide Movement," Carrie Chapman Catt, who had previously disapproved of parades as too militant, led the first section of women from countries where women were enfranchised. There were twenty-six floats, ten bands, including Alma Nash and her Missouri Ladies Military Marching Band, six brigades of horsewomen, six golden chariots, and six mounted heralds. There were writers wearing white gowns, artists clad in pink, and musicians in red. Workers rode on a float depicting the inside of a sweatshop, holding a banner "We Want to Protect Our Children."

Dawn Mist, an American Indian woman, led a division. General Jones and her army received a loud ovation. Senators and representatives from equal-suffrage states marched with a banner inscribed "Women Helped Elect These Men." Wearing academic gowns and caps, twenty-two black women, founding members of Delta Sigma Theta at Howard University, and honorary member Mary Church Terrell, marched in the college division. They had been invited by a white woman in charge of organizing that division, Elsie Hill, who had attended Vassar College around the same time as Inez Milholland and Lucy Burns. "The Allegory of Women," a tableau featuring a hundred women and children and culminating with the release of white doves, was performed in front of the Treasury Building.

A line of Boy Scouts and some male college students along the march did their best to restrain men determined to disrupt the parade. But, they were overwhelmed while many police officers stood idly by. Rampaging men blocked the parade, forcing marchers to fight their way through. A girl on a float was grabbed and kicked in the face. Women were spat on and manhandled. Men shouted ribald jeers and vile insults. Suffragists on horseback, including Inez Milholland and an outrider with the

Illinois delegation, bravely rode into the mob, pushing it back on the sidewalk. Confronted by a menacing line of twenty men with their arms locked, a young woman, who "was really terrified," braced herself and shouted: "Girls, get out your hatpins, they are going to rush us."[25] The men backed off.

It took the arrival of three cavalry troops from Fort Myer to finally control the crowd, allowing marchers to triumphantly complete the historic parade. More than a hundred women were taken to the hospital. Headlines across America announced the melee. In New York City, a front-page headline read: WOMEN BATTLE HOSTILE MOBS IN CAPITAL PARADE.[26] A Senate committee investigated police conduct during the parade. The chief of police lost his job. The treatment of women, according to Grace Trout, "aroused the indignation of the whole nation and converted many men to the suffrage cause."[27]

Several weeks after the grand parade, in the Territory of Alaska that had been recently created by the United States Congress, the legislature, composed of seven senators and fifteen representatives, unanimously voted to enfranchise women. The only senator who opposed the bill, Elwood Brunner of Nome, "had the good sense or caution to absent himself during the roll call."[28] It was the first bill passed by the legislature and signed by Governor J. F. A. Strong. Two years later, Governor Strong said that voting by women had not "unsexed them nor caused them to take on 'unwomanly attributes' or unfitted them to become wives and mothers, or to attend to their domestic duties."[29]

Alice Paul would have had every reason to think that President Woodrow Wilson was well informed about woman suffrage. He was well educated and experienced in dealing with public issues as a professor, college president, and governor of New Jersey. He knew that instead of welcoming him when he arrived in Washington, D.C., a huge crowd was watching the grand suffrage parade. But shortly after the parade, Alice Paul led a small deputation to ask President Wilson to request that Congress consider woman suffrage, and he replied that the issue was new to

138

him. He would have to learn more about it. Over the next few months, Alice Paul sent four more deputations to educate him.

In April, she formed the Congressional Union (CU), a companion organization to NAWSA's Congressional Committee, the committee to which NAWSA had appointed Paul and Burns as the chair and vice chair. Paul's decision to found another organization did not concern the NAWSA leaders, at least not yet. On July 31, a motorcade of eighty gaily decorated automobiles, with suffragists from across America gathered in Hyattsville, Maryland, and, with Alice Paul riding in the lead car, drove five miles to the capitol to deliver petitions with 75,000 signatures.

On October 26, 1913, Emmeline Pankhurst arrived in New York harbor aboard the steamship *Provence*. Immigration officials refused her entry, taking her instead to Ellis Island. There she was interrogated by a board of special inquiry that had acquired a complete dossier of her arrest record from British authorities. (Since July 1912, she had been imprisoned twelve times, each time going on a hunger strike.) The board ordered her deportation as an "undesirable alien on the grounds of 'moral turpitude.'"[30]

Alva Belmont provided an attorney who appealed the case to the Commissioner of Immigration in Washington, D.C. who referred it to President Wilson. Besieged with appeals by Jane Addams and other prominent people, Wilson ordered Pankhurst's release. "Whoever was responsible for my detention," she later wrote, "entirely overlooked the advertising value of the incident. My lecture tour was made much more successful."[31] Widespread newspaper coverage included a three-quarter-length photograph on the front page of a newspaper in Nashville, Tennessee, with a caption hailing her as "England's famous fighting suffragette." The banner headline across the front page of a San Francisco newspaper read: MRS. PANKHURST ENTERS N.Y. IN TRIUMPH.[32]

In Hartford, Connecticut, Emmeline Pankhurst gave her speech, now known as her "Freedom or Death" speech. Citing suffragettes' resolve to continue hunger strikes, she declared that "the enemy (i.e., the government) . . . will have to choose between giving us freedom or giving us death."[33] Inspired by her speech, Katharine "Kit" Houghton Hepburn (mother of the famous actor Katharine Hepburn, who was then six years old), and Emily Pierson revitalized the fight for the vote in Connecticut, where no gains had been made since 1893, when women won limited school suffrage.

Lucy Burns introduced Emmeline Pankhurst, her mentor and longtime friend at gatherings in Delaware and Maryland. On a Sunday afternoon, Pankhurst addressed a standing room crowd at the Columbia Theater in Washington, D.C. Several days later, she left New York City on board the *Majestic*, knowing that she might be rearrested under the Prisoner's Temporary Discharge of Ill Health Act, dubbed the "Cat and Mouse Act." Parliament had passed the act, authorizing the release of dangerously ill suffragettes, who, once they recovered were rearrested, to prevent the martyrdom of hunger-striking suffragettes.

NAWSA's Forty-Fifth Annual Convention opened in Washington, D.C. on November 29, 1913. One of the speakers, Margaret Hinchey, a laundry worker, "made a deep impression" on the delegates as she described women "working seventeen and eighteen hours a day standing over heavy machines." She told how the mayor of New York City, George B. McClellan, Jr., had denied a request for a parade permit during the 1909 strike, saying the striking women "are of no account to me." Would he have said that, Hinchey asked, if they had been "women with votes?"[34]

As head of NAWSA's Congressional Committee and president of the CU, Alice Paul gave a report detailing a whirlwind of agitation: the grand parade; campaigns by a paid organizer from North Carolina to Rhode Island; daily news items sent to newspapers across the country; distribution of thousands of pieces of literature; establishment of a Men's League; from five to ten outdoor meetings held daily; numerous deputations to President Wilson; and testimonies before congressional committees.

She announced the publication of the *Suffragist,* the CU's official weekly newspaper. Edited by Rheta Childe Dorr, a prominent journalist, the *Suffragist* was full of editorials, many written by Lucy Burns; articles and commentary; updates, poems, sketches, and cartoons by well-known artists such as Nina Allender. Allender's depiction of a suffragist—young, energetic, competent, intrepid—became known as an "Allender girl." Her work was infused with "a woman's vivacity and a woman's sense of humor, a humor which plays keenly and gracefully about masculine insensibility."[35]

Although NAWSA leadership appreciated Paul's achievements, a breach was in the making over the strategies of solely focusing on the federal amendment, and of holding the party in power responsible for the failure to enfranchise women. There was also the matter of the CU, Alice Paul's new organization. Carrie Chapman Catt pointedly asked Paul where was her allegiance—to NAWSA's Congressional Committee or to the CU? Who would have control of the money that Paul was so good at raising? NAWSA leaders were particularly apprehensive that Paul and Burns would introduce militant tactics. When, in a widely publicized incident, Lucy Burns was arrested and fined $1 for using chalk to write a notice for a mass meeting on a sidewalk in Washington, D.C., Anna Howard Shaw publicly chastised her. When Alice Paul and Lucy Burns welcomed Emmeline Pankhurst, Anna Howard Shaw told a reporter, "I disapprove of her methods."[36]

Before the year ended, NAWSA's leadership gave Alice Paul a choice: She could either resign as president of the CU or be replaced as chair of the Congressional Committee. Paul refused to resign. NAWSA re-formed the Congressional Committee with Ruth Hanna McCormick and Antoinette Funk and Elizabeth K. Booth, co-workers in the successful Illinois campaign.

NAWSA's convention ended on December 5, the day that Emmeline Pankhurst was rearrested at sea. The night before the *Majestic* arrived in Plymouth, England, she received a wireless message alerting her that the government had decided to rearrest her. The *Majestic*, under orders by the police, came to anchor in the outer harbor. Two "huge gray warships" were in the inner harbor. From the deck, Pankhurst watched as a speeding boat "dashed across the harbor, directly under the nose of the grim war vessels." Two women, drenched from the spray of the waves, stood in the boat.

"The Cats are here, Mrs. Pankhurst!" they shouted through megaphones as their boat raced past the *Majestic*. Another speeding boat brought seven policemen and a wardress from Holloway Prison to arrest her. "Following my firm resolve not to assist in any way the enforcing of the infamous law," Emmeline Pankhurst later recalled, "I refused to go with the men, who thereupon picked me up and carried me to the waiting police tender."[37]

She was imprisoned in Exeter primarily, a sympathetic prison official told her, to prevent her from appearing at the massive meeting that had been arranged to welcome her home. She immediately went on a hunger strike. Given her prominence, prison authorities did not dare to force-feed her. After three days, she was released. Nine days later, she was rearrested and imprisoned. For four days, Emmeline Pankhurst refused food and water and added a "sleep strike," keeping herself awake "as far as was humanly possible."[38] MILITANTS BURN MANSION TO AVENGE MRS. PANKHURST WHO COLLAPSES IN PRISON, read the front-page headline in a New York City newspaper.[39] Another headline in the same newspaper read: MILITANT METHODS NOT FOR AMERICANS, SAYS DR. ANNA SHAW.[40]

The morning of the fifth day, an ambulance took Emmeline Pankhurst to a hospital. Many days passed before she recovered even a small fraction of her usual health.

Throughout 1913, American suffragists had peacefully soldiered onward. In New York City, 10,000 suffragists marched eight abreast, accompanied by thirty-five bands in a parade that went on for hours. In New York, Pennsylvania, and Iowa, states that required two successive legislatures to approve a woman suffrage amendment, suffragists prepared for the second year of their campaigns. Campaigns were underway in seven states, where woman suffrage amendments were on the ballot in 1914.

A resolution proposing a federal woman suffrage amendment to the Constitution was before committees in the House of Representatives and in the Senate. But, it could no longer be the Sixteenth Amendment. In 1913, two new amendments had been added to the Constitution: the Sixteenth gave Congress the power to impose and collect taxes, and the Seventeenth established the direct election of senators. Alice Paul, Lucy Burns, and the CU were geared up to make woman suffrage the Eighteenth Amendment, as was NAWSA. Surely Congress would soon pass a federal woman suffrage amendment to the Constitution.

PART IV

Chapter 10

Hard-Fought Campaigns: 1914

Here we are—all bound for the field of battle. —Jessie Hardy
Stubbs

"All over the country women are asking for the vote. We are a force in life, a factor which must be considered," declared Jeannette Rankin on May 2, 1914—Suffrage Day. Organized by the CU, Suffrage Day was a first-of-its-kind event. WHOLE NATION OBSERVES WOMAN'S DAY, read a newspaper headline in Missoula, Montana.[1]

In Louisville, an orchestra played in Lincoln Park while children danced around a maypole. Eleven girls, dressed as yellow butterflies, represented the nine states and one territory with equal suffrage and Illinois with presidential suffrage. A boy, dressed as a cocoon, represented Kentucky, a state "almost ready to leave its dark habitation."[2] In Hartford, Connecticut, Ethel Murray, dressed as Joan of Arc, wearing chainmail and a helmet and astride a white horse, led a parade of floats and thousands of marchers. A team of oxen pulled a cart inscribed with the words: "Connecticut Trying to Catch Up." At many events, suffragists adopted a resolution demanding action on the federal woman suffrage amendment, now known as the Bristow-Mondell Resolution, for Representative Frank Bristow and Senator George Mondell, who had reintroduced the measure in Congress.

Not everyone celebrated. In Boston, anti-suffragists sold red roses, the symbol of their opposition, claiming that 100,000 were worn during the day. In Belleville, Illinois, some husbands refused to allow their wives to participate. Alda Robins Black, an organizer from Chicago, reported that some women said "that they have been beaten by their husbands for voting, and others have been locked up and intimidated to keep them from voting."[3]

A week later hundreds of Suffrage Day resolutions, including two delivered by carrier pigeons, were presented to a delegation of senators and representatives in Washington, D.C. After gathering in a mass meeting at the grandiose Belasco Theatre, more than five hundred women wearing long white dresses and "Votes for Women" sashes marched in perfect formation to the capitol. There, the women who represented every congressional and senatorial district in America, arranged themselves on the stairs, filling all three hundred and fifty-six steps. A group of women in the front row sang "The March of the Women," WSPU's anthem composed by Dame Ethel Smyth, with lyrics by Cicely Hamilton. Entering the building, they marched into the ornate rotunda where they presented the resolutions.

Suffragists with long-handled brushes and buckets of glue pasted notices for events on buildings. This one was for the procession to deliver May Day resolutions to the Capitol and the White House on May 9, 1914. (Library of Congress)

The May demonstrations were part of the CU's ongoing efforts to pressure the recalcitrant Congress to pass a federal woman suffrage amendment. After ten days of debates, the amendment had won a majority vote in the Senate, but not by the necessary two thirds. In the House, the Rules Committee voted against forming a Woman Suffrage Committee. Democrats were in the majority in the House, and the Democratic Caucus, a decision-making group of all Democratic representatives, could have ordered the House Rules Committee to create the committee. They refused, despite intense pressure from the CU. Instead, the Democratic Caucus passed a resolution stating that the "question of Woman Suffrage is a State and not a Federal question."

"Unless the Democratic Party reconsiders its present position," the CU warned, it would send organizers to the nine equal-suffrage states to campaign against Democratic candidates.[4] Employing a different tactic, NAWSA's Congressional Committee introduced a new federal woman suffrage amendment that set up a process to be used at the state level. Senator John F. Shafroth of Colorado and Representative Alexander M. Palmer of Pennsylvania introduced the measure, known as the Shafroth-Palmer Resolution. The multi-step process included securing an initiative petition with the number of signatures exceeding eight percent of all those who voted at the last general election. "Incredibly cluttered and cumbered," dismissively asserted the CU.[5] Having acted before getting the approval of NAWSA's board, the Congressional Committee's action caused serious discord among board members and consternation throughout NAWSA's membership.

The British fight for the vote was upended on August 4, 1914, when Great Britain entered World War I. This war, as had the Civil War in the 1860s in America, posed stark choices: war work, suffrage work, peace work, or a combination. Emmeline and Christabel Pankhurst quickly made their choice and negotiated a deal—the government would release all imprisoned suffragettes and the WSPU would end its militant campaign and do war work. MILITANTS END HOSTILITIES IN GREAT BRITAIN, announced the front-page headline in a Boston newspaper.[6] Although many suffragettes objected to the Pankhursts' "autocratic decision," they complied and ceased their militant activities.[7] Nonmilitant suffrage organizations, including the National Union of Women's Suffrage Societies (NUWSS), also suspended their political activities and joined the war effort. British women were acclaimed for their war work. "Newspapers were full of the praises of women; financiers, statesmen, economists, and politicians declared that without the aid of women it would be impossible to win the war," wrote Millicent Garrett Fawcett, president of the NUWSS, "The anti-suffragism of Mr. Asquith even was beginning to crumble."[8]

Sylvia Pankhurst wept over her mother's and sister's decision. A pacifist, she joined with Emmeline and Frederick Pethick-Lawrence to lead an international peace movement. With others, they also formed a new organization to continue the fight for the vote: The Women's Freedom League and the United Suffragists. "To keep the suffrage flag flying throughout the war is, we believe, an act of the greatest service to the community as well as to our particular cause," declared Evelyn Sharp, a writer and editor for the Pethick-Lawrence's publication *Votes for Women*.[9] Emmeline Pankhurst publicly repudiated and condemned Sylvia.

On the last days of August, purple, white, and gold banners (the CU's official colors) illuminated by floodlights decorated Alva Belmont's mansion in Newport, Rhode Island, for the first meeting of the CU's Advisory Committee. Announcing that she "was tired of having to pull along with me a heavy mass of suffrage conservatism," Alva Belmont had left NAWSA and contributed much-needed money to the "fearless group unafraid to fight for its principles."[10] Alice Paul had recruited prominent longtime ardent suffragists to serve on the Advisory Committee: Inez Milholland, who was now a lawyer; author Charlotte Perkins Gilman; labor reformer Florence Kelley; Mary E. Woolley, the president of Mount Holyoke College; Helen Ring Robinson, a senator in the Colorado legislature; and Lavinia Dock, the nurse educator and General Jones's "Surgeon General."

Lucy Burns gave a speech, pointing out that President Wilson, a Democrat, had rebuffed seven deputations requesting his support of a federal woman suffrage amendment, including one with four hundred wage-earning women representing fifty trades. Burns described in detail how the Senate and House, both under Democratic control, had maneuvered to block progress. Therefore, Alice Paul said in a follow-up speech, the Democratic Party was "responsible for the non-passage of our measure." It was "the enemy." The question was "how shall the enemy be attacked?"

Their plan was to send organizers to the nine equal-suffrage states with four million women voters—Wyoming, Colorado, Utah, Idaho, Washington, California, Arizona, Kansas, Oregon—and conduct a campaign against every Democratic candidate, even pro-suffrage ones, on the ballot in the November election. "The mere announcement of the fact that Suffragists of the East have gone to the West with this appeal will be enough to make every man in Congress sit up and take notice," declared Alice Paul.[11] WAR ON CONGRESSMEN, trumpeted a newspaper headline in Washington, D.C.[12] Josephine Jewell Dodge, President of the NAOWS, denounced the campaign as an "endeavor to import from England its discarded militancy."[13] The CU's plan, replied Alice Paul, "is militant only in the sense that it is strong, positive, and energetic."[14]

The Advisory Committee approved the pioneering tactic and raised the money to finance it. On September 14, a farewell garden party was held for the fifteen national organizers who would open their headquarters in a key city. Lucy Burns went to San Francisco with trade union organizer Rose Winslow. Born Ruza Wenclawska in Poland, Rose Winslow had worked in a hosiery factory from the age of eleven until nineteen, when she contracted tuberculosis. Doris Stevens and Ruth Astor Noyes went to Denver. Stevens had met Alice Paul at the 1913 parade and cancelled plans to take a vacation with her friends, having succumbed to Paul's request that she stay and help the fledging

CU. Noyes had left NAWSA and organized CU demonstrations, such as the recent motorcade to the capitol. Josephine Casey, a member of the Chicago Union of Elevated Car Employees, went to Phoenix, Arizona, with labor union organizer Jane Pincus. Kansas City, Kansas, was the destination for Lola Carson Trax, who had a knack for staging publicity stunts, and Edna Story Latimer, president of a suffrage league in Baltimore that had organized twenty-five open-air meetings.

Jessie Hardy Stubbs, a "war correspondent" who had hiked with General Jones and was the CU's press secretary, and Virginia Arnold, who had left college to fight for suffrage, went to Portland, Oregon. Margaret Fay Whittemore, the granddaughter of a prominent suffragist in Michigan, and Anne McCue, a factory worker from Pennsylvania, went to Seattle. Three organizers worked solo. Gertrude Hunter, founder of the Wage Earner's League in Minneapolis, Minnesota, set up headquarters in Cheyenne, Wyoming. Elsie Lancaster took a suffrage slide show to present in moving picture theaters in Salt Lake City, Utah. A widow, Helena Hill Weed, made arrangements for her three children, in order to spend six-weeks in Boise City, Idaho.

Seven NWP organizers posed before boarding a train headed west, from left, Rose Winslow, Lucy Burns, Doris Stevens, Ruth Astor Noyes, Anne McCue, Jane Pincus, Jessie Hardy Stubbs. (Library of Congress)

A photograph of Winslow, Burns, Stevens, Noyes, McCue, Pincus, and Stubbs, smiling and dressed in stylish suits and hats, was widely distributed by the CU's Press Department, headed by the enterprising Florence Brewer Boeckel. A newspaper in Lehi, Utah, published it with the headline: SUFFRAGISTS WHO HAVE INVADED THE WESTERN STATES.[15]

Energetic and enthusiastic, the young organizers distributed massive amounts of literature; showed pro-suffrage silent films; gave countless speeches; and canvassed from door to door in big cities, small towns, little settlements, mining camps, and the lone residence in a remote area.

"Here we are—all bound for the field of battle," Jessie Stubbs reported from on board the North Coast Limited. "We have put up signs in each car that there will be a meeting tonight in the observation car . . . sold ten *Suffragists* today on board the train, secured new subscribers . . . and contributions to the campaign." While traveling from Phillipsburg to Osborne, Kansas, on board a freight train, Lola Trax held a meeting in the caboose with about a dozen passengers. In Wyoming, Gertrude Hunter braved high winds and snow to speak in a town "consisting of a station, a store, and post-office. Not a residence in the place." People came from "miles and miles to attend . . . on horseback, in wagons, buggies, and autos."[16] In Arizona, Jane Pincus was amused to find every Democratic candidate declaring that he and his mother and his grandmother believed in woman suffrage.

A record number of seven states held woman suffrage amendment referenda in the November 1914 election: the second time in Ohio and Nebraska; the fourth time (three referenda for equal suffrage, one for school suffrage) in South Dakota; the first time in Missouri, North Dakota, Nevada, and Montana. Supporters enthusiastically joined the campaigns: homemakers, industrial workers, business owners, clerks, teachers, writers, farmers, students, spiritualists, and socialists.

In Ohio, suffragists decided to use the initiative and referendum process, realizing that there was "no hope" that the legislature would authorize a woman suffrage amendment referendum. Thousands of volunteers set out to get the number of legally required signatures, ten percent of the number of voters at the last election, or 130,000 names. On July 30, 1914, women and men carrying petitions with 131,271 names marched into the State House, moving some witnesses to tears.

"Everything which had been tried out in any campaign was done. Constant work from the beginning of 1913 to Nov. 1914," reported Harriet Taylor Upton, president of the state suffrage association.[17] Florence Goff Schwarz, who was billed as "the most feared anti in Ohio," led the opposition. A newspaper headline warned readers that Schwarz: WIELDS TRENCHANT PEN.[18] Anti-suffragists toured county fairs and conducted statewide automobile tours to spread "the gospel of anti-suffragism."[19] Several days before the election, Upton spied a man distributing literature paid for by the liquor industry with instructions on how to vote against Amendment 3, the Ohio Women Suffrage Amendment of 1914.

Male voters defeated the measure by a majority of 182,905: 335,390 yeas, 518,295 nays. Since Ohio was a "home rule state," meaning that local governments could pass laws and ordinances, suffragists shifted their strategy to securing woman suffrage at the city level.

In Missouri, the 1911 visit by Emmeline Pankhurst had helped invigorate suffragists. Her "charming personality had set at rest all fears as to the ill effects of suffrage, even of the 'militant' variety." Sylvia Pankhurst appeared shorty after her mother, and was also "most gratifying to the friends of suffrage."[20] Edna Fischel Gellhorn, a highly respected civic leader and president of the state suffrage association, campaigned with her six-year old daughter Martha (later a legendary war correspondent). The public was assured—"There is to be nothing militant about the organization.

While we shall be aggressive, vigorous and energetic in a way, it will always be within good form and good taste."[21]

Suffragists sidestepped a hostile legislature and conducted a successful initiative campaign to get a woman suffrage measure on the ballot. The slogan "Suffrage for Women in 1914" was printed on posters, leaflets, advertisements. Lola La Follette from Wisconsin spoke several times, including at the Men's City Club. A popular actor, she regularly performed in *How the Vote Was Won*, a one-act comedy spoofing the idea that men protected women.

Male voters defeated the Missouri Suffrage Amendment, known as Issue 13, by a majority of 140,206: 182,257 yeas, 322,463 nays.

Antoinette Funk, described by a reporter as "a little woman who does not weigh more than 100 pounds," had worked in the Illinois campaign. She traveled more than 8,000 miles to campaign in the remaining five states. Consumed by the fight for the vote, Funk, who was first widowed then separated from her second husband, had sent her two young daughters to stay with relatives. She kept in touch with them by sending letters and postcards.

In Nebraska, Funk found "almost unbelievable conditions of opposition" to a woman suffrage amendment to the state constitution.[22] Powerful brewing interests activated a network of opposition and formed an enforcement committee to suppress the campaign. Businessmen, merchants, tradesmen, bankers, lawyers, and doctors were warned that they would lose business if they donated money. When a man's wife was identified as a suffragist, he received an intimidating visit from a committee member. Thirty of the most influential men in Omaha formed The Nebraska Men's Association Opposed to Woman Suffrage. Their nine-page anti-suffrage manifesto asserted that the right to vote "is a privilege of government granted only to those whom the government sees fit to grant it." Women were not "fit" because they do not "always think coolly and deliberate calmly." Women's place is in "the realm of gentler and holier and kindlier attributes that make the name of wife, mother and sister next to the name of God himself."[23] (According to the 1910 census, there were two men to every woman residing in Nebraska. One can only wonder why the Omaha men were so resistant.)

The German-American Alliance that had ties to the brewing industry issued an appeal written in German, urging their members to defeat the amendment to avoid the "yoke of prohibition on our necks." The Alliance also declared—"Our German women do not want the right to vote."[24] Another anti-suffrage group sponsored a half-page advertisement in a newspaper, warning that if the amendment passed women would be "compelled to serve on juries" and "good women" would be associated with women like Inez Milholland, "an acknowledged leader of the Woman Suffrage Movement as well as of the 'Feminist' Movement."[25] Josephine Jewell Dodge and Minnie Bronson, the president and general secretary of the NAOWS, came from New York to speak at a large public meeting. They reiterated that women did not want the vote.

Suffragists strenuously fought back. Speakers and organizers undertook automobile tours to reach voters in the large state, traveling over 20,000 miles to five hundred towns and villages. NAWSA contributed $4,000 and sent two organizers. Anna Howard Shaw gave countless speeches. General Rosalie Jones arrived in August to hold the first street meeting in Omaha. In October, Jane Addams gave several speeches.

Male voters defeated the Nebraska Women's Suffrage Amendment, known as Amendment 4, by a majority of 10,104: 90,738 yeas, 100,842 nays.

In South Dakota, Antoinette Funk traveled by stagecoach, speaking in small cities and villages. Along with Mary Shields Pyle, president of the Universal Franchise League, Funk spent a week at the State Fair in Huron that was attended by as many as

50,000 people a day. The grounds, buildings, "every prize-winning animal, every racing sulky, auto and motorcycles" were bedecked with "Votes for Women" pennants. During their dances, Native American women waved suffrage banners. A snake charmer held a suffrage pennant as an "enormous serpent coiled around her body."[26]

There was minimal opposition, only a few anti-speakers who were paid $100 a week. Nevertheless, male voters for the sixth time "denied their women the right of representation" by a majority of 11,914: 39,605 ayes, 51,519 nays. Suffragist leaders declared that they were "not in the least daunted or discouraged" because the amendment had been defeated by a little over half the number of "no" votes cast in the 1910 referendum. That gave South Dakota suffragists "every reason to believe the next one would be successful."[27]

In North Dakota, Antoinette Funk was sent to "untilled suffrage field," places never visited by a suffrage speaker or an organizer. She "zigzagged across" the vast state from the "southeast to the northwest corners." In Minot, she was arrested for speaking in public. Funk, a lawyer, knew that she was just being harassed by a "town official unfavorable to women." The judge agreed with her and remitted her $5 fine.[28]

Every year between 1901 and 1911, a woman suffrage measure had been introduced to the North Dakota legislature. In 1912, during her return trip to America, Sylvia Pankhurst's speech to a small group of women and men had prompted the formation of the Votes for Women League with the astute Clara L. Darrow as president. Invigorated suffragists, along with WCTU members, progressives, and socialists, successfully pressured the legislature to authorize a woman suffrage referendum for November 1914. It would be a "hard and hopeless campaign" because of a provision in the 1889 constitution requiring that a woman suffrage measure had to be approved by a majority of the voters "voting at the election," not a majority voting on the measure itself.[29]

Suffragists waged a thorough campaign. A full-page newspaper advertisement declared, 40,000 NORTH DAKOTA WOMEN ASK FOR THE BALLOT.[30] The North Dakota Association Opposed to Woman Suffrage countered with anti-amendment advertisements and distributed literature. Male voters defeated the North Dakota Women's Suffrage Referendum by a majority of 9,139: 40,209 yeas, 49, 348 nays (with nays and blanks counted together as required by the 1889 constitution). Suffragists maintained that if the blanks had not been counted against the measure it would have passed.

In Montana, a state bordered on the south by Wyoming, where women had been voting for forty-four years (with the social order still intact, despite the anti-suffragists' dire predictions), Antoinette Funk found a high level of interest and an "undertow of fierce opposition."[31] The politically powerful Amalgamated Copper Company, fearful that women workers would support pro-worker legislation, had teamed up with the liquor interests. Jeannette Rankin, chair of the Montana Woman Suffrage Association, led the 1914 campaign.

A reporter and suffragist, Belle Fligelman, described Jeannette Rankin's appearance at a rally: "When Miss Rankin came forward to speak, the air became electric. She immediately dispelled the notion that suffragists were all middle-aged and masculine. Young, attractive, energetic and flowing with friendliness and reason. . . . She wore a gold-colored velvet suit." Fligelman's male colleague said that Rankin "looked like a young panther ready to spring."[32]

After Belle Fligelman made her first suffrage speech on a street corner in Helena, her "horrified" mother told her not to come home if she did it again. She spoke again and spent the night in a hotel that she charged to her father. "After that," she recounted, "I was allowed to speak on street corners, although Mother was still horrified in spite of her feelings that what I was doing had a high purpose. As time went on, she had to accept even more 'unladylike' techniques from me and other campaigners for the rights of women. We had a long way to go."[33]

Jeannette Rankin, the oldest of seven children, was born in 1880 on a ranch six miles from Missoula. Her suffrage work began during the 1910 suffrage campaign in Washington. A graduate student at the University of Washington, she had responded to an advertisement asking for volunteers to hang suffrage posters in Seattle. "I had thought the only reason women didn't have the vote was because they hadn't asked for it," she once recalled.[34] Discovering that women had been asking for the vote for years motivated Rankin. She became a hired organizer for NAWSA and campaigned in fifteen states before returning to Montana.

The referendum campaign lasted eleven months. Jeannette Rankin undertook a nine thousand-mile speaking tour, talking to miners, farmers, city dwellers, and homesteaders. WCTU members canvassed door to door in every county. Bird May Wilson, a lawyer and stockbroker who owned a ranch and had interests in several mines, traveled by horse and buggy throughout the southern part of the state. Belle Fligelman and Lucille Topping drove a buggy pulled by two horses up a steep mountain road to speak at a remote gold-mining town. After their talk at Miners Hall, "someone got out a fiddle." The miners, still wearing their "high rubber boots," lined up to dance with them. Belle and Lucille "pushed these men in their rubber boots around the dance floor," all the while thanking "them earnestly for the votes they were going to give us in November." Later that night, Lucille drove the horses down the treacherous road while Belle "stretched forward and held a lighted kerosene lantern over the horses' tails so that she could see the road."[35]

The campaign culminated with Anna Howard Shaw leading a spectacular suffrage parade in Helena. As many men as women marched in the parade. Male voters approved the Montana Women's Suffrage Amendment by a majority of 3,714: 41,302 yeas, 37,588 nays—equal-suffrage state number ten!

In Nevada, Anne Martin, "a marvelous horseback rider and camper and also an almost fierce woman suffragist," had the campaign so well organized that Antoinette Funk felt superfluous.[36] By the time she was twenty-two years old, Anne Martin had earned several college degrees and founded the Department of History at Nevada State University. Having done that, she, like Alice Paul and Lucy Burns, went abroad to study and travel. Like them, she got involved with the WSPU and Emmeline Pankhurst. On November 11, 1910, during a demonstration at the House of Commons, Anne Martin had been arrested, along with 114 women and four men. They were released after their bail was paid and the charges were dropped the next day. (Martin's friend Lou Hoover had sent her husband Herbert, who was in London, to bail her out, but Frederick Pethick-Lawrence had already done that. Yes, the same Herbert Hoover who would become president of the United States.)

She returned to Nevada in 1912, was elected president of the Nevada Equal Franchise Society, and spent two years canvassing the state with its rugged mountain ranges and deserts. Antoinette Funk noted that Anne Martin appeared to know every voter's name. Suffragists held street meetings, distributed literature, and secured the support of labor unions, the governor, and prominent businessmen. The day before the election, anti-suffragists placed a quarter-page advertisement in a newspaper announcing a free picture show and a speech, "The Last Word AGAINST Woman Suffrage," by Minnie Bronson.

Nevada Constitutional Amendment No. 1: Suffrage was approved by a majority of 3,714: 41,302 yeas, 37,588 nays— equal-suffrage state number eleven!

The seven hard-fought campaigns in 1914 yielded five defeats and two victories. Women in eleven states—Wyoming, Colorado, Utah, Idaho, Washington, California, Arizona, Kansas, Oregon, Montana, Nevada—plus women with presidential suffrage in Illinois had national voting power. Women voters, Harriot Stanton Blatch wrote in a letter to a New York City newspaper, "are ready to act as levers in bringing pressure on Congress."[37]

Of the forty-three Democratic Party candidates on the ballot in equal-suffrage states, twenty-three were defeated in November. The CU claimed credit for helping to defeat many of them. Even more important, from the CU's perspective, its campaign had made woman suffrage a highly visible issue in equal-suffrage states. NAWSA adamantly disagreed, insisting that the tactic alienated elected officials, including President Wilson. In Oregon, the CU's campaign against Senator George Chamberlain, a pro-suffrage Democrat who was running for reelection, caused a rancorous disagreement among local suffragists. The CU was unconcerned. (Chamberlain was reelected.)

NAWSA celebrated the progress at its Forty-Sixth Annual Convention in Nashville. Dissension over the Congressional Committee's controversial Shafroth-Palmer Amendment, a multi-step process at the state level for securing equal suffrage, dominated the discussions. "More bitterness was shown than ever before at one of these annual meetings."[38] Anna Howard Shaw was reelected president, although many blank ballots were submitted as a protest vote. Shortly after the convention, NAWSA's board voted to drop the Shafroth-Palmer Amendment, that had been designed to appease states' rights proponents. Their timing was undoubtedly hastened by the fact that massive campaigns for woman suffrage referenda were underway in four large eastern states: New Jersey, Pennsylvania, Massachusetts, and New York. This was no time for suffragists to be distressed and distracted.

158

Chapter 11

Undauntable Suffragists: 1915

Getting about a million ideas. —Gertrude Watkins

The weather prediction was unsettled, probable showers for Saturday, August 7, 1915, the day about a dozen suffragists wearing stylish hats, white dresses, and "Votes for Women" sashes marched up the gangplank to board a tugboat, the *W.S. Holbrook.* The tug was named after its owner, who had donated its use for the suffrage cause. A motion picture man and reporters followed along. Louisine Waldron Elder Havemeyer cradled a carved piece of wood painted bronze, about two and a half feet long—the Torch of Liberty, a replica of the Statue of Liberty's torch. It was Harriot Stanton Blatch's idea to appropriate the iconic image of the torch as the emblem of woman suffrage. She and Louisine Havemeyer had displayed it during their ten-day speaking tour across New York, from Long Island to Buffalo, in support of the upcoming woman suffrage referendum. Unable to attend the day's event due to the recent death of her husband, Blatch had appointed Havemeyer as the guardian of the Torch of Liberty.

A philanthropist and innovative art collector, sixty-year-old Louisine Havemeyer grew up in New York City. Her father died when she was eighteen and her mother took the family for an extended stay in Europe. In Paris, she met Mary Cassatt, a well-known artist who tutored her in modern art and advised her as she began collecting art. In 1883, she married Henry O. Havemeyer, head of American Sugar Refining Company and an avid art collector. During frequent trips abroad, they consulted with Cassatt, buying paintings, including some of Cassatt's.

In 1907 and 1908, Louisine Havemeyer suffered devastating tragedies—the untimely deaths of her husband, her mother, and twin grandchildren. At the same time, she dealt with a federal suit charging her late husband's company of not paying duty on tons of imported sugar. During a voyage to France in 1909, she tried to throw herself overboard. Determined to get her deeply depressed friend reengaged with life, Mary Cassatt, an "ardent suffragist," urged her to "work for suffrage, for it is the women who will decide the questions of life or death for a nation."[1]

Cassatt's idea resonated with Havemeyer who recalled: "My mother and her associates were interested in it, and were friends of the pioneers of the movement." She joined the Women's Political Union (WPU), the renamed Equality League for Self-Supporting Women founded by Harriot Stanton Blatch. Havemeyer later wrote that Blatch was her "guide and friend . . . who insisted that I could speak; that I must speak; and then saw to it that I did speak."[2]

Docked at Pier A at the Battery in New York City, the *W.S. Holbrook* was bedecked with suffrage publicity. A huge purple, white, and green banner, the colors of the WPU, advertised the upcoming New Jersey woman suffrage referendum. Attached to the side railing and the front of the wheelhouse was a huge banner: VOTE YES FOR WOMAN SUFFRAGE OCT. 19th. Two more banners were on the front railing. Across the Hudson River at a dock in Jersey City, Mina A. Van Winkle, president of the New Jersey WPU, led suffragists aboard the festooned tugboat, the *A.W. Smith*. Hundreds of spectators watched from both shores.

Shortly after eleven o'clock, the *Holbrook* and *Smith* met each other in the middle of the Hudson River, amid "a tremendous shrieking of whistles and the undivided attention of hundreds of persons aboard tugs, liners, and ferries" in the river. The tugboats were tossed about as crewmen struggled to lash them together. Once secured they "bumped and scraped" up against each other.[3]

Standing in the bow of the W. S. Holbrook, *Louisine Havemeyer, wearing a hat topped with flowers and a "Votes for Women" sash slung over her white dress, holds up the Torch of Liberty. (Library of Congress)*

Louisine Havemeyer, rallying from a bout of seasickness, gave a short speech, exhorting New Jersey men not to misfire when they cast their vote. Then, leaning over the railing and reaching across the water, she placed the Torch of Liberty into the outstretched hand of Mina Van Winkle, transferring "the sacred token of liberty, the beloved torch, to our sisters in the neighboring State."[4] Just as the torch was passed, the "sun broke through the gray bank of clouds . . . another omen of victory," according to suffragists.[5] Newspapers around the country published photographs of the dramatic transfer.

The next day, Havemeyer took the ferry across the Hudson River to "start the torch upon its way in New Jersey." In Newark, on a day so hot that the "asphalt was soft and gooey," she held the torch aloft and told the crowd: "Men, look to it that some day your daughters don't turn upon you and say: 'Father, oh, father, why didn't you give us the right to help make the laws which might protect us, and which might affect every condition under which we live?" With a group of young New Jersey suffragists, she toured with the torch through towns along the Jersey Shore, trying to convert vacationers.

Finally, "worn down with the heat and fatigue," she left the torch "in the custody" of the young women: "'Remember, young ladies,' I called to them as I motored away; 'the torch is not an easy thing to take care of.'" It was "stolen" the very next day. Havemeyer was "heart-broken," not knowing that the theft, Mina Van Winkle later revealed, was a publicity stunt to garner headlines, and an opportunity to refurbish the well-worn torch.[6] Had she been informed she would have surely approved of the stunt. "Publicity was our greatest asset," she had asserted, "that open-sesame to the ignorant and uninterested feminine mind—publicity which awakened their curiosity and their intelligence."[7]

In time, a young lawyer found the Torch of Liberty, neatly wrapped in a package tied with purple, white, and green ribbons on a streetcar in Philadelphia. He refused to take the fifty-dollar reward because he supported woman suffrage, more pro-amendment fodder for reporters.

The possibility of victory in one or more of these four industrialized, populous, electoral-votes-rich eastern states—New Jersey, Pennsylvania, Massachusetts, and New York—galvanized suffragists across the country. Anne Martin from Nevada; Jeannette Rankin from Montana; and Rose Bower from the Black Hills of South Dakota who used her skills whistling and playing her trumpet to announce street meetings, arrived in New Jersey.

The "Arkansas Flying Squadron," three women from Little Rock, went to New York City to help and to get "suffragistically educated." Gertrude Watkins was excited about "getting about a million ideas to take back." Street meetings, said Florence Cotnam, "sounded like a fairy tale to us. It has not yet struck Arkansas, but it will when we get back." Alice Ellington wanted to "change the impression some have that Southern women don't want the vote. We do, thousands of us. We feel, too, that if New York gives the vote to women. . . . One after another of our States will come in because the Southern man will not stand for the imputation that he is less just and generous to his women than his Northern brother."[8]

Cotnam and Ellington were hosts at the "Votes for Women Hopperie," a fundraising attraction created by suffragist Vira Boarman Whitehouse, who joined the cause in response to the mob violence at the 1913 grand parade. The pro-suffrage managers of Luna Park, an amusement park in Coney Island, had provided a rent-free space beside the bandstand. For a nickel donation, customers could try to hop up to the summit of a spiral staircase 136 feet long. On opening night, two suffragists had hopped to the top and "tossed 200 small boxes of caramels down the incline" to the hundreds of spectators.[9] Cotnam and Ellington handed out small bags made in suffrage colors and filled with Arkansas rice.

The tugboat transfer of the torch and hopping up the "Hopperie" were just some of the attention-getting tactics suffragists used in the four campaign states throughout the summer and fall of 1915. There were mass meetings, street meetings, street dances, suffrage balls, suffrage schools, pageants, plays, parades, picnics, teas, block parties, door-to-door canvassing, outdoor concerts, moving picture shows, slide shows, torchlight rallies, squadrons of automobiles whisking speakers here and there, and contests with rewards such as two chickens for the best suffrage speech. Suffragists opened suffrage stores. Wearing sandwich boards emblazoned with slogans, they walked the streets. They plastered posters and placards on the sides of buildings and billboards. Spectacular events were undertaken by daring suffragists who went up in hot-air balloons and biplanes and dropped leaflets on crowds below. Boundless energy and optimism infused suffragists in all four campaign states.

A profusion of suffrage novelties and ephemera inscribed with "Votes for Women" and other slogans attracted attention, spread the message, generated enthusiasm, raised money, and demonstrated solidarity. Anti-suffragists produced material, but on a much smaller scale. The years between 1908 and 1917, according to historian Kenneth Florey, are "The Golden Age of Suffrage Memorabilia."

The paraphernalia inscribed with suffrage slogans included: balloons, buttons, badges, ribbons, pins, pennants, and chocolates; ceramic objects—cat-shaped bud vases, salt and pepper shakers, and an inkwell figurine; porcelain objects—candle snuffers, figurines, hand bells, cups and saucers; sterling silver spoons—grapefruit, demitasse, and bon bon—engraved with a bust of Susan B. Anthony on the handle; calendars, clocks, watches and fobs; cosmetics; dust mops; facecloths; handheld fans with the phrase, "Keep Cool and Raise a Breeze for Suffrage!"; flyswatters; board games, toys (including a Sojourner Truth Wind-Up Toy), dolls, and playing cards; a novelty telescope with a portrait of Elizabeth Cady Stanton; miniature liberty bells; packets of a variety of yellow flower seeds; paper bags and cups; holiday cards, postcards, stationery, pens, pencils, paper weights and ink blotters; rolling pins; rubber stamps; sashes and scarves; hatpins and hat bands; shirts and socks; soaps; statues; and sheet music and records. Thousands of matchboxes were inscribed—"The more light you throw on woman suffrage the better it strikes you."[10]

In Massachusetts, suffragists flew huge kites inscribed with "Votes for Women." On July 15, "Suffrage Blue Bird Day," they tacked up 100,000 twelve-by-four-inch brightly painted blue birds on telephone poles and fences. Made of tin, each bluebird's head was turned toward the viewer with its beak open, as if to chirp the words inscribed down its yellow breast and tail: "Votes for Women Nov. 2nd."

In Pennsylvania, Katherine Wentworth Ruschenberger financed the making of the Women's Liberty Bell, also called the Justice Bell, a one-ton copy of the iconic Liberty Bell without the crack and with the words "establish justice" added to the inscription.

A ceremony for the casting of the Justice Bell included children with Katherine Wentworth Ruschenberger who commissioned the bell; suffragists with banners; and young women with a garland of flowers. The workers in the background paused for the photograph. (Library of Congress)

The clapper was chained to prevent it from ringing until women were enfranchised. Carried about on the back of a truck, the bell traveled more than five thousand miles through all sixty-seven counties. Large crowds and marching bands met it at stops along the way. Suffragists gave speeches from the back of the truck. At one stop, silent film actor Raymond Hitchcock, who was on location filming a moving picture, jumped on the truck and proclaimed: "I am a showman . . . I believe in giving the girls a fair show and therefore believe me, I'm with you."[11]

In New York, Louisine Havemeyer designed a "Ship of State" that she commissioned to be made and rigged to look like the *Mayflower*, the ship that brought English colonists to America. An electric light was at the end of each spar. A green and red light was at the port and starboard beams. The electric wiring was attached to a battery that she carried in her automobile. The centerboard was taped onto a stick for her to hold so she could control the lighting with a handheld button.

"No matter where I went from the largest city to the smallest village, I had but to light my little 'Ship of State' to collect a crowd," Havemeyer later recalled. "The 'Ship' flashed out its lights up to the very day" before the election.[12]

In New York City, "suffrage days" were arranged to appeal to specific groups of men, including firemen, bankers, and street cleaners, who received souvenirs of tiny brooms. On the Night of the Interurban Council Fires, huge bonfires were lighted on high bluffs in the five boroughs of New York City. There was a pageant and music and illuminated balloons with suffrage messages, and fireworks at each location.

On January 12, 1915, for the first time since 1878 when the Sixteenth Amendment was introduced, the House of Representatives had debated and voted on a federal woman suffrage amendment resolution. The debate lasted an uninterrupted ten hours. A record-breaking crowd of pro- and anti-suffragists had watched the contentious proceedings. A banner headline across the top of the front page of a Tulsa, Oklahoma newspaper reported the result: SUFFRAGE RESOLUTION VOTED DOWN IN THE HOUSE YESTERDAY.[13] The vote was 204 to 174.

Josephine Jewell Dodge, the president of NAOWS, heralded the defeat as a sign that suffragists' "wave of hysteria . . . will be on the wane." Anna Howard Shaw countered that the very fact of the vote indicated that woman suffrage was now a matter of "national importance."[14] Alice Paul announced that the CU would immediately begin work to get the Senate to vote on an identical resolution. But, despite their dogged efforts, the Senate did not vote before the final session of the Sixty-Third Congress ended on March 3.

Determined to get the Sixty-Fourth Congress to pass the federal woman suffrage amendment, Alice Paul vowed "to make Woman Suffrage the dominant political issue." Congressmen, she said, would feel the force of "a veritable suffrage cyclone."[15]

On March 31, at the CU's Advisory Committee meeting in New York City, Alice Paul and Lucy Burns presented ambitious plans to formally establish the CU as a national organization, and to send organizers into the states to recruit members. In equal-suffrage states, the CU organizers would organize a state convention for voting women where delegates would be selected to attend the first and "epoch-making" event: the National Convention of Woman Voters. The goal was to "convince the doubting" members of Congress that "the voting women of the west . . . are anxious to help their sisters of the east." In a statement, Alice Paul underscored the power of women voters to influence politics: "One-fourth of our national senate, one-sixth of the national house of representatives, and one-fifth of the votes for president come from states where women are voters."[16]

The CU's plan was a direct challenge to NAWSA that had spent years building a national network of state auxiliary associations, sending organizers, speakers, money, literature, and convening state and national conventions. NAWSA protested the CU's foray into its territory. Unfazed and driven to intensify pressure on Congress, Alice Paul dispatched ten skilled organizers to establish the CU as a force to be reckoned with throughout America. The breach between the two organizations widened: SUFFRAGE WAR, proclaimed a newspaper headline in Washington, D.C.[17]

Alice Paul arranged a dramatic meeting place for the upcoming National Convention of Women Voters—the grandiose world's fair, the Panama-Pacific International Exposition (PPIE) meeting in San Francisco. PPIE marked the recent opening of the Panama Canal, the 400th anniversary of Balboa's discovery of the Pacific Ocean, and San Francisco's recovery from the 1906 earthquake. The Tower of Jewels, a forty-three-story marvel, covered with 100,000 dangling pieces of illuminated, colored, cut-glass jewels, dominated the landscape. Eleven splendid Beaux-Arts palaces were adjoined by three courts: the Court of the Universe, the Court of Four Seasons, and the Court of Abundance. More than eighteen million people paid a daily fee of fifty cents to gape at dazzling displays, including a huge, four-ton Underwood typewriter that printed the daily news, and to indulge in fun and food.

The CU opened an exhibit in the Palace of Education. Purple, white, and gold pennants filled the exhibit, dubbed the "freedom booth." A large portrait of the "firmly-sweet face of Susan B. Anthony" hung on the wall.[18] The Sixty-Third Congress's record on the woman suffrage amendment, along with each representative's voting record, was on display. The Great Demand Banner was prominently displayed on the back wall. Every visitor was asked to sign a petition. Attention-getting, but unsubstantiated, claims were soon attributed to the petition. SUFFRAGE PETITION 18,333 FEET LONG, enthused a newspaper headline in Washington, D.C.[19] "This petition bears over a half million signatures," raved a Chicago newspaper.[20]

Alice Paul had big plans for the petition—a cross-country road trip, a novel and arduous venture. (At the time, the transcontinental Lincoln Highway was comprised of stretches of concrete, gravel, sand, and dirt. Heavy rains turned sections into axle-deep mud.) She had recruited an envoy, Sara Bard Field, a poet and organizer, to ride in an automobile across the country to Washington, D.C., where she would present the petition to President Wilson. Field had worked in the 1912 Oregon and 1914 Nevada campaigns. In Nevada, she met national organizer Mabel Vernon, who had told her about Alice Paul: She is "no bigger than a wisp of hay, but she has the most deep and beautiful violet-blue eyes, and when they look at you and ask you to do something you could no more refuse."[21]

Sara Bard Field, who was divorced, had two children who lived with their father. She visited them on weekends and the idea of not seeing each other for months was painful. But, she later recalled: "They both understood what my mission was to be and were very brave in accepting the fact that I ought to go."[22]

Paul recruited a second envoy, Frances Joliffe. The automobile was provided by two businesswomen and suffragists from Providence, Rhode Island, who had come by ship to PPIE: Ingeborg Kinstedt and Maria Kindberg. Sturdy, stern-faced Swedish immigrants, Kinstedt and Kindberg bought an Overland Six, model 82, a seven-passenger touring car with a six-cylinder engine from the Willys-Overland Company, an exhibitor at the Palace of Transportation, for $750. (The Ford Motor Company exhibit featured a small assembly line, where workers assembled eighteen cars a day that were then sold.)

Alice Paul planned a spectacular send-off on the last day of the three-day National Woman Voters Convention. Three thousand delegates from equal-suffrage states, representing 400,000 women voters attended the convention, held in the Palace of Progress. Alva Belmont, dressed in a purple, white, and gold gown, gave the opening address, exhorting enfranchised women to "use the power of her ballot" to pressure Congress to give their disenfranchised "sisters justice and freedom."[23] Notable women spoke. The novelist and journalist Cora Miranda Baggerly Older said that she had once thought that "Woman Suffrage was like Utopia," and that men would give it to women—"But I have learned that Utopias are not given away; they must be fought for."[24]

On the last day of the convention, September 16, 1915, thousands of people, plus a crowd of onlookers, gathered in the Court of Abundance. There were girls dressed in the native costumes of other countries. A huge women's chorus sang a song that included the line: "We are women clad in new power." The crowd sang the song of the British suffragettes, "The March of the Women," that begins, "Shout, shout, up with your song!" The lights were darkened and thousands of women formed a procession: "Orange lanterns swayed in the breeze; purple, white and gold draperies fluttered, the blare of the band burst forth, and the great surging crowd followed to the gates."[25] Maria Kindberg, the driver, was sitting behind the wheel of the automobile covered with suffrage streamers. Ingeborg Kindstedt, the "machinist," sat beside her. To the cheers and shouts of farewell, Sara Bard Field and Frances Joliffe climbed in the back seat. The ornate gates swung open and the automobile disappeared into the darkness. ON TO WASHINGTON SUFFRAGE WAR CRY, exclaimed a newspaper headline in Bismarck, North Dakota.[26]

The transcontinental travelers for the cause posed for a photograph, from left, Sara Bard Field, suffrage envoy; Maria Kindberg, the driver; Ingeborg Kindstedt, the "machinist." The Great Demand Banner is displayed on the car. (Library of Congress)

The 5,000-mile journey lasted an eventful three months. The intrepid suffrage travelers—Field, Kindberg, and Kindstedt—endured miserable weather from dust storms to blizzards. (Frances Joliffe soon returned home due to illness. After recovering, she completed the trip by train.) In Nevada, they spent a night lost in the Great American Desert (now the Great Basin Desert): "The bitter cold of the night and the utter desolation of the whole country and the fear that we would not have enough gasoline to get to a filling station kept us agitated and in a good deal of physical distress," Sara Bard Field recalled.[27]

Late one rainy night in Kansas, their car got stuck in a humongous mud hole. After shouting for help until they were hoarse, Sara Bard Field, a small woman, managed to haul herself out of the car, finding herself in a slough. "I kept sinking into the mud; I didn't have boots, and the mud began to get up to my knees," she said, describing her slippery, gooey walk back to a farmhouse that they had passed earlier in the evening. She roused the farmer who returned to the scene with her in his truck. To haul the car out of the mud, he brought along two draft horses. "You girls got guts," he told her.[28]

At stops along the way, Sara Bard Field spoke at welcoming events arranged by Mabel Vernon, an indispensable strategist and fundraiser. Imaginative, resourceful, and tireless, Vernon preceded the suffrage car by train. In Salt Lake City, a cavalcade of automobiles met them. Sara Bard Field gave her speech from the steps of the new capitol, and met the venerable suffragist, eighty-seven-year old Emmeline Wells. The biggest parade was in New York City. "Fifth Avenue rubbed its eyes when the weather-beaten automobile, bearing the slogan 'On to Congress!' and followed by a hundred other cars, blazed a path of purple and gold down the great thoroughfare," wrote one reporter.[29]

By the time the intrepid travelers reached Washington, D.C., male voters had decided the fate of woman suffrage amendments in New Jersey, Pennsylvania, Massachusetts, and New York. New Jersey was the bellwether of the four woman suffrage referenda in 1915, with a special election scheduled on October 19. The stakes were high; suffragists believed that a victory in a large eastern state would cause a cascade of victories elsewhere, even in resistant Southern states. Property-owning women had voted in New Jersey for thirty-one years (1776–1807). Generations of suffragists had fought to restore the right to vote that they once had. In 1911, the four main suffrage groups formed a united committee to focus on securing a state referendum on woman suffrage. That same year, Anna Dayton organized the New Jersey Association Opposed to Woman Suffrage. Prominent men formed the Men's Anti-Suffrage League. James R. Nugent, a political boss in the thrall of the liquor industry, marshaled his considerable resources to defeat the amendment.

Cavalcades of automobiles, with "Vote 'Yes' Oct 19" banners on the back and the front and flags flying from the windshield, traversed the state. President Wilson, a resident of New Jersey, announced he would vote for the amendment, reiterating his position that the issue should be decided by the states, not the federal government. Special efforts were made in racially and ethnically diverse sections of the state, with speeches, buttons, and literature delivered in different languages. Minnie Reynolds, a seasoned organizer from Colorado, coordinated the "biggest colored mass meeting ever held in Newark for any purpose."[30] Florence Spearing Randolph, a minister in the African Methodist Episcopal Zion church, organized the New Jersey State Federation of Colored Women's Clubs that supported the woman suffrage amendment.

Male voters defeated the woman suffrage amendment by a majority of 51,110: 133,281 yeas, 184,391 nays. James Nugent gloated that "sober-minded Jerseymen" had defeated "long-haired men and short-haired women. . . . Women in the home, and not in politics . . . is what New Jersey voters stand for."[31] Mina Van Winkle denounced James Nugent and the "rottenness of the political leaders who conducted the campaign against us."[31]

In Pennsylvania, the campaign was led by Jennie Bradley Roessing, president of the Pennsylvania Woman Suffrage Association, who traveled with the Justice Bell, passionately speaking to rouse support. The campaign was carefully planned with the state divided into divisions and organized by political districts. Workers at the headquarters of the Pennsylvania Woman Suffrage Association in Harrisburg, the capital, scrambled to keep up with orders for novelties and supplies: fans, buttons, paper napkins, pennants, notepaper, drinking cups, lanterns, lead pencils, candy, children's toys, attractive boxes with seeds for yellow flowers, the color of suffrage—marigolds, sunflowers, hollyhocks, and roses. The publicity department organized events to plant suffrage gardens. Three full-time writers turned out pro-suffrage literature. The speakers' bureau provided a steady supply of speakers. The African-American activist writer and journalist, Alice Dunbar Nelson worked as a field organizer, speaking to diverse audiences. Advertisements were placed in streetcars. There were auto tours and open-air meetings. Money and workers came from other states. Suffragists conducted an exhaustive and exhausting campaign.

Male voters overwhelmingly defeated the woman suffrage amendment by a majority 55,688: 385,346 yeas, 441,034 nays. Eighty percent of the negative vote was cast in Philadelphia, the "stronghold of the saloon vote."[32]

In Massachusetts, women had won the right to vote in school committee elections in 1879. The following year, Louisa May Alcott, the celebrated author of *Little Women* and a dedicated suffragist, was the first woman to register to vote in Concord: "Trying to stir up women to vote," she wrote in her journal. "So timid & slow. . . . So hard to move people out of old ruts." After voting on March 29, 1880, with a group of 19 other women, she reported: "No bolts fell on our audacious heads, no earthquake shook the town."[33]

Many years later, in 1914, the first suffrage parade was held in Boston. It had caused a sensation. There were singers and marchers from throughout New England and one from Australia. Descendants of historic suffragists marched: Lucy Stone's daughter; Angelina Grimke's daughter-in-law; Louisa May Alcott's grandniece; a son, three grandsons, a granddaughter, and two granddaughters-in-law of William Lloyd Garrison. An even more sensational parade, the Victory Parade with thirty bands, was held on October 16, 1915.

In protest, the Massachusetts Association Opposed to the Further Extension of Suffrage to Women (MAOFESW) produced 100,000 red paper roses, the official badge of the anti-suffragists, to distribute to the spectators at the Victory Parade. Anti-suffragists who lived in buildings along the parade route draped their balconies in red cloth and posters with anti-suffrage messages. (The red rose had been adopted in 1914 by the NAOWS as a visual symbol of their opposition to woman suffrage and their disapproval of suffragists flouting of societal conventions of womanly behavior.) Anti-suffragists held indoor meetings; advertised in streetcars, newspapers, and magazines; distributed a lavishly produced pamphlet; and published a song "The Anti-Suffrage Rose" with the line, "We're going to show them who's right."[34]

Suffragists used all the tactics employed in other states. Florence Luscomb, an architect who had studied the British movement, described being on an automobile tour and arriving in a tiny town at dusk, "By the light of the store we made out a shadowy group on the porch, . . . such a greeting they gave us! . . . I just talked in the darkness, heart to heart."[35]

On Election Day, November 2, 1915, 8,000 women stood outside polling places throughout the state, holding placards inscribed: "Show your Faith in the Women of Massachusetts; vote 'Yes' on Woman Suffrage." The liquor industry passed out pink slips promising, "Good for two drinks if woman suffrage is defeated."

Male voters in Massachusetts defeated the referendum by a majority of 132,083: 163,406 yeas, 295,489 nays. In the aftermath, Massachusetts suffragists turned their attention to passing a federal woman suffrage amendment.

New York had the largest population and the most electoral votes for president and vice president of the United States. A win would greatly increase women's political leverage. Beginning in 1854, a woman suffrage measure was presented annually to the legislature. Despite constant efforts, the gains had been incremental. Only women who lived in villages and country districts were granted limited school suffrage. Tax-paying women in villages and towns could vote on measures dealing with taxes and bonds.

In 1911, Carrie Chapman Catt formed the Empire State Campaign Coordinating Committee (ESCC) to unite the many suffrage societies in New York City and throughout the state. Two successive legislatures were needed to pass a bill authorizing a woman suffrage amendment referendum. In January 1913, the first legislature approved the resolution. Twenty-eight paid organizers worked throughout 1914 to ensure passage by the second legislature that convened in 1915. Carrie Chapman Catt conducted suffrage schools to train volunteers to conduct house-to-house canvasses; undertake automobile tours; conduct open-air mass meetings; and fire a barrage of pro-amendment press releases, articles, and letters to the editor. Early in 1915, the legislature passed the bill authorizing a woman suffrage amendment referendum at the November 2 election.

Suffragists conducted a colossal campaign. Forty paid organizers and an estimated 200,000 women worked constantly. Gertrude Foster Brown, the concert pianist turned suffrage leader, recorded her speech, "Why Women Want the Vote," on a phonograph record. On October 23, a sunny day with a bitterly cold wind, dense crowds lined Fifth Avenue to watch the grandest suffrage parade ever held in New York City. Carrying banners, 30,000 to 45,000 women, according to various estimates, marched clad in white with their "Votes for Women" sashes across their chests. There were sixty equestrians; women from other states and countries; working women from factory workers to doctors and nurses to a lifeguard; marching bands; and floats, including one featuring the popular Kewpie dolls with a poster inscribed: "Isn't It a Funny Thing That Father Can't See Why Mother Should Vote."

Suffragists from New Jersey carried banners inscribed: "Not Down and Out, but Up and Doing." Five thousand men marched in the parade singing, "I'm going to vote for woman suffrage . . . On next election day," to the tune of "Tramp, Tramp, Tramp, the Boys are Marching." 45,000 MARCH FOR

SUFFRAGE BRAVING WIND AND DARKNESS IN GREATEST WOMAN'S PARADE, declared the headline in a New York City newspaper.[36]

On November 2, 5,000 suffragists, including Maud Malone, took their position as poll watchers. Male voters defeated the woman suffrage amendment by a majority of 194,984: 553,348 yeas, 748,332 nays. At campaign headquarters in New York City, Anna Howard Shaw asked Carrie Chapman Catt, "How long will it delay your fight, Carrie?"

"Only until we can get a little sleep. Our campaign will be on again tomorrow morning—and forever until we get the vote," Catt replied.[37]

On December 6, the transcontinental suffrage car arrived in Washington, D.C. The Sixty-Fourth Congress convened that day, just as Alice Paul had planned. A large procession gathered in front of the capitol. One hundred feet of the long petition was unrolled and carried on a white cloth by twenty bearers led by a mounted escort of twelve women on horseback, wearing purple, white, and gold cloaks and representing the eleven equal-suffrage states, plus the Territory of Alaska. A long line of suffragists marched with military precision: women bedecked in "Votes for Women" sashes, young girls dressed in white, flag-bearers carrying the American flag and the Susan B. Anthony banner, a group representing the thirty-seven unenfranchised states, the Justice Bell, and a military band. The petition-bearers marched up the east steps of the capitol, where they were met by a congressional delegation.

After a ceremony of music and speeches, a detachment of suffragists marched to the White House. At a meeting in the East Room, Anne Martin introduced Sara Bard Field and Frances Joliffe to President Woodrow Wilson. Field said she hoped that he would support the federal woman suffrage amendment. She asked Wilson to examine the petition. He studied the long list of names: citizens, governors, mayors, state legislators. He assured the gathering of ever-hopeful but frequently disappointed suffragists: "This visit of yours will remain in my mind, not only as a very delightful compliment, but also as a very impressive thing which undoubtedly will make it necessary for all of us to consider very carefully what is right for us to do."[38]

December 6, also marked the beginning of CU's first national convention. The weeklong event was held in their new headquarters, the Cameron House, just a short walk across Lafayette Square from the White House. The mansion, known as "Little White House," had been the meeting place for generations of politicians. The CU's move from their original headquarters in a basement office on F Street to such a prestigious and strategic location established it and its agenda as a force to be reckoned with. The convention ended at the nearby Belasco Theatre with a huge mass meeting and a presentation of the Susan B. Anthony pageant, directed by Hazel MacKaye, a renowned pageant director. "For the purpose of propaganda," said MacKaye, "a pageant can hardly be surpassed."[39]

Shortly after the CU's convention, NAWSA held its annual convention in Washington, D.C. The entire tenth floor of the new Willard Hotel was festooned with flags and banners. Anna Howard Shaw noted the presence of many young women among the veteran suffragists, "All hail to the new and thank God for the old!"[40]

The vexing issue of the CU's 1914 campaign in equal-suffrage states to defeat Democratic candidates was on the agenda. Many delegates were outraged that even pro-suffrage Democratic candidates were targeted. Pro-suffrage Representative Carl Hayden, of Arizona, whose mother, Sallie Davis Hayden, was a suffragist, had denounced the campaign as "political treachery without parallel in the history of the suffrage movement."[41] People and reporters who did not know the difference between the two organizations blamed NAWSA for the campaign.

Attempting to mediate the situation, the popular and prolific writer Zona Gale, who believed that "all suffragists have a common cause at heart," proposed a resolution that was adopted, appointing a committee of five people to meet with the CU to discuss the "question of cooperation."[42]

In late November, Anna Howard Shaw had announced that she would not run for reelection as president of NAWSA. A close friend of Susan B. Anthony and an internationally acclaimed orator, Anna Howard Shaw had unceasingly worked to enfranchise women for thirty years. She could claim significant successes: woman suffrage had become a national issue, and NAWSA's membership had grown from 17,000 to more than 200,000, with a commensurate increase in auxiliary societies. There were eleven equal-suffrage states, up from four, plus the Territory of Alaska, and presidential suffrage in Illinois. The gains, however, did not compensate for an even larger number of losing referenda, the rivalry with Alice Paul, controversy over the Shafroth Amendment, inadequate fundraising, and the fact that Shaw had not been able to shape NAWSA and its state auxiliaries into a cohesive, harmonious entity. Many longtime members were demoralized and discontented. Young members criticized NAWSA's hidebound ways and for years they had been trying to replace Shaw. Finally, now, in 1915, at the age of sixty-eight, Shaw announced her resignation.

Anna Howard Shaw's most likely successor was Carrie Chapman Catt, who had served as president from 1900 to 1904. But Catt, the president of IWSA, was devoted to advancing the international suffrage movement. She was also a key leader in the upcoming New York "Victory in 1917" referendum campaign. During the convention, delegates persistently pressured Catt to agree to be NAWSA's next president. A committee of one hundred prominent delegates insisted that she accept the position. "It will kill me, I think," Catt confided to her coworker and confidante Mary "Mollie" Garret Hay.[43]

Carrie Chapman Catt capitulated after Gertrude Foster Brown agreed to head up the New York campaign. Equally important, she was given the sole authority to appoint her own national board of directors.

In a ceremony of genuine appreciation for Anna Howard Shaw's heroic years of service to the cause, a brass band played as a procession of national leaders, state presidents, and committee chairs bearing huge bouquets and cornucopias filled with yellow flowers, marched around the room singing patriotic songs. The audience, who had been "asked to help themselves to the great quantities of flowers on the tables," joined in the singing. Sitting in a plush chair, Shaw had a golden laurel wreath around her neck and a long garland of flowers across her lap. State presidents laid their bouquets at her feet "until they were banked as high as the arms of her chair." When she stood to speak, the "whole audience sprang to their feet and commenced to shower her with roses until she was almost lost to sight."

Anna Howard Shaw was made an honorary president, and given a generous annuity so that she would continue her suffrage work. "I cannot think what to say except that I'm very happy," she said. Then, she went to Carrie Chapman Catt, who was sitting in the back of the room. Taking her hand, Shaw led her to the front and presented her as NAWSA's next president. When the cheers subsided, Carrie Chapman Catt said, "I'm old, I'm unhealthy, and I'm tired out, but I will do my best!"[44]

On December 17, the contentious "question of cooperation" between NAWSA and the CU was discussed at a meeting between NAWSA's committee (Carrie Chapman Catt, Ruth Hanna McCormick, Katherine Dexter McCormick, Antoinette Funk) and the CU's committee (Alice Paul, Lucy Burns, Dora Lewis, and Anne Martin).

Catt, a fifty-six-year-old, strong-willed leader, threw down the gauntlet: Alice Paul would have to "guarantee that the CU would observe" NAWSA's policy of nonpartisanship: "To neither support nor oppose any political party, nor to work for or against any candidate except as to his attitude toward woman suffrage."[45] The equally strong-willed, thirty-year-old Alice Paul refused to acquiesce to Catt's ultimatum. The two groups never met again, but both relentlessly, in their own way, continued to fight for the vote.

Chapter 12

Battle Cry: 1916

We have waited long enough. —Anna Howard Shaw

On Valentine's Day, February 14, 1916, suffragists fired an artillery barrage of valentines at congressmen, particularly opponents of the federal woman suffrage amendment. Robert Lee Henry from Texas, chairman of the House Committee on Rules, received an acrostic, with each letter of HENRY decorated with a cupid or hearts or flowers:

H is for Hurry —
  Which Henry should do

E is for Every —
  Which includes women too.

N is for Now —
  The moment to act.

R is for Rules —
  Which you must bend to the fact.

Y is for You —
  With statesmanlike tact.

Edward W. Pou (pronounced *pew*) from North Carolina, a member of the Rules Committee, received a valentine illustrated with a gentleman presenting a bouquet to a maiden dressed in ruffles with the verse: "The rose is red / The violet's blue / But VOTES are better / Mr. Pou." Edwin Y. Webb from North Carolina, chairman of the House Judiciary Committee that was considering the suffrage amendment received a valentine pointing out his hypocrisy: "Federal aid he votes for rural highways / And Federal aid for pork each to his need / And Federal aid for rivers, trees, and harbors / But Federal aid for women?—No, indeed!" [1]

Regardless of suffragists' efforts, it was clear that the Sixty-Fourth Congress was not going to pass the federal woman suffrage amendment. In the Senate, the Woman Suffrage Committee had issued a favorable report, but pro-suffrage senators decided that the time was not right to bring it to a vote. In the House, Chairman Webb, a virulent anti-suffragist, blocked any action on the amendment, by "postponing it indefinitely."[2]

In January, Carrie Chapman Catt had issued a battle cry in a letter to state presidents of NAWSA's affiliates: "Let's make this old world hum with 'Suffrage first'; Suffrage by the Federal route, Suffrage by the State route, Suffrage East and Suffrage West, until our dear lawmakers surrender. There are enough of us to give them no rest if we 'get together' and pull together. It is worth it."[3]

In February, she set off on an extensive and arduous tour to assess the functioning of the state affiliates and rally the troops. In a fiery speech in Minneapolis, Minnesota, Catt "charged the suffrage organizations all over the country with inefficiency." According to a report in the widely read *Woman's Journal*, "She made those who had supposed themselves the most ardent feel that their zeal hitherto had been a pale and ineffectual flame, and she aroused it to an intenser glow."[4]

Carrie Chapman Catt's "Winning Plan" was a key in winning women's fight for the vote. She was president of NAWSA, the International Woman Suffrage Alliance, and founded the League of Women Voters. (Library of Congress)

On April 6, at Columbus Circle in New York City, Carrie Chapman Catt broke a pint bottle of gasoline over the radiator of the "Golden Flier," also called the "Yellow Flier," a small yellow Saxon roadster automobile. (She dented the radiator on her first try. On her third try, she broke the bottle.) The ceremony signaled the start of a two-way transcontinental tour by suffragists Nell Richardson and Alice Snitje Burke and their kitten named Saxon.

That same week, at a meeting of the CU's Advisory Council, Alice Paul proposed her next plan—the creation of an "organization of a political Party of women voters," the National Woman's Party of Western Women Voters, commonly known as the Woman's Party. (The Woman's Party was organized in equal-suffrage states. The CU remained in states without equal suffrage.) Now was the time, Paul said, to show the administration and majority party in Congress that women voters were a "power to be feared . . . that it really will be dangerous to oppose" them.[5] As always, Paul's plan included a publicity-generating component. Prominent suffragists from non-suffrage states would travel on a chartered train, dubbed the "Suffrage Special," to equal-suffrage states to recruit voting women to organize a state branch of the Woman's Party, and to attend a convention in Chicago in June.

On April 7, five hundred members of the CU and a brass band gathered at Pennsylvania Station in New York City to celebrate the departure of the "Women Envoys to the West." Envoys from New York City were onboard, including Harriot Stanton Blatch. (After the 1915 referendum defeat in New York, key members of Blatch's WPU joined the CU. In January 1916, Blatch merged the WPU with the CU.) The rest of the envoys representing working women, college students, and pioneer suffragists would board in Washington, D.C. Two days later, with a signal from two buglers and "the cheers of 5,000 banner-carrying, flag-waving, flower-laden" supporters, the "Suffrage

Special," draped with purple, white, and gold streamers, left Union Station in Washington, D.C., heading west.

Twenty-three suffragists from twelve states, led by Lucy Burns, were on board for thirty-eight days, with stops in the eleven equal-suffrage states, plus Illinois. Enthusiastic crowds welcomed them along the way. In Wyoming, a facsimile of the 1869 act enfranchising women was presented to Harriot Stanton Blatch. In Spokane, Washington, the envoys participated in a tree-planting ceremony in honor of a leader of the victorious 1910 campaign, May Arkwright Hutton, who had recently died. In Seattle, Lucy Burns scattered leaflets from an open-cockpit hydroplane.

Lucy Burns in a hydroplane, piloted by Lieutenant Terah "Tom" Maroney. As she dropped leaflets over Seattle, her "Votes for Women" sash blew off and landed on a roof. (Library of Congress)

The "Suffrage Special" tour culminated in a convention in Salt Lake City. Delegates passed resolutions demanding a federal woman suffrage amendment, which were carried by women voters onboard the "Suffrage Special" back to Washington, D.C. The CU staged a spectacular event for the presentation of the resolutions to congressmen. Women in white holding purple, white, and gold ribbons, formed an aisle up the steps of the capitol. Two women buglers stood at the top of the capitol's long stairway. A huge women's chorus sang "America the Beautiful," with lyrics by suffragist Katharine Lee Bates.

A few months later, Nell Richardson, Alice Burke, and their now almost full-grown cat Saxon ended their trip in the "Golden Flyer," having driven 10,700 miles down the East Coast, through the Southern states, up the West Coast, and back east through the northern states to New York City. They had survived four days lost in the desert near Phoenix, a shoot-out between Mexican and American soldiers along the southern border, and the worst roads in America. In an article headlined: SUFFRAGE AUTOISTS MOTOR 10,700 MILES, a reporter noted that Richardson and Burke "were well." Their "little yellow car," however, "had a worn look," covered with supporters' signatures and mottos such as "Eat Raisins in California."[6] The six-month tour sponsored by NAWSA garnered publicity, although considerably less than the CU's five-week "Suffrage Special" train trip.

June 5, was the first day of the Woman's Party three-day convention in Chicago. "A new force marches on to the political field," declared Maud Younger in her stirring keynote speech.[7] Ida Tarbell, a famous investigative reporter who was in Chicago to cover the Republican National Convention that began on June 7, warned against "underestimating" the new Woman's Party: "It sailed into port here last night, the purple, white and yellow banners standing straight out to the wind, and such a landing as it made. . . . It knows exactly what it wants. Moreover, it knows its power." (Publicity-savvy Paul had scheduled her convention to capitalize on reporters who would be in Chicago for the Republican Convention.)

On the second night of the Woman Party's convention, representatives from the various political parties appealed for votes. "Never have I seen gentlemen pass so quickly from amused and interested confidence to puzzled and irritated humility—or plain scared—as at the meeting on Tuesday night," Tarbell wrote.[8] (Believing that women were best suited for the domestic role, excepting herself, Ida Tarbell opposed woman suffrage.) A Republican was jeered when, instead of suffrage, he promised protection from foreign forces that were in the throes of World War I. Representatives from the Progressives, Prohibitionists, and Socialists affirmed their support of woman suffrage, eliciting a round of cheers and banner waving.

On the last day of the Woman Party's convention, the Republican Party opened its national convention in the huge Coliseum in Chicago. Dubbed "rival national suffrage organizations" by the Associated Press, members of the Woman's Party and NAWSA were there to demand that the Republican Party's Resolutions Committee include a woman suffrage plank in the party platform.[9] At three o'clock in the afternoon, when the Resolution Committee was meeting in the Coliseum, two women buglers in Grant Park signaled the start of a rain-soaked, wind-buffeted suffrage parade, organized by NAWSA. Carrie Chapman Catt had offered to cancel the parade due to the weather. "NO!" suffragists shouted. "Good," Catt replied. NAWSA paid $2, 250 for raincoats and boots.

Braving a biting wind and unrelenting deluge, thousands of suffragists, estimates ranged from 5,500 to 40,000, marched from Grant Park, on the shores of storm-roiled Lake Michigan, to the Coliseum. Portia Willis, a young suffragist from New York, drove two elephants, the symbol of the Republican Party, their trunks curled around the ends of a wood plank inscribed with SUFFRAGE PLANK. There were twenty-four bands, a bagpiper, and the Justice Bell. Accompanied by a band playing "Hail, The Gang's All Here," the soggy suffragists marched into the Coliseum just as an anti-suffragist was telling the Resolutions Committee—"Women do not want the ballot."[10]

The Resolutions Committee worked through a contentious night to craft a party platform. Three committee members, including chairman Senator Henry Cabot Lodge from Massachusetts opposed woman suffrage, two members supported a federal suffrage amendment, and one supported suffrage by the state-by-state method. The next day, suffragists crowded the gallery to hear Lodge read the Republican Party Platform. Having been up all night, he "looked smaller and whiter than usual," an observer reported. Suffragists erupted in shouts of joy when he read: "The Republican party . . . as a measure of justice to one-half the adult people in this country, favors the extension of the suffrage to women." The triumph turned bittersweet when Lodge added a qualifier: "But we recognize the right of each state to settle this question for itself."[11]

The following week, the Democratic National Convention opened in St. Louis. A headline in a New York City newspaper declared: WOMEN MOVE ON ST. LOUIS TO DEMAND EQUAL RIGHTS. The sub-headline announced suffragists' tactics: "Plan 'Golden Lane,' Parades, Tableaus and Constant Demonstrations to Win from Democrats a Full-Fledged Suffrage Plank." The "Golden Lane" was the brainstorm of Emily Newell Blair, a writer and publicity chair of Missouri Equal Suffrage Association. Eight thousand suffragists participated in what a reporter dubbed a "talkless, as well as a walkless 'parade.'" Wearing white hats, white dresses, a gold "Votes for Women" sash worn diagonally across their chest, and carrying gold parasols, women and girls of all ages stood four feet apart in an almost mile-long line along Locust Street, the main street from the hotel district to the convention hall.

There was a double line for the first part of the demonstration (a row of women standing behind a row of women seated in chairs at the edge of the sidewalk): "The effect of this living hedge on either side, blazing with gold, but absolutely silent despite the great number of women, was remarkable, and caused considerably more comment during the rest of the day than the convention itself," wrote a reporter. (Suffragists' plan to have a donkey, the Democrats' symbol, pull a donkey cart with several suffragists failed when the donkey balked at Twelfth Street and Locust. "When last seen," a reporter noted, "two big policemen were holding the animal's head, urging him to be reasonable."[12])

About midpoint in the "Golden Lane," a stunning tableau was dramatically arranged on the steps of the building that had once housed the Museum of Fine Arts: At the top of the long stairway, representing the Goddess of Liberty, stood a woman wearing a flowing white robe and holding a torch high above her head adorned with a crown with seven spikes. Arranged before the goddess were thirteen white-clad women holding large shields emblazoned with the names of equal-suffrage states and the Territory of Alaska, plus Illinois, the presidential suffrage state. To the right, in a diagonal line down the steps, was a group of gray-clad women, representing partial-suffrage states. To the left, stood sorrowful-looking women clad in black, with their hands bound by chains, representing states where women had no voting rights. In front, stood women dressed in the costume of countries that had enfranchised women: Isle of Man, New Zealand, Australia, Tasmania, Finland, Norway, Denmark, and Iceland. The "Golden Lane" prompted a St. Louis newspaper to publish a poem that read in part: "How the Democrats did hate / Marching down the Golden Lane."[13]

Like the Republicans, the Democrats' Resolutions Committee worked all night drafting the party platform. Representatives of NAWSA and the Woman's Party kept watch outside the closed door, ready to lobby any member who might appear. Conflict over the woman suffrage plank broke out about 3 a.m. Angry voices were heard. By morning, the Resolutions Committee endorsed a woman suffrage plank that favored the extension of suffrage to women, state by state. An anti-woman suffrage minority report was approved by four committee members, including Governor James Ferguson of Texas.

Both reports were presented at the convention for delegates' approval or disapproval. Suffragists armed with golden flags, banners, handkerchiefs, umbrellas, and streamers filled the visitors' gallery. They loudly booed and hissed while the Texas delegation raucously cheered Ferguson's anti-woman suffrage minority report. When Senator Key Pittman of Nevada chastised the Texans, suffragists shouted and cheered, turning the gallery into a kaleidoscope of waving golden "Votes for Women" flags, banners, handkerchiefs, streamers and bobbing umbrellas.

"It was the first time," wrote a reporter, "that one of the great cheering demonstrations of a National Convention had been a woman's cheer . . . and the thought seemed to flash to the minds of that Texas delegation that it would not be the last. They sank into their seats silenced."

During the voting on the reports, suffragists in the gallery made a show of recording each vote as it was cast. "The sight of them," doing that, noted a reporter, "had a most unnerving effect upon the delegates." When the Texas delegation announced 38 yeas and 8 nays for the anti-suffrage minority report, suffragists let out a "long steady stream of hisses . . . so loud, so sharp, so fierce."[14] The majority of delegates, however, approved the pro-woman suffrage plank. Thus, for the first time, the Democratic and Republican parties both included a woman suffrage plank in their platform.

Suffragists' satisfaction at this achievement, however, was mitigated by the addition of the state-route qualifier. Jennie Roessing and Hannah Patterson, leaders of the Pennsylvania Woman Suffrage Association, who had kept the all-night vigil when the Democrats met, were "mad all the way through."[15] It was just "'political exigency'" that prompted the parties to include "'some kind of a suffrage plank,'" asserted Carrie Chapman Catt, "and they thought to hoodwink the women by a jumble of words. They in no sense succeeded."[16] (As they had for years, the Progressive, Socialist, and Prohibition parties included a woman suffrage plank without a qualifier.)

The Democrats nominated President Woodrow Wilson to run for reelection. The Republican candidate was Charles Evans

Hughes, who had resigned his position as an associate justice of the United States Supreme Court to accept the nomination. Alice Paul and Carrie Chapman Catt mobilized their corps of suffragists to bombard Hughes with letters, telegrams, and personal visits. Paul and Catt paid him separate visits. They pressured Republicans to pressure Hughes. Finally, in August, Charles Evans Hughes became the first presidential candidate of a major political party to announce his support of a federal woman suffrage amendment.

President Wilson was intransigent. The CU sent deputations of prominent Democratic women, to no avail. At a Fourth of July event, while President Wilson was addressing the crowd, Mabel Vernon, whose voice was noted for its "clear, ringing quality," called out: "Mr. President, if you sincerely desire to forward the interests of all people, why do you oppose the national enfranchisement of women?"[17] The second time she called out, the Secret Service escorted her off the premises.

NAWSA also applied pressure to President Wilson, although employing more decorous tactics. Carrie Chapman Catt and Jennie Roessing, armed with irrefutable facts and data, privately met with Wilson at the White House. They documented the charges of fraud in the defeats of woman suffrage amendment referenda in Michigan, Nebraska, and Iowa. They showed him onerous, if not insurmountable, provisions in state constitutions that suffragists were up against. They tallied the financial, emotional, and physical costs of suffrage campaigns. All to no avail.

Carrie Chapman Catt and NAWSA's Board of Officers called an Emergency Convention to meet in Atlantic City, New Jersey, from September 4–10, 1916. (A resort city with a famous boardwalk and a beautiful beach, Atlantic City was chosen to entice delegates accustomed to meeting later in the year.) Catt titled her presidential address "The Crisis." She compared the state of the movement to Niagara Falls—"a vast volume of water tumbling over its ledge, but turning no wheel. Our machinery is set for the propaganda stage, not for the seizure of victory." She underscored the obstacles to amending many state constitutions, asserting that only a federal amendment would ensure equal suffrage in every state. Issuing a clarion call, Catt declared—"If we are to seize victory, there must be a change in mental attitude. THAT CHANGE MUST TAKE PLACE IN THIS HALL, HERE AND NOW. Women, arise! Demand the vote! . . . DEMAND THE VOTE! WOMEN, ARISE!"[18]

Catt presented her strategy for victory in a secret meeting with national officers and state presidents. Maud Wood Park later recalled, "I shall always remember the crowded, stuffy room . . . the tired faces of the women; the map of the United States on the wall; most vividly of all, I remember Mrs. Catt's calm demeanor."[19] Her plan, dubbed "The Winning Plan," included continuing the appeal for a federal woman suffrage amendment; organizing congressional districts; mobilizing enfranchised women to exert "direct political action" on state and federal politicians; and increasing the number of equal-suffrage states.[20] She, however, insisted on several radical changes. State organizations could no longer function autonomously. (This provision caused a breach with Laura Clay and Kate Gordon, Southern states' rights suffragists who used their autonomy to exclude black suffragists.) A million-dollar war chest must be raised. Thirty-six state organizations must sign "a solemn compact . . . that we *do* want enfranchisement by the Federal route." (Thirty-six was the number needed for ratification of a federal amendment.)

Thirty-six state presidents signed the compact, vowing to conduct a "red-hot, never-ceasing campaign" to get a federal amendment approved and ratified. They also agreed to simultaneously and vigorously conduct state campaigns for full or presidential suffrage in states that appeared winnable. Catt's presentation was replete with martial language: "bombardment . . . mobilization . . . great army . . . divisions . . . general . . . attack upon the enemy at a fortified point." She warned that "any pusillanimous coward among us who dares to call retreats, should be court-martialed." Participants agreed not to reveal the comprehensive nationwide strategy so that the enemy would not "discover where the real battle is" going to be waged. Catt predicted that the "end of our struggle would be won by April 1, 1922, six years hence." [21]

On the fifth day of the convention, President Wilson arrived, looking dapper in white shoes, pants, shirt and tie, topped by a dark blazer. His entourage included his wife, whose secretary had called Catt, inquiring as to the proper attire. Catt assured her that there was no set standard. Edith Wilson arrived wearing a white dress, a hat with a single feather plume, and a luxurious white fox stole, complete with the fox's head and tail over her coat. President Wilson declined Carrie Chapman Catt's offer to speak first. He patiently sat through the program, while his wife fanned him with her elegant fan.

When President Wilson rose to speak, the audience greeted him with applause and cheers. He made no promises, just said that "there has been a force behind you . . . and for which you can afford a little while to wait." When he finished, Anna Howard Shaw rose to her feet and pointedly replied, "We have waited long enough for the vote, we want it now and we want it to come in your administration!"[22] Wilson smiled and bowed, then left the platform, as the audience stood and applauded.

In 1916, the entire membership of the House of Representatives, one fourth of the Senate, and President Wilson were up for reelection. Women voters and non-voters enthusiastically participated in the fall election campaign. Suffragist Frances Kellor, a well-known social worker and founder of the National League for the Protection of Colored Women, organized the "Women's Campaign Train" for the Republican presidential nominee, Charles Evans Hughes.

Nationally known speakers on the Campaign Train included Elisabeth Freeman who had hiked with General Jones. In her speeches to black audiences, Freeman decried the unjust treatment of "colored people" of the country by President Wilson, who had reinstated segregation in the federal civil service. Wilson told a group of prominent black men protesting his action that "segregation is not a humiliation but a benefit, and ought to be so regarded by you gentlemen."[23]

In May, the National Association for the Advancement of Colored People (NAACP) asked Elisabeth Freeman, who was in Dallas, to go to nearby Waco and investigate the mutilation, burning, and lynching of Jesse Washington, a black, illiterate teenage farmhand. Under the guise of promoting suffrage, she went to Waco and disarmed people into revealing horrific descriptions of the lynching. Her shocking report of the "Waco Horror," accompanied by gruesome photographs, appeared in the NAACP's magazine *The Crisis*, edited by W.E.B. Du Bois, who had spoken on the "Democracy of Sex and Color" at NAWSA's 1912 Convention. Elisabeth Freeman's report drew national attention to lynching, an "institution of American barbarism."[24]

During the 1916 campaign, NAWSA remained nonpartisan, although many members campaigned for pro-suffrage candidates and for Woodrow Wilson, whose slogan was "He Kept Us Out of the War." (Since beginning on April 28, 1914, World War I had spread from western Europe to Russia and Japan.) "He Kept Us Out of Suffrage," countered the CU. Just as they had in 1914, but on a larger scale, the CU launched an anti-Democrat, hold-the-party-in-power-responsible campaign in the equal-suffrage states. The Woman's Party that had pledged to use its best efforts to defeat Democratic candidates joined them. Their campaign, according to Carrie Chapman Catt, was a "tactical blunder."[25] The prominent historian Charles Beard, who coauthored books with his wife, Mary Ritter Beard, a historian and an original member of the CU, defended the tactic in a letter to Catt, asserting: "All that was got" at the Democratic and Republican conventions, was because the politicians feared the "impending danger" of an anti-Democrat campaign aimed at western women voters. If Catt thought that NAWSA's parade at the Republican

Convention converted "anti-suffrage leaders," Beard wrote, "then you do not know these men as I do."[26] Catt remained unconvinced.

Equal-suffrage states were blanketed with pro-federal suffrage amendment and anti-Democrat campaign literature; purple, white, and gold banners, flags, pennants; signs and posters; and huge across-the-street streamers and billboards. Lucy Burns, Louisine Havemeyer, Sara Bard Field, Maud Younger, Elizabeth Kent, and Anne Martin fanned out across the western equal-suffrage states in what a Washington, D.C. newspaper dubbed the "Western invasion." Elsie Hill, having just recovered from a serious illness, went to Denver. In Chicago, Minnie Brooke started conducting street meetings, as many as ten a day. Rose Winslow spent more than a month in Arizona. Her speech in the mining town of Bisbee was announced in the local newspaper and illustrated with a full-length photograph of her. Described as "that astonishing young Polish-American factory girl," the article noted her "especially poignant appeal to the men and women of labor."[27] Women and men in the "mines and lumber camps . . . and the remote Arizona towns, listened to her with tears pouring down their faces."[28]

On October 19, violence broke out in Chicago at a silent protest held by a hundred members of the Woman's Party. While President Wilson was speaking in an auditorium, women stood outside holding signs reading: WILSON IS AGAINST WOMEN; PRESIDENT WILSON HOW LONG DO YOU ADVISE US TO WAIT? A mob of men swarmed the women, pushing, shoving, kicking, knocking them down, tearing their clothing, destroying banners and signs. In another attack, two men assaulted Minnie Brooke, tearing a small suffrage flag from her hand and throwing her in the street. A hotel doorman rushed to rescue her from the oncoming automobiles. In Denver, Elsie Hill was arrested for distributing literature. In Colorado Springs, the police removed a large banner and locked it in a jail cell for the night.

When President Woodrow Wilson gave a campaign speech in Chicago, suffragists held a legal demonstration. They were violently attacked by a mob of men—for the first, but not the last, time. (Library of Congress)

Inez Milholland Boissevain, along with her younger sister Vida, a concert singer who gave up her career to work for suffrage, set off on a whirlwind speaking tour. (Inez had married a Dutch citizen, Eugen Boissevain. Under American law, at that time, upon marriage, a woman had to take the man's nationality; thus she lost her American citizenship. Friends could not teasingly call her "Dutchy" for long: "I'm going to get him naturalized right away, quick," she told them. That she did and regained her American citizenship.")[29]

Dubbed the "flying envoy," the widely recognized, glamorous, charismatic Inez Milholland Boissevain garnered enormous publicity. A newspaper in Topeka, Kansas, simply announced in a front-page headline: SHE COMES HERE.[30] In an article headlined, MANY TURN OUT TO HEAR THE BEAUTY, a reporter in Cut Bank, Montana, noted that "gallant men and fair women" attended her speech at the train station. As her train left, "several sentimental young men were yelling 'votes for women.'" However a "few ladies were seen to turn up their noses and heard to remark that she wasn't 'awful purty.'"As for "one or two married men, they "were heard to declare the lady was not better looking than their own wives."[31]

Inez Milholland Boissevain's tour was exhausting. She had not been well before she had set out. Her sister, her parents, her husband, and her doctor urged her not to go, but she insisted. Day after day, she gave impassioned speeches. Train schedules required her to leave and arrive at all hours of day and night. Her energy flagged. Her tonsil became severely infected. Still, she soldiered onward. In San Francisco, she addressed an audience of fifteen hundred people. "Miss Milholland, her Diana-like figure gowned in white, was a flaming personification of the equality of women," wrote a reporter. The audience "vigorously cheered . . . as she flayed President Wilson and the Democratic party for their refusal to confer national suffrage on women." Afterward, she answered questions and graciously talked with women waiting in line to meet her. She was on her feet for hours.

In Los Angeles, on October 23, 1916, Inez Milholland Boissevain fainted while speaking and was carried off the stage: "It was a dramatic scene. A moment before, this remarkable woman, the charms of whose personality have not been exaggerated, held the great audience with the fire and emotion of her oratory. In the middle of an intense sentence, she crumpled up like a wilted white rose and lay stark upon the platform, while one of those eloquent silences befell the expectant crowd."[32]

Ten minutes later, she returned, pale, barely able to stand. Sitting in a chair, Inez Milholland Boissevain finished speaking; her last words were said to be: "President Wilson, how long must women wait for liberty?"[33] She was rushed to a hospital. Vida remained at her side, awaiting the arrival of their parents and Eugen Boissevain. A month later, on November 25, Inez Milholland Boissevain died of aplastic anemia, despite receiving transfusions from blood that Vida and friends had donated. She was thirty years old. Newspapers across the country reported her death. "She was one of Nature's noblewomen," read a tribute in a Tacoma, Washington newspaper.[34]

An extraordinary memorial service was held for Inez Milholland Boissevain on December 25 in National Statuary Hall in the United States Capitol. Purple, white, and gold banners hung from the pillars and balcony. A purple, white, and gold flag was placed beside each chair. A solemn procession was led by a boys' choir, followed by a suffragist wearing white carrying a duplicate of the first banner Inez Milholland carried in the 1910 New York City parade with the inscription: "Forward, out of error, / Leave behind the night: / Forward through the darkness, / Forward into light. The procession continued with three divisions of young women each wearing surplices, the first group in purple, the second in white, the last in gold.

The acoustics of Statuary Hall made the music "seem to come from above." The boy choristers and the Mendelssohn Quartet sang. The organist played. Anne Martin introduced the many people who spoke. Elizabeth Kent read two resolutions. Maud Younger gave the eulogy, saying, in part: "And so ever through the West, she went. . . . There where the sun goes down in glory in the vast Pacific, her life went out in glory in the shining cause of freedom. . . . With new devotion we go forth, inspired by her sacrifice to the end that this sacrifice be not in vain." The procession regrouped and marched out, as the choristers sang "For All the Saints." The audience sat "spellbound by all the beauty and grief." Then the stirring sounds of the "Marseillaise" "burst from the organ like a call to the new battle."[35]

Three woman suffrage amendment referenda were held in 1916: Iowa and West Virginia for the first time, and South Dakota for the sixth time. In Montana, Jeannette Rankin was a candidate for a seat in the House of Representatives.

In Iowa, where women had the right to vote on bond and tax issues, victory seemed a sure thing. Carrie Chapman Catt, who grew up in Iowa, spent six weeks campaigning there. "Suffrage is coming from every direction. You can't stop it," she told an overflow audience at the Grand Opera House in Dubuque.[36] But, anti-suffrage forces were greatly aided by the arrival from California of seventy-three-year-old John Irish, a former Iowa legislator who had once supported woman suffrage. Now, a for-hire anti-suffragist, Irish told audiences that he changed his mind after living in California, where women had voted since 1911. Gullible audiences were swayed by his bogus claims that voting women led to higher taxes, moral decay, delinquent children, worry lines on women's faces, and men who no longer took their hats off in the elevator.

Male voters defeated the Iowa Women's Suffrage Amendment by a majority of 10,081: 162,849 yeas, 172,930 nays. An investigation by the WCTU "revealed that the victory was literally stolen from the women of Iowa." Unregistered voters by the thousands had been allowed to vote on the amendment. In many counties, the number of ballots on the amendment exceeded the number of voters who had been checked off as having voted. But, nothing could be done—there was no process for challenging the results. Iowa suffragists reorganized: "Every one was sad but no one resigned and those who had worked the hardest and sacrificed the most were the first to renew their pledges for further effort."[37]

In West Virginia, the ten-month campaign was hard fought. Lenna Lowe Yost, the president of the WCTU and newly elected president of the state suffrage association, reported working seventeen hours a day in the headquarters she set up in her home. A "flying squadron" of speakers blanketed the state.[38] Ida Craft, the colonel in General Jones' army, held a suffrage school for women in Charleston.

Male voters defeated the Women's Suffrage Amendment by a record-setting majority of 98,067: 63,540 yeas, 161,607 nays. A factor, according to the report in the *History of Woman Suffrage*, was the "use made of by the opposition of the negro question." Black male voters were told that white women voters would "take the vote away from them and also establish a 'Jim-Crow' system" of discriminatory laws. White women were told that "the negro women outnumbered them and would get the balance of power." The oppositions' methods were "reprehensible."[39] Suffragists also blamed the usual villains: liquor and business interests.

In South Dakota, male voters defeated the woman suffrage referendum for the sixth time, (including the defeat of a women's school suffrage referendum in 1894) by a majority of 4,918: 53,432 yeas, 58,350 nays. Although disappointed, suffragists were heartened that the opposing majority was considerably less than the opposing majority in 1914. The loss, according to South Dakota suffragists, "was the same old story, principally the foreigners, especially the Germans, had once more denied to American women the privilege which they, themselves, had acquired so easily." Members of the state association optimistically noted that for the first time the anti-suffragists "deemed it necessary" to intensify their opposition in South Dakota.[40]

In Montana, Jeannette Rankin had traveled the state, talking to voters in dance halls, lumber camps, and street corners. She promised to fight for a federal suffrage amendment, child-welfare reforms, an eight-hour workday, prohibition, and, as a pacifist, she vowed to work for peace. Before all the votes were counted on Election Day, a reporter told her that she had lost. The next day, the newspaper confirmed that news. Two days later, however, the final vote count gave the victory to Jeannette Rankin, the first woman elected to Congress. She would join 434 men in the House of Representatives. "Breathes there a man with heart so brave that he would want to become one of a deliberative body made up of 434 women and himself?" was the question posed by a newspaper in Kentucky.[41]

Woodrow Wilson was reelected the President of the United States. On December 2, 1916, he was on board the presidential yacht anchored near the Statue of Liberty in New York Harbor.

He was there to send a wireless signal to switch on a new illuminating system to light up the statue. On nearby Staten Island, suffragists posed for a photograph in front of a two-seater biplane about to take off towing a huge banner: "WOMEN WANT LIBERTY TOO." The pilot, "petite, plucky" Leda Richberg-Hornsby, declared: "This is war for woman's rights." Her passenger Ida Blair was armed with leaflets. But, their plan to "bomb" Wilson's yacht was foiled by high winds that forced Richberg-Hornsby to crash land in a swamp. Dubbed SUFF BIRD WOMEN, Richberg-Hornsby and Blair survived with a few bruises.[42] (At the dedication of the statue in 1886, suffragists staged a protest, pointing out the hypocrisy of representing liberty as a woman.)

Two days later, President Wilson made no mention of woman suffrage when he addressed the Sixty-Fourth Congress on December 4. Tipped off, Alice Paul had planned a surprise. Arriving early enough to be at the head of the line for seats in the gallery, five CU members got prime seats in the front row, facing the desk where President Wilson would speak. Under her oversize cape, Mabel Vernon was concealing a large banner made of yellow sateen that was pinned to her skirt. Five long pieces of tape were attached to the top of the banner. Surreptitiously, she unpinned the banner and dropped it to the floor. As President Wilson was recommending more freedom, including voting rights for Puerto Rican men, Mabel Vernon whispered the go-ahead signal. In one swift movement, each woman picked up a piece of tape, lifted and swooped the banner over the gallery railing, and held on while it unfurled to display the question inscribed in large, bold letters: MR. PRESIDENT, WHAT WILL YOU DO FOR WOMAN SUFFRAGE?

Wilson looked up and kept reading. A young page jumped up and tore down the banner. Guards headed for the gallery. After President Wilson left, "every Congressman was on his feet staring up at the gallery."[43] The CU distributed press releases that had been prepared the night before, garnering more publicity than the President's speech. Carrie Chapman Catt denounced the

CU's demonstration as "cheap publicity." She urged the press to "make a clear distinction" between the CU's tactics and NAWSA's, where women "are doing constructive educational work in the most dignified and reasonable way possible." The women, Catt insisted, "had nothing to do with the demonstration; they do not approve of it, nor of similar demonstrations which, without doubt, will come in the future."[44]

PART V

Chapter 13

Silent Sentinels: January-April 1917

Patience ceases to be a virtue. —Olympia Brown

On the afternoon of January 9, 1917, a deputation of three hundred women led by Sara Bard Field waited for President Wilson in the East Room of the White House. The President had been putting off the meeting. He had instructed his aide to tell Alice Paul that the "days and the hours" she proposed for their meeting "are impossible," adding, "I would like to avoid seeing them altogether, but if I do see them, it will be at the time of my own selection."[1] Alice Paul, as always, persisted until he finally set a day and a time. The women were there to present the memorial resolutions for Inez Milholland. President Wilson entered the room surrounded by Secret Service men.

Smiling, he greeted Maud Younger and shook her hand. She briefly replied, handed him several resolutions, and introduced Eunice Dana Brannan, head of the CU's New York branch and a member of the Executive Committee. Brannan, the publicity-savvy daughter of the founder of the *New York Sun*, wore her hair in an elegant updo and had a steely gaze. She handed Wilson the New York resolution that included the plea: "We ask you with all the fervor and earnestness of our souls to exert your power over Congress in behalf of the national enfranchisement of women in the same way you have so successfully used it on other occasions and for far less important measures."[2]

Sara Bard Field spoke, reminding President Wilson of their previous visit to present the petition with 500,000 signatures: "In the light of Inez Milholland's death, as we look over the long backward trail through which we have sought our political liberty, we are asking, how long, how long, must this struggle go on? We have come here to you in the name of justice, in the name of democracy, in the name of all women who have fought and died for this cause. We have come asking you this day to speak some favorable word to us that we may know that you will use your good and great office to end this wasteful struggle of women."

President Wilson "listened cordially" as she "talked very nobly and beautifully." (Younger described her as "small, delicate Sara Bard Field, a woman of rare spirituality and humor.") Suddenly his countenance froze, his "manner chilled." Field later said that the "look in his eyes became so cold that . . . the words almost froze on her lips." The cause of his mood change, it appeared, was that she quoted Charles Evans Hughes, Wilson's rival who had narrowly lost the election, and who supported a federal woman suffrage amendment. In addition, President Wilson had been told that the women were merely there to present the resolutions, not to ask for his support. "Icy stillness" was what Younger felt when Wilson spoke. His views were unchanged, he said; he would not "dictate to his Party," a claim that infuriated suffragists, who noted the many issues on which Wilson had dictated to "his Party," including tariffs and preparedness for war. It was up to them, Wilson said, to "concert public opinion."

Then, "with a last defiant glance at us all" President Wilson "abruptly left the room," reported Maud Younger. "Stunned, talking in low, indignant tones," the women returned to their headquarters. The President had "said we must concert public opinion," Younger mused. "But how? For half a century women had been walking the hard way of the lobbyist. We had had speeches, meetings, parades, campaigns, organization. What new method could we devise?"[3]

Alice Paul had anticipated the question and gotten the approval of the CU's Executive Committee for an unprecedented tactic—to picket the White House. At what a reporter dubbed an "indignation meeting," Harriot Stanton Blatch presented the idea:[4] "We can't organize bigger and more influential deputations. We can't organize bigger processions. We can't, women, do anything more in that line. . . . Won't you come and join us in standing day after day at the gates of the White House with banners asking, 'What will you do, Mr. President, for one-half the people of this nation?' Stand there as sentinels—sentinels of liberty, sentinels of self-government, silent sentinels."

The women, whom President Wilson had rebuffed one too many times, enthusiastically agreed: "We could wait no longer . . . the fight was on," recalled twenty-nine-year-old Doris Stevens, a national organizer.[5] Stevens "espoused a new woman feminism," writes historian Linda Ford, "believing that women should take power for themselves,".[6] She had "her own charm and her own beauty and her own great ability," said Sara Bard Field.[7]

The next day, January 10, 1917, at 10 a.m., Alice Paul led a somber, dignified procession of twelve women, including women from Illinois, Arkansas, and California. Each woman wore a purple, white, and gold "Votes for Women" sash across her coat and carried a large banner. Valiantly marching the short distance from the Cameron House across Pennsylvania Avenue, they took up their post at the two main gates of the White House, the East Gate and the West Gate.

Four of the banners were inscribed with a message, including: MR. PRESIDENT / HOW LONG / MUST / WOMEN WAIT / FOR LIBERTY?, and MR. PRESIDENT / WHAT / WILL YOU DO / FOR / WOMAN SUFFRAGE? The new tactic achieved Alice Paul's goal of keeping woman suffrage before the public. WOMEN BEGIN SILENT PICKET read the front-page headline in an Ogden, Utah newspaper.[8] In

Marshalltown, Iowa, a front-page headline announced: SUFFS PICKET WHITE HOUSE.[9]

Teams of pickets stood in front of the White House six days a week from 10 a.m. to 5:30 p.m., regardless of the weather. They were undeterred by steamy hot days, or days with rain, snow, hail, cold wind, and icy sidewalks. Sympathetic women dispensed drinks, scarves, mittens, coats, boots, and galoshes. The janitor at the Cameron House brought hot bricks for them to stand on to keep their feet from freezing.

Day after day, side by side, a kaleidoscope of pickets (more than 2,000 women over two and a half years), took their place: factory workers and society women; relatives of prominent men, including a former ambassador's daughter, admiral's wife, former vice president's niece; celebrities and pioneer suffragists; professional women and college students. Nell Mercer, a young black businesswoman who owned a hardware store, came from Virginia. Eighty-two-year-old Olympia Brown came from Wisconsin. A former vice president of NAWSA, Olympia Brown had embraced Alice Paul's vigorous tactics. "Patience ceases to be a virtue. We cannot allow our cause to rest, or to be overlooked, or over-shadowed," Brown declared.[10]

The first woman reporter in Buffalo, Ada Davenport Kendall, who would soon join the picket line, wrote: "There is nothing hysterical or violent in their method. Although men have thought it glorious to slay their brothers and raze cities for liberty these women have raised neither hand or voice. They speak no words and do not attempt to defend themselves if attacked. With their silent appeal they have made woman suffrage the vital issue from coast to coast."[11]

Silent Sentinels with purple, white, and gold and lettered banners stood in front of the White House. (Library of Congress)

With her genius for communicating with images, Alice Paul ensured that the picket lines and banners were beautiful and ever changing. The banners—rectangular, square, occasionally notched or pointed at the bottom edge, embellished with fringe and tassels—ranged in size from six feet by six feet to five feet by two feet. Some were attached to a long pole. Other banners were handheld. Slogans on banners were painted or had applique letters or were stenciled on a variety of fabrics: cotton sateen, linen, light wool, silk. The messages were artistically lettered in easy-to-read bold type.

In February, Alice Paul planned special event days. College Day brought students from thirteen schools across the country. Women from Maryland came to picket on Maryland Day, the first of many state days. There were days for specific groups, such as teachers, nurses, doctors, writers, lawyers. Labor Day was held on a Sunday so that factory and office wage-earning women could picket. New banners appeared inscribed with quotes by Susan B. Anthony and excerpts from President Wilson's speeches and books.

The pickets provoked a range of emotions. The CU lost some members and subscriptions to the *Suffragist.* Other members supported the decision. When she received a phone call inquiring, "Will you come to picket the White House this afternoon?" Mary Church Terrell, who lived in Washington, D.C. recalled, "As a rule, I complied." Several times, she took her daughter Phyllis with her "to swell the numbers."[12] Elizabeth Selden Rogers, a pioneering suffragist from New York City, where she was a prominent civic reformer for public education, wrote: "I think the picketing is *splendid* and I will come and do it myself."[13] A forceful speaker on the Suffrage Special, Rogers's "whole soul" was always "fuming for militant action."[14]

Some elderly gentlemen, however, who watched the pickets from their nearby club were scandalized by the "shameless" women and their "shocking" picket.[15] NAWSA's leaders were agitated. "No one can feel worse that I do," said Anna Howard Shaw, "over the foolishness of their picketing the White House."[16] The tactic was "unwise and unprofitable to the cause," asserted Carrie Chapman Catt. It was "childish reasoning" to think that picketing would "force the President of the United States to act," fumed Gertrude Foster Brown, president of the State Woman Suffrage Association in New York, where another woman suffrage referendum was on the ballot in November.[17]

Representative Henry Emerson from Ohio ranted: "If men did these things, they would be put in jail." The pickets' action was "outlawry," sputtered Representative William H. Stafford from Wisconsin. Representative J. Thomas Heflin from Alabama, an unvarnished advocate of white supremacy, denounced the pickets as "monstrous, disloyal, unpatriotic."[18]

As for President Wilson, he appeared unbothered by the pickets, and sometimes, he seemed "amused and interested."[19] On a particularly nasty weather day, he instructed his staff to invite the pickets to come in and get warm in the White House, an offer they refused. One day, when he was returning from his morning golf game, he noticed new banners with quotes from his book, *The New Freedom.* According to a reporter, he "surveyed" the banners "critically for a minute." Apparently pleased, he "rewarded the pickets with his most genial smile . . . then doffed his hat and the automobile shot through the west gate, on either side of which were massed sentinels."[20] Shortly after that encounter, however, Wilson rejected a request to meet with leaders of the CU.

On February 1, 1917, Germany resumed unrestricted submarine warfare. Two days later, February 3, newspapers across the country announced the news that President Wilson had severed diplomatic relations between Germany and the United States. NATION ON VERGE OF WAR, announced the banner headline in a Bismarck, North Dakota newspaper.[21] Carrie Chapman Catt called a meeting of NAWSA's Executive Council to deal with the question: "What shall we do if the United States enters the war?"[22] The meeting was held at Suffrage House, NAWSA's elegant new headquarters in a twenty-six-room house not far from the White House.

The meeting was a volatile mix of militarists and pacifists, of disagreements over strategy: Should NAWSA prioritize war work or woman suffrage? It was a "difficult meeting," according to Mary Gray Peck, NAWSA's corresponding secretary. "The national officers and state presidents were women of strong personality and decided views."[23]

Since 1914, Catt, a pacifist, had been dividing her time between two causes: peace and woman suffrage. Almost 2,000 women wearing black armbands had marched in a Women's Peace Parade on August 29, 1914, in New York City, led by Fanny Garrison Villard, a suffragist, pacifist, and a co-founder along with Mary Church Terrell, W.E.B. Du Bois, and others of the National Association for the Advancement of Colored People (NAACP). In 1915, Catt's international coworkers, Emmeline Pethick-Lawrence, the British suffragette and pacifist, and Rosika Schwimmer, a suffragist and pacifist from Hungary, had toured America, advocating peace. They joined with Catt and Jane

Addams to form the Woman's Peace Party that sent representatives to a conference at The Hague, the Netherlands.

But now, in 1917, Carrie Chapman Catt prioritized suffrage, believing that it was the right that was "protective of all other rights."[24] A two-part resolution was passed at a mass meeting. The first part listed specific things NAWSA would do to support the government in case of war, such as training women for agricultural work to increase the food supply, and cooperating with the Red Cross. The second part stated that war work should not interfere with the primary objective—submission of the federal amendment. In the end, Catt "carried the day with her conviction," recalled Maud Wood Park. "We must do both."[25] (Catt was repudiated by the New York branch of the Woman's Peace Party.)

On March 2, 1917, at a joint convention in Washington, the CU merged with the Woman's Party under the name the National Woman's Party (NWP). The merger, proclaimed Alice Paul, would bring about a "unity in organization" and a "unity of spirit in the whole Suffrage movement." Paul was elected the chair, Anne Martin, vice chair, Mabel Vernon, secretary. Members of the Executive Board included Lucy Burns, Alva Belmont, Maud Younger, Doris Stevens, and Dora Lewis. The NWP's "sole purpose" was "immediate passage of the National Suffrage Amendment."[26] A dramatic demonstration was planned—a "Great Delegation of Voting Women Accompanied by Unenfranchised Women" marching around the White House. "The President admired persistence," wrote Doris Stevens. "He also said he appreciated the rare tenacity shown by our women. Surely now he would be convinced!"[27]

The demonstration took place on March 4, the day of President Wilson's inauguration for a second term. It was a day of "high wind and stinging, icy rain." A thousand women, an "Army with Banners," circled the White House.[28] Each woman gripped the pole, "struggling against the gale to keep" their waterlogged banners upright.[29] Marching single file, a banner length apart, the women, some but not everyone, wearing slickers, rubber hats and galoshes, marched around the White House four times, a total distance of about four miles. A band led the way, playing the "Marseillaise" and various hymns. Then came Vida Milholland, carrying a banner inscribed with her sister Inez's last words: MR. PRESIDENT, HOW LONG MUST WOMEN WAIT FOR LIBERTY? The Great Demand banner was next: WE DEMAND AN AMENDMENT TO THE CONSTITUTION OF THE UNITED STATES ENFRANCHISING WOMEN.

There were girls and women of all ages, representing all forty-eight states arranged in line alphabetically. Gilson Gardner, a prominent journalist and the husband of one marcher, Matilda Hall Gardner, wrote: "To see a thousand women—young women, middle-aged and old women . . . . marching in a rain that almost froze as it fell . . . losing only those who fainted or fell from exhaustion, was a sight to impress even the dulled and jaded senses of one who has seen much."[30] Twenty-two-year-old Beulah Amidon, a former law student and the NWP's press secretary, who had been with Inez Milholland when she collapsed, carried a replica of the first banner Inez Milholland had carried:

FORWARD, OUT OF ERROR,

LEAVE BEHIND THE NIGHT:

FORWARD THROUGH THE DARKNESS,

FORWARD INTO LIGHT.

Armed with a copy of NWP's resolution to present to President Wilson, a committee of women led by Anne Martin tried to enter a gate to the White House. It was locked. Blocked from having a meeting with Wilson or any of his staff, the women left a letter and a copy of the resolution with the police officer on guard, Sergeant McQuade, who said he could not promise them that Wilson would ever get their messages. While Anne Martin was dealing with McQuade, President Wilson and his wife Edith exited in their limousine. Stony-faced, they stared straight ahead, passing by six "dripping banner bearers" lined up on either side of the driveway.[31]

Two months of persistent picketing and provocative banners had clearly gotten under the Wilsons' skin. The drenched, icy cold suffragists, a reporter noted, were "incensed at the treatment accorded them." It was a defining moment, recalled Doris Stevens: "All the women who took part in that march will tell you of the passionate resentment that burned in their hearts on that dreary day."[32]

President Wilson called for a special session of Congress to convene on April 2, 1917. His purpose was to ask Congress to declare war on Germany. "We shall fight," he declared, 'for the things which we have always carried nearest our hearts . . . for democracy, for the right of those who submit to authority to have a voice in their own Government."[33] Since it was the first session of the Sixty-Fifth Congress, it included the swearing in of members who had been elected in the November 1916 election. Cheers and applause welcomed Jeannette Rankin as she took her seat as a representative from Montana, the first woman elected to Congress.

Earlier in the day, she had been feted at a breakfast sponsored by NAWSA in the elegant Shoreham Hotel. Two hundred women gathered to celebrate Rankin, who sat between Alice Paul and Carrie Chapman Catt. "The day of our deliverance is at hand," declared Catt, "and I know, and we all know, that this deliverance is to be at the hand of a woman." When Alice Paul rose to speak, a reporter noted that "everyone in the room arose as a silent tribute to the energy with which Miss Paul had directed suffrage work in Washington."[34] It would be the last time Alice Paul and Carrie Chapman Catt appeared together.

After the breakfast, Catt whisked Rankin away to the Suffrage House. Standing on a balcony, she briefly spoke to an excited crowd standing on the sidewalk. From there, Rankin and Catt rode in a procession of automobiles emblazoned with suffrage banners and flags to the Capitol.

Jeannette Rankin speaking from the balcony of NAWSA's headquarters. Above her on the right, is NAWSA's blue suffrage flag with yellow stars for the twelve equal suffrage states. (Library of Congress)

The wife of a Texas congressman seated in the gallery reported that Rankin was surrounded by congressmen who wanted to shake her hand. "I rejoiced to see that she met each one with a big mouthed, frank smile and shook hands cordially and unaffectedly," noted the eyewitness. Rankin had not "smirked or giggled or been coquettishy." Or, even worse, that if "she had been masculine and hail-fellowish." That would have been "sickening."[35]

That same day, the federal woman suffrage amendment was reintroduced in Congress. Pickets stood outside the White House and, for the first time, they stood outside the Capitol. The new message on their banner read:

RUSSIA AND ENGLAND ARE ENFRANCHISING THEIR WOMEN IN WAR-TIME. HOW LONG MUST AMERICAN WOMEN WAIT FOR THEIR LIBERTY.

Two recent international events had inspired that message. In Petrograd, Russia (now St. Petersburg), a march of 40,000 women, enflamed by scarcity of food and the carnage of the war, had sparked the Russian Revolution in March (in February on the Julian calendar used in Russia then). With the abdication of Czar Nicholas II and the end of centuries of imperial rule, a new provisional government took control. The new government instituted liberal reforms, including universal suffrage. WOMEN OF RUSSIA TO VOTE FOR ASSEMBLY, read the headline in a New York City newspaper.[36]

The second event took place in England in the House of Commons when David Lloyd George, the new prime minister, announced his support of woman suffrage. The proposed legislation included a qualification of either 30 or 35 years of age. The voting age for men was twenty-one. The age difference ensured that women would not be in the majority, due to the loss of men in the war. It was necessary in order to get the bill passed, Lloyd George told a deputation of women from groups that had suspended their fight for the vote to do war work, including Emmeline Pankhurst. Sylvia Pankhurst, a pacifist who had broken with her mother and sister Christabel and had continued to work for suffrage during the war, objected. Citing census figures, she pointed out that most working women were between the ages of 20 and 25: "To exclude them from the franchise is most unjust."[37]

SUFFRAGISTS IN U.S. BUOYED BY BRITISH ACTION, read a newspaper headline in Washington, D.C. "Unquestionably the British action on woman suffrage will advance our federal amendment in Congress," asserted Ruth White, a NAWSA lobbyist. "Surely we don't want the country from which we wrested our independence to forge ahead of us when it comes to democratization in any form."[38] Alice Paul believed that Britain's example would "prove the final push needed for getting us the ballot during the coming session."[39]

Jeannette Rankin's first vote was on the issue of whether the United States should enter the war. Watching from the gallery was Maud Wood Park, now head of NAWSA's Congressional Committee, dubbed the "Front Door Lobby" because they eschewed backdoor methods of stealth and secrecy. Rankin, a "thorough-going pacifist," was under enormous pressure.[40] People urging her to vote "yes" included her brother Wellington, who had financed and run her campaign. A "no" vote, he told her, would end her political career. Carrie Chapman Catt and other NAWSA members aggressively pressured her. A "yes" vote, they believed, would gain allies for the suffrage resolution and prove women's mettle for war, the traditional domain of men. Alice Paul and Hazel Hunkins, an organizer and picketer from Montana, visited Rankin. "We told her," Paul later recalled, "we thought it would be a tragedy for the first woman ever in Congress to vote for war, that the one thing that seemed to us so clear was that the women were the peace-loving half of the world and that by giving power to women we would diminish the possibilities of war."[41]

Jeannette Rankin sat through the first roll call. Before the second roll call began, Park noticed that Rankin's brother, accompanied by a Montana suffragist who had donated to her campaign, summoned his sister to come to the door and listen to their pleas one more time. Returning to her seat, Rankin voted "no." Although she was "entirely out of sympathy" with Rankin, Maud Wood Park "knew that her vote was heroic."

Reports that Jeannette Rankin cried appeared in many newspapers. If so, Park wrote, her tears "were not evident in the gallery." However, Park did see that the Democratic floor leader, Claude Kitchin from North Carolina, "the nth degree of the he-man type," broke down and wept both audibly and visibly during his speech against the resolution." (Six senators and fifty representatives also voted against the war resolution.)

Later, when Rankin asked Park if her vote had harmed the cause, Park replied, "That I feared it had, temporarily, but that I was glad she had voted against the resolution, for, with her convictions, she could not honorably have done otherwise." Rankin said that her "uppermost thought" was that as a "woman without children" she should not "cast a vote that might send the sons of other women to their death."[42] Years later, Rankin said that she felt that the "first time the first woman had a chance to say no to war she should say it."[43]

Far more than Rankin's vote, it was America's entry into the war that harmed the cause. The federal woman suffrage amendment was reintroduced. But so were a slew of war measures and leaders in Congress agreed to give them precedence. That decision, according to Park, plunged NAWSA's "Congressional Committee into a serious dilemma . . . should we or could we go on with our work for the amendment at that time?" Intense discussions resulted in a compromise: The committee would scale down its efforts and just focus on getting a hearing before the Senate Committee on Woman Suffrage. Catt's plan of state campaigns "carried on simultaneously all over the country" would continue.[44]

Chapter 14

Tireless Struggles: January-April 1917

I vote 'Aye,' and I can't explain my vote. —William "Bill" Martz

In North Dakota in 1917, a woman described as "small in stature but big in fighting spirit," Elizabeth Preston Anderson, president of the WCTU, asked Senator Robert M. Pollock to write a presidential and municipal suffrage bill based on the Illinois bill.[1] Anderson, who had witnessed the political trickery in 1893 that had "lost" the suffrage bill passed by the legislature, teamed up with Grace Clendening and Mary Darrow Weible. (During Sylvia Pankhurst's second speaking trip in 1912, Weible's mother, Clara L. Darrow, had arranged for her to speak in Fargo and stay at Weible's house. Pankhurst's speech reinvigorated suffragists.) Together, Anderson, Clendening, and Weible lobbied to get the requisite votes for passage. They were aided by a new group of legislators, the Nonpartisan League (NPL). Composed of farmers, the NPL supported woman suffrage. Enfranchised women, they argued, would be "better mothers and more interesting wives."[2] Finally approved by the legislature, the bill was signed into law by the governor. The Anti-Suffrage Association tried to repeal it, but their petition fell short.

The North Dakota campaign was just one of a record number of eleven partial-suffrage campaigns between January and April 1917. Suffragists were doggedly determined to win the right to vote, even if only bits and pieces. The record of their tireless struggles should give pause to anyone who has the right to vote but does not exercise it.

In Tennessee, two early leaders were sisters-in-law. Elizabeth Avery Meriwether was known for the "keen sarcasm, wit and

216

humor" she displayed while speaking that "caused frequent bursts of laughter and applause" from audiences.[3] Lide Smith Meriwether wrote a "confession of faith" stating why the "women of Tennessee, do and should want the ballot." Hundreds of women signed her manifesto that included: "Being 21 years old, we object to being classed with minors . . . paupers, convicts and pardoned criminals, lunatics and the idiot. . . . We taxpayers claim the right of representation; We married women want to own our clothes; . . . We mothers want an equal partnership in our children."[4]

Suffragists' activism was hampered because many "feared to violate the conservative traditions of their southland."[5] It was not until 1917 that four young women introduced street speaking in Jackson and Memphis. That same year, acting on NAWSA's advice, Anne Dallas Dudley, president of the Tennessee state suffrage association, launched a campaign to secure presidential and municipal suffrage.

Considered a "legendary beauty," the wealthy Dudley was the mother of a young daughter and son who appeared with her in photographs and led parades with her. She pitched her appeals to men in the South, where the notion of chivalry still held sway: "I don't want to usurp your place in government, but it is time I had my own," she sweetly assured them.[6]

Hearing Dudley, who served on NAWSA's board, speak at a convention, Maud Wood Park worried that Southern men would dismiss her as a "honey-tongued charmer" sent by NAWSA "to cajole them." Not to worry, a Southern coworker told her, "southern men were so accustomed to that sort of persiflage they would think a woman unfeminine if she failed to use it."[7] Dudley led a vigorous campaign. Petitions and endorsements were submitted to legislators. Suffragists testified. President Wilson sent a telegram urging passage.

The legislature defeated the bill by a majority of 25: 46 yeas, 71 nays. "We are not crybabies. . . . We will simply work harder for suffrage in Tennessee," said Anne Dallas Dudley.[8]

In Ohio, suffragists changed their tactics, having won only limited school suffrage in 1894, and having lost two woman suffrage referenda (1912 and 1914). By 1917, they had succeeded in getting women municipal suffrage in three charter cities, or cities that define their own form of governance: East Cleveland, Lakewood, and Columbus. Attempting to win presidential suffrage, they were joined by Representative James Reynolds who agreed to sponsor the bill. An anti-prohibitionist, Reynolds "fought the battle for it against great odds," placing his sense of duty to his pro-suffrage constituents over his alliance with the liquor industry.[9] The legislature passed the bill by a majority of 26: 92 yeas, 66 nays. The governor signed it into law.

Opponents launched a campaign for a referendum to repeal the law. Petitions were posted in saloons where a signature earned a free drink. Scores of fraudulent signatures were obtained. Despite being burdened with war work, suffragists investigated signatures, filed lawsuits, went before election boards, and appeared in courts, exhausting themselves and their funds until they were overwhelmed and outspent. Male voters repealed the law by a majority of 146,120: 422,262 for retaining the law, 568,382 for repealing it.

In Indiana, the state suffrage association was founded in 1851 by hatmaker and temperance lecturer Amanda Way who declared: "Unless women demand their rights politically, socially, and financially, they will continue in the future as in the past."[10] In 1875, a legislator converted Zerelda G. Wallace to the cause. The former First Lady of the state and president of the WCTU, Wallace had addressed the legislature about the effects on a family when men abuse alcohol, and presented a petition signed by thousands of women. Legislators reacted rudely, ridiculing and denouncing the idea of temperance. Her petition, one senator told her "might as well have been signed by 10,000 mice."[11] Shaking his hand, Zerelda Wallace thanked him for making her a suffragist.

In 1917, victory seemed possible with the support of a newly elected pro-woman suffrage governor. Two suffrage groups opened headquarters; one founded by Grace Julian Clarke, daughter of George Julian, who had introduced the first woman suffrage amendment into Congress in 1868. Catharine Waugh McCulloch, the lawyer who had helped win presidential suffrage in Illinois, came to help. A presidential and municipal suffrage bill was approved by a majority of 59: 99 yeas, 40 nays. As usual, opponents launched a court challenge. The Indiana Supreme Court declared the bill unconstitutional, although by then between 30,000 and 40,000 women in Indianapolis had registered to vote, now to no avail.

In Arkansas, seventy-five women organized the Political Equality League (PEL) in 1911. Twenty-one-year-old Mary Fletcher, PEL's president, who was a graduate of Vassar College, had attended the suffrage meeting in the cemetery organized by Inez Milholland. Legislators repeatedly resisted PEL's efforts to secure any measure of suffrage. In 1917, the newly elected governor, Charles Hillman Brough, urged legislators to grant women primary suffrage. (A one-party state, whoever won a primary in Arkansas was sure to win the election.) Representative John Andrew Riggs, known as the "father of women's suffrage in Arkansas," wrote and introduced the bill[12] Opponents tried all their tricks to kill it, but in the end it was passed by a majority of 52: 87 yeas, 35 nays.

A photographer took pictures of happy suffragists standing with Brough, who was wearing a white shirt, suit, and shoes, and a black bow tie, on the steps of the capitol in Little Rock. A drum corps led a lively parade to the Marion Hotel for an exuberant mass meeting. Arkansas was a significant win, noted a St. Louis newspaper: "It is the first state of the old South to go this far in the recognition of women's rights."[13]

For almost fifty years, the "thinking men and women of New Hampshire," including the revered philanthropic reformers Armenia and Nathaniel White, had been fighting to "secure changes in laws in behalf of women."[14] Legislators repeatedly repelled suffragists' efforts with the exception, in 1878, of granting women the right to vote for members of the school board and for the appropriation of money. In 1903, male voters defeated a women suffrage amendment referendum. Still, suffragists labored onward. NAWSA sent paid workers to help organize the state. Jeannette Rankin and other prominent speakers from across America gave lectures. The Finnish suffragist, Anina Johanssen, came to speak.

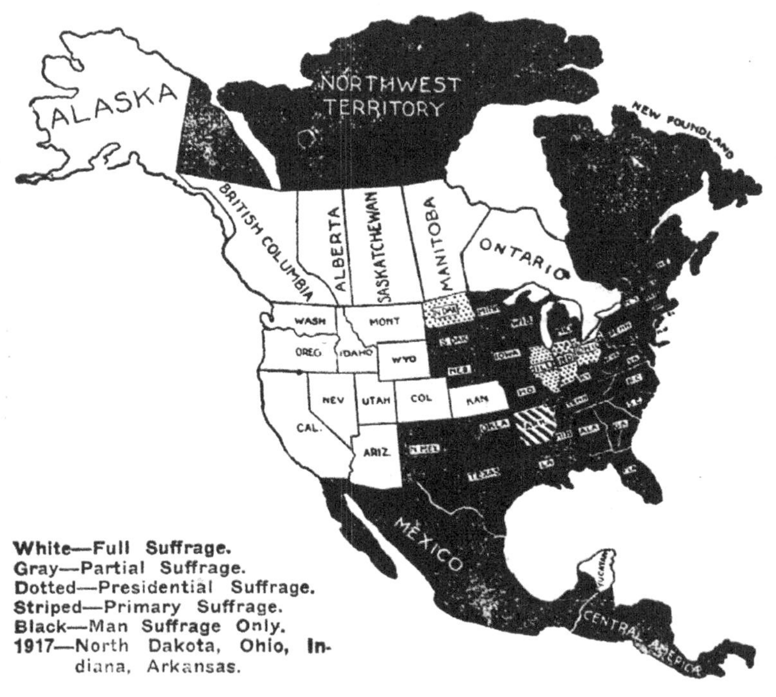

Suffragists produced a vast array of material to educate and persuade people. This map illustrated a newspaper article, "Sweeping Gains in 1917 Shown By Statisticians of Suffragists." Five types of suffrage were shown: full, partial, presidential, primary, man suffrage only. (Library of Congress)

In 1915, a large illuminated "suffrage map" had been installed in the State House in Concord, the capital. Legislators received valentine cards and tickets for the suffrage film "Your Girl and Mine." NAWSA furnished templates for a suffrage section that appeared in many newspapers. In 1917, legislators voted on a bill granting presidential, county, and municipal suffrage. Representatives had invited women to sit in their chairs and spectators were crowded in the gallery. The bill was approved by a majority of 9: 16 yeas, 7 nays. A month later, however, after a heated debate, senators defeated it. Suffragists across America were all too familiar with having a woman suffrage amendment or a bill passed by one legislative branch and defeated by the other. In time, they had seen it for what it was—a ploy to string them along.

In Vermont, an equal suffrage amendment had been resoundingly defeated in 1870. In 1879, tax-paying women won the right to vote and hold office in school districts. A municipal suffrage bill was routinely introduced, but never passed. Six different woman suffrage bills were introduced during the 1916–1917 legislative session. Grace Sherwood, a physician and president of the state suffrage association, reported that their opponents used "every trick that legal minds could devise and employ to retard or defeat their passage."[15]

But, one bill got through. After five days of hearings in March, the legislature granted women town and municipal suffrage by a majority of 9: 120 yeas, 111 nays. The governor signed it into law.

In Rhode Island, Paulina Wright Davis, a reformer who used a realistic mannequin to teach women anatomy and health, was the first president of the Rhode Island Woman Suffrage Association, founded in 1868. She was succeeded by Elizabeth Buffum Chace, an ardent reformer. In 1887, a woman suffrage amendment referendum was defeated by a majority of 15,068: 6,889 yeas, 21,957 nays. Five years later, Henry Blackwell promoted the strategy of obtaining presidential suffrage at RIWSA's annual convention. Seizing on the idea, suffragists pressured legislators, year after year. Once, an aggravated senator threw a copy of the bill on the floor, stomped on it, and swore: "I will kill woman suffrage."[16]

Finally, on April 11, 1917, the legislature passed the presidential suffrage bill. SUFFRAGE BREAKS THROUGH, proclaimed the headline in a New York City newspaper.[17] "It was a small victory, but a momentous one. . . . The solid block of the conservative East had been broken," declared Maud Wood Park.[18]

Emily Pierson, who had revived the Connecticut Woman Suffrage Association, announced that she was buying a farm in Rhode Island in order to establish residence and vote in the 1920 presidential election. Then, she would return to her suffrage work, although she was "pretty nearly tired of trying to penetrate the official brain" of Connecticut legislators who had repeatedly defeated woman suffrage bills.[19]

In Nebraska, legislators had granted women limited school suffrage in 1869, repealed it, except for widows and unmarried women in 1875, then restored it in 1881. Twice, male voters had soundly defeated a woman suffrage amendment referendum (1882 and 1914). With that history undoubtedly in mind, when a presidential and municipal suffrage bill was introduced in January 1917, Edna M. Barkley, president of the Nebraska Woman Suffrage Association, tended the bill with "careful and consistent 'mothering' . . . watching over it for months."[20] In February, the bill passed the House, accompanied by applause from suffragists crammed into the gallery. After a delay of two months, the Senate passed the bill and the governor signed it into law.

Anti-suffrage forces immediately launched an initiative petition for a referendum on the law. If the petition drive succeeded, the law would be suspended until the referendum was held in the 1918 general election in Nebraska. In July, a petition with more than the required 29,147 signatures was presented to Secretary of State Charles W. Pool. Pool, who was not required by law to check the validity of the signatures, announced that a referendum would be on the ballot for the November 1918 general election.

Edna Barkely rallied suffragists to fight back. She pressured Pool to give them access to examine the signatures. She filed a suit for an injunction against him. Grace Richardson and Katherine Sumney led the arduous effort to scrutinize 18,000 signatures in Omaha. Teams of suffrage workers uncovered massive fraud and forgery: false addresses, including ones in the middle of cornfields and the Missouri River and signatures of fictitious people.

The signatures of dead people were on some petitions, prompting one newspaper to publish a tongue-in-cheek comment that "many dead and gone . . . apparently returned to Earth to fight suffrage." The case, *Barkley v. Pool*, dragged on for two years, until a district court judge issued a permanent injunction, preventing the secretary of state from placing a referendum on the ballot. The Nebraska Supreme Court upheld the judge's decision on June 28, 1919, affirming the 1917 victory. Suffragists declared it a "glorious victory."[21]

In Maryland, the record of Mistress Margaret Brent's request for not just one, but two votes from the Colonial Assembly in 1648 had been carefully preserved in the state archives. Her bold demand and her recognition of the political power of the vote was a touchstone story among suffragists; that truth was recalled at conventions. From its inception in 1889, the state suffrage association focused on education. Suffragists hung pictures of pioneer suffrage leaders in the schools. Copies of a multivolume set of the *History of Woman Suffrage* were donated to public libraries. In 1908, the state association's slogan was "Convert the public school teachers." Olympia Brown of Wisconsin and Emma Smith DeVoe of Washington state were invited to speak at a special mass meeting for teachers.

Maryland's legislators were particularly resistant to the idea of enfranchising women. In 1906, suffragists had reported that their request for partial suffrage was treated "as a joke."[22] In 1910, the Equal Suffrage League of Baltimore, founded in 1909 by Elisabeth King Ellicott, a wealthy energetic reformer, tried again. After an acrimonious debate, the Maryland House of Delegates defeated a municipal suffrage bill. Opponents voiced concerns that "racial integration of black and white women at the polls might lead to trouble." A second similar bill was likewise defeated. Ellicott submitted the bill for the third time in 1914. ANOTHER INNING FOR WOMEN: MRS. W. M. ELLICOTT SAYS SUFFRAGISTS OUGHT TO FEEL EMPOWERED, read the front-page headline in a Baltimore newspaper. [23]

But, legislators refused to deal with Ellicott's bill. Suffragists were rudely told: "Don't come asking us for the ballot. We won't give it to you. You are not wanted in the Legislative halls. Go home and take care of the boys and girls."[24] That same year Elizabeth King Ellicott died of pneumonia at the age of fifty-six. She bequeathed her large estate to "woman suffrage and the education of the negroes."[25] In 1917, the presidential suffrage bill was defeated by a majority of 3: 59 yeas, 62 nays. It was now two hundred and sixty-nine years since Mistress Margaret Brent had stood before the Colonial Assembly and asked for a "Vote . . . and Voyce."

In Michigan, in the House of Representatives on April 18, 1917, William "Bill" Martz of Detroit, known for the "tremendous power of his booming voice, roared: 'I vote 'Aye,' and I can't explain my vote." Martz was voting on a presidential suffrage bill. Stunned silence greeted his announcement, then applause, for Martz was an avowed foe of woman suffrage—unless, it turned out, his wife was sitting about three feet away from him and "happily smiling."[26] The bill that had already been passed in the Senate passed by a majority 84 votes: 135 yeas, 51 nays. Margaret Whittemore, a NWP organizer whose Quaker grandmother was a pioneering suffragist in Michigan, was elated by the news: "It is with a new sense of political power that I continue my work in organizing women for national suffrage."[27]

Of these eleven state partial-suffrage campaigns in the first four months of 1917, there were eight victories: North Dakota, Ohio, Indiana, Arkansas, Rhode Island, Vermont, Nebraska, and Michigan. But in the fall, two of the victories were overturned: in Ohio by a referendum and in Indiana by a court ruling. In Nebraska, the victory was suspended due to litigation. Subtracting Ohio, Indiana, and Nebraska from the eight victories and adding them to the three losses (Tennessee, New Hampshire, Maryland) adds up to more defeats (six) than victories (five), a fact that opponents frequently cited as proof that women did not want the vote. That claim—affirmed by all too many women— would hound suffragists throughout the fight for the vote.

Longtime suffragist Charlotte Perkins Gilman described six types of anti-suffrage women in her poem, "The Anti-Suffragists": *Fashionable women in luxurious homes. . . . Successful women who have won their way. . . . Religious women of the feebler sort. . . . Ignorant women—college bred sometimes. . . . And selfish women— pigs in petticoats. . . . And, more's the pity, some good women too. . . . These tell us they have all the rights they want.*[28]

Chapter 15

Arrests!: Spring-September 1917

There is no law against what we are doing, remember that. —Dora Lewis

"I have been lobbying a lot lately," Hazel Hunkins, a twenty-seven-year-old, freckle-faced field organizer, and a picket, wrote to her mother in Billings, Montana. "Can you imagine saying that women don't need the vote; that they are represented by men; that man is naturally woman's superior. . . . If there is anything that can make me boil it is to be told by some great big fat pompous slobby dirty dishonest politician that women weren't capable of voting correctly and in the same breath say with a smirk that he'd do anything for the ladies!"[1]

Hunkins, the valedictorian in high school and a Vassar College graduate, wanted a job as a chemist: "I applied from New York to California, answering every ad . . . I got stacks of letters back. A big stack. Every single one read, 'You are qualified, but we do not employ women.' I was indignant." She joined the NWP after meeting Clara Louise Rowe, a national organizer who spoke in Billings during the 1916 anti-Democratic campaign. She had her first ride in an airplane, distributing suffrage leaflets over a crowd in San Francisco. Campaigning in Colorado Springs, Hunkins met Alice Paul: "We were on street corners. . . . She turned to me and said, 'Go on, say something.' I looked at her, she had such blue eyes, no they were so dark, they were purple. One didn't disobey Alice Paul. She was such a compelling person. I got on the truck and have no idea what I said. Later she told me I was wonderful."[2]

In the spring of 1917, Hazel Hunkins was one of a nationwide army of suffragists intensely stirring up support for passage of a federal woman suffrage amendment. Letters piled up in congressmen's offices. Legislatures in equal-suffrage states sent pro-federal woman suffrage amendment resolutions to Congress. In Congress, ever-present NAWSA and NWP lobbyists strategized, persuaded, and tallied votes. When the Senate Woman Suffrage Committee (first formed in 1882) held a series of hearings in a meeting room filled with suffragists, Carrie Chapman Catt brought a prop—a flag stand with silk flags, representing the countries where women had the right to vote. "We teased her a great deal about her toys," recalled Maud Wood Park.[3]

It was inexcusable that the United States lagged behind other countries in enfranchising women, Catt told committee members. May the glaring gap be "visualized before your eyes," she said, as, one by one, she held up a flag: Australia, New Zealand, Canada, Finland, Norway, Denmark, Iceland, and Russia. Her bare-knuckle conclusion left no doubt that she was done listening to their "mumbo jumbo" of excuses that belonged "on the scrap-heap of outworn opinion. . . . We ask you, gentlemen, to wait no longer."[4]

Senator Andrieus Aristieus Jones, chairman of the Senate Woman Suffrage Committee, was from New Mexico, the only western state where women had no form of suffrage, and no possibility of securing the sky-high number of votes required to amend the constitution. Jones, whom Park described as a "slow-spoken man of middle age with astonishingly blue eyes in a brown face," promised he would expeditiously report the committee's recommendation.[5]

In the House of Representatives, suffragists strategized at getting a Woman Suffrage Committee created. Since the 1870s, woman suffrage proposals had been referred to the Judiciary Committee. An implacable foe of woman suffrage, Edwin Y. Webb from North Carolina had been the chairman since 1914. Creating a

Woman Suffrage Committee solely dedicated to the federal amendment would break Webb's stranglehold. In a letter to the pro-suffrage Speaker of the House of Representatives, James Beauchamp "Champ" Clark from Missouri, Carrie Chapman Catt wrote: "We beg you to recommend to the House the establishment of a Woman Suffrage Committee."

Along with her deferential use of the word "beg" (a word not in Alice Paul's vocabulary), Catt issued a warning that women might be less motivated to do essential war work "if they are forced to carry a conviction that the monarchies of the world have been more just to their women citizens than this Republic has been to us."[6] Catt also wrote to Alice Paul, asking her to withdraw the pickets from the White House and the Capitol. As the president of NAWSA, she pointed out, she led an organization with two million members. The picketing by Paul's much smaller organization was harming "the great cause for which all suffragists are working" by arousing "serious antagonism in the minds of people who would otherwise be friends of the suffrage movement."[7] As an example, she cited a member of the House Rules Committee, Bryon Patton Harrison from Mississippi who said he would not vote for a Woman Suffrage Committee as long as there were pickets.

Edward Pou from North Carolina, "a rigid, grayish man, with . . . the proverbial poker face," was now the chairman of the Rules Committee.[8] Early in May, NAWSA lobbyist Helen Gardener informed President Wilson that Pou was awaiting his opinion regarding the creation of the House Woman Suffrage Committee. (Wilson considered the diminutive, graciously feminine Gardener to be an acceptable suffragist, unlike the pickets.) In a letter dated May 14, Wilson informed Pou that he approved of the idea, as a "very wise act of public policy and also an act of fairness."[9]

Pou granted a hearing, during which Maud Younger, the NWP's lobbyist, recalled the night President Wilson gave his war message to Congress. She described listening to Wilson eloquently talk about what America would fight for—"for democracy, for the right of those who submit to authority to have a voice in their own government." And while members of Congress applauded, she said, "some of us there in the gallery thought of the 20,000,000 of women in our own country who 'submit to authority' without a voice in their own government."[10]

On June 6, by a single vote, the Rules Committee approved a resolution calling for the creation of a Woman Suffrage Committee. Like Senator Jones, Representative Pou promised to promptly report the Rules Committee's action to the House for a vote. Suffrage lobbyists were optimistic that the report would be favorable. "But as week after week went by without a report," Maud Wood Park later recalled, "we grew increasingly uneasy."[11]

Alice Paul resisted enormous pressure to cease picketing once America went to war. She knew her history. During the Civil War, suffragists dismissed Susan B. Anthony's objection and heeded men's requests to suspend their campaign and do war work, believing they would be rewarded with enfranchisement. Elizabeth Cady Stanton later confessed: "I was convinced at the time that it was the true policy. I am now equally sure it was a blunder."[12] Nothing could dissuade Alice Paul from her determination to keep the woman suffrage before the public and the president. She was unmoved by warnings that picketing the White House would be seen as disrespectful, even treasonous. That she was sending unarmed pickets into a "big cyclone."[13]

The cyclone touched down the day a Russian delegation arrived at the White House, June 20 at 12:30 p.m. CAPITAL POLICE STOP PICKETING, read the front-page headline in the Night Extra edition of a Philadelphia newspaper. The continuation of the story on page three was illustrated by three photographs grouped together: a large banner with the headline—TO THE ENVOYS OF RUSSIA; a resolute suffragist, "under police guard bearing a new banner replacing one destroyed in the rioting"; and a group of agitated men "tearing a banner to bits." The headline for the photographs read: MOB

ATTACKS SUFFRAGISTS IN STREETS OF WASHINGTON.[14]

The mob's attack was precipitated by the banner, known as the Russian banner. Stretched between two standards, it was in response to reports that Elihu Root, the head of a delegation sent to Russia, had claimed that there was universal suffrage in the United States, an obviously refutable lie that the NWP could not, and would not, ignore. The banner charged Wilson and Root with "deceiving Russia," pointing out that "twenty million American women are denied the right to vote." Appealing to Russians, who in a recent revolution had overthrown their autocratic government, the banner pleaded: "Help us make this nation really free. Tell our Government that it must liberate its people before it can claim free Russia as an ally."

William S. Timmis, an architect from New York City, had led the attack, rushing at Lucy Burns and Dora Lewis, pushing them back, ripping the banner from its wooden frame. Four men jumped in, shredding the banner to pieces. Lucy Burns and Dora Lewis stood erect, holding the empty frame. Shouts of "treason" and "it is an outrage," resounded. Dee Richardson, a worker in the War Department, screamed, "You are a friend to the enemy, and a disgrace upon your country."[15]

The next day, a group of boys destroyed a new Russian banner carried by Lucy Burns and Katharine Morey, an NWP organizer and the daughter of Agnes Morey, head of the NWP in Massachusetts and a stellar speaker on the "Suffrage Special." Burns and Morey returned to the Cameron House to eat lunch. Hazel Hunkins took a position in front of the White House, holding a banner inscribed: DEMOCRACY SHOULD BEGIN AT HOME. (A newspaper in Billings would label her "part of the lunatic fringe which hangs forever around the edge of the suffrage cause."[16])

Suddenly, the sound of pandemonium reverberated in the Cameron House. Rushing out, Katharine Morey witnessed an attack on Hazel Hunkins, who had climbed up the concrete base of the iron fence surrounding the White House. With her banner held high, she clung to the fence. Shouting "traitor," Richardson wrenched her free.[17] A mob of men joined in and tore the banner to pieces, trampling the remnants on the pavement. Swarming to the West White House Gate, they destroyed another banner.

Mabel Vernon, known for her fearlessness, quickly organized a line of four pickets and led them out of the headquarters. Nobly bearing NWP's tricolor banners, they marched with military precision across Lafayette Park and Pennsylvania Avenue. The crowd, estimated in the thousands, hesitated, unsure of what to do, perhaps awed by the women's boldness. In that interval, the police, who had been summoned by a riot call, arrived and escorted the pickets to the White House gates. The crowd was dispersed and a burly policewoman arrested Dee Richardson, who was later released.

Sensational headlines appeared in newspapers across the country. In Ardmore, Oklahoma the headline declared: SUFF BANNERS RIPPED AGAIN.[18] The pickets' actions were championed. "From all my heart and soul I am proud of the courage of American women, who so boldly demand real liberty and democracy," a member of the Russian mission wrote to Alice Paul.[19] Representative James Heflin from Alabama raged: "The flaunting of this banner was unpatriotic, disloyal, and outrageous." The banner was "reprehensible," fumed Anna Howard Shaw. [20] Doris Stevens unabashedly declared: "We believed the truth must be told at all costs."[21]

After two days of attacks, Major Raymond W. Pullman, Chief of Police for the District of Columbia, called Alice Paul, having consulted with the president of the district commissioners, Louis Brownlow, who was appointed by President Wilson. Stop sending the pickets, Pullman told her, or they will be arrested. Picketing was legal, according to their lawyers, Paul replied. "Certainly it is as legal in June as in January. The picketing will go on as usual."[22] The next day, Friday, June 22, 1917, Major

Pullman ordered rows of policemen and policewomen to line up outside the NWP headquarters. "The period of leniency has passed," he declared.[23]

The only activity at the headquarters was the coming and going of individual suffragists. Mabel Vernon departed, carrying a box. A little later, Lucy Burns appeared and strolled off in one direction. Then, Katharine Morey, "a frail, little girl," according to a reporter, sauntered off in another direction. Rendezvousing at the East Gate of the White House, Burns and Morey unfurled a banner inscribed with Wilson's words that had been concealed in Vernon's box. "The little devils!" shouted an unsuspecting policeman.[24] Arrested and taken to the police station, Lucy Burns and Katharine Morey waited for hours before being charged with obstructing traffic and released on their own recognizance. (Journalist Gilson Gardner, whose wife was a picket, opined: "When President Wilson's administration ordered the arrest of the suffrage pickets—and of course the police have taken their orders in this matter directly from the White House—the administration did a very stupid thing."[25])

Pickets continued to be arrested and released: four on one day, twelve on another day. On June 26, more were arrested, but for the first time, six pickets were singled out and told to return to court the next day for a trial: Katharine Morey; Mabel Vernon; the nurse and hiker Lavinia Dock; national organizer Virginia Arnold; Maud Jamison, a teacher and businesswoman; and Annie Arniel, a munitions factory worker who was recruited by Mabel Vernon.

On June 27, Judge Alexander Mullowney found the six women guilty "of obstructing traffic," and imposed a fine of $25, or three days in the District of Columbia Jail. To Mullowney's surprise, the convicted women refused to pay the fine. Without hesitation, they chose to spend three days and two nights in the District Jail.

At a time of rampant and legal segregation, the white suffragists were confined with black inmates, an obvious attempt to humiliate the white women. The imprisoned women, however, got along. One day, a black inmate persuaded the matron to let them leave their cells and listen to music. When she asked if anyone could play the jail organ, Mabel Vernon volunteered that she could play a few hymns. The inmate told Vernon: "Ask Evelyn what she would like to hear." Evelyn, a quiet girl with a drug addiction, requested, "God Be with You Till We Meet Again." Mabel Vernon played the hymn, and, as she later recalled, "We all proceeded to sing."[26]

The day the pickets were released a hundred women from across America attended a reception breakfast in the garden of the Cameron House. Mabel Vernon spoke and insisted that they were not martyrs: "It was a very simple thing to do." But, she continued, "I do not want to go back to jail, and I do not want others to go, *because it should not be necessary.*"[27]

On July 4, Independence Day, Dora Lewis, a member of the NWP Executive Committee, mailed a postcard to her eighty-one-year old mother, who had sent Dora a jar of jelly:

> Dearest Mother, . . . We are going out presently carrying our banner—Policemen and policewomen & plain clothes men on the sidewalks thick as blackberries. There is no law against what we are doing, remember that. Love to Father. . . . I'm expecting to enjoy that jelly in jail.
>
> Your loving D.[28]

Two groups of pickets demonstrated, carrying banners inscribed with words from the Declaration of Independence: GOVERNMENTS DERIVE THEIR JUST POWER FROM THE CONSENT OF THE GOVERNED. Dora Lewis was in the second group. A crowd of about 2,000 people shoved and insulted them. Hostile spectators and the police grabbed at the banners, engaging in a fierce tug-of-war with the pickets.

Eleven women were arrested and appeared before Judge Mullowney: Lucy Burns, Dora Lewis, Vida Milholland, and Margaret Whittemore; Elizabeth Stuyvesant, a dancer and a socialist; Frances Green, a new recruit; and Joy Young, a small woman whom it took three policemen to subdue. Four more women were first timers: Helena Hill Weed, a geologist; Iris Calderhead, an indefatigable speaker; Gladys Greiner, a star athlete in basketball, tennis, and golf; and Lucille Shields, a singer and regular on the picket line from Amarillo, Texas.

Lucy Burns and Helena Hill Weed argued their case before Judge Mullowney. They pointed out inconsistency: Picketing was legal from January 10 to June 22, then it was not. The police would sometimes control the crowd, sometimes just stand by, sometimes manhandle pickets and confiscate their banners. Mullowney had previously said they could picket as long as they kept moving, which is what they were doing; still they were arrested.

"It is evident," Lucy Burns told Mullowney, "that the proceedings in this court are had for the purpose of suppressing our appeal to the President of the United States, and not for the purpose of accusing us of violating the police regulations regarding traffic."[29]

Dressed in prison garb, from left, Doris Stevens, Alison Turnbull Hopkins, and Eunice Dana Brannan. Stevens included an annotated list of suffrage prisoners in her firsthand account, Jailed for Freedom. (Library of Congress)

Judge Mullowney sentenced the women to three days in the District Jail. Any pickets who appeared before him again, he sternly warned, would get long terms in the Occoquan Workhouse in Lorton, Virginia.

Eleven days later, Mullowney did just that. On July 17, he sentenced sixteen pickets on the charge of obstructing traffic to sixty days in Occoquan Workhouse. They had been arrested during their demonstration on Saturday, July 14, marking Bastille Day, an event that commemorated the beginning of the French Revolution in 1789. Three groups of pickets carrying banners had marched single file, one after another, to the East and West Gates of the White House. Among the dazzling array of banners was one inscribed: LIBERTY, EQUALITY, FRATERNITY, the motto associated with the French Revolution.

The pickets, who came from nine states, ranged in age from twenty-two to sixty-two. Among them were Anne Martin, Doris Stevens and Eunice Dana Brannan; Janet Fotheringham, a physical education teacher; and Beatrice Reynolds Kinkead, a journalist with four children who had fought in California's suffrage campaigns. Florence Bayard Hilles was head of NWP in Delaware, a munitions worker, and the daughter of a former ambassador to Great Britain. Betsy Graves Reyneau was a portrait painter, despite the disapproval of her father and husband who thought that women were not fit to be artists.

The crowd, attracted by the sight of the police and their patrol wagon, was subdued. Doris Stevens noted that "an intense silence fell on the spectators, as they saw not only younger women but white-headed grandmothers hoisted into the crowded police vehicle, their heads erect and their frail hands holding tightly to the banner until wrested from them by superior force."[30] Suffragists and banners were crammed into patrol wagons and driven to police headquarters.

The Omaha Bee, Doris Stevens's hometown newspaper, published a "message" from her on its front page, illustrated with her picture: "I was arrested today for carrying a purple, white and gold banner to the White House. We were peacefully and lawfully protesting against the injustice of the national government in refusing to enfranchise women. The government was the aggressor. . . . It does not hesitate unlawfully to arrest us in its attempt to crush out this demand." The article noted that Stevens was "one of the first to switch" from NAWSA to the CU, and that she "is a personal friend of Mrs. O. H. P. Belmont of New York, and has been a frequent guest at her home and on her private yacht."[31]

The women defended themselves at a trial that lasted two tense days. "What a spectacle it must be to the thinking people of this country to see us urged to go to war for democracy in a foreign land," said Florence Bayard Hilles, "and to see women thrown in prison who plead for that same cause at home." Judge Mullowney pronounced a draconian sentence: "Sixty days in the workhouse in default of a twenty-five-dollar fine." Clearly, the sentence was intended to coerce the convicted women into paying the fine. Shocked and shaken but unwavering they replied: "We protest against this unjust sentence and conviction but we prefer the workhouse to the payment of a fine imposed for an offense of which we are not guilty." Then, according to Doris Stevens, "We filed into the 'pen' to join other prisoners waiting to be carried off to prison."

Loaded into the airless police wagon, the women were taken to the train station where they boarded a train to Virginia. It was dark when they arrived at a small station in the middle of nowhere. "Even the bravest member of our party was struck with a little terror," admitted Doris Stevens. Transferred to locked vans, they endured a rocky, rough ride. At Occoquan, they were registered and stripped of everything from wedding rings to eyeglasses, assigned a number, and informed that they would be punished if they broke the "rule of silence."

After a supper of "dirty, sour soup," they were forced to strip naked, shower, and change into shapeless, coarse prison clothes.[32]

236

Although Virginia had rigid segregation laws, they were placed in a dormitory with black women, once again an attempt to humiliate and frighten the white women into ceasing to picket. They were "put with colored women as an insult," stated Eunice Dana Brannan, "but the colored women were kind to them and indignant at their treatment."[33] When they went to sleep, their "thoughts turned to the outside world."[34] Would there be a public protest? Would the government be forced to enfranchise women?

Newspapers across the country carried the news. An Ogden, Utah newspaper reported: SUFFRAGISTS ARE IN JAIL DRESS.[35] President Wilson's longtime friend, Dudley Field Malone, whom Wilson had appointed to a lucrative government position, personally lodged a protest. When Wilson professed ignorance, Malone told him, "After this, Mr. President, you *do* know."[36] Malone threatened to resign, an act that would have greatly embarrassed Wilson.

Telegrams and letters condemned the harsh sentence. Women, even some who objected to picketing, protested. The government's action, Doris Stevens wrote later, "had made women feel sex-conscious. Women were being unjustly treated . . . women stood up and objected to our treatment." A notable exception was the lack of any solidarity and protest from NAWSA's leaders, including Carrie Chapman Catt.

The imprisoned suffragists were assigned to work in the sewing room. No talking was allowed, although occasionally they managed to talk to the other inmates. One night, they were ordered to sit in a recreation room until bedtime. "We tried to sing," Doris Stevens wrote, "the negroes joined in and soon outsang us with their plaintive melodies and hymns." On the third day of the sixty-day sentence, President Wilson issued a pardon. Before they left, Superintendent Raymond Whittaker venomously told Lucy Burns, who had arrived to escort the pickets: "Now that you women are going away, I have something to say to *you*. The next lot of women who come here won't be treated with the same consideration that these women were."[37]

Since January 1917, Catherine Flanagan had been eager to join a picket line. A young stenographer and member of the Connecticut Woman Suffrage Association (CWSA), Flanagan lived with her widowed mother Bridget in Hartford. Finally, on August 1, the first day of her vacation, she left for Washington, D.C. Her decision roiled the CWSA. The association "most emphatically does not endorse picketing at the White House," stated vice president Grace Thompson. The CWSA's president, Katharine Houghton Hepburn, whom Flanagan had consulted before she left, disagreed: "It behooves those who are less public spirited to try to comprehend her unselfish devotions."[38]

The daily pickets had resumed on July 23, and Flanagan joined them on August 5. On August 14, the pickets displayed a new, deliberately provocative banner drafted by Lucy Burns. The inscription addressed to KAISER WILSON, charged him with caring more about establishing democracy for Germans than for American women. The slogan ended with: TAKE THE BEAM OUT OF YOUR OWN EYE, a Biblical phrase referring to a hypocrite.

"For a half an hour people gathered about the banner," recounted Catherine Flanagan. "You felt there was something brewing in the. . . . Suddenly, it came—a man dashed from the crowd and tore the banner down." Other banners were destroyed. Flanagan and the other banner bearer returned to Cameron House to get reinforcements and more banners. Just behind them was "the crowd, which was fast changing into a mob." When they emerged with new banners, the mob "jumped them," screaming insults and throwing rotten eggs.

A sailor slugged Elizabeth Stuyvesant and tore off her blouse. A ladder appeared and another sailor climbed up and yanked down the American flag that hung over the front door beside the NWP's purple, white, and gold flag. Other sailors used a ladder to climb up and destroy banners that hung over the third-floor balconies. Lucy Burns barely managed to shake off two men who were trying to drag her over the edge.[39] Catherine Flanagan was on the stairs when a shot was fired through the second story window and embedded itself in the ceiling. The .38-caliber bullet had passed twelve inches above the heads of three suffragists who were sitting on a window seat.

Five minutes later, Catherine Flanagan and Katharine Morey were asked to go to the White House and hold a banner. Going out the back way, they climbed a back fence and made their way to the White House. Soon a sailor spotted them and destroyed their banner, dragging them along the pavement. A policeman standing beside them did nothing.

During the riot, President Wilson and his wife left the White House, clearly witnessing the attacks on the pickets. Police reserves arrived about five o'clock and cleared the sidewalk. Seeing an opening, the pickets, bearing their purple, white, and gold banners, returned to the White House where they marched back and forth three times. On their way back, the crowd jumped them in Lafayette Park, destroying their banners. Madeleine Watson, a NWP state officer from Illinois, was pushed down and kicked so hard she had to be carried into the Cameron House. Throughout the night, suffragists heard the sounds of men trying to get in.

The next day, one Kaiser banner and fifty tricolor banners were destroyed. Small boys and ruffians taunted the pickets, spitting, and shouting nasty comments. Alice Paul, a small woman, was knocked down three times. Grabbing her sash in an attempt to tear it off, a sailor dragged her thirty feet along the sidewalk, inflicting a severe gash on her neck. A soldier struck Elizabeth Stuyvesant. Beulah Amidon was thrown to the pavement. Waves of impassioned suffragists surged forth from headquarters to replenish the supply of banners and flags and take their place on the picket line.

On August 16, fifty policemen led the attack on the pickets. They "fell upon these young women with more brutality even than the mobs," wrote Doris Stevens.[40] Three policemen attacked

Virginia Arnold, Elizabeth Stuyvesant, Lucy Burns, and Natalie Gray, whose mother, a state NWP officer, had sent her to "fight for democracy at home," since she did not have a son to "fight for democracy abroad."[41] Abandoning their poles and wooden frames, relay teams of women took up their position and held up banners that they had smuggled out, concealed under their hats, pinned to the underside of skirts, or folded up in a newspaper.

Seven waves of pickets were repeatedly attacked by forty policemen and women, who destroyed their banners. When the crowd swelled in the late afternoon, the police let the mob take over. Fifty-six Kaiser banners were captured and one hundred and forty-eight flags destroyed. Two men who tried to help the pickets were arrested.

On August 17, with the pickets obviously unstoppable, Major Pullman notified Alice Paul that they would be arrested. At noon, six women, including Catherine Flanagan and Madeleine Watson, took their posts at the White House gates. A policeman warned them that they would be arrested if they did not move. But, they did not move, nor were they arrested, just repeatedly warned.

When their shift ended at 3:15 p.m., Flanagan and the other women ate lunch at the Cameron House and returned to picket at 4 p.m. A crowd started to form as government workers got out of work. It seemed to Catherine Flanagan that the police were waiting for the crowd to get big enough to justify arresting them for obstructing traffic. Then, at 4:30 p.m., Captain Carl Flather walked through the crowd and headed straight toward her. "Move on," he ordered, "you are under arrest."[42] A photographer took a picture of a large policewoman looming between Flanagan, who was holding a large tricolor banner, and Watson, who held a banner inscribed: MR. PRESIDENT HOW LONG MUST WOMEN WAIT FOR LIBERTY.

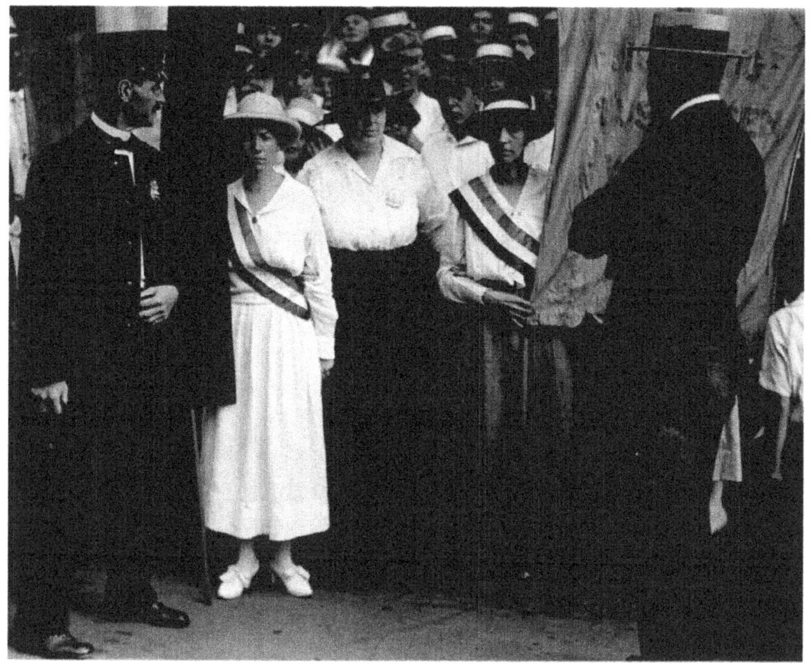

The arrest of Catherine Flanagan, holding a tricolor banner, and Madeleine Watson, holding a lettered banner. The policewoman with the badge on her white shirt escorted them to the prison van. They were sentenced to thirty days in Occoquan workhouse. (Library of Congress)

Six pickets were arrested, tried, refused to pay the fine, and sentenced to thirty days in Occoquan workhouse: Catherine Flanagan, Madeleine Watson, Natalie Gray, Lavinia Dock, Lucy Ewing, the niece of a former vice president of the United States; and Edna Dixon, a public school teacher in Washington, D.C. After two weeks of enduring squalid conditions and foul food, Dock, Ewing, Watson, and Gray were hospitalized. In Washington, D. C., a newspaper headline read: SUFF PICKETS GO TO HOSPITAL.[43]

Suffragists' reports of unsanitary, harsh conditions were confirmed when Virginia H. Bovee, a prison matron at Occoquan, who was fired for being friendly with the pickets, signed a sworn affidavit. Bovee's complaints included prisoners "being put on bread and water, or by being beaten"; filthy bed linens; and worms in "the beans, hominy, rice, cornmeal and cereal . . . on the top of the soup."[44] The reports of the intolerable conditions prompted a firestorm of telegrams and letters to elected officials, demanding an inspection and investigation. Not surprisingly, Superintendent Whittaker personally conducted sanitized tours for several congressmen who found nothing to complain about. The NWP, however, filed a formal complaint. PICKETS BRING CHARGES, reported a newspaper in Washington, D.C.[45]

In the fall of 1917, NAOWS had announced a national campaign to awaken opposition to woman suffrage. Their first target was Maine, where a woman suffrage amendment referendum was scheduled for September 10. NAOWS flooded the state with speakers from Massachusetts, Iowa, and Colorado. Local suffragists battled back. NAWSA sent a campaign manager, Deborah Knox Livingston, and speakers. More than a million leaflets were circulated.

Male voters defeated the measure by a majority of 18,154: 38,838 nays, 20,684 yeas. Livingston cited numerous reasons for the defeat from "inherent conservatism and prejudice" to "resentment at the 'picketing' at the White House by the 'militant' suffragists."[46] NAOWS trumpeted the news that Maine was the twelfth suffrage referendum to be defeated since 1914, compared to only two wins in Montana and Nevada.

The week before the Maine election, thirteen pickets had been arrested while demonstrating at a parade of drafted soldiers, attended by President Wilson. Three of the women had been arrested before—Maud Malone, Lucy Burns, and Annie Arniel. Some of the others included Mary Winsor, one of three sisters from a prominent Quaker family, all of whom would go to jail; Edith "Aingy" Ainge, an expert in caretaking, calming, and cheering up; and Lucy Branham, a graduate student who had received a Carnegie Medal for saving two people, a woman from drowning and a man who tried to save her, but then needed to be saved himself. (Lucy's suffragist mother with the same name would later go to jail.) Julia Emory was a bespectacled young woman who longed "to start a feminist revolution."[47] Pauline Fortall Adams, a militant Irish immigrant, had invented two suffrage games to raise money. Abby Scott Baker, once described by a reporter as having a "magnetic personality," was head of the NWP's Press Committee."[48] Her three sons were fighting in World War I.

Their trial before Judge Pugh (Mullowney was on vacation) on September 4, was "sensational in the extreme," according to a reporter. Julia Emory's mother gave a tearful plea to spare her daughter from jail. Over Julia's objections, Pugh paroled her to the custody of her mother. Then, he increased the pickets' sentence from thirty to sixty days in Occoquan. Sixty days, he warned them, would become the "fixed" sentence if they did not stop what they were doing. "I want to tell you, Judge Pugh, that democracy will never be suppressed by prison wall," Pauline Fortall Adams shouted. "And I want to say to you that suffrage will never be obtained as long as these methods of yours prevail," Pugh bellowed back.[49]

Alice Paul and her indomitable pickets were keeping suffrage in the news across America, alongside war news. And Paul had a supply of ideas for generating publicity. She dispatched four groups of compelling speakers, including Louisine Havemeyer and Dora Lewis, on a nationwide "The Truth About Occoquan" lecture tour. On September 11, she held a banquet at the Cameron House, honoring the first women to be released from Occoquan—the pale, weak, much thinner Catherine Flanagan, Madeleine Watson, Lavinia Dock, Lucy Ewing, Natalie Gray, and Edna Dixon. Alva Belmont, always a sure bet to attract reporters, was the main speaker. Elegantly dressed and "bedecked with jewels," Belmont praised the freed women, who had served twenty-five days, with five days off for good behavior, and issued a warning to President Wilson: "Such an administration, if it does not cease its cowardly persecution, should be shorn of power in the next Congressional elections."[50]

A few days before the banquet that he undoubtedly attended, Dudley Field Malone resigned, seriously embarrassing President Wilson. MALONE QUITS RICH OFFICE AS REBUKE TO THE PRESIDENT, read the front-page headline in a Phoenix newspaper.[51] (Wilson replaced Malone with Byron R. Newton, who said suffragists were "a menace to civilization . . . restless, abnormal women who seem to have a perverted and diseased ambition . . . freaks of their sex."[52])

On September 14, Senator Andrieus Jones visited Occoquan workhouse. That same day, six pickets arrived to serve a thirty-day sentence. Two of the convicted women were Russian immigrants. Nina Samarodin was a labor organizer who urged "working women" to "arise now and demand your political rights." Anna Gwinter was a member of the Women's Waistmaker's Union. Ruth Crocker, said, "I guess they can make us sick but they can't make us quit."[53] Katharine Rolston Fisher, a teacher and writer, wished there was another way than going to jail, "but the fight must be won."[54] When Judge Mullowney had asked if they would pay a fifty-cent fine, Ada Davenport Kendall, the reporter, defiantly replied, "Not if you made it five cents."[55] The sixth woman turned out to be an F.B.I. plant.

The day after his visit to Occoquan, Senator Jones, after a six-month delay, finally released the Woman Suffrage Committee report recommending passage by the Senate of the federal woman suffrage amendment. Nine days later, Representative Pou finally presented the House Rules Committee's report recommending the creation of a House Woman Suffrage Committee. A heated two-hour debate ensued. Representative Joseph Walsh of Massachusetts angrily belittled the proposal as resulting from "the nagging of iron-jawed angels" who were "bewildered, deluded creatures with short skirts and short hair."[56]

244

When the roll call finally began, Maud Wood Park, who was sitting in the gallery, recalled, "It was the first of many times, when I was to sit in a Congressional gallery, with my heart in my throat, checking up on our polls as the votes were recorded."[57] The measure passed by a majority of 77: 181 yeas, 104 nays. The next task was appointing a chairman and members to the Woman Suffrage Committee. Opponents, however, were determined to derail, or at least impede, the process.

By mid-September, just as Superintendent Whittaker had threatened, harsher treatment was being meted out to imprisoned pickets. Instead of being assigned to the sewing room, they were now forced to do hard manual labor. When Ada Davenport Kendall said that she was too debilitated from lack of nutrition to scrub a bathroom floor on her hands and knees and asked for another assignment, she was put in the "punishment cell," or solitary confinement, and fed three thin slices of bread and water in a leaky paper cup for seven days. Her toilet was an open bucket. She was knocked around by a matron and several attendants. Back home, Kendall had a parrot named Pol; in her cell at Occoquan, she befriended a rat that she named Machiavelli. When Lucy Burns attempted to talk to Kendall to find out how she was, Burns too, was put in the "punishment cell" and fed bread and water. Ada Davenport Kendall would denounce Occoquan as "a place of chicanery, sinister horror, brutality and dread."[58]

Chapter 16

Night of Terror:
September-December 1917

They tried to terrorize and suppress us. They could not. —Alice Paul

The first question Katherine Hodges asked Ernestine Hara, a small, thin-faced young woman with large, dark eyes, was how old she was. She had just turned twenty-one, Hara replied. Hodges, who lived in Everett, Washington, had come to New York City to attend a Socialist Party convention. Hara, who was born into an anarchist family in Romania, had come to America when she was eleven years old and lived just around the corner from the Party headquarters. Although she was not a member, she helped in the office where she met Hodges. Knowing that Alice Paul needed pickets, Hodges told Hara about NWP's picket lines and the possibility of going to jail.

"Well, I'd never been to jail," Hara recalled. "It was kind of romantic in my mind. I thought it would be a thrilling experience." But, it was also more than that for Hara: "As a radical, I believed in justice . . . it was highly undemocratic and an outrage that so much opposition had been placed" against women getting the vote. "That's why I went down to Washington, D.C."[1]

Ernestine Hara (later Ketter) was with the third group of pickets sentenced to thirty days that arrived at Occoquan on September 26, 1917. Two other women came from New York City: Hilda Blumberg, a Russian immigrant, trade unionist, and a teacher; and Peggy Baird Johns, an artist and journalist for a socialist newspaper. A fourth woman, Margaret Wood Kessler, was from

Denver, a "frail" woman, described as "all spirit and fire—a dauntless lover of liberty and justice."[2] Before going to Occoquan, they spent one night in the District Jail where Hara said they embraced Peggy Johns's idea that since they were "unjustly arrested" they were "political prisoners." That idea, Hara said, "really gave quite a different tinge to the whole struggle."

At Occoquan, they had an "immediate discussion" with the other imprisoned pickets who enthusiastically embraced the idea.[3] In solidarity, they refused to work. Clandestinely circulating a piece of paper, they created and signed a historic document, demanding to be treated as political prisoners. They demanded access to legal counsel, books, letters, newspapers, writing materials, food sent in from the outside, permission to see each other, visits from family and friends, and the release of Lucy Burns from solitary confinement.

The document, arguably the first organized group demand for political prisoner status in America, was smuggled out and served on the district commissioners. A Washington newspaper printed the "Text of the Ultimatum" and the names of the eleven imprisoned signers: "Mary Winsor, Lucy Branham, Ernestine Hara, Hilda Blumberg, Maud Malone, Pauline Fortall Adams, Eleanor A. Colman [Calnan], Edith Ainge, Anna [Annie] M. Arniel, Dorothy Jones Bartlett, Margaret M. Fotheringham."[4] Responding that "we do not know what is meant by 'political prisoners,'" the commissioners ordered that they rescind their demands.[5] When they refused, the eleven signers and Lucy Burns were transferred to the District Jail in Washington, D.C., and placed in solitary confinement.

Recently released from jail, from left, Lucy Branham, Dorothy Jones Bartlett, Lucy Burns, Annie Arniel, Pauline Fortall Adams, Mary Winsor, Eleanor Calnan, Edith Ainge, and Margaret Fotheringham staged a demonstration, demanding political prisoner status for imprisoned pickets. The reference on a sign to Russia and Miyukoff, a political agitator, highlights suffragists' attention to international affairs. (Library of Congress)

After she was released, Ernestine Hara was "tempted to go back again on the picket line." But, she "wasn't courageous enough to" risk going back to jail. She "felt horrified by the different things that could happen to you in prison."[6] There was also the stigma, as Hara pointed out: "Jails had a very bad reputation for anyone, especially for women. If you were a jailbird, you were a fallen woman." Effie Boutwell Main's husband filed for divorce "on account of the disgrace" of her serving a ten-day sentence. Hazel Hunkins's half-brother paid for a newspaper notice, informing readers that she "had been deluded by people in Washington" and "was not that kind of girl."[7] Several women were fired from their jobs, including Janet Fotheringham, for setting a bad example for her students.

Nevertheless, women joined the picket line, fully aware of the risks. Many women went to jail again and again. Lavinia

Dock, three times, and Edith Ainge, five times. After her second imprisonment in 1917, Annie Arniel had returned to Wilmington, Delaware, to recuperate. Although she was "much broken in health," according to a reporter, she predicted that her "experience may have to be repeated before the great cause for which we women have endured so much is finally won."[8] Arniel served eight jail terms, totaling 108 days. Lucy Burns, who endured punishment in solitary confinement wrapped in a blanket, having been stripped of her clothes, spent the most time in jail of any suffragist. Sisters went to jail: the Grams, Winsors, Fotheringhams, Crockers, Youngs, Elsie Hill and Helena Hill Weed, as did mothers and daughters—the Moreys and the Branhams.

To sustain their spirits in vermin-infested cells, pickets composed songs, each woman adding to the lyrics, a phrase, a line that they called out from cell to cell. Accompanied by a hair comb played by Annie Arniel, the women created a doggerel to Woodrow Wilson, nicknamed "Woody-Wood," a reflection of their disdain for him. They created the stirring anthem *Shout the Revolution of Women* with the line—"Invincible our army, forward, forward."[9] Prisoners taught classes in foreign languages, literature, and physical culture.

Katharine Rolston Fisher, who spent thirty days in Occoquan Workhouse, wrote poems, one in which she decried the night a prison matron roughly rebuffed Lucy Burns's efforts to obtain water for a suffering prisoner. Mary Winsor, who spent sixty days in Occoquan Workhouse, created prayers in which she would detail the "daily cruelties." One of "cruelties" was the barbarous punishment known as "the greasy pole" where the regular prisoners, "girls with their hands tied behind them," were strapped to a greasy pole and partly suspended, causing them to slide down with their arms wrenched above their head.[10]

On October 3, an incident had occurred that a Washington, D.C. newspaper labeled "a race riot and a free-for-all fight." The sensationalized front-page headline read: OCCOQUAN 'SUFF'

RIOT.[11] It started when Peggy Baird Johns, who had been hospitalized for several days, was taken to the warden's office and told that she was being taken somewhere, but not told where. Alarmed that she was being taken to a psychopathic ward, a place where people could be locked up indefinitely with no legal rights, she shouted for help. Ernestine Hara, Maud Malone, and Ada Davenport Kendall, who had just recently been released from solitary confinement, and others rushed to help her. "We're here Peggy," they shouted. "They are taking me away! Help me! Save me!" Johns cried out. They ran for safety in the sewing room, but "three husky guards appeared."[12]

"Then," reported Ernestine Hara, "of all the dirty tricks," the "Negro girls" were ordered to beat them up, with the threat that they would be punished if they refused. "I'm telling you, they beat the hell out of us," she recalled. Hearing the ruckus and cries for help, other imprisoned pickets arrived. Lucy Burns rushed to use the telephone. But, Acting Superintendent Tweedale, who was filling in for Whittaker, who had been suspended during an investigation of the NWP's complaints, "just tore the phone right of the wall."[13] Finally, allowed to call, Lucy Burns alerted the NWP's lawyer, who made sure that Peggy Johns, who had been whisked away in an automobile, was taken to the District Jail hospital, not the dreaded Washington Asylum Hospital.

The use of the imprisoned "Negro girls" to attack the white women was a deliberate tactic to debase and terrorize the imprisoned pickets. For the black women, the threat of punishment if they did not comply was a reminder of their powerlessness, not that they needed reminding. Ordering the attack also was an effort to alienate the two groups of imprisoned women that were showing compassion for each other. Although they risked punishment, black women tended to Dorothy Jones Bartlett, who had played the piano in the "colored department," when she was sick. Kate Heffelfinger, an art student from Pennsylvania who was repeatedly put in solitary confinement, where she was "wild with madness or mad with wildness," wrote in a letter to Beulah Amidon: "Especially the Negroes are good to us," although "it was penalty of solitary for them if they were seen talking to us." Some of the white imprisoned pickets protested for better conditions for all prisoners, not just themselves. Ernestine Hara pointed out that black prisoners had fewer blankets and no exercise. Mary Winsor contacted Dudley Field Malone, now NWP's lawyer, to help a black girl that Whittaker had whipped.

The Wilson administration's policy of imprisoning the pickets radicalized many of the white and black inmates. Ada Davenport Kendall wrote in her newspaper column: "My bed will not be soft nor my food pleasant nor will any of the comforts of life be mine until the suffering of those people is ended." A black prostitute who was constantly harassed by the police told Doris Stevens that she hoped they would get the vote "and fix SOME THINGS for women." As for Stevens, she came out of prison "hot with indignation."[14]

The "riot," according to prison officials, was caused by the suffragists' refusal to obey the rules. Commissioner Louis Brownlow used it as an excuse to postpone the investigation that was underway into the complaint filed by the NWP. Imprisoned suffragists were warned "that unless they obeyed the rules of the institution and discontinued their acts of insubordination and riot, they will be removed from Occoquan to the city jail and placed in solitary confinement."[15] Superintendent Whittaker was reinstated.

On October 6, 1917, the day the War Session of the Sixty-Fifth Congress adjourned having failed to adopt a federal suffrage amendment, Alice Paul led a picket line of ten women to the White House gates. Her hands grasped a pole much taller than she was. Attached to the pole was a large banner inscribed with the insistent and persistent question: MR. PRESIDENT WHAT WILL YOU DO FOR WOMAN SUFFRAGE? Pauline Jacobson, a reporter for a San Francisco newspaper, observed the scene. Paul, Jacobson wrote, was "frail and slight, and very pale, her eyes and face really lit with exaltation of purpose." She watched as Paul's banner with its simple question and three other banners were "torn and mutilated." When the women were arrested, Jacobson felt "something majestic even in the way each stooped her head to enter the small door of the patrol wagon." She followed the suffrage pickets to the police station, where they were charged with "obstructing traffic." The women were released on bail for a trial on Monday.

At their trial, Alice Paul and the women introduced a new tactic. They refused to participate in the proceedings: "We do not consider ourselves subject to this Court since, as an unenfranchised class, we have nothing to do with the making of the laws which have put us in this position." A flummoxed Judge Mullowney pronounced a suspended sentence and restored the bail they had paid. Paul released a statement: "We are glad that the authorities have . . . grown wary of prosecuting women for peacefully petitioning for political liberty. . . . We will use our unexpected freedom to press our campaign with ever-increasing vigor."[16]

On October 15, four women, who were under the suspended sentence, were arrested for picketing again: Rose Winslow, Maud Jamison, Kate Heffelfinger, and Minnie Hennesy, a businesswoman from Connecticut. "We thought that by dismissing the Suffragists without sentence this Court had finally decided to recognize our legal right to petition the government," Rose Winslow told the judge.[17] Mullowney pronounced an unprecedented sentence for obstructing traffic—six months in Occoquan Workhouse. Five days later, Alice Paul led three pickets to the West Gate of the White House. Paul's banner was inscribed with Wilson's words from a poster to sell war bonds: THE TIME HAS COME TO CONQUER OR SUBMIT. FOR US THERE CAN BE BUT ONE CHOICE. WE HAVE MADE IT. They were arrested and tried on October 20.

Given the courage of the dauntless pickets, it is hard to imagine that anyone thought that even stiffer sentences would stop them. Yet, Mullowney imposed extreme sentences to be served in the District Jail in Washington, D.C.: seven months for Paul and Caroline Spencer, a physician from Colorado who had carried banners; thirty days for Gladys Greiner and Gertrude Crocker. He added a month to the six-month sentences he had already given Rose Winslow, Kate Heffelfinger, Minnie Hennesy, and Maud Jamison. That same day, Alice Paul wrote a letter to her mother, telling her that she was going to the District Jail for seven months and that Dora Lewis would be the acting chair of the NWP. "Please do not worry," she concluded. "It will merely be a delightful rest. With love, Alice."[18]

Two weeks later, Alice Paul and Rose Winslow decided "upon a hunger strike, as the ultimate form of protest" against intolerable prison conditions and the government's refusal to treat them as political prisoners.[19] On November 5, 1917, they refused to eat. Seventy-eight hours later, W. E. Gwynne Gardner, the district commissioner in charge of prisons and hospitals, issued the order to force-feed Paul and Winslow. On the afternoon of November 8, A. J. Gannon, the jail physician, poured a mixture of eggs and milk into a rubber tube that he shoved down their throats.

That evening, Mary Law, an enterprising reporter for a Washington, D. C. newspaper, went to the hospital at the District Jail and uncovered the news that Alice Paul had been transferred to the psychopathic ward, a place where she could be held indefinitely. "We moved her from the receiving ward to the psychopathic ward three or four hours ago," an "amiable" man unwittingly told her. "The psychopathic ward! Has she lost her mind?" an astonished Law asked him. "No more'n usual, I guess,' he said cheerfully."[20]

Mary Law relayed the news to the NWP headquarters. Early in the evening of November 9, Helen Paul, Alice Paul's sister, and Agnes Morey prowled the grounds of the hospital, searching for the building where Alice Paul was imprisoned. Suddenly they heard her voice from an upstairs window and called up to her. Talking though the barred window, she confirmed that she was in the psychopathic ward: "I am being systematically persecuted in an effort to break my will . . . I asked for air and they boarded up my window; I asked for privacy and they took down the iron door, leaving only the bars, while scores of men walk through the corridors." A nurse who was ordered to observe her flashed a light in her face at night, preventing her from sleeping. "This ordeal was the most terrible torture," she said, "as it prevented my sleeping for more than a few minutes at a time."

As for being force-fed, she emphatically said, "I have fought every effort to feed me."[21] On tiny scraps of paper that were smuggled out of the jail, Rose Winslow described the brutal treatment: "One feels so forsaken when one lies prone and people shove a pipe down one's stomach. . . . Don't let them tell you we take this well. Miss Paul vomits much. I do too. . . . We think of the coming feeding all day. It is horrible." In a note to Lucy Burns, Winslow wrote: "The feeding gives me a severe headache. My throat aches afterward, and I always weep and sob, to my great disgust, because I try to be less feeble."[22]

Dr. Gannon told reporters that they offered no resistance to the forced-feedings. Warden Louis Zinkhan said that they "took it like little lambs."[23] Newspapers across America covered the story, and most rejected their lies. TUBE EMPLOYED FOR FEEDING TWO SUFFRAGISTS IN HUNGER STRIKE, read the headline in an Albuquerque, New Mexico newspaper. Protests poured into the White House—telegrams, letters, phone calls. Alva Belmont denounced the "barbarous and inhuman" treatment, warning President Wilson that "this latest persecuting by the administration is causing a dangerous popular revolt."[24] Helen Paul confronted Warden Zinkhan: "How could such a horrible brutal thing be thought of. . . . She has never done anything except work for the freedom of the women of this country."[25] If her sister died, Helen Paul told Zinkhan, he would "have to answer for her murder."[26] Zinkhan replied, "If these women don't eat. It is their own fault."[27]

In analyzing Alice Paul's nonviolent and rhetorical strategies, scholars Katherine H. Adams and Michael L. Keene write: "The story became now . . . the repeated tortures enacted by a tyrannical government on its unrepresented citizens and the valor or those using nonviolent techniques to fight back."[28] Just what

Alice Paul had intended: "We'll have ammunition against the Administration," she wrote to Dora Lewis, "and the more harsh and repressive they seem the better."[29]

Meanwhile, Carrie Chapman Catt and Anna Howard Shaw rode in a parade of gaily decorated automobiles to the White House to meet with President Wilson. Three days earlier, on November 6, male voters in New York had approved a woman suffrage amendment by a majority of 102,353: 703,129 yeas, 600,776 nays—equal-suffrage state number twelve! Catt and Shaw planned to effusively thank President Wilson, who had strongly endorsed the measure, and to urgently solicit his support for the federal amendment to the Constitution.

The New York campaign had been well financed by a generous gift from Miriam Folline Leslie, who had resurrected her deceased husband's bankrupt publishing empire. When Leslie died in 1914, an astonished Carrie Chapman Catt learned that she had willed more than a million dollars for Catt to use for the cause of woman suffrage. The settlement included a suitcase full of jewels that was delivered to her office. Before sending the jewels to be sold, Catt, who had never met Miriam Leslie, spread the emeralds, rubies, diamonds, and pearls on her desk. A staff member, who was admiring the dazzling display, placed a diamond-studded tiara on Catt's head.

During the massive campaign in New York, an overtly patriotic parade of 20,000 women had marched up Fifth Avenue in New York City. A highlight was the creative display of the petition with the names of more than one million women that repudiated the canard that women did not want the vote. The many signed pages of the petition had been pasted to eight hundred large square pieces of sturdy cardboard, each one carried by two women. Marching eight abreast, their line stretched almost a mile.

More than two million women were now enfranchised in a state with forty-five electoral votes. "The victory is not New

York's alone. It's the nation's. The 65th Congress will now pass the federal amendment," declared a jubilantly optimistic Carrie Chapman Catt.[30]

The timing of the visit by Carrie Chapman Catt and Anna Howard Shaw to President Wilson may or may not have been coincidental, but it occurred the day before the NWP held a demonstration at the White House that Alice Paul had planned shortly before she was sent to jail. In a letter to NWP members, she had written: "Dear Suffragist, . . . We are working for a particularly long picket line on Saturday, November tenth. . . . Will you help? We need you urgently. All who picket must be prepared for imprisonment . . . . Very sincerely yours, Alice Paul"[31]

Forty-one women from across America came to picket. The night before the demonstration, a group of them went to the jail yard to try and talk with Alice Paul. (Previously, Doris Stevens and Catharine Flanagan had gone and made contact with her. Vida Milholland stood under her window and sang to her.) First, Katharine Morey and Catharine Flanagan checked on the whereabouts of Warden Zinkhan, whose house was next to the building where Alice Paul was confined. While the group of women silently waited, the two young women rang the doorbell.

Informed that Zinkhan was ill, they signaled that the coast was clear and the group rushed to stand under Alice Paul's boarded-up window, calling up their names, telling how much money had been raised, and shouting out that forty-one women, from as far away as Oklahoma, Utah, Louisiana, Minnesota, and California, had come to demonstrate in her behalf. Alice Paul "raised her hand . . . she was clearly silhouetted as she stood in the window," wrote a reporter for a New York newspaper.[32] The women left a bouquet of chrysanthemums with a guard who shooed them away.

The next day, five contingents of women bearing purple, white, and gold banners and flags demonstrated. Eunice Dana

Brannan led the first group of pickets, marching with military precision. Captain Carl Flather blocked their way, telling them to "move on." Brannan replied "that they intended doing no such thing." Flather nodded to six policemen to take them to the police van. As soon as they were arrested, the second group appeared, stood in silent protest, were arrested and taken away, still carrying their flags and banners. And so it went for each group. ARREST 41 PICKETS FOR SUFFRAGE AT THE WHITE HOUSE, reported the front-page headline in a New York City newspaper.[33] Carrie Chapman Catt accused the pickets of making "a psychological mistake. . . . We stand on the threshold of final victory, and the only contribution these women make to it is to confuse the public mind."[34]

Forty-one women were tried on November 12; Judge Mullowney dismissed them. Within an hour, a picket line went out again. Two men in uniform destroyed some banners. Dora Lewis was knocked down by some boys. Agnes Morey was jabbed in the face with the broken end of her pole. The pickets were arrested and released. Thirty-one women went out again the next day and were arrested. On November 14, Mullowney pronounced sentences, ranging from six days for the elderly Mary Nolan, a longtime suffragist from Florida, to seven months for the indomitable Lucy Burns. When Mullowney suggested that Mary Nolan might not survive a prison term, she declared: "Your Honor, . . . I should be proud of the honor to die in prison for the liberty of American women."[35]

Mullowney had sentenced the women to serve in the District Jail. Instead, the district commissioners ordered them sent to Occoquan Workhouse, perhaps because they were afraid to have such a large group of suffrage pickets in the jail with Alice Paul, or perhaps they had something else in mind for them.

The women ranged in age from seventy-three-year-old Mary Nolan to nineteen-year-old Matilda Young, the sister of Joy Young. Seven of the women had already served prison sentences: Lavinia Dock, Dora Lewis, Hilda Blumberg, Eunice Dana

Brannan, Peggy Baird Johns, Julia Emory, and Lucy Burns. First-timers included Emily DuBois Butterworth, a craftswoman who once won first prize for best suffrage parade hat; Dorothy Day, a journalist and free speech advocate; Elizabeth Hamilton, whose mother worried that she might go on a hunger strike; Leda Richberg-Hornsby, a pioneering aviator who once flew her biplane, "Sweetheart," in a publicity stunt for NAWSA; Paula Jakobi, a playwright and expert in prison reform; and Cora Weeks, an artist.

Two sisters, Betty Gram, who had abandoned her promising acting career, and her sister Alice, both in their early twenties, came from Portland, Oregon. Mary "Minnie" Quay came from Utah "to do her bit for the freedom of [the] enslaved millions of sisters in . . . our fair land."[36] Alice Cosu, a state NWP officer, came from New Orleans. Kate Stafford of Ardmore, Oklahoma, whose arrest was front-page news in her hometown, was a noted civic reformer and the mother of six children. Kathryn Lincoln, a sociologist from Delaware, was the author of "A Picket Song" that began with the lyrics: "I will sing to the Cause of Woman / That unites from every walk in life / That inspires to any sacrifice."[37]

(NWP officers Anna Kelton Wiley, a founding member of the NWP, and Elizabeth Thacher Kent appealed their sentences. They were later sentenced to fifteen days. Wiley refused to pay the fine and went to jail. Kent's husband, a former congressman from California and a newly appointed member of a government agency, paid his wife's fine without her permission. Elizabeth Kent, strenuously but unsuccessfully objected.)

They arrived at Occoquan Workhouse in the early evening of November 14, 1917. Whittaker was not there, and Dora Lewis, the "velvet-voiced and immovable" acting chair of the NWP, refused to give their names to Minnie Herndon, the matron in charge.[38] Intending to state their demand to be treated as political prisoners, Lewis insisted on waiting for Whittaker, who was at a meeting with the district commissioners at the White House.

Whether Whittaker, a man with "blazing little eyes," was following district commissioners' orders is unknown.[39] But, when he finally arrived, he ordered a brutal attack on the women by at least forty men. "Suddenly the door literally burst open and Whittaker, burst in like a tornado; some men followed him," reported Mary Nolan, who vividly described what became known as "The Night of Terror":

> We could see a crowd of them on the porch. They were not in uniform. Mrs. Lewis stood up. Some of us had been sitting and lying on the floor, we were so tired. She had hardly begun to speak, saying we demanded to be treated as political prisoners, when Whittaker said, "You shut up. I have men here to handle you." Then he shouted, "Seize her!" I turned and saw men spring toward her, and then someone screamed, "They have taken Mrs. Lewis." A man sprang at me and caught me by the shoulder. I remember saying, "I'll come with you; don't drag me; I have a lame foot." But I was jerked down the steps and away into the dark.[40]

"Whittaker in the center of the room directed the whole attack, inciting the guards to every brutality," reported Eunice Dana Brannan. They were "thrown, dragged, and hurled out of the office, down the steps, and across the road and field to the Administration Building, where another group of bullies was waiting, some of them burnishing billy clubs."[41] The guards hauled and dragged, the women into a "perfectly dark hall" with stone cells, "punishment cells," on each side. Pushed into a "filthy cell," Mary Nolan lost her balance and "fell against the iron bed." A guard shoved Alice Cosu in the cell, throwing two mats and two dirty blankets in after her.

> We had only lain there a few minutes, trying to get our breath, when Mrs. Lewis was literally thrown in. Her head struck the iron bed. We thought she was dead. She didn't move. We were crying over her as we lifted her to the pad on my bed, when Mr. Whittaker came to the door and told us not to dare to speak, or he would put the brace and bit in our mouths and the straitjackets on

our bodies. We were so terrified we kept very still. Mrs. Lewis was not unconscious; she was only stunned. But Mrs. Cosu was desperately ill as the night wore on. She had a bad heart and was then vomiting. . . . The guards paid no attention.

Dorothy Day, a "frail girl," was manhandled by two guards "twisting her arms above her head. Then suddenly they lifted her up and banged her down over the arm of an iron bench— twice."[42] Leda Richberg-Hornsby fought a guard to free Dorothy Day. Emily DuBois Butterworth was taken to the male section of the jail and told that "they could do what they pleased with her."[43] Just as Kathryn Lincoln, who kept a diary while imprisoned, caught a glimpse of a calming smile from Eunice Brannan: "Mr. W. suddenly appears wild with fury, his fists clenched. Abuse rains from his crooked mouth and ends with 'or I'll gag you and put you in a straight jacket [sic] for the night.'"[44]

Lucy Burns, who fiercely resisted, was overpowered and thrown in a cell. She began calling out the roll "in her clear, beautiful voice . . . to see if all were there and alive. The guards called, 'Shut up!' but she paid no more attention to them than if they had not spoken."[45] She continued calling the roll. Guards threatened her with a straitjacket and a gag. They handcuffed her to the cell door with her arms stretched above her head. Julia Emory, a small woman whom Whittaker had grabbed by the neck and thrown in the same cell, raised her arms and stood beside Lucy Burns all night long.

The next morning the battered and traumatized suffragists repeated their demand to be treated as political prisoners. Lucy Burns and Dora Lewis started a hunger strike. Other women joined them. They were tempted with toast and milk, an egg and coffee, bouillon and bread. On the third day, fried chicken and salad was delivered to them. "I think this riotous feast which has just passed our doors is the last effort of the institution to dislodge all of us who can be dislodged. They think there is nothing in our souls above fried chicken," Lucy Burns wrote in a note that circulated in secret. While fasting, Paula Jakobi later wrote, she progressed from "weakness" to "slight nausea and headache" . . . fever and dizziness . . . very dry, peeling skin and swollen lips . . . increasing weakness and aphasia." She could not remember names and "it was quite impossible to read."[46]

A detachment of Marines had been summoned to the workhouse to guard the grounds the night the women arrived. The day after the attack, Whittaker refused to admit Matthew O'Brien, the NWP's lawyer. The following day, armed with a court order, O'Brien was able to confer with Lucy Burns and Dora Lewis. Katharine Morey, who had accompanied him, hoping to see her mother Agnes, was turned away. "I am sorry to do this, but we are under military orders," a Marine told her. "What would you do if I refused to obey your orders? Would you shoot?" Katherine Morey asked. "I cannot say what I would do, but I have strict orders, Madam," he replied.[47]

Determined to free the imprisoned women, Doris Stevens, who was now in charge of the NWP headquarters, and O'Brien obtained a writ of habeas corpus, a legal procedure that would force the government to bring the women to court. But first the writ had to be served on Whittaker by a deputy marshal; the administration conspired to impede the process. Deputy marshals suddenly became hard to secure. Superintendent Whittaker disappeared. It took six failed attempts before he was finally flushed out late one night at his home and served.

Meanwhile, Lucy Burns and Dora Lewis had grown so weak that they were force-fed. Dr. Gannon and Whittaker tried to whitewash the procedure, but Burns and Lewis managed to write grisly descriptions on scraps of paper that were smuggled out and released to the press. Lucy Burns was "held down by five people at legs, arms, and head." When she refused to open her mouth, Dr. Gannon "pushed the tube up the left nostril . . . makes nose bleed freely. . . . Operation leaves one very sick. Food dumped directly into stomach feels like a ball of lead."[48] Dora Lewis described "gasping and suffocating with the agony of it."[49]

Convinced that Burns and Lewis were the ringleaders of the hunger strike, Whittaker had them moved to the District Jail. Then, he intensified his futile efforts to force the remaining women to eat: bullying, offering bribes, harassing by constantly interrogating them. The force-feedings continued in a particularly brutal way that could only be seen as an attempt to terrorize the women.

Mary Nolan, who had received a six-day sentence because of her age, emerged from Occoquan to tell of the horror. Teams of NWP organizers on speaking tours related graphic details to audiences across the country. Upon their release, the survivors of "The Night of Terror" wrote affidavits. *The Suffragists* published shocking accounts. Ada Davenport Kendall wrote to the head of the Secret Service in New York, W. G. Flynn, who protested to President Wilson that the suffragists were "being treated very harshly." Wilson replied that he did not think Kendall "is in the condition of mind to discuss the matter." Joseph Tumulty, Wilson's chief of staff, replied to protests lodged by Mary Ritter Beard and a group of New York suffragists that "the treatment of the women picketers has been grossly exaggerated."[50]

In mid-November, Wilson ordered an investigation by Commissioner Gardener, the man who had ordered the force-feeding. Not surprisingly, Gardener gave the jail a "clean bill of health."[51] Government officials pressured reporters to downplay the reports of abuses. John Arthur Seavey, a reporter for a New York City newspaper, claimed to have toured the District Jail and talked with Alice Paul and Rose Winslow. The women looked "well" and that he "found not a trace of vermin."[52] (David Lawrence, a prominent columnist with connections to Wilson, spent time in the jail talking with Alice Paul and Lucy Burns. A story emerged that he was an emissary from Wilson, although there is no evidence of that.)

Anna Howard Shaw, a friend of Dora Lewis, so thoroughly subscribed to the official line that she refused Shippen Lewis' plea to help his mother, Dora. "No sane person" could think that picketing helped the cause, Shaw wrote to her once-upon-a-time friend's son. The claims of abuse were "without foundation. . . . The government has been more mistreated than pickets."[53]

After undergoing a five-day hunger strike, Dora Lewis returned to the NWP headquarters. Barely able to walk, she was assisted by Clara Louis Rowe (left) and Abby Scott Baker (right). Gertrude Crocker, Katharine Fisher, Hazel Hunkins, and Julia Emory were also released barely able to walk. (Library of Congress)

The hearing before Federal Judge Edmund Waddill, Jr. on the writ of habeas corpus took place on November 23. Superintendent Whittaker, Warden Zinkhan, and Matron Minnie Herndon appeared with the "haggard, red-eyed, sick" imprisoned suffragists. Doris Stevens observed, "Some were able to walk to their seats; others were so weak that they had to be stretched out on the wooden benches with coats propped under their heads for pillows. Still others bore the marks of the attack of the 'night of terror.' Many of the prisoners lay back . . . hardly conscious of the proceedings."[54]

Dudley Field Malone and Matthew O'Brien presented the argument that it was illegal for prisoners sentenced for offense in the District of Columbia to be imprisoned in the state of Virginia. Eunice Dana Brannan's husband, John Winters Brannan, a prominent physician, testified in behalf of the allegation of cruelty: "It is evident that the suffrage prisoners were deliberately terrorized . . . and were treated with great brutality by the male guards who handled them and knocked them about with the fury of thugs under the immediate direction of Mr. Whittaker himself."[55]

Ruling that the confinement in Virginia was illegal, Judge Waddill ordered the prisoners to be remanded to the custody of the District Jail in Washington, D.C. After the imprisoned suffragists were transferred there by automobile, three things were clear: the District Jail could not force-feed that many hunger-striking women, the administration could not afford to let the women die, and the suffrage prisoners could not be broken. On November 27 and 28, Judge Mullowney ordered the release of all the imprisoned suffragists.

MILITANTS WIN OUT FOR HUNGER STRIKE, read the front-page headline in a Rock Island, Illinois newspaper. No official explanation was given for their release: "Jail official could not be found," wrote one reporter, "to explain the release of the women."[56] A "very pale and thin" Alice Paul, who had served only five weeks of her seven-month sentence, said: "We are put out of jail as we were put into jail, at the whim of the government. They tried to terrorize and suppress us. They could not, and so freed us."[57]

A week later, seventy former suffrage prisoners, clad in white, carrying purple, white, and gold banners, marched down the aisle of the crowded Belasco Theater and onto the stage. One after another they stepped up to Elizabeth Kent to receive a small silver "Jail Door Pin," a small silver jail door with a chain attached to a heart-shaped lock, modeled by Alice Paul on the British suffragette Holloway Broach that she had been awarded. Alice Paul was greeted with a "storm of applause and cheers," led by

Dudley Field Malone and Maud Younger. Elizabeth Kent embraced and kissed Mary Nolan. Katharine Houghton Hepburn appealed for funds and raised pledges of $86,000. An eight-year-old girl in a yellow dress donated $5 from "the girls of the United States who are going to vote someday."[58]

On December 12, 1917, a newspaper headline in Washington D. C., warned: SUFFRAGIST ARMY INVADES CAPITOL.[59] This time, however, the "suffragist army" was composed of NAWSA delegates, who were attending the Forty-Ninth Annual Convention—five hundred of them. Divided into forty-four groups, the swarm of suffragists flexed their muscles, patrolling the marble corridor of Congress and soliciting votes for the federal woman suffrage amendment. They had come from across America, many traveling through horrendous weather: "below zero, snowstorms and washouts . . . delegates from the South were in two train wrecks." In Washington, D.C., despite the challenges of wartime conditions—accommodations crowded with soldiers and their families, scarce food and inflated prices—the "tried and loyal suffragists, being accustomed to hardships and self-sacrifice," carried on.[60]

Clearly out of patience, the delegates adopted a resolution, warning elected officials that if the Sixty-Fifth Congress failed to pass the federal woman suffrage amendment, NAWSA would end its nonpartisan position and vigorously work to elect pro-suffrage politicians and defeat opponents.

The year 1917 was a year of world war and revolution abroad and the exhilarating victory in New York, juxtaposed against the brutal treatment of suffrage pickets. In December, the liquor and brewery industries' heavily financed opposition to woman suffrage became pointless when Congress passed the Eighteenth Amendment, establishing the prohibition of "intoxicating liquors," and referred it for ratification by the states. Passage of that federal amendment exposed the hypocrisy of the states' rights argument against a federal woman suffrage amendment.

In December, in Great Britain, the House of Commons took the penultimate step in the fight for the vote, approving the Representation of the People Act that did away with property qualification for men and enfranchised women over the age of thirty who were university graduates or who occupied or were married to occupiers of a certain amount of property. "Even those of us who had striven to the last for the full solution," wrote Sylvia Pankhurst, "knew now that the breach in the sex barrier had been made."[61]

In America suffragists steadfastly soldiered on.

PART VI

Chapter 17

Fiery Tactic: January–October 1918

I think there's a possibility. —Maud Wood Park

On the afternoon of January 9, 1918, in the House of Representatives Office Building, Maud Wood Park ran into Ruth Hanna McCormick. "I can't see any possibility of our getting through, can you?" she asked Park. "I think there's a possibility," Park replied.

Sworn to secrecy, Park could not yet tell McCormick that, "at that very moment," the chairman of the House Woman Suffrage Committee, John E. Raker from California, had taken a small delegation of Democratic representatives to meet with President Wilson. The next day, January 10, the House was scheduled to vote on the federal woman suffrage amendment, and Raker hoped that Wilson would publicly urge Democrats to vote for it. Approval of the measure required a two-thirds majority; the Republicans promised overwhelming support. But the powerful contingent of Southern Democrats was strongly opposed. Too many other Democrats were still "doubtfuls."

"We scarcely ate and were too tired to sleep because of the innumerable last things to be attended to," Maud Wood Park reported. They had fired off telegrams and letters to suffrage workers in every congressional district where there was even "the faintest chance" of converting an uncommitted, a doubtful, or even an anti-suffragist legislator.

A "doubtful" who was traveling by train through Florida was joined on board by NAWSA's state president.[1] Suffragists greeted him at every stop along the way. A worker with a brother who was friends with an "uncommitted" legislator prevailed on her brother, whose wife was pregnant, to talk to him. The legislator finally agreed that if the baby was a girl, he would vote "yes," if a boy, "no."[2] (It was a girl, and the legislator kept his word.)

Maud Younger, the NWP's chief lobbyist, knew that they lacked sixty votes: "We worked day and night," she later wrote. Our friends in Congress, brightly hopeful, told us we had votes to spare, but we knew the truth."[3]

On January 9, while Raker and his delegation met with President Wilson, reporters stood in the snow outside the White House. It seemed like a long wait before Raker appeared to report that Wilson had publicly declared his support for the federal woman suffrage amendment, and that he "will stay home from his game of golf tomorrow morning to see any Congressman who wishes to consult him about it."[4] Wilson's decision was big news. An Albuquerque, New Mexico newspaper published two headlines— a banner stretched across the top of the front page: VOTES-FOR-WOMEN AMENDEMENT IS EXPECTED TO WIN IN LOWER HOUSE TODAY, and a front-page article: PRESIDENT THROWS FULL WEIGHT OF INFLUENCE IN FAVOR OF AMENDMENT FOR NATION-WIDE SUFFRAGE.[5] Park was elated that Wilson had finally "come openly into the fight," but she had begun to doubt "the practical value of" his support. That night she went to bed "tired and depressed." By her careful count, they had "barely enough votes . . . if nothing slipped, and I felt as if some calamity would be sure to intervene."[6]

On January 10, the calamities that Maud Wood Park had feared, happened. Clifford Ireland from Illinois was delayed by a train wreck. Henry Barnhart from Indiana had been taken to the hospital. James Robert Mann from Illinois remained hospitalized after six months. The ardent suffragist wife of New York Representative Frederick Hicks had died during the night. Thetus Sims from Tennessee had slipped on ice and broken his shoulder.

The good news was that Sims was there, although in agonizing pain having refused to have his shoulder treated for fear that the procedure would keep him away from voting. Hicks arrived, having been sent to vote by his dying wife. Suddenly, the door opened and a "pale and trembling" Barnhart was brought in on a stretcher that was set down by the Speaker's desk.[7] Mann appeared, as "a wave of applause and cheers swept over the floor."[8]

At 11 a.m., the daily opening ritual began: the Sergeant-at-Arms walked down the aisle holding the ceremonial ebony and silver mace, topped by a silver eagle. Behind him walked Speaker James Beauchamp "Champ" Clark from Missouri, wearing a tan frock coat with a white flower in the buttonhole. There was a prayer, routine business, and then a long day of speeches, and sometimes bitter debate. "Beset by nauseating fear," Maud Wood Park listened.[9]

William Gordon from Ohio accused the "women militants" of "coaxing, teasing, and nagging the President . . . to club Congress into adopting this joint resolution." James H. Mays from Utah countered that, instead of decrying the pickets "we should be ashamed of the unreasonable stubbornness on the part of the men who refused them the justice they have so patiently asked."[10] The amendment would enfranchise "colored women" and undercut "Southern States . . . struggling to maintain law and order and white supremacy," warned John A. Moon from Tennessee. Park "choked with anger" at Moon's "dastardly appeal . . . to the prejudices of Southern members."[11]

She was thrilled when Jeannette Rankin from Montana rose to speak: "No woman among us . . . failed to rejoice that at last a woman's voice could be raised in the Congress in behalf of her own sex." Rankin challenged her colleagues: "How shall we explain the meaning of democracy if the same Congress that voted for war to make the world safe for democracy refuses to give this small measure of democracy to the women of our country?"[12]

The clerk called the roll. From the gallery, suffragists anxiously watched as their friends and opponents "were scurrying around," hustling for votes. Sims, "his arm in a sling, was going to one after another on the Democratic side," trying to convince "one or two of his Southern friends to our side or to prevail upon them to not vote at all."[13]

After two roll calls, the vote was still in doubt. It was hard for the suffragists to hear what was happening in the chaotic scene below them. Agitated representatives crowded around the speaker's desk, with suffrage supporters "in the thick of the confusion." After the third roll call, James Campbell Cantrill from Kentucky shouted up to Maud Wood Park: "It's close, but we've won, I think."[14] Then, an opponent from Virginia demanded a recapitulation. Suffragists held their breath. Finally, the clerk announced the vote as 274 yeas, and 136 nays, the necessary two thirds, with just one vote to spare!

Pandemonium erupted in the gallery and on the floor of the House—women and men shouting, cheering, shaking hands, hugging, crying for joy. Outside the gallery door, a woman started singing the hymn "Praise God from Whom All Blessings Flow" and a multitude of voices joined her. That night in her diary Anna Howard Shaw wrote: "A great day!" She wished that Susan B. Anthony "had been there and yet she must know. Heaven could not be heaven if such a thing could happen and she not know it."[15]

January 10, 1918, coincidentally, was the same day that the House of Lords passed the Representation of the People Act, thus enfranchising 8.4 million women over the age of thirty in the United Kingdom. Carrie Chapman Catt and Millicent Garrett Fawcett, head of the non-militant NUUWSS, exchanged letters of congratulation, proposing that January 10 should be a national holiday.

Alice Paul's insistence that picketing was legal was vindicated on March 4, 1918. The United States Federal Appeals Court ruled that the arrests and detainment of the pickets were unconstitutional. ARREST OF PICKETS AT THE WHITE HOUSE ILLEGAL, SAYS COURT, stated the headline in a New York City newspaper.[16]

Three weeks after the ruling, striking cigar workers were not arrested for picketing in Washington, D.C. An article in a Duluth, Minnesota newspaper touted "the value of the all-summer struggle of the suffrage pickets to keep their banners flying in front of the residence of the president. Nearly 200 of them went to jail, many were beaten and manhandled, many went on hunger strike until their health was permanently injured. But they stayed in the fight."[17]

March 4 was also the day Anne Martin announced her candidacy for senator from Nevada. The first woman to run for the United States Senate, her announcement was reported in newspapers throughout the country. "Persons who have never seen a feminist and have illusions about them would be shocked by Anne Martin," wrote a reporter. "She is not a tall, gaunt, hard, steely-eyed, pioneering woman, with a talking delivery comparable to a steel trap making a ration of ten-penny nails." Not at all, she is rather a "gentlewoman . . . with thoughtful blue eyes, dark brown hair, a low, clear voice that deliberates as it talks."[18] When she was asked—"Why a woman should be in the Senate?"—Martin had replied: "Because they are people and they must take an intelligent and active part in the government under which they live."[19]

The Senate vote was the next battle in the fight for the vote. "It was only the clever vision, the intense conviction, and the unhesitating persistence of Miss Paul and the Woman's Party that kept the amendment to the front and carried it to the point where it now stands, simply awaiting final action by the Senate," wrote a reporter for a Bridgeport, Connecticut newspaper.[20]

Suffrage lobbyists carefully assessed the likely pro-amendment votes. They were at least ten short of the sixty-four votes needed for a three-fourth majority. "Put on your armor, mobilize your army," Carrie Chapman Catt exhorted state presidents in a letter she wrote the day after the House victory. "We won by a single vote in the House; we may be beaten by a single vote in the Senate. Leave no stone unturned."[21]

Suffragists across America did just that, signing petitions, besieging their senators with telegrams and letters, activating influential people to exert pressure, and writing articles and letters to editors to create the perception of a strong demand for woman suffrage. Suffragist lobbyists spent endless hours walking through the long marble corridors, calling on senators, developing relationships, cajoling, persuading. Pro-amendment senators were enlisted to convert opponents and doubtfuls, although sometimes that approach backfired. When Maud Younger asked Senator Irvine L. Lenroot, a supporter from Wisconsin, to talk to Senator William Borah from Idaho, Lenroot "viciously" said: "Nagging! If you women would only stop nagging!" Making "a savage face" at her, he "hurried down the hall."

Stunned, Maud Younger "stood still . . . I wondered if he thought we liked 'nagging'; if we liked going to the Capitol day after day, tramping on marble floors, waiting in ante-rooms—sometimes rebuffed, sometimes snarled at. I wondered if he thought we could do it for anything but a great cause—for the thousands of women toiling in the factories, for the thousands struggling under burdens of home. And then I bit my lips to keep back the tears."[22]

Suffrage lobbyists slowly shifted one senator after another from a "no" or "doubtful" to a "yes" position. Maud Younger got Porter McCumber from North Dakota to acknowledge that he would "feel obliged to" vote "yes," if the legislature of his state asked him to vote for it.[23] Younger relayed that information to Beulah Amidon who sent a slew of telegrams to influential people, including her father, a prominent judge in North Dakota. Straightaway, the legislature passed a resolution calling on McCumber to vote "yes." Alice Henkle from Utah, who was the captain of the pickets, set off a successful bombardment of pro-suffrage resolutions from a host of civic and religious organizations that convinced Senator William H. King that his constituents wanted him to vote for it.

When it appeared that there were enough "yes" votes, Senator Andrieus Aristieus Jones from New Mexico, chairman of the Woman Suffrage Committee, announced he would bring up the amendment for a vote on May 10. Maud Younger described that day: "Victory seems in our hands. . . . The galleries were filled. The senators came in all dressed up for the occasion—here a gay waistcoat or a bright tie, a flower in a button-hole, yonder an elegant frock coat over gray trousers."[24]

But then, the opposition took over the proceeding. Sensing defeat, Senator Jones withdrew the motion to vote on the woman suffrage amendment. In the gallery, Maud Wood Park "felt humiliated through and through."[25] Carrie Chapman Catt was furious. "The whole dastardly business of delay, and backing and filling, and hauling and yanking, has rasped CCC sometimes beyond endurance," wrote Clara Hyde, Catt's personal secretary.[26]

The NWP had relocated their headquarters to a magnificent mansion on Lafayette Park. It was just a short walk across Pennsylvania Avenue to the White House. A large statue of Marquis de Lafayette, a Frenchman who fought in the American Revolutionary War, stood in the southeast corner of the park. On a Tuesday afternoon, August 6, 1918, the day that Inez Milholland would have turned thirty-two years old, Hazel Hunkins led a line of almost one hundred women wearing white gowns and bearing purple, white, and gold banners and flags to the statue of Lafayette. Mary Gertrude Fendall, NWP's treasurer who excelled at recruiting women for picket duty, stood on a platform that had been set up at the base of the statue. Her banner bore Inez Milholland's last words: HOW LONG MUST WOMEN WAIT FOR LIBERTY?

Standing beside her were two women holding a large banner stretched between two poles that read in part: WE CONDEMN THE PRESIDENT AND HIS PARTY FOR ALLOWING THE OBSTRUCTION OF SUFFRAGE IN THE SENATE. A phalanx of banner bearers stood on both sides of the statue. The dignified, gray-haired Dora Lewis stepped forward and declared, "We are here because when our country is at war for liberty and democracy . . .," at which point she was roughly arrested and taken away.[27] Hazel Hunkins took her place and was arrested, and again and again and again one woman replaced another and was arrested, until forty-eight women were crammed into patrol wagon after patrol wagon, including Alice Paul, who was standing in the street. PICKET SUFFS ARRESTED BY PARK POLICE, read the front-page headline in a Washington, D.C., newspaper. (Beside it was the headline: CITY'S HOTTEST RECORDED DAY; the temperature had reached 106 degrees![28])

Lucy Branham, flanked by suffragists holding an American flag and banners, spoke during a demonstration in 1918 at the statue of Lafayette. (Library of Congress)

NAWSA officers were outraged. Mollie Garrett Hay, characterized the pickets as "fanatics," and their method "foolish and futile" that "again has brought the cause of woman suffrage into disrepute." Hay declared that NAWSA considered President Wilson a "friend and champion." She asserted that "quiet, patient methods of work" would result in victory.[29] (Hay and Catt had lived together since Catt's second husband died.)

The women were released, and their trial was postponed until the government could figure out how to charge them. Ten days later, they were charged, tried, and convicted for "holding a meeting in public grounds," and for "climbing on a statue."[30] Refusing to participate in the court proceedings, the silent, stolid women read, knitted, and napped until the judge pronounced the sentence: ten days for holding a meeting or fifteen days for climbing on a statue. WOMAN SUFFRAGISTS ARE SENT TO JAIL, read a newspaper headline in Phoenix, Arizona.[31]

Instead of being sent to the District Jail, twenty-four women, including Dora Lewis, Lavinia Dock, Mary Winsor, Lucy Burns, Hazel Hunkins, and Edith Ainge were incarcerated in an old jail, a rat-and-vermin infested hellhole that had been declared unfit for human habitation in 1909. Placed in underground cells with little light and no fresh air, just the sickening odor of sewer gas, caused the women, in quick order, to become violently ill.

To escape the vile smell in their small cells, they took their thin straw mats and stretched out in the corridor, defying the guards who ordered them to return to their cells. Lying on their mats, they commenced a hunger strike. The NWP publicized the horrendous conditions. Telegrams and letters urged senators and representatives to intervene on behalf of the imprisoned women. Maud Younger took Senator Jones to see for himself. Five full days later, the women were released "trembling with weakness, chills, and fever, scarcely able even to walk to the ambulance or motor car."[32]

In September 1918, President Wilson engaged in subterfuge. The NWP had announced a September 16 protest meeting to be held at 4 p.m. at the base of the Lafayette Monument. On that day, Wilson met with a delegation of Southern and Western women, and assured them that he "heartily" supported the amendment and would fully exercise his power "to urge the passage of the amendment by an early vote." However, two pro-suffrage senators told the NWP that Wilson knew that the amendment would not be considered before Congress adjourned in a few days. For the NWP, Wilson's deviousness "was intolerable." They changed their "planned demonstration to a more drastic form of protest."[33]

Evelyn Wotherspoon Wainwright, a founding member of the NWP and the socially prominent wife of Rear Admiral Richard Wainwright, set the stage with a dramatic invocation before an enthusiastic gathering of spectators and suffragists. Standing in front of the Lafayette Monument, with a line of pickets holding purple, white, and gold banners behind her, Wainwright called out—"Lafayette, we are here! We, the women of the United States, denied the liberty which you helped to gain." Lucy Branham moved in front of the crowd. With her, holding a flaming torch, was Julia Emory. "We want action, not words," Branham boldly stated. Receiving the torch from Emory, she burned a paper inscribed with the words Wilson had spoken to the delegates. "The torch which I hold symbolizes the burning indignation of women. . . . We, therefore, take these empty words, spoken by President Wilson this afternoon, and consign them to the flames."[34] Spectators cheered and donated money. The police escorted the suffragists back to their headquarters.

The NWP's nonviolent, militant, theatrical tactic appeared to have worked. The next day, Senator Andrieus Jones stood up on the floor of the Senate and announced that he would bring up the woman suffrage amendment for a vote on September 26, and not withdraw it until the vote took place. Suffragists from across America rushed to Washington. "Suffrage House is crowded from roof to cellar," wrote Rose Young, the editor-in-chief of *The*

Woman Citizen, NAWSA's official journal, formerly the *Woman's Journal.*[35]

On September 26, suffragists crammed together in the Senate gallery to watch the proceeding. "Discussion began. Discussion went on," recalled Maud Younger. "For five whole days it lasted, with waves of hope and waves of dismay, and always an undercurrent of uncertainty. Thursday, Friday, Saturday, the speeches went on."[36] Some senators ranted against "negroes" (Vardaman from Mississippi), immigrants (Frelinghuysen from New Jersey), and suffrage lobbyists (Reed from Missouri). Others extolled state's rights (Underwood from Alabama).

McCumber from North Dakota and King from Utah groused that they had to vote "yes" because they represented an equal-suffrage state. In contrast, Ransdell from Louisiana declared that he would vote "yes," despite his state legislature's recent resolution opposing the measure. Williams from Mississippi proposed an amendment enfranchising only white women. McKellar from Tennessee "made a new point, that it was unfair to have some women voting in some states and not in others." Furious that the amendment was two votes short, Pittman from Nevada "worked himself into a tense fury that made his eyes blaze and his voice sting like a whiplash."[37]

On the fifth day, Monday, September 30, at the personal behest of Carrie Chapman Catt, President Wilson made a dramatic decision to personally appeal to the Senate. He appeared at 1 p.m., along with Vice President Marshall and many cabinet members. Passage of the federal woman suffrage amendment, Wilson told the senators, was "vitally essential to the prosecution of the great war of humanity in which we are engaged." He echoed what generations of suffragists had repeatedly proclaimed: "Democracy means that women shall play their part in affairs alongside men and upon an equal footing with them."[38]

In the gallery, suffragists were thrilled. For Doris Stevens, it was "a truly beautiful and memorable appeal."[39] But, on the floor, the opposition immediately went to work to undo President

Wilson's plea. Senator Oscar Underwood from Alabama, whom Maud Wood Park characterized as "easily the ablest of our opponents," spoke at length "to refute the war argument and to rattle once more the dry bones of the states' rights and negro objections." Smith from South Carolina, Lodge from Massachusetts, and Martin from Virginia continued the onslaught. Kendrick from Wyoming finally spoke for the amendment. But he was followed by an opponent, Bankhead from Alabama. Maud Wood Park later wrote, "I felt as if I were at a funeral service, waiting for the arrival of the officiating clergyman."[40]

The next day, October 1, the woman suffrage amendment was defeated, two votes short of the required three fourths. Senator Jones immediately changed his vote to a "no," a parliamentary tactic in order to move to reconsider the measure. "Stunned, as though unable to grasp it, hundreds of women sat there," recalled Maud Younger. "Then slowly the defeat reached their consciousness, and they began slowly to put on their hats, to gather up their wraps, and to file out of the galleries, some with a dull sense of injustice, some with burning resentment.[41] Alice Paul hastened back to headquarters to plan their next campaign. Maud Wood Park, Helen Gardener, and Mollie Garrett Hay, "with heads as high as we could get them," went to thank senators who voted for the amendment. The next day Park persuaded Carrie Chapman Catt, who was profoundly "disappointed and upset," to go talk to supportive senators. "We've got to act like merry sunshine . . . for we can't afford to have anybody know that we feel beaten," Park told her.[42] Catt went with Park, but she vowed to never again witness a vote, even a guaranteed victory.

President Wilson had "done something, . . . but there was a great deal more that he could have done," concluded Maud Younger.[43]

Chapter 18

Assault on Congress:
October - December 1918

We burn his words on liberty today. —Elizabeth Selden Rogers

A global influenza pandemic, dubbed the Spanish flu, was first confirmed in the United States at a military base, Fort Riley in Kansas. A mess cook reported ill on March 11, 1918. Within days, more than 533 soldiers were in the hospital. During the first phase, most people recovered. But then, the influenza virus mutated to a virulent form and deadly epidemics swept across America. In October, almost 200,000 people died.

To combat the disease, many public officials shut public buildings, banned gatherings and meetings, and distributed gauze masks. The number of people on a streetcar was limited. Some movie theaters sold half the number of tickets to reduce crowding. People were advised to keep their distance from each other. Spitting in public was illegal. Bodies piled up in the street. Coffins were in short supply. In the eighteen months the virus ravaged America, an estimated 675,000 people died. Under these dire conditions, suffragists conducted campaigns for a woman suffrage amendment referendum in five states: Louisiana and Texas for the first time, Oklahoma for the second time, Michigan for the fourth time, and South Dakota for the seventh time.

In Louisiana, the 1918 campaign was openly fractious. Kate Gordon, a key suffragist who openly uttered racist invectives, was an ardent "states' rights suffragist."[1] She insisted that Southern states keep control of voter qualifications, thus maintaining the discriminatory state laws aimed at excluding black voters.

Wealthy and socially prominent, Kate Gordon lived with her sisters: Jean, an activist to end child labor, and Fannie who ran the household. After a stint as NAWSA's corresponding secretary, Gordon had resigned when it became clear that NAWSA was working for a federal woman suffrage amendment. "She believed," writes historian Elna C. Green, "that federal action would lead automatically to black suffrage, an unacceptable outcome for those, like her, determined to protect the South's hard-won white supremacy."[2]

In 1913, Gordon helped organize and became president of the Southern States Woman Suffrage Conference (SSWSC). "State sovereignty and white supremacy were inextricably connected," she declared. At the same time, two moderate Louisiana suffragists, Sake Meehan and Lydia Holmes who rejected Kate Gordon's racist states' rights suffragism, and her "imperious ways and contentious personality," formed the Woman Suffrage Party (WSP) of Louisiana that was admitted as a NAWSA affiliate.[3] "If Miss Kate could be silenced or eliminated some way, the cause of suffrage in La. would certainly benefit. . . . In plain words—she is a d--- nuisance," Sake Meehan wrote in a letter to a coworker.[4]

Unable to reconcile, the SSWSC and the WSP launched independent campaigns to secure passage of a woman suffrage amendment to the state constitution. Severely hampered as the influenza epidemic spread through New Orleans, and by constant rain that made roads impassable throughout the state, their efforts failed. Male voters defeated the suffrage amendment by a majority of 3,504: 19,573 yeas, 23,077 nays. Most of the negative votes were cast in New Orleans, where the mayor was an anti-suffrage political boss.

In Michigan, after losing three referenda (1874, 1912, 1913), women had won the right of presidential suffrage in 1917. Many women had shifted their attention to war work. The belief was widespread that men would reward their support of the war and just give them equal suffrage. Carrie Chapman Catt strongly disagreed. She requested a meeting with the Michigan Equal Suffrage Association where she aroused the delegates to adopt the plan that NAWSA had prepared for state campaigns, including a budget of $100,000 and a massive petition campaign.

More than 200,000 women signed the petition. Names were published day by day in a newspaper in Grand Rapids. Pages and pages of the petitions were hung on the walls of the women's section at the state fair. Organizations throughout the state supported the campaign with money and workers. NAWSA's tireless head of campaigns and surveys, Nettie Rogers Shuler, who had moved from Buffalo to New York City to work for NAWSA after the death of her husband, returned three times to train local suffragists and conduct speaking tours. Massive amounts of suffrage material were distributed—500,000 pieces of literature and 50,000 buttons in Detroit. Thousands of posters were put in store windows and 174 large billboard posters were displayed. Streetcars and newspapers carried paid advertisements, exhorting men to vote "yes." On November 6, 1918, male voters in Michigan finally approved a woman suffrage amendment by a majority of 34,506: 229,790 yeas, 195,284 nays—equal-suffrage state number thirteen!

In Oklahoma, the governor opposed woman suffrage and the Oklahoma Woman's Suffrage Association, led by Adelia C. Stephens, was neither well organized nor well funded. NAWSA strongly advised against conducting a campaign. Nevertheless, the state organization struggled onward and sent urgent pleas to NAWSA for help. In April, NAWSA agreed to direct the campaign and provide organizers, money, and literature.

Suffragists' efforts were greatly complicated when the second, more lethal, wave of the Spanish flu hit Oklahoma. The first case quickly spread from twenty cases to more than three hundred in the small town of Wilburton to more than a thousand in Oklahoma City. The state commission of health closed all public buildings. All kinds of remedies were tried, including lying in a tub full of chopped onions. The 1918 flu peaked in Oklahoma in October and November, killing more than 7,000 Oklahomans.

With the limits on public gatherings, suffragists ramped up their efforts to get publicity and circulate literature. A branch of the NWP led by Kate Stafford, a picket who was jailed and manhandled during the "Night of Terror," pasted posters and broadsides on farmers' wagons, barns, fences, telephone poles, and the sides of buildings. Almost 60,000 women signed a pro-amendment petition. On September 1, Nettie Rogers Shuler and her daughter, Marjorie, NAWSA's publicity director, went to Oklahoma and took over the campaign. About the same time, Sarah C. White of NAOWS, arrived to assist the Oklahoma Anti-Suffrage Association. Espousing the sanctity of separate spheres for men and women and distributing anti-suffrage literature, the anti-suffragists held numerous tea parties and luncheons.

The campaign was beset with obstructions. Claiming that the secretary of state had not sent the text of the amendment soon enough, the election board refused to print it on the ballot. Ordered by a judge to print the text, the election board created a separate suffrage ballot. In October, suffragists discovered that soldiers in several military camps who had already voted had not received the suffrage ballot. That mattered because if a voter did not mark the amendment it was counted as a "silent vote" against the measure.

On Election Day, women poll watchers stood outside and inside the polling places. The goal was high: The amendment had to win by a majority of the total number of votes cast in the general election. Male voters approved State Question 97, striking out the word "male" in the voter qualifications section of the constitution, by a majority of 25,428: 106,909 yeas, 81,481 nays. Another victory, or so it seemed until opponents raised questions that prevented the election board from certifying the results. Finally, on December 3, the board declared that the woman suffrage amendment had carried—equal-suffrage state number fourteen! Oklahoma became the first Southern state to grant equal suffrage rights.

In Texas, the fight for the vote had a slow start-and-stop trajectory. Over the years, key women had advocated for woman suffrage: the Finnigan sisters, Annette, Elizabeth and Katharine, who helped found the state suffrage association; Helen M. Stoddard, president of the WCTU; Mary Eleanor Brackenridge, a prominent clubwoman and president of the Equal Franchise Society; and Minnie Fisher Cunningham, president of the Texas Equal Suffrage Association. In 1917, suffragists had vigorously supported the successful impeachment campaign against the corrupt Governor James E. Ferguson, an irredeemable foe of woman suffrage. Ferguson's successor, William P. Hobby, the beneficiary of the women's efforts to oust Ferguson, advocated for voting rights for women at all primary elections, including for two senators and eighteen representatives to Congress. Since Texas was virtually a one-party state, winning a primary nomination was the equivalent to winning an election.

On March 26, the primary suffrage bill passed the legislature by a majority of 63: 101 yeas, 38 nays. Representative C. B. Metcalfe purchased a fancy fountain pen for the bill-signing ceremony. After Governor Hobby signed the bill, he gave the pen to Minnie Fisher Cunningham.

In South Dakota, for the seventh time, male voters considered a woman suffrage referendum that included a provision adding citizenship and a five-year residence requirement to voter qualifications. Suffragists had long attributed their defeats to lax voting requirements for newly arrived male immigrants, whom opponents would bribe with money and/or alcohol to vote against woman suffrage. In April, Nettie Rogers Shuler set up suffrage schools. Experienced instructors such as Florence Cotnam of Arkansas taught novice suffrage workers how to organize, lobby, raise money, and campaign.

NAWSA sent two field workers, speakers, and money. Carrie Chapman Catt had planned to campaign, but much to the disappointment of state suffragists she came down with the flu. (In New York, where women had won the vote in 1917, Catt, despite her illness, insisted on going with Mollie Garrett Hay on Election Day to vote for the first time. They were met by a horde of photographers and reporters.)

Campaign workers, an "efficient, faithful little band, conducted "persistent, intensive, quiet work."[5] On Election Day, male voters finally—after six defeats—approved the woman suffrage amendment referendum by a majority of 20,384: 49,318 yeas, 28,934 nays. South Dakota was equal-suffrage state number fifteen!

Both women who ran for the United States Senate lost: Anne Martin in Nevada and Jeannette Rankin in Montana, where she had run for a Senate seat after the district she represented in the House of Representatives was reapportioned to her disadvantage. (In Nevada, a woman would not be elected to Congress until Catherine Cortez Masto was elected to the Senate in 2017. In Montana, Jeannette Rankin served another term in the House of Representatives from 1941–1943, but since then no woman has represented Montana in Congress.)

Throughout the fall campaign, Alice Paul orchestrated a picket assault on Congress. Teams of women from California, Texas, Minnesota, and elsewhere repeatedly picketed the capitol and the Senate Office Building. Anti-suffrage senators were targeted. A banner was inscribed: WE PROTEST AGAINST THE 34 WILFUL SENATORS WHO HAVE DELAYED THE POLITICAL FREEDOM OF AMERICAN WOMEN. The NWP's tactic seriously aggravated Senator Reed Smoot, a pro-suffrage Republican from Utah. Suffragists standing with banners were not going to change senators' minds, he told Maud Wood Park. "Who are they, anyway?" he said, "fairly chocked with indignation. . . . . Little young things, just out of school or old ladies who ought to be at home enjoying their grandchildren." Despite his ire, Park suspected that Smoot cooperated with the

NWP "a good many times because he regarded them as opponents of President Wilson, whom he detested."[6]

Pickets who demonstrated in front of the Capitol and the Senate Office Building were handled roughly by policemen. (Library of Congress)

Capitol police aggressively stopped the women, blocking them from marching up the capitol steps, manhandling them, confining them in the detention room in the basement, and confiscating their banners. On October 28, a line of twenty-one women, led by Alice Paul and including Lucy Burns, Edith Ainge, Annie Arniel, and Julia Emory, was halfway up the capitol steps when the police attacked. Annie Arniel was knocked down. A large photograph of a policeman grabbing a picket and other policemen seizing banners appeared in a North Platte, Nebraska newspaper with the headline, SUFFFRAGETTE INVASION OF THE SENATE FOILED.[7]

A week later, a group of women with simple black bands, the sign of mourning, around their arms solemnly walked up and down in front of the Senate Office Building, decrying "the death of justice" in America.

World War I ended on November 11, 1918. Ten days later, the Senate declared a recess. Protesting the Senate's inexcusable inaction on the federal woman suffrage amendment, Alice Paul led eleven pickets to the capitol, bearing banners boldly and confrontationally inscribed:

AMERICAN WOMEN PROTEST AGAINST THE SENATE'S RECESSING WITHOUT PASSING THE SUFFRAGE AMENDMENT.

AMERICA . . . . PREACHES DEMOCRACY FOR ALL EUROPE WHILE AMERICANS ARE ARRESTED FOR ASKING FOR IT AT THE CAPITOL.

Outnumbering the women two to one, a horde of police assaulted them. Clara Wold, a journalist from Oregon, who was "knocked down twice on the Senate steps; was shaken like a rat." Alice Paul was "dragged and pushed."[8] Elizabeth Green Kalb, a young graduate student from Texas who had won the Carnegie Peace Prize in a statewide oratory contest, declared that women in Texas would "join the protest of and for American womanhood" once they knew that women were "fallen upon by a set of ruffianly police, mauled about, dragged and struck in the most outrageous manner." Such treatment, she wrote, "makes one sick with shame for our boasted democracy."[9]

On December 4, 1918, thousands of people stood along the waterfront, cheering the departure of President Wilson on board the steamship *George Washington*, bound for the Paris Peace Conference that would establish the terms of peace with Germany. Five destroyers escorted the ship out of the New York Harbor, with a dozen more waiting to escort the ship another 100 miles or so beyond the last point of land. Two army airplanes put on a show of aerial acrobatics that thrilled the spectators, and undoubtedly the president and his entourage. President Wilson waved and doffed his hat as his ship passed a transport ship loaded with returning soldiers waiting to dock. The presidential flag was hoisted and the five destroyers fired off a thunderous twenty-one-gun salute. It was the first trip to Europe by a sitting American president.

286

Two days before President Wilson departed, the Sixty-Fifth Congress had reconvened for its final session. For the first time in one of his regular addresses to a joint session, President Wilson had requested that Congress make women "the equals of men in political rights."[10] But for the NWP, Wilson's plea was too late, just superficial, hollow words, not backed by substantive actions, as he "sailed serenely off to France" in order "to secure freedom for everyone but his own people."[11]

Time was running out for the Sixty-Fifth Congress to approve the federal woman suffrage amendment. NAWSA ratcheted up its efforts. Mass meetings were held with war workers. Appeals were written and sent to the Senate. Maud Wood Park initiated a "new kind of letter-writing campaign." Previously she had instructed suffragists to write to their own senator; now she wanted them to write to every senator. "Will you help with such a bombardment?" she asked, clearly a rhetorical question, for she continued with instructions: "The letters should begin to come in on December 2 and should continue until a vote is taken on the Amendment."[12]

The demand that NAWSA's members keep up a steady bombardment of ammunition—telegrams, letters, resolutions, personal appeals—was just one of the reasons NAWSA did not hold an annual convention, for the first time since 1890. Other factors were the influenza; war work; and the state campaigns in Michigan, South Dakota, and Oklahoma that had exhausted NAWSA's field organizers, especially Nettie Rogers Shuler.

Alice Paul summoned national and state leaders to a three-day conference, a war council, in December, where a unanimous decision was made to escalate the burning of Wilson's words. As always, the NWP's press bureau sent out a press release announcing the demonstration: SUFFS ALL PEEVED AT WILSON; WILL BURN HIS BOOKS, read a front-page newspaper headline in Topeka, Kansas.[13]

On December 16, four hundred women—"pioneer suffragists, munitions workers, women of the West, toilers, the unenfranchised women of America"—led by Anna Kelton Wiley, carrying the American flag, marched to the foot of the Lafayette Monument. A large, mostly respectful crowd, watched the solemn procession of women clad in white, half of whom carried lighted torches, while the other half carried purple, white, and gold banners. A slight mist was falling, recounted Doris Stevens: "Massed about that statue, we felt a strange strength and solidarity, we felt again that we were a part of the universal struggle for liberty." A large Grecian urn rested on the base of the statue. Pine logs in the urn were set ablaze as Vida Milholland sang the "Woman's Marseillaise." Elizabeth Selden Rogers said: "Our ceremony today is planned to call attention to the fact that President Wilson has gone abroad to establish democracy in foreign lands when he has failed to establish democracy at home. We burn his words on liberty today, not in malice or anger, but in a spirit of reverence for truth."

The few hecklers in the crowd were silenced at the sight of an aged, diminutive woman, eighty-three-year-old Olympia Brown from Wisconsin, who threw a copy of the speech Wilson made when he arrived in France into the flames, declaring: "I have fought for liberty for seventy years, and I protest against the President's leaving our country with this old fight here unwon."

Agnes Morey burned Wilson's book *The New Freedom.* Eunice Dana Brannan burned Wilson's speech on opening a Liberty Loan Campaign to raise money for the war. Doris Stevens burned his statement to Democratic women before the recent election: "The flames burned brighter and brighter as the night grew black. The White House was empty, but we knew our message would be heard in France."[14]

Chapter 19

Escalation: January-March 1919

Where was my Uncle Sam? —Louisine Havemeyer

On the afternoon of January 1, 1919, the tolling of a large bell at the NWP headquarters, signaled the start of Alice Paul's fiery new tactic—continual "Watchfires of Freedom." The fire burned in a large Grecian urn located on the sidewalk in front of the White House. Into the flames, Dora Lewis solemnly dropped "scraps of paper" inscribed with excerpts from recent speeches by President Wilson, who was still in Europe. Four silent sentinels, bearing purple, white, and gold banners and holding unlit torches, flanked the urn. Annie Arniel and Mary Dubrow, a teacher from New Jersey, unfurled a large banner lettered with a scathing indictment of President Wilson, accusing him of "deceiving the world when he appears as the prophet of democracy," and being "responsible for the disfranchisement of millions of Americans."[1]

As Helena Hill Weed was speaking, a band of soldiers, sailors, and civilians rushed the women, destroyed the banners, and broke the urn. The sentinels lit their torches from the spilled embers and held them high. CROWD CHARGES WOMEN PICKETS, read an attention-getting newspaper headline in San Francisco.[2] The skirmish was interrupted when the crowd was diverted by the sight of flames erupting from a bronze urn on a pedestal in Lafayette Park. Hazel Hunkins stood by the flames, holding aloft a purple, white, and gold banner. The women were arrested, but later released because no one knew what misdemeanor or crime they had committed.

Through rain, snow, and sleet for four days and four nights, shifts of women kept the watchfire burning in a metal washtub, and then in a new stone urn in front of the White House. As each shift changed, the bell tolled. Mobs of men and boys periodically broke up the fire, scattering embers on the sidewalk that caused the pavement to buckle. PAVEMENTS EXPLODE AS SUFF FIRE BURNS, reported a newspaper in Washington, D.C.[3]

A continual "Watchfire of Freedom" ablaze in a large Grecian urn in front of the White House. (Library of Congress)

The police began to use fire extinguishers to put out the fires, but watchfires kept bursting out in Lafayette Park, and in front of the White House, even on the lawn where Hazel Hunkins started two fires after climbing the White House fence. Mildred Morris, a well-known reporter from Denver, was particularly adept at lighting asbestos coils to start fires. Morris, who had fiery red hair "with streaks of white as it stood out in all directions," was, according to Hunkins, "cynical, thin and wiry. . . . [She] stopped at nothing . . . she slept where she happened to be . . . ate when she had money, drank too much and smoked endlessly."[4]

On January 5, Annie Arniel, Julia Emory, Mary Dubrow, and Phoebe Munnecke, who had come from Michigan to help organize meetings and demonstrations, were arrested and charged with building a "bonfire on a public highway between sunset and sunrise."[5] The next day at 9 a.m., they, along with Alice Paul and

Dora Lewis, were tried in police court before Judge Hardison. Paul, Lewis, and Arniel were sentenced to five days in the District Jail; Emory, Dubrow, and Munnecke received ten days. Locked in their prison cells, the women went on a hunger strike. "They will not eat food as a protest against their arrest, which we feel to have been unwarranted and illegal," announced Lucy Burns, who was in charge while Alice Paul was imprisoned.[6]

The NWP sent out a press release announcing another watchfire would be built at 5 p.m., in front of the White House on January 7. Harriet Andrews, a war worker from Missouri; Kate Winston from Maryland who was "obeying her conscience and fighting for the right"; and Rebecca Winsor Evans from Pennsylvania, one of the three Winsor sisters who went to jail, kept the fire going for three hours.[7] Wilson's recent speech on democracy was burned.

Later that same day, two more women burned Wilson's words: Matilda Young and Josephine Day Bennett, an advocate for wage-earning women in Connecticut. All five women were arrested and were sentenced to five days in jail. Bennett's husband, M. Toscan Bennett, a lawyer and "her co-worker in the cause of democracy" for twenty years, wrote a letter in which he imagined himself addressing the judge: "My wife was arrested the other day. Yesterday she was sent to jail. We are sick of a democracy which is always just around the corner. . . . Your Honor must know, as every intelligent person knows, that the charges . . . are ridiculous charges."[8]

By January 8, eleven hunger-striking women were in jail, including some first-timers: Mary Dubrow, Phoebe Munnecke, Harriet Andrews, Kate Winston, and Josephine Day Bennett. Others were veteran "jailbirds": Alice Paul and Matilda Young for the second time, Edith Ainge and Julia Emory for the third time, Annie Arniel and Dora Lewis for the fourth time.

Five days later, on the afternoon of January 13, twenty-five suffragists, bearing banners, built a watchfire in front of the

White House. As usual, the NWP had sent out a press release announcing the demonstration. A crowd gathered. The police moved in and arrested three women. More police, armed with shovels and fire extinguishers, put out the fire by stomping on the dying embers. The women rekindled it. The police arrested seventeen more women. A blaze flared up in Lafayette Park, attracting a crowd. A mob of men split off and proceeded to attack the NWP's headquarters. Riotous men tore down the American flag and the large bell from the front of the building.

Throughout the evening women were arrested, released on bail, and returned to build and guard watchfires. By 10 p.m., twenty-three women were under arrest and sent to the House of Detention for the night, including Elsie Vervane, president of the Woman's Machinist Union of Bridgeport, Connecticut, who had come with a group of union women; Carrie Weaver and her daughter Eva, both munitions workers, who had come in solidarity to protest the arrest of Josephine Day Bennett; and Elizabeth Green Kalb who said: "As long as women are not free we are going to protest at the cost of health and strength against our political bondage."[9]

The twenty-three women were tried before Judge McMahon and an audience of suffragists who applauded when the women appeared. McMahon ordered the applauders removed, shouting: "See that they do not return. And lock the doors."[10] He sentenced the women to five days in the District Jail, where they joined twenty-two already imprisoned, hunger-striking women. He also sentenced four of the applauders to twenty-four hours in jail. SUFFRAGISTS WHO BURNED SPEECHES ALL GO TO JAIL, declared a newspaper in New York City.[11] (Another headline on the same page read: DUTCH CABINET SUPPORTS WOMAN SUFFRAGE BILL. Carrie Chapman Catt's longtime friend, Aletta Jacobs, the first woman physician in the Netherlands and head of the Society of the Right of Women in Holland, was confident of victory. The article noted: "Carrie Chapman Catt and the woman suffragists of America are generously cabling sincerely good luck notes across the Atlantic.")[12]

On January 19, the elderly Mary Nolan, who had survived the "Night of Terror," and Berthe Arnold from Colorado, a kindergarten teacher, were arrested. At her trial, Nolan proclaimed: "I am willing to do or suffer anything to bring victory to the long courageous struggle. I have fought this fight for many years . . . I have seen children born to grow to womanhood to fight by my side. I have seen their children grow up to fight with us."[13]

Suffragists who were watching the proceeding burst into applause. McMahon, thoroughly infuriated, immediately tried thirteen of the applauders for contempt of Court and sentenced them to forty-eight hours in jail, including Lucy Burns, Edith Ainge, Mary Gertrude Fendall, Phoebe Munnecke, Lucy Branham, Annie Arniel, Matilda Young, Gertrude Crocker, and Lucille Shields. Arnold was sentenced to five days. Reluctant to jail the frail Mary Nolan, the judge released her.

"No picketing and no prison for me, I don't like the thought of either one," Louisine Havemeyer had "always laughingly" told Alice Paul, who was thirty years younger than the sixty-four-year-old Havemeyer. A member of the Advisory Council and generous contributor, Havemeyer, who had vigorously campaigned with the Suffrage Torch and Ship of State, was ambivalent about picketing and had shifted her attention to doing war work. Nevertheless, when Alice Paul called and asked her to participate in a demonstration and pack a valise "in case we should have to go to prison," Havemeyer left her three-story marble mansion that housed a world-famous art collection and a fleet of Rolls-Royce motor cars, and took the train from New York City to Washington, D.C. (The valise was to include "a warm wrapper and a bottle of disinfectants.")

She arrived at NWP headquarters on the day before the vote in the Senate, and the day the NWP had announced a demonstration to burn an effigy of President Wilson. The atmosphere was aswirl with activity—suffragists assembling and gathering banners, and spectators congregating in Lafayette Park and along Pennsylvania Avenue in front of the White House.

"My heart began to beat fast," Louisine Havemeyer recalled as Alice Paul ushered her into her office. Paul briefly explained her plan to send a train, called the "Prison Special," around the country with speakers who had been imprisoned to arouse the public to pressure Wilson and the Democrats to pass the federal suffrage amendment. Even if the Senate passed the amendment the next day, the train would still go to whip up support for ratification by the required thirty-six states. Alice Paul wanted experienced speakers and women who would attract curious crowds and reporters. Havemeyer, a prominent philanthropist and a witty, down-to-earth, even sometimes risqué speaker, fit both categories.

In her usual no-small-talk, direct manner, Alice Paul, her "little ninety-pound figure erect and expectant," said: "We need you, Mrs. Havemeyer, for our speaker on the Prison Special. If you remain in prison only a short time, you are qualified; . . . Now, will you carry the American flag and lead the procession? I think the crowd will be friendly, although it is known we are going to burn the President in effigy."

Looking at Paul with "her great, dark, earnest eyes" Havemeyer replied, "Yes, what am I to do?"

"Lucy Burns has charge of the demonstrations. Do as she says, and leave your bag where we can send it to you."

"Well," recalled Havemeyer, "there I was—can you imagine how I felt?—heading the demonstration, when fifteen minutes before the very thought of it had sent my heart beating."[14]

With her head high and the American flag held even higher, Louisine Havemeyer marched down the center of Pennsylvania

Avenue as the crowd "fell back on each side." More than a hundred women marched. Elizabeth McShane, a teacher who had traveled with the Justice Bell, carried the urn that Havemeyer likened to a "twelve-inch flower-pot." The pint-sized, "bright and mischievous" Sue Shelton White, who left NAWSA to lead the Tennessee NWP, carried a small cartoon of Wilson that she would drop in the flames. Twenty-six women carried wood. Unmolested, the line of women arrived at the White House.

"Here we are, Mrs. Havemeyer! Now make your speech," Lucy Burns commanded. So she did: "I planted my feet firmly, held up my flag, and very deliberately repeated our message to the President and the people . . . 'We women of America are assembled here today to voice our deep indignation that while such efforts are being made to establish democracy in Europe, American women are still deprived of a voice in their government here at home.'"

Thirty-nine women were arrested, including Havemeyer, although her arrest took some doing after Lucy Burns instructed her to light a match and she botched repeated attempts. All the while Captain Flather pleaded with Lucy Burns:

"Please, Miss Burns, don't let her do it! You know we don't want to take her. Please don't . . ."

"Go on, Mrs. Havemeyer. Don't pay any attention to him," Burns instructed her.

Back and forth they went, until Louisine Havemeyer finally loudly whispered to Lucy Burns that in order to get arrested, "I believe I will have to kick him."[15]

With that, Flathers gave up and had her arrested. SUFFRAGISTS BURN WILSON IN EFFIGY; MANY LOCKED UP, read the sensational front-page headline with a sub-headline: MRS. HAVEMEYER ARRESTED, in a New York City newspaper.[16] (Havemeyer later wrote that her children were shocked to "read in the morning papers that their little mother was in prison."[17]) Mollie Garrett Hay, on behalf of NAWSA, denounced the "outrageous performance," claiming that it brought "shame and stigma" to the women of America and questioned the NWP's motives: Did they want "success of the amendment or publicity for their organization?"[18] As always, Alice Paul ignored the condemnation. Years later, she said, "We had opposition to everything we did. Everything."[19]

The next morning, February 10, while Havemeyer and the other women waited in a jail attached to the courthouse for their trial, Senator Andrieus Jones told Maud Wood Park that they were still one vote short. The last chance had appeared to be Senator John Sharp Williams, of Mississippi—a close ally of Wilson who had received several cables from the president, urging him to vote "yes." But now, according to Williams, not even the president could convince him to "support a cause advocated by such outrageous methods."[20] In fact, his criticism was most likely irrelevant, given that he had never wavered in opposing woman suffrage.

The amendment was defeated, one vote shy of victory. SENATE REJECTS SUFFRAGE FOR FOURTH TIME, stated a front-page headline in South Bend, Indiana.[21] A Boston newspaper announced: WOMAN SUFFRAGE LOSES BY ONE VOTE.[22]

Soon after the Senate voted, the judge started the proceeding. Each woman was sentenced to a five-dollar fine or five days in jail. Refusing to pay the fine, they were taken to jail in the prison van—"A huge tin box on its side with slits—just a few on top for gasping air only—and narrow seats that you slipped off of. We did not, for they crowded us in so tightly that there was one row on the seat and another row on that row's knees," wrote Louisine Havemeyer.

Much to their disbelief, they were taken to the condemned jail where previous suffrage prisoners had suffered from breathing fumes of poisonous gases. Entering the "pestilential jail," Havemeyer reported: "My very heart stood still for an instant, and then bounded beneath my ribs and crackled as the sparks of indignation snapped within. Where was my Uncle Sam? Where was the liberty my fathers fought for? Where the democracy our boys were fighting for?"

The women immediately went on a hunger strike, knowing that it would hasten their release. Public pressure had recently forced the government to cease force-feeding hunger strikers. The women also knew that the government was loath to let them die, thus creating martyrs for the cause. That night, as Havemeyer readied herself to lie down on a mat of dirty straw, a young suffragist, "a little slip of a factory worker," came to "say 'Goodnight'" and "slipped her a real little pillow she had smuggled in." Lying alone in a jail cell, Louisine Havemeyer wondered, "For what?" She thought of women in Europe, including in Germany, "the enemy," who had been enfranchised. She thought of all the war work she and millions of American women had done. "And here I am, lying on an armful of dirty straw," she said aloud.[23]

On February 15, the "Prison Special," a chartered train nicknamed "The Democracy Limited," left Washington, D.C., with twenty-six suffrage prisoners who had been imprisoned for a total of 1,064 days. "From Prison to People" was the slogan, along with the teaser: "When 200 American Women Are Willing To Go To Prison There's A Reason." A newspaper in Morgan City, Louisiana, described the Prison Special as "one of the most significant suffrage events in some years . . . these women represent the rebellion in the present demand of women for the vote."[24]

Alice Paul and Joy Young had done superb advance work setting up welcoming events at fourteen stops during the three-week transcontinental train trip: Charleston, Jacksonville, Chattanooga, New Orleans, San Antonio, Los Angeles, San Francisco, Denver, Chicago, Milwaukee, Syracuse, Boston, Hartford, New York City. The articulate and dignified former prisoners, who wore their prison pin, were dressed in a replica of the prison garb—a long-sleeve, high-neck, ankle-length shapeless dress and apron made of coarse material.

Lucy Burns, who was in command, usually asked Louisine Havemeyer to be the first speaker. That was because she was small, Havemeyer told the audiences, thus a "difficult target," if an "audience were disposed to be hostile."[25] Vida Milholland sang suffrage songs composed in jail. Lucy Burns gave graphic details of the horrors of being force-fed. Sarah Tarleton Colvin, a nurse who titled her autobiography *A Rebel in Thought*, described the rats: "I can still hear them squeaking and fighting and the sound they made as they fell from the table to the floor and scurried away."[26] Maud Vernon asked for contributions. "Many have asked us," said Abby Scott Baker, "why we were not satisfied with President Wilson's words?" Her pithy reply prompted laughter: "Shall we be satisfied when the captain of the boat offers us a gangplank a foot too short?"[27]

In New York City, the "prison specialists" staged a pageant at Carnegie Hall. Vida Milholland, representing Liberty, stood on the stage, holding a flaming torch. Girls dressed in black with long mourning veils stood with Rhoda Hunt, who portrayed "Shackled America." Women dressed in the traditional garb of equal suffrage nations marched down the aisle and onto the stage. Raising her torch high, Vida Milholland sang the "Women's Marseillaise." Louisine Havemeyer declared: "The militants are here, and we haven't broken anything, not even broken down."[28] The Prison Special, a uniquely Alice Paul–created spectacle, attracted huge crowds, generated positive publicity, energized supporters, gained converts, raised money, challenged the claim Wilson had done enough, and dispelled the image of the NWP as the refuge of dangerous radicals.

On February 24, President Wilson returned to America to discuss the proposed peace treaty that would require approval by two-thirds of the Senate. He disembarked in Boston, where welcoming festivities were planned. Agnes Morey, who had endured the "Night of Terror," and her daughter Katharine, a member of the first group to go to jail, organized a demonstration. With Katharine carrying the American flag, they led twenty-two women bearing banners to the front of the reviewing stand, where Wilson would speak.

Marching in front of a line of Marines, the women formed a line close to the front of the reviewing stand. "They ought to be home, darning their husbands' socks," a spectator shouted.[29] Forty-five minutes passed before the police, "in an exceedingly gentlemanly manner," arrested the women. Charged with "loitering more than seven minutes" they spent the night in the House of Detention, a "dirty, filthy hole under the Court House," where they slept on iron shelves two feet wide, reported Katharine Morey. "The place slowly filled up during the night with drunks and disorderlies until pandemonium reigned."[30]

The women, along with three other suffragists who burned Wilson's words at a demonstration on Boston Common, protested Judge Bolster's decision to try them one by one in a closed court. They refused to give their names, using "Jane Doe" instead. Bolster pronounced sentences of eight days in the Charles Street Jail. "He had imprisoned . . . these bothersome women who had dared to stand quietly in the streets of Boston, (alongside thousands of others standing there much less quietly) and hold up banners which asked for freedom," wrote a reporter.[31] A few days later, a man, unknown to the suffragists, paid their fines, and against their will they were forced from the jail, two of them carried out. FINES PAID THEY REFUSE TO QUIT JAIL—EJECTED!! read the front-page headline in a Phoenix, Arizona newspaper.[32]

After the February 10 defeat in the Senate, Maud Wood Park reported that several attempts were made to get the federal woman suffrage amendment passed by the Sixty-Fifth Congress before it adjourned on March 3. A revised suffrage amendment was proposed that allowed the states to enforce the suffrage amendment, a concession to the states' rights senators. The revised amendment won the vote of Senator Edward James Gay, a Democrat from Louisiana, thus ensuring its passage. However,

Senator Andrieus Jones's attempts to get the unanimous consent needed in order to introduce it for a vote was blocked by two anti-suffrage Republican senators, Weeks of Massachusetts and Wadsworth of New York, who took turns filibustering. Thus, the opponents guaranteed that suffragists would have to start anew in both the House and the Senate of the Sixty-Sixth Congress.

Since most state legislatures, at that time, met in biennial regular session, the anti-senators' successful filibuster also complicated the process of the required next step after Congressional approval—ratification, or getting the approval of two thirds, or thirty-six state legislatures. Forty-one state legislatures were still in session; whereas, later in 1919, only ten would hold a regular session. "By delaying submission to a legislative off-year," wrote Mary Gray Peck, a NAWSA officer, "the opponents of the measure had compelled the women to ask the majority of states to call a special session to ratify, with all the trouble and expense entailed. They hoped by so doing to delay ratification long enough to prevent women from voting on a nation-wide scale in the next presidential election. Also no doubt they wanted to make ratification as hard as they could!"[33]

Having consulted with the Senate about the proposed peace treaty, President Wilson returned to France on March 5. He embarked from New York City, where huge crowds greeted him when he arrived the day before his departure. That evening, March 4, Wilson spoke at the Metropolitan Opera House, located at Thirty-Ninth Street and Broadway. Marching from their New York headquarters on Forty-First Street, Alice Paul led a picket line of twenty-five women, bearing purple, white, and gold banners and a lettered banner with the enduring question: MR. PRESIDENT HOW LONG MUST WOMEN WAIT FOR LIBERTY?

As always, the NWP had announced the plan to burn Wilson's speech. Doris Stevens recalled that it was "a clear, starry night" when they encountered a phalanx of policemen at Fortieth Street and Broadway.[34] When the women tried to get through the police line, they were attacked. "It was a merry fight, or sickening or disgusting as one looked at it," wrote a reporter at the scene.[35] As Doris Stevens "looked at it," the fight was terrifying: "As we neared the corner opposite the Opera House two hundred policemen in close formation rushed us with unbelievable ferocity. They spoke not a word but beat us back with their clubs with such cruelty as none of us had ever witnessed before."[36]

A mob of soldiers and sailors joined the police. One soldier jumped Margaretta Schuyler, twisted her arms, tore the flag from the pole, and broke the pole over her head. Women were knocked down, trampled, hit with fists, kicked. Banners were shredded, poles broken, then used as weapons against the suffragists. Doris Stevens, Alice Paul, and four other women were arrested. Taken to the Thirtieth Street police station, they refused to give Lieutenant Henry Hellmers their names, so he booked them as "Jane Doe." After a short time in a cell, the women were suddenly and inexplicably released.

They returned to the scene, where suffragists kept trying to move forward to burn President Wilson's speech. Police, reinforced with more officers, violently blocked them.

When Marya Ratavitch, "a tiny thing with bobbed hair" from Chicago, tried to use her "puny strength" to break through the police line, two officers shouted: "You want to get through. We'll take you through." Seizing her, they used her as a battering ram. "Shot through as it were," into the open space, a hatless, disheveled Marya Ratavitch collapsed.[37] Soldiers and sailors inflicted repeated "knee kicks" on Grace Cross, a physician, causing her "excruciating pain." A policeman kicked her in the ankle, rupturing a tendon.[38] Bruised, battered, and bloodied, the suffragists were heartened when Elsie Hill managed to burn a paper with Wilson's speech. "We never turn back . . . and we won't until democracy is won!" she shouted.[39]

About 11 p.m., the "bannerless procession" of suffragists returned to their headquarters. At the door, a man, swinging a heavy banner pole, hit Doris Stevens on the side of her head, knocking her unconscious. Her hat was burned in the street, along with a stash of banners that a mob had discovered when they vandalized their headquarters.

Several newspapers appeared to blame the suffragists: SUFFS CHARGE THE POLICE IN NEW YORK, erroneously declared a Boston newspaper.[40] "It hurt to have the world think we had attacked the police," wrote Doris Stevens, "but that was not important, for the President . . . as he sailed away to Europe. . . . He knew that we were not submitting in silence to his inaction."[41]

The Metropolitan Opera House demonstration was the last of the NWP's "dramatic acts of protest." Their "martyrdom"— arrests, imprisonment, physical attacks, forced-feedings—"was the conscious voluntary gift of beautiful, strong and young hearts. But it was never martyrdom for its own sake. It was martyrdom used for a practical purpose"—victory in the fight for the right to vote, explained Doris Stevens.[42]

Chapter 20

On the Brink: March-June 1919

At the dawn of woman's political power in America. —Maud
Younger

The sound of music coming from the back of the Odeon Theater in St. Louis interrupted a mass meeting of suffragists. It was March 28, 1919, the last evening of NAWSA's Golden Jubilee Convention, marking the fiftieth anniversary of the enfranchisement of women in the Territory of Wyoming in 1869. The music announced the arrival of four Missouri suffragists with the news that the legislature had just passed a presidential suffrage bill. Led by Edna Fischel Gellhorn, holding a banner—NOW WE ARE VOTERS—the women marched to the stage amid a standing ovation of "deafening cheers and wild waving of handerchiefs."[1]

They had spent ninety-six days in Jefferson City, the capital, working to get the bill passed. The House easily passed it in February. But opponents in the Senate came close to killing the bill. The women had outwitted them by chartering a train to bring a staunch supporter, Senator Howard Gray, back in time to cast the winning vote. "A dead silence fell upon the room," recalled Marie B. Ames, when Gray walked into the Senate chamber: "Gloom was upon the countenance of those who had hoped to send the bill to its defeat. In the battle of wits the side of right and justice triumphed."[2]

Presidential suffrage measures were also on the ballot in Iowa, Ohio, Indiana, Wisconsin, Maine, Minnesota, and Tennessee. After a hard fight, the measure was approved in Iowa. In Ohio and Indiana, where opponents had overturned presidential suffrage victories in 1918, presidential suffrage was approved for the second time. In Wisconsin, the measure passed without much difficulty.

In Maine, the anti-suffragists put up a hard fight. They were defeated after a six-month campaign of "quiet, continuous and intensive political work."[3] In Minnesota, a state with an impossible constitution to amend and a history of defeating presidential suffrage bills, the victory was won by the low-key efforts of a small group of women. In Tennessee, the presidential suffrage bill included municipal suffrage. The victory was won with the incessant hard work of seven paid organizers, the tireless work of the legislative committee, and a supportive telegram from President Wilson.

Suffragists' state victories had exponentially increased women's voting power. Steadfastly, they continued their efforts. At the federal level, they had to start anew to get the woman suffrage amendment approved by the Sixty-Sixth Congress. It had to be re-passed by the House of Representatives and passed by the Senate. "Our faces must be turned to our new campaign," Maud Wood Park wrote to NAWSA's state presidents. It was "urgently necessary," she wrote, for them to get written pledges of support from reelected and new members of the next Congress. "The enemy will leave no stone unturned to pledge men against us."[4]

The NWP kept constant pressure on President Wilson to secure the last vote in the senate, the sixty-fourth, needed for victory. The most likely person was the newly elected senator from Georgia, William J. Harris. Alice Paul sent a cable to Wilson in France at the Paris Peace Conference, and lobbied influential Democratic leaders to contact him. Well aware that the NWP could resume militant activities and embarrass Wilson at the Paris Peace Conference, his allies sent him a telegram, suggesting he meet with Harris. Wilson contacted Harris who happened to be in Italy. They met in France and Harris pledged his support of the suffrage amendment. With the last vote secured, Wilson sent a cable calling a special session of the Sixty-Sixth Congress on May 19. "It seems to me" he wrote in a message to Congress, "that every consideration of justice and public advantage calls" for passage of the federal woman suffrage amendment.[5]

James Robert Mann from Illinois, the man who had left his hospital bed to vote for the amendment on January 10, 1918, was the new chairman of the House Woman Suffrage Committee. "I was terribly scared of him," confessed Maud Wood Park, because he always started "by growling and telling me all the things I did not know." Each time they met, she reminded herself that "he soon quieted down and gave me the advice I wanted. And extremely valuable advice it always was." Mann planned to get the amendment approved by the House of Representatives on the third day of the special session. "I could not believe my ears," recalled Park.[6] But he did just that. On Wednesday morning, May 21, 1919, Park, "still chill with apprehension," took a seat in the gallery, alongside Helen Gardener and Mollie Garrett Hay.[7] The debate was limited to two hours.

Now that the fight for the vote was on the brink of victory, both political parties were angling to take credit and secure the loyalty of women voters. Democrat Claude Kitchin from North Carolina reminded Republicans, now the party in power, that from 1897 to 1911 the Republican Party had controlled Congress, yet failed to pass the amendment, lest they assume that women would reward Republicans with their votes. Democrat Thomas L. Blanton from Texas said, "I think my wife and daughter are as capable of voting as most men in this country are."[8]

Die-hard anti-suffrage representatives had their say. Democrat Frank Clark from Florida announced that he would not "drag" woman "from the lofty pedestal on which she has been placed by the undying love of the American man—the pedestal of sisterhood, wifehood and motherhood—to the low level of war politics, God forbid!" Republican Benjamin Focht from

Pennsylvania read a letter from the Pennsylvania Association Opposed to Woman Suffrage.

When the roll was called, the yeas came so fast Maud Wood Park had trouble keeping up: "There was no scurrying for one more vote, no sick men coming in to record their support." Instead, there were "gusts of laughter and applause. . . . Everybody was jovial. I hardly recognized our cause in its new setting of gaiety."[9]

The vote was 304 yeas, 89 nays, 42 votes more than required. Theodora Youmans from Wisconsin had watched the proceeding from the gallery in a section reserved for "Mrs. Catt's ladies," located between the press section and the NWP section: "There was no excitement, no jubilee on our side. . . . The fight had been so long and the victory had come so gradually that it was difficult to grasp. We filed out smiling quietly to each other and that was all."[10]

Maud Wood Park, NAWSA's head lobbyist, whose astute social skills and grasp of legislative processes and politics were indispensable in dealing with members of Congress. (Library of Congress)

HOUSE ADOPTS SUFFRAGE AMENDMENT, proclaimed the banner headline stretched across the front page of a newspaper in El Paso, Texas.[11] The next day, Park received an urgent message to meet Representative Mann at the capitol. Rushing there, she found him standing on the steps with a motion picture crew. Following instruction, she walked to Mann and shook his hand "as enthusiastically" as she could. But she "shook so long and so hard that the camera man finally yelled, 'Let go of his hand, Lady! Let go of his hand!'" The movie, which was shown as a news item before feature films, prompted audiences to laugh at the sight of her abruptly dropping "Mr. Mann's hand, after shaking it as if it had been a pump-handle."[12]

In the Senate on May 23, James Eli Watson from Indiana, the new chairman of the Woman Suffrage Committee, released the Committee's unanimous favorable report, and announced that he would call up the woman suffrage amendment for a roll-call vote on June 3. Two more senators had pledged to support the amendment; victory was assured, or so it seemed. (Senators had defeated the suffrage amendment in 1887, 1914, 1918, and January 1919.)

June 3, 1919, was a hot, humid day in Washington, D.C. The Senate gallery was filled with suffragists. Alice Paul and Carrie Chapman Catt were elsewhere. Catt was at NAWSA's headquarters in New York City. (After witnessing senators debate and defeat the amendment on October 1, 1918, she had vowed to stay away.) Confident of victory, Alice Paul was traveling in Massachusetts, Illinois, Pennsylvania, Michigan, and Minnesota, meeting with state officers to plan ratification campaigns.

Maud Wood Park was not so confident. She worried that "some harmful, but seemingly innocuous, amendment might be tacked on to our resolution by the opponents." She "was most afraid" of Senator Underwood's amendment to require ratification by state conventions, instead of state legislatures. She was "quite beside" herself when she learned of Senator Phelan's plan to add an amendment regarding the selection of delegates to a state convention.[13]

For Maud Younger, the day was anticlimactic: "For the fifth time in a little more than a year, we sat in the Senate gallery to hear a vote on the Suffrage Amendment. The new Congress, coming in on March fourth, had brought us two more votes. There was no excitement. The coming of the women, the waiting of the women, the expectancy of the women, was an old story."[14]

Confident of victory and eager to vote, only a few pro-suffrage senators spoke. Opponents voiced their anti-suffrage amendment tirades: states' rights; fear of enfranchising "the dark sisters of the South;"; and the "menace to the peace and welfare of the Nation."[15] Four amendments to the amendment, including one to enfranchise only white women, were voted on and defeated. On June 4, the final roll-call vote began on a proposed amendment to the Constitution that read: "The right of citizens of the United States to vote shall not be denied or abridged by the United States or by any State on account of sex. Congress shall have power to enforce this article by appropriate legislation."[16]

Maud Wood Park kept track: "Ashurst's aye was followed by four noes in succession from Bankhead, Beckham, Borah and Brandegee. Then came five C's in favor; Capper, Chamberlain, Culbertson, Cummins, and Curtis. . . . Through the F's and K's . . . the M's and N's, P's and S's . . . and up to the last favorable vote, which was Watson's, nothing slipped." The final vote was 56 yeas, 25 nays, just two votes more than required. Maud Wood Park "sat still trying to realize" that—"The end of the fight in Congress had come."[17]

Mollie Garret Hay left the gallery to call Carrie Chapman Catt. Maud Younger read a statement by Alice Paul: "The women of this country will vote in the 1920 election. There is no doubt of immediate ratification. We enter upon this final stage . . . joyously, knowing that women will be enfranchised citizens of this great democracy within a year."[18]

Maud Younger later wrote that she, along with Julia Emory, Abby Scott Baker, Elizabeth Selden Rogers, and others "walked slowly homeward, talking a little, silent a great deal. This was the day toward which women had been struggling for more than half a century! We were at the dawn of woman's political power in America."[19] In a note to Alice Paul, Elizabeth Selden Rogers wrote: "Your unconquerable soul in that frail little body has done it all. I can hardly believe it is really true. I had so little faith in men, I feared they would play tricks at the end."[20]

Newspapers across the country spread the news. In Washington, D. C., WOMAN SUFFRAGE VICTORIOUS IN SENATE, proclaimed the banner headline stretched across the top of a newspaper.[21] In Los Angeles, an exuberant headline read: SUFFRAGE IS WINNER.[22] The issue of race, a through-line in American history, was reflected in a headline and subheadline in an Elizabeth City, North Carolina newspaper, evoking the issue of maintaining white supremacy: SUFFRAGE STRENGTHENS SOUTH'S WHITE VOTE / NUMBER OF WHITE WOMEN IN SOUTH FAR EXCEEDS NUMBER OF NEGROES OF BOTH SEXES.[23]

The anti-suffragists conceded the passage of the amendment, but not its ratification: ANTIS LINING UP NEW FIGHT, read the headline in a Seattle newspaper.[24] The math favored the anti-suffragists. Ratification required approval by thirty-six of the forty-eight state legislatures, with just thirteen state legislatures needed to block ratification. Opponents could prolong the suffrage struggle for years. THE RACE FOR SUFFRAGE IS NOW ON, signaled the headline in a Logan, Utah, newspaper.[25]

PART VII

Chapter 21

Up to the States: June-December 1919

Telephone and telegraph wires were kept humming. —Ruth B. Hipple

WOMEN'S SUFFRAGE NOW UP TO THE STATES, reported a Boston newspaper.[1] The race was on to be the first state to ratify the federal woman suffrage amendment. "We of Wisconsin have been extremely ambitious to secure for our state the honor of being the first state to ratify," declared Theodora Winton Youmans.[2] But, the Illinois General Assembly ratified the Nineteenth Amendment first by a majority of 132: 135 yeas, 3 nays, on the morning of June 10, 1919. An hour later, the Wisconsin Legislature followed suit by a majority of 75: 78 yeas, 3 nays. At two in the afternoon, the Michigan Legislature unanimously ratified. Each state's governor ceremoniously signed the certificate. In Illinois, a Rock Island newspaper celebrated with a front-page headline: ILLINOIS BY APPROVAL IS FIRST TO ACT.[3]

Each state ratification certificate had to be certified by the Secretary of State in Washington, D.C. Illinois's certified copy was returned with a mistake and it had to be redone. Meanwhile, David James, a former Wisconsin legislator and father of suffrage leader Ada James, had returned from Washington, D.C., with an official document attesting to the fact that Wisconsin's certified copy was the first to be received. Thus, both states won first placc, Illinois for the first ratification and Wisconsin for the first certification.

Alice Paul sewed three large gold stars on the ratification flag, a ritual that garnered publicity with photographs of her seated with the flag, sewing needle in hand. (The flag that was hung vertically was a large banner with wide purple, white, and gold stripes. The stars would be sewn in the white stripe in two rows of eighteen stars each, one row of gold stars and other of blue, representing the thirty-six ratification states.)

Mary Burnett Talbert was a national and international suffragist and activist who called on women of all races to work together. At an event in Washington, D. C., "Votes for Women: A Symposium by Leading Thinkers of Colored Women," Talbert declared that "the colored woman has. . . exactly the sort of powers which are today peculiarly necessary to the building of an ideal country." (Black Past)

Alice Paul and Carrie Chapman Catt commanded an army of suffragists united in the fight for ratification. Both NAWSA and the NWP had planned campaigns in every state. Maud Younger set up her famous card index chock-full of personal and professional information concerning governors and state legislators, the ammunition of lobbying. NAWSA was similarly armed. Their publicity bureaus churned out massive amounts of press releases and articles. A press release that appeared in newspapers across America featured Alice Paul, dubbed "Joan of Arc," and touted her "ability to fight to the finish."[4] It was accompanied by a serene photograph that belied her militant reputation. WOMEN ARE SURE OF VICTORY, SAYS MRS. CATT, read the headline of a lengthy interview with Carrie Chapman Catt, illustrated with a dignified photograph of her in a Washington, D.C. newspaper.[5]

Alice Paul dispatched seasoned national organizers throughout the country, including many jail veterans. Julia Emory went to Maryland. "Good-by, good luck and don't come back until Maryland ratifies," coworkers wished her as she left to meet with the governor. She later wrote in the *Suffragist*, the NWP's widely read weekly publication:

> "It's good of you to come," Governor Emerson Harrington greeted me.
>
> "Not good of me, but necessary, Governor, to let you know how much women need a special session in Maryland, now. Not just the 15,000 Maryland women . . . who have asked me to come to you, but all the women in the United States."
>
> "Ah," said he. "You ladies are too impatient."

Harrington reiterated that special sessions were expensive and unpopular with legislators. Emory set off to poll the legislators; many of whom, she soon discovered, lived "far apart and in such inaccessible places." One man was in his wheat field threshing wheat. Women could not "pitch hay," he dismissively told her. Borrowing his pitchfork, she lifted a fork full of hay up in the hay wagon, three times! "Well, I'll be jiggered," he exclaimed, "labor is scarce and now I'll know where to look for help when I need it!"

"What we need," Emory replied, is "your vote."[6]

On June 16, three states ratified the federal woman suffrage amendment: Kansas, Ohio, and New York. In Kansas, where women had won equal suffrage in 1912, after two referenda defeats, Governor Henry J. Allen was the first governor to call a special session of the legislature that unanimously ratified the amendment. In Ohio, the grueling fight finished with "nothing but good will from the men" who ratified by a majority of 94: 103 yeas, 9 nays.[7] In New York, Carrie Chapman Catt pressured Governor Alfred E. Smith to call a special session. After only one negative speech, the amendment was unanimously ratified. Alice Paul sewed three more stars on the ratification flag.

In Pennsylvania, where women had no rights to vote, Dora Lewis, head of the NWP's National Ratification Committee and Lucy Kennedy Miller, president of the Pennsylvania Woman Suffrage Association, a NAWSA affiliate, led the fight. On June 24, the General Assembly ratified by a majority of 135: 185 yeas, 50 nays. Suffragists jammed in the aisles and galleries erupted, cheering and waving banners and flags. Helium-filled balloons soared above the jubilant crowd. The celebration spilled into the street with a spontaneous victory parade. Newspapers published a photograph of Governor William Sproul, as he signed the ratification certificate with a feather pen. Standing at his right side was Dora Lewis, who had served four jail sentences, totaling more than eighty days, and survived the "Night of Terror."

Two more states ratified in June: Massachusetts and Texas. In Massachusetts, anti-suffragist Sara White proposed holding a state referendum on the federal amendment. White's proposal was one of the anti-suffragists' tactics aimed at delaying and potentially defeating the amendment. A fervent force of suffragists fought back, speaking in hearings and debates, lobbying, and generating letters, telegrams, and resolutions of support. On June 25, after defeating the resolution calling for a state referendum, legislators ratified by a majority of 167: 219 yeas, 52 nays. Massachusetts, the birthplace of Susan B. Anthony and Lucy Stone, and the historic stronghold of anti-suffragists, became the seventh state to ratify the federal woman suffrage amendment.

Opponents obstructed, delayed, harassed, heckled, threatened, and filibustered in Texas. When anti-suffragists tried to lure senators out of town to break the quorum, friendly legislators and suffragists scrutinized the passengers on all the outbound trains. On June 27, the House voted 18 yeas, 9 nays. The next day, the Senate, by a viva voce vote, (a quicker, simpler method that did not record each senator's vote, than the roll call method), ratified the amendment.

Ratification Scoreboard June 1919
Victories: 9 of 36, Defeats: 0 of 13

On July 2, Iowa became the tenth state to ratify. The next day, in Missouri, at 10 a.m., a line of women marched to the capitol in Jefferson City: club women, WCTU women, NWP and NAWSA women. Many were carrying yellow parasols as they had during the Golden Lane demonstration at the 1916 Republican Convention in St. Louis. Women with suffrage buttons, banners, ribbons, flowers, and "Votes for Women" sashes filled the galleries. The resolution to ratify was approved by a majority of 118: 125 yeas, 7 nays.

The victories in Iowa and Missouri were tempered by the news that Anna Howard Shaw had died. Mentored by Susan B. Anthony, Shaw had devoted close to forty years to the fight for the vote. GREAT SUFFRAGE WORKER DIES ON EVE OF FRUITION OF HER LIFE'S ENDEAVOR, read the headline in a Great Falls, Montana newspaper.[8] She had not slowed down when she resigned in 1916 after twelve years as NAWSA's president. In early May, Shaw gave a speech at the first National Conference on Lynching in which she denounced lynching as "public murder."[9] Later in May, she became the first woman to receive the government's highest civilian award, the Distinguished

314

Service Medal, for her work as head of the Woman's Committee of the Council of National Defense. She was on a tour to promote peace when she was stricken with pneumonia. After seeming to recover, Shaw collapsed with a high fever and chills. Her life partner, Lucy Anthony, for whom Anna Howard Shaw was her "precious love," was at Shaw's side when she died "looking out towards the setting sun."[10]

In Alabama, President Wilson had sent a telegram, expressing his "very earnest hope that the Suffrage Amendment . . . be ratified." Josephus Daniel, the Secretary of the Navy and a Southerner, wrote that it would be a "loss to southern chivalry and southern prestige" if Alabama "halted this great reform."[11] The Ratification Committee of the Alabama Equal Suffrage League, led by Patti Ruffner Jacobs, battled the Women's Anti-Ratification League, led by Marie Bankhead Owen. Betty Gram and Sue Shelton White, the NWP's superb organizers, joined the fight. Representatives of the liquor industry boldly plied their influence. On July 17, women from across Alabama filled the gallery and watched senators defeat ratification by a majority of 6: 13 yeas, 19 nays. The House vote was delayed. For now, anti-suffragists had won their first victory—half a state.

In Georgia, Emily McDougald, president of the Equal Suffrage League of Georgia, led the fight. Veteran suffragists Dora Lewis, Anne Martin and Mabel Vernon came to help the NWP branch in Georgia. President Wilson sent a supportive telegram, for which he was dismissed as a "meddler."[12] Opponents, according to a pro-suffrage legislator, were "bloodthirsty and vindictive." Hostile legislators denounced the federal woman suffrage amendment as "a vicious piece of legislation" that would "equalize white women with Negro women." They accused outside suffragists of trying to "induce Georgia women to refuse to bear children which was the sole aim and end for having women at all, according to Bible doctrine."[13]

On July 24, the Georgia General Assembly defeated ratification by a majority of 127: 44 yeas, 171 nays. (Ratification was finally approved on February 20, 1970.)

Four days later, on July 28, Arkansas governor Charles Hillman Brough called a special session of the legislature. Carrying yellow "Votes for Women" banners, suffragists watched the debate, surprised to "find a few real enemies and moss grown arguments" openly expressed.[14] "I'd rather see my daughter in her coffin than at the poll," announced one legislator.[15] Senator Henry Ponder, who introduced the bill in the Senate, countered that "he believed his children would be prouder of that act of his than of anything else he might ever do."[16] The amendment was ratified by a majority of 59: 74 yeas, 15 nays.

Ratification Scoreboard June–July 1919
Victories: 12 of 36, Defeats: 1½ of 13

The precipitous drop in the number of victories, from nine in June to three in July, alarmed suffragists. Their battle plans understandably calculated that the twenty-six states where women had equal or presidential suffrage, in particular the pioneering equal-suffrage states in the West, would quickly ratify the amendment. But Western governors were stalling. Some cited the extra expense of a special session. Others said that their women already had suffrage. Some Western women agreed. "Why should we incur the expense of extra sessions for something we ourselves do not need?" asked one enfranchised woman.

Reports of such insular comments were "criticized and resented by women in all parts of the country." Vivian Pierce, co-editor of *The Suffragist*, disdainfully said: "This attitude was least of all expected in the West, cradle of humanitarian and liberal sentiment and overwhelmingly pro-suffrage."[17] A New York City newspaper declared: RATIFICATION OF THE SUFFRAGE AMENDMENT AT A STANDSTILL.[18]

Carrie Chapman Catt deployed four envoys, two Republicans and two Democrats, to the Western states to scout the situation, and to fire up the politicians, the public, and the press. The governor of Minnesota, Joseph A. A. Burnquist, who was at his remote ranch, rode a horse bareback for four miles, and then rode a long way in a car to meet the Republican envoys in a little town. He promised to call a special session in September. In Arizona, the Democratic envoys tracked down the governor, who was on vacation, and got his pledge to call a special session, sometime.

Two states ratified on August 2. In Montana, Emma Ingalls—feminist, writer with a "caustic pen," and publisher of a county newspaper—was a member of the House of Representatives.[19] At a special session, she introduced the ratification resolution and legislators unanimously approved it. In Nebraska, suffragists arranged to coordinate their 1919 convention in Lincoln, the capital, with the special session called by Governor Samuel R. McKelvie, "a consistent friend of the cause." On August 2, suffragists went *en masse* to the capitol to have "the joy of being present" as the amendment was ratified and signed by Governor McKelvie.[20]

In September, there were only three ratification victories. In Minnesota, on September 8, women arrived at the capitol in St. Paul in automobiles with "suffrage" written on the windshield and decorated with sunflowers, goldenrod, and yellow bunting. In a special session, legislators ratified by a majority of 169: 180 yeas, 11 nays. Cheering, laughing, hugging, waving suffrage colors, suffragists celebrated. In the rotunda, a band played the "Battle Hymn of the Republic," the song composed by pioneer suffragist Julia Ward Howe. The state suffrage association treated legislators and the governor to a specially prepared chicken dinner.

In New Hampshire, suffragists enlisted prominent men to organize the Men's Committee for Ratification; from past experience they knew that women could have little influence. Carrie Chapman Catt sent Marjorie Shuler to help with the campaign. On September 10, at a special session, legislators ratified by a majority of 73: 226 yeas, 153 nays.

In Alabama, on September 22, despite a massive effort by pro-amendment forces, the House rejected the amendment by a majority of 29: 31 yeas, 60 nays, thus ending the possibility that the Senate would reconsider its rejection in July. (Ratification was finally approved on September 8, 1953.)

In Utah, Governor Simon Bamberger had needed prodding to call a special session. In Washington, D.C., Alice Paul sent Anita Pollitzer, known for her charming persuasiveness, to the capitol to tell Utah's congressman, Milton Welling, a friend of Bamberger, that the NWP was holding the Democrats responsible for the delay. Wary of riling up the NWP's anti-Democrat militancy, Welling sent a forceful telegram to Bamberger, who responded by calling a special session on September 30. State Senator Elizabeth Hayward introduced the resolution for ratification. By a unanimous vote, Utah became the seventeenth state to ratify.

Ratification Scoreboard June–September 1919
Victories: 17 of 36, Defeats: 2 of 13

Late in October 1919, Carrie Chapman Catt packed the ratification dress she had made after the House of Representatives passed the federal woman suffrage amendment on January 10, 1918 ("so hopeful of early victory"), and headed west on a "Wake up, America!" tour.[21] Catt and some of her best campaign speakers barnstormed through twelve states in eight weeks, rallying women, pressuring governors, and persuading legislators to ratify the amendment. At a mass meeting in South Dakota, where she had campaigned for the 1890 state suffrage referendum, Catt asked if there were any veterans of that fight in the audience—twenty-five women stood up!

She was depressed before she left, writing to Mary Grey Peck in late September: "It is fall and the wretched rain is rotting everything, and my governors politely tell me they will call their special session when they are ready and not before. . . . So with the rain and the rot and the governors, I have been down to the bottom of the dumps today." But, wherever Carrie Chapman Catt went, wrote Mary Gray Peck, "the political atmosphere changed from quiescent to violent activity."[22] Before the end of 1919, governors had called special sessions in California, North Dakota, South Dakota, and Colorado. The governors of Oregon and Nevada pledged to call special sessions. Carrie Chapman Catt returned from her trip, again predicting victory before February 1, 1920.

In California, Governor William B. Stevens finally called a special session. He had been bombarded by letters, telegrams, telephone calls, petitions, resolutions, and personal visits. Genevieve Allen, head of the state NWP, and organizers Vivian Pierce and Abby Scott Baker had stirred up the onslaught through a newspaper campaign. On November 1, legislators ratified by a majority of 71: 73 yeas, 2 nays.

Eighteen states had now ratified the federal woman suffrage amendment—six of them unanimously, but Maine was worrisome. Anti-suffragists had used the initiative petition to get a referendum on presidential suffrage on the ballot in the 1920 general election. Next they got a resolution introduced in the legislature to postpone ratification of the federal woman suffrage amendment until after the referendum on the presidential suffrage bill. The powerful state affiliate of the American Federation of Labor (AFL) came out in support of that resolution.

Alice Paul hastened to Maine to join forces with Dora Lewis and the head of the state NWP, Florence Brooks Whitehouse, a wealthy and prominent former member of NAWSA. In a flurry of activity, Alice Paul persuaded the head of the AFL in Washington to write a letter supporting ratification. Whitehouse distributed the letter to newspapers and legislators. She persuaded the state labor organization to change its position to support ratification. Pro-suffrage Governor Carl Milliken called a special session, declaring: "If only one woman in Maine wanted to vote she should have the chance."[23] On November 5, the legislature ratified, but by the closest margin to date, a majority of 23: 96 yeas, 73 nays.

In December, in North Dakota, party politics threatened to sabotage ratification. The political party in control, the Non-Partisan League, held a grudge. Women, who had school suffrage, had not voted for a League candidate in a recent school election. Nevertheless, indomitable suffragists convinced the governor to call a special session. On December 1, legislators ratified by a majority of 133: 143 yeas, 10 nays, 3 absent.

In South Dakota, the fight for ratification played out in the middle of winter and the dark of night. Mary Shields Pyle, president of the state association, and the NWP organizers ceaselessly pressured Governor Peter Norbeck to call a special session. In Washington, D.C., Alice Paul and Anita Pollitzer lobbied national politicians to send telegrams to the governor. After legislators agreed to pay their own expenses, the governor, on very short notice, announced a special session in December. "It was the dark of winter," wrote Ruth B. Hipple. "Telephone and telegraph wires were kept humming for the next thirty-six hours and the men coming from all directions." A man who lived far from a train station "used up three automobiles getting to the train . . . as the snow made the roads almost impassable."[24]

On December 3, beginning at 7 p.m., the legislative process was quickly accomplished; the resolution was introduced to the Senate and the House, given the first and second readings, and referred to the proper committees. As required, the Legislature adjourned until the next legislative day, which was one minute after midnight on December 4. Convening at that time, South Dakota legislators unanimously ratified at 12:44 a.m., in time for them to catch the trains that left in both directions about 2 a.m.

The final 1919 victory was in Colorado, on December 15. Suffragists had offered to serve as unpaid clerks and pages for a special session. Governor Oliver Shoup refused their offer, unless they raised $15,000 to cover the entire cost. His demand backfired when suffragists exposed his demand as far in excess of the actual cost of a special session. Relentless pressure finally forced Shoup to call a special session.

The resolution for ratification bore the names of three women legislators: Senator Agnes Riddle, and Representatives May Bigelow and Mabel Ruth Baker. May Bigelow was given the honor of wielding the gavel from the Speaker's rostrum when the unanimous vote for ratification was announced.

The victory in Colorado was number twenty-two, far short of suffragists' expectations. The opposition was relentless. "Opponents had begun a series of systematic attempts to find legal flaws in the ratification votes or to have them held up by a referendum to the voters. . . . the opposition had grown exceedingly bitter," wrote Maud Wood Park.[25]

Desperate to stop the Prohibition Amendment that had been ratified and was due to go in effect January 1, 1920, "wet" forces in Ohio had used the initiative and referendum provision in the state constitution to secure a state referendum in Ohio on the Prohibition Amendment that the Ohio Supreme Court upheld as constitutional. Although the Ohio legislature had already ratified the federal woman suffrage amendment, the court's decision meant that a statewide referendum might be necessary: Ohio's place on the ratification list was in question. An apprehensive Harriet Taylor Upton told reporters, "We are ready to vote and most of us eager for the privilege. But we believe we shall have to sit back and wait for other states to make it possible."[26] Emboldened anti-suffragists quickly circulated petitions in the twenty-one additional states with initiative and referendum provisions in their constitution.

Pro-suffrage forces appealed the court's ruling. NAWSA hired Charles Evans Hughes, a former member of the United States Supreme Court. Dora Lewis's son, Shippen, joined the NWP's team of lawyers.

Ratification Scoreboard: June–December 1919
Victories: 22 of 36; Defeats: 2 of 13

Chapter 22

Unite Again: January-July 1920

Suffragists of the country, do not lay down your arms! —Kenyon Hayden Rector

Madeline McDowell Breckinridge, president of the Kentucky Equal Rights Association, watched the ratification proceeding from the gallery along with a crowd of suffragists. As a young woman, she had had tuberculosis of a leg bone. When part of that leg was amputated, she used a wooden leg. Undaunted, Breckinridge, who was noted for "her speaking ability and humor," became a leading civic reformer and suffragist. An observer described how "in a strong voice coming from a slim and often weak body," she would ask audiences to "look at male-led Kentucky, with its poor schools, violence, and corrupt politics" then, pointedly ask, "if the question should not be whether women were fit for suffrage but whether men were."[1]

In the spirit of bipartisanship, a Republican presented the resolution for ratification in the Senate controlled by Democrats and a Democrat presented it in the Republican-controlled House. It was ratified by a majority of 69: 102 yeas, 33 nays.

In Rhode Island that same day, January 6, suffragists from around the state filled the galleries "to witness the final scene in a fifty years' drama." Governor Robert Livingston Beeckman recommended ratification—"an act of justice long delayed."[2] The House voted 89 ayes, 3 nays. The Senate ratified by a *viva voce* vote, with one dissenting vote. Suffragists celebrated their victory at a gala event attended by Jeannette Rankin.

Three more states—Oregon, Indiana, Wyoming—ratified in January. On January 13, the Oregon legislature claimed it set a record by unanimously ratifying in thirty minutes. On January 16 in Indiana, Helen Benbridge, president of the Franchise League, sat at the rostrum in the Senate Chamber and listened to "the last wail" of the three anti-suffrage senators.[3] Legislators ratified by a majority of 40: 43 yeas, 3 nays in the Senate, and unanimously in the House. A brass band signaled the victory with a lively rendition of "Glory, Glory, Hallelujah." In Wyoming, where women had been voting since 1869, legislators unanimously ratified on January 27 in a special session that the governor called after months of ignoring suffragists' requests. Theresa Jenkins, a veteran of the fight for the vote, thanked the politicians "for their action in behalf of women of the State, the United States and the world."[4]

The next day, despite suffragists' ardent efforts, the South Carolina General Assembly refused to ratify by a majority of 101: 24 yeas, 125 nays. (Ratification was finally approved on July 1, 1969.)

Ratification Scoreboard January 1920
Victories 27 of 36, Defeats 3 of 13

The surge in January continued into February, as six more states approved ratification: Nevada, New Jersey, Idaho, Arizona, New Mexico, and Oklahoma where a young woman had sacrificed her life.

In Nevada, suffragists in Carson City, the capital, provided legislators with free room and board. At a special session on February 7, Sadie Dotson Hurst, the first and only woman legislator, was given the honor of presiding over the proceedings in the Assembly. Fifty of her constituents came to witness the historic event in a train car on which they attached a "Suffrage Special" banner. (They used seventy-five tacks that, an annoyed conductor said, defaced railroad property.) The Assembly voted: 25 yeas, 1 no. The Senate vote was unanimous.

Lillian Feickert and Alison Turnbull Hopkins led a "terrific fight" in New Jersey.[5] Alice Paul sent Catherine Flanagan and Betty Gram. "Every organizer of the Woman's Party who had worked in the State," said Gram, "whispered in my ear, 'don't try New Jersey—it will never ratify.'" It was with "reluctance" that she had "invaded the territory of the enemy."[6]

Feickert, president of the New Jersey Woman Suffrage Association (NJWSA), formed the Ratification Committee, a coalition of pro-ratification groups, including the State Federation of Colored Women's Clubs, led by the Reverend Florence Randolph. She excluded the NJNWP because of its militancy. In January, NJWSA held an extravaganza in Trenton, the capital, highlighted by the choreographed presentation of a ratification petition with 140,000 names.

On February 2, the New Jersey Senate ratified by a majority of 16: 18 yeas, 2 nays. In the Assembly, on February 9, several pro-suffrage legislators were absent, infected with influenza. The opposition stalled, filibustered, and played parliamentary tricks. James Nugent, the powerful political boss, stood in the corridor, sending messages with tantalizing offers to lure legislators. "Debate lasted until one o'clock Tuesday morning—five hours of continuous fiery combat," recalled Betty Gram. Then, the roll call and victory by a majority of 10: 34 yeas, 24 nays: "Silence followed for long seconds and then the wild, almost hysterical cheers of women . . . and out of the galleries poured countless smiling women—bearing banners of victory, to take their places among the liberated people."[7]

On February 11, Idaho became the thirtieth state to ratify. Representative Emma F. A. Drake, a physician and the prolific author of books for women, including *Maternity Without Suffering*, introduced the resolution in the House where the vote to ratify was unanimous. The Senate voted 29 yeas, 6 nays. On February 12, there was "scarcely a ripple of excitement" in Arizona. Four women legislators introduced the resolution for ratification that passed unanimously. Several anti-suffragists from the Iowa and Virginia were listened to with "good-natured amusement."[8]

That same day, the Virginia General Assembly defeated the ratification resolution. The state Equal Suffrage League, led by Lila Meade Valentine, had conducted a ceaseless campaign, securing the endorsement of prominent men, and holding a mass meeting where Carrie Chapman Catt electrified supporters. NAWSA and the NWP sent organizers, speakers, and thousands of pieces of literature—all to no avail. (Ratification was finally approved on February 21, 1952.)

Nine days later, on February 21, the New Mexico Legislature ratified by a majority of 38: 53 yeas, 15 nays. On February 28, Oklahoma became the thirty-third state to ratify by a majority of 84: 109 yeas, 25 nays.

The suffrage martyr of Oklahoma, thirty-three-year-old Aloysius Larch-Miller, had died on February 2 in Shawnee. The day before, although ill with influenza, she had debated "one of the ablest orators," Attorney General S. P. Feeling, "a bitter opponent" of ratification, at a convention of Democrats. They had met to discuss a resolution requesting the obstinate governor to call a special session. Aloysius Larch-Miller's "enthusiasm and eloquence" won the debate and convention delegates overwhelmingly adopted the resolution requesting a special session. "She gave her young life as the supreme sacrifice for the cause she loved."[8] Memorial resolutions were passed in Aloysius Larch-Miller's honor. The flag at the capitol in Oklahoma City was flown at half-mast. Children and local citizens raised money to create the Larch-Miller Park in Shawnee. A plaque affixed to a boulder reads: IN MEMORY OF ALOYSIUS LARCH-MILLER WHO GAVE HER LIFE FOR THE ENFRANCHISEMENT OF WOMEN.

From February 12-18, 1920, NAWSA held its Fifty-First Annual Convention, the "Victory Convention," at Chicago's posh Congress Hotel. Delegates had been summoned to celebrate "our ever-buoyant hope, born of the assurance of the justice and inevitability of our cause, which has given our army of workers the unswerving courage and determination that has at last overcome every obstacle."[9]

In her presidential speech, Carrie Chapman Catt said: "Ours has been a cause to live for, a cause to die for if need be. It has been a movement with a soul, a dauntless, unconquerable soul ever leading onward." She set off a wild celebration, declaring—"Oh, women, be glad today and let your voices ring out the gladness in your heart!"[10] Suffragists wearing sashes, badges, pins, and armed with all types of horns, let loose a cacophonous clamor. They jockeyed to pull the cord on a huge bell that hung from the ceiling. State delegations, "tooting and shouting and singing" and calling out state "yells," marched around the magnificent white and gold ballroom. "It was a joyous occasion and a good noisy one, just as it should have been," remembered Theodora Winton Youmans.[11]

Half of the weeklong convention was devoted to organizing the League of Women Voters (LWV), a new nonpartisan organization dedicated to the education of women citizens that Catt had proposed as the successor to NAWSA. Numerous suffrage associations in states that had ratified had already re-formed themselves into a state LWV. A ratification banquet featured "sparkling speeches," a "program of well-known songs cleverly adapted to suffrage," and a large blue and silver "living ratification valentine," with an opening in the middle. One by one, the state presidents from ratifying states appeared in the opening and recited critical but humorous rhymes aimed at women in states "still in outer darkness."[12]

The final night of the convention began with a community sing-along and featured women dressed in the actual clothes of various periods in the fight for the vote. Each woman took a seat in tiers on the stage, a "lovely spectacle." As Carrie Chapman Catt presented honor roll awards to pioneers and veterans, Harriet Taylor Upton interrupted her. In the name of "countless suffragists," Upton presented Catt with an elegant piece of jewelry—a platinum brooch with a large sapphire surrounded by

326

diamonds. Overcome with emotion, Carrie Chapman Catt signaled to Upton to say something. A delighted Harriet Taylor Upton said "this was the first time she ever was able to do something that Mrs. Catt could not."[13]

Ratification Scoreboard: January–February 1920
Victories 33 of 36, Defeats 4 of 13

Jesse A. Bloch, a businessman and influential member of the West Virginia Senate, was on vacation in San Francisco when he read in a newspaper that his vote was needed to ratify the federal woman suffrage amendment. NWP organizers Mary Dubrow and Betty Gram, who had worked in seven ratification campaigns, had been initially optimistic. Soon they were alarmed; legislators who had pledged to ratify were "wavering . . . It was an opposition stampede—nothing less," recalled Betty Gram.[14]

The source was twofold: partisan bickering and outside pressure, including a committee from the Maryland General Assembly that was sent to West Virginia to protest ratification because it would impose woman suffrage on states that did not want it. Suffragists vociferously affirmed their confidence that the West Virginia Legislature was "perfectly qualified and competent" to make their own decision.[15] The House ratified: 47 yeas, 40 nays. The vote in the Senate was a tie: 14 yeas, 14 nays.

Meanwhile, Senator Bloch and his wife Jessie were aboard a special train, breaking speed records in a five-day race across the country. At a stop in Chicago, they were offered a ride in an airplane delivering mail, but Jessie refused. WIFE WON'T LET LEGISLATOR FLY TO SAVE SUFFRAGE, read a front-page headline in New York City newspaper.[16]

While legislators waited in Charleston, vigilant suffragists kept them from leaving town. Mary Dubrow "hovered round and about" the fourteen pro-suffrage senators "trying, with radiant cheerfulness, to instill into everyone the feeling: 'Senator Bloch is on his way and all is well with the world.'" Telegrams arrived noting his presence in "remote places that gradually grew nearer." Pro-suffrage senators "carried pillows in their hands and playing-cards in their pockets."[17] Suffragists supplied them with sandwiches and coffee. Opponents in the House tried to reconsider the resolution. They attempted to have a recently retired anti-suffrage senator, A. R. Montgomery, reseated. They tried tricks and lies. Alice Paul decried their tactics, charging that interests opposed to suffrage "are making another desperate stand in West Virginia."[18]

On March 10, cheers and applause greeted Senator Bloch when he took his seat in the Senate. Suffragists crowded the gallery and Senate floor. An intense debate went on for hours. At 6 p.m., the Senate, with Block voting, ratified the federal woman suffrage amendment. A newspaper in Washington, D. C. printed a photograph of a smiling Jesse Bloch standing between a tired-looking Betty Gram and Mary Dubrow with the caption: THEY SAVED SUFFRAGE IN WEST VIRGINIA.[19] Both Alice Paul and Carrie Chapman Catt touted the West Virginia victory as the stepping stone to final victory. A confident Catt prepared to leave for Geneva, Switzerland, for the eighth meeting of the International Woman Suffrage Alliance, of which she was still the president.

On March 22, 1920, Washington became the thirty-fifth state to ratify. Emma Smith DeVoe thanked the legislators in the name of "early suffrage workers." Suffrage pioneer Carrie Hill, "a tiny figure whose white hair was scarcely on the level with the top of the Speaker's desk," thanked the WCTU and the leaders of civic organizations and the cause of labor.[20] WOMAN SUFFRAGE BUT ONE NOTCH AWAY, announced a newspaper headline in Norwich, Connecticut.[21]

Four days later, led by a brass band, suffragists marched into the Maryland State House. They watched as legislators refused to ratify by a majority of 38: 45 yeas, 83 nays. Reassembled outside, the band led suffragists who marched two by two around the State House, holding high NAWSA's yellow flags and the NWP's purple, white, and gold banners. Spectators cheered them on. Before dispersing, they held a meeting and passed resolutions of appreciation to the pro-amendment legislators, the "brave men who had fought so

328

valiantly for democracy."[22] (Ratification was finally approved on May 29, 1941. It was certified on February 25, 1958.)

On March 30, suddenly and surprisingly, it appeared that the thirty-sixth state would be Mississippi. By a vote of 23 yeas and 22 nays, the Mississippi Senate ratified. News of that vote activated pro- and anti-ratification forces. Telegrams flooded the state, including one from the anti-ratification Speaker of the House in Delaware: "Stand firm against ratification. Delaware Legislature still firm for State's rights and will not ratify."[23]

(The doctrine of states' rights had been used by Southern politicians to disenfranchise black men who had been granted the right to vote by the Fourteenth and Fifteenth Amendments. To date, although Congress had the power to enforce those amendments, it had done nothing to protect black men's right to vote. "Many southern politicians feared that if the woman suffrage amendment was approved, the federal government would then enforce the Fourteenth and Fifteenth Amendments," write historians Marjorie Julian Spruill and Jesse Spruill Wheeler."[23])

On March 31, legislators in both Mississippi and Delaware were scheduled to vote on a resolution to ratify. FATE OF SUFFRAGE RESTS WITH TWO STATES TODAY, read the banner headline in a Bismarck, North Dakota newspaper.[24] In Delaware, the vote was delayed.

In Mississippi, raucous legislators bollixed the proceedings, shouting, hooting, jeering, interjecting hostile remarks. "I would rather die and go to Hell than vote for woman suffrage!" raged Representative R. H. Watts.[25] Pro-suffrage legislators who tried to give speeches were drowned out. The resolution to ratify was defeated by a majority of 71: 23 yeas, 94 nays. "Thus was banished forever," wrote Lily Wilkinson Thompson, president of the Mississippi Woman Suffrage Association, "the dream of Mississippi suffragists that the women would receive the ballot from the men of this great state."[26] (Ratification was finally approved on March 22, 1984.)

Ratification Scoreboard January–March 1920
Victories: 35 of 36, Defeats: 6 of 13

The fight for final victory continued. The way ahead was fraught with frustration and futility. The Republican governors of Vermont and Connecticut were particularly irksome. In Vermont, Governor Percival Clement adamantly refused to call a special session. On April 21, a deputation of four hundred women who had traveled over muddy, rocky, nearly impassable roads, with one woman walking five miles, arrived in Montpelier, the capital. The band of "loyal, ardent soldiers" was led by Lillian Olzendam on a bitterly cold day, through drenching rain along the streets of Montpelier, up the capitol steps, and into a room where Clement sat in a chair. Fourteen women briefly presented their arguments. Clement replied that "he did not wish to make a decision at present."[27] Suffragists kept up the pressure, arranging to have thousands of letters and telegrams sent to him, urging him to call a special session.

In Connecticut, the anti-suffrage governor, Marcus H. Holcomb, claimed that the state constitution limited him to calling a special session only "on special emergencies." Petitions, appeals, resolutions, and lobbying failed to change his mind. Katharine Ludington, president of the Connecticut Woman Suffrage Association, created a Suffrage Emergency Corps, composed of prominent women from across the country: scientists, doctors, lawyers, educators, civic leaders, and labor organizers. For a week in May, dubbed "Special Emergency Week," the women fanned out across the state, speaking in thirty-six towns. Holcomb remained unmoved. SUFFRAGISTS FAIL TO SWERVE HOLCOMB, reported the front-page newspaper headline in a Bridgeport, Connecticut newspaper.[28] The majority of legislators sent a petition, asking the governor to call a special session. Still he refused. (Ratification was finally approved on September 14, 1920.)

In Delaware, on May 5, the Senate had ratified by a majority of 5: 11 yeas, 6 nays. But on June 2, the House refused to consider the resolution. It was a bitter end for suffragists who had conducted an intense and costly campaign with mass meetings, petitions, speeches, automobile parades, and a parade of suffragists' children riding ponies and bicycles and being pushed in carriages. (Ratification was finally approved on March 6, 1923.)

"Suffragists of the country, do not lay down your arms!" warned Kenyon Hayden Rector in her pamphlet "Women Awake!" The first woman licensed architect in Ohio and a member of the NWP's Advisory Council, Rector urged, "You soldiers who hold the cause dear, unite again for the final struggle!"[29]

From left, Sue Shelton White, Benigna Green Kalb, Kenyon Hayden Rector, Mary Dubrow, Alice Paul, and Elizabeth Green Kalb posed in front of the NWP headquarters with a banner they displayed at the 1920 Republican National Convention: "No self respecting woman should wish or work for the success of a party that ignores her sex. Susan B. Anthony, 1872." (Library of Congress)

Suffragists celebrated a victorious court decision on June 1: The United States Supreme Court unanimously ruled that the anti-prohibitionists' tactic to require a statewide referendum on federal amendments was invalid. OHIO REFERENDUM LAW KNOCKED OUT BY SUPREME COURT, read the front-page newspaper headline in Marshalltown, Iowa.[30] The Ohio Legislature's ratification of the federal women suffrage amendment was secure.

That news prompted Florida suffragists to realize that the provision in their state constitution was no longer valid, and appealed to Governor Sidney J. Catts to call a special session. He refused. He had tried to get it through the last session and the same anti-senators were still in power. Senator Murray Sams of Volusia Country opposed woman suffrage "unconditionally and unqualifiedly" because it was "impossible for women to be equals of men." Senator George G. Brooks of Monroe County did not "care to lower women from the pinnacle. . . . Politics is a dirty game . . . and women can not mix with filth without some of it sticking."[31] (Ratification was finally approved on May 13, 1969.)

In Louisiana, suffragists squared off against states' rights suffragists Kate and Jean Gordon, who had joined local anti-suffragists and paid organizers from the NAOWS. On June 9, the Louisiana Senate voted to indefinitely postpone a vote on ratification. The House defeated it on June 15 by a majority of 23: 44 yeas, 67 nays. Lydia Wickliffe Holman, head of the Joint Ratification Committee, confronted Governor Parker, citing his glaring lack of leadership. He rudely dismissed her. "The responsibility for the failure of this Federal Amendment to enfranchise 27,000,000 women, including those of Louisiana, rests on Governor John M. Parker," she fired back in a public statement.[32] Early in July, Representative Conrad Meyer reintroduced the ratification resolution. His motion was defeated, one vote short of the necessary two thirds. Another attempt failed and the Louisiana Legislature adjourned on July 8. (Ratification was finally approved on June 11, 1970.)

Four days later, another state was ruled out when Governor Clement of Vermont finally replied to the "Suffrage Emergency Corps," and officially refused to call a special session. WOMEN SLAPPED IN FACE BY G.O.P. GOVERNOR, was a graphic newspaper headline in Atlanta, Georgia.[33] (Ratification was finally approved on February 8, 1921.

Chapter 23

Justice Bell: August-September 1920

The vote is the emblem of your equality. —Carrie Chapman Catt

By August it was clear—the fight for the thirty-sixth state was down to North Carolina and Tennessee. The battle was front-page news across America: SUFFS' EYES ON RACE TO RATIFY ACT, read a headline in Rock Island, Illinois.[1] President Wilson sent telegrams to the governors of both states. They agreed to call a special session, although North Carolina Governor Thomas Bickett replied that he hoped the Tennessee Legislature would ratify first to spare North Carolina from "the feelings of bitterness that would surely be engendered by debate on the subject."[2]

Marjorie Shuler, NAWSA's publicity director and a veteran of the Oklahoma campaign, had assessed the situation in both states. Worried about ongoing political feuds and powerful anti-suffragists in Tennessee, Shuler summoned Carrie Chapman Catt, who had recently returned from Europe.

In 1918, the Tennessee legislature had granted women the right of presidential and municipal suffrage. For the 1919 municipal election, Catherine Talty Kenny, head of the Ratification Committee of the Tennessee Equal Suffrage League (TESL), worked closely with Juno Frankie Pierce, founder of the Nashville Federation of Colored Women's Clubs, to register black women and get out the vote. In May 1920, Kenny, "reaching out across the color line," invited Pierce to speak at the first convention of the Tennessee League of Women Voters (TLWV), the successor of TESL.

At the convention, held in the House chambers of the capitol, Pierce, the daughter of a house slave of a former Tennessee legislator, told the gathering of white women: "What will the Negro woman do with the Vote? . . . We are optimistic. . . . We are asking only one thing—a square deal."[3] Abby Crawford Milton, the former president of TESL, was elected president of the TLWV. Kenny, Milton, and Anne Dallas Dudley would lead the ratification fight. Pierce would do what she could within the confines of segregated Nashville.

Carrie Chapman Catt arrived in Nashville on July 17, an oppressively steamy day. She set up her headquarters in the elegant Hermitage Hotel, located near the capitol. In advance of her arrival, she had sent a four-page, single-spaced letter to Kenny replete with warnings and tactics. In particular, she insisted Kenny establish a Men's Ratification Committee: "No matter how well the women may work, ratification in Tennessee will go through the work and action of men, and the great motive that will finally put it through will be political and nothing else. We have long since recovered from our previous faith in the action of men based on love of justice."[4]

Catt stressed the importance of sending a deputation of "earnest and well-informed local women" to visit every legislator before the special session began. She later described what that extraordinary effort had required of the women: "The Southern summer heat was merciless and many legislators lived in remote villages or on farms miles from any town. Yet the women trailed these legislators, by train, by motor, by wagon and on foot, often in great discomfort, and frequently at considerable expense to themselves. They went without meals, were drenched in unexpected rains, and met with 'tire trouble,' yet no woman faltered."[5]

Catt herself, along with Abby Crawford Milton, undertook an extensive speaking tour. It is possible that a recently widowed woman who ran a farm in Niota, Phoebe "Febb" Ensminger Burn, heard Catt speak. A college graduate, Febb Burn had been interested in suffrage "for years" and liked "the militants as well as the others." Her son Harry had been elected to the state legislature in 1918 at the age of twenty-two. His mother, he once wrote, was "a student of national and international affairs who took an interest in all public issues."[6]

On August 1, the NWP set up headquarters at the Tulane Hotel. Sue Shelton White, the dynamic head of the state branch noted for her political acumen, was in charge. Veterans of many ratification campaigns, including Betty Gram and Catherine Flanagan, came to canvass the state, recruiting legislators to sign pledges in support of ratification.

Josephine Anderson Pearson, the state president of the Tennessee Association Opposed to Woman Suffrage, spearheaded an aggressive anti-ratification campaign aimed at appealing to anti-suffragists throughout the South. She fired a barrage of broadsides, pamphlets, letters, and circulars. One letter exhorted women to fight three "deadly principles" lurking in the federal woman suffrage amendment: "1. Surrender of state sovereignty. 2. Negro woman suffrage. 3. Race equality."[7] Nashville was awash with suffrage and anti-suffrage paraphernalia, and filled with people sporting pro-suffrage yellow roses or anti-suffrage red roses. The ratification battle was dubbed the "War of the Roses."

On August 9, Governor Albert Roberts addressed the opening session of the Tennessee Legislature: "The eyes of all America are upon us. Millions of women are looking to this Legislature to give them a voice and share in shaping the destiny of the Republic."[8] Suffragists were sure of ratification in the Senate. In the House, sixty-two of ninety-nine members had pledged to ratify the amendment. Some of the pledged members, however, were fickle, easily enticed by liquor, susceptible to bribes, or cowed by threats, all of which the anti-suffragists provided.

The next day, Governor Thomas Bickett addressed the opening session of the North Carolina Legislature. He confessed that he had "never been impressed with the wisdom of or the necessity for woman suffrage in North Carolina." Nevertheless, he concluded, "Woman suffrage is at hand . . . the better part of wisdom and grace is to accept the inevitable and ratify the amendment."[9] Four days later, on August 13, the North Carolina Senate Committee on Constitutional Amendments released a favorable report: 7 yeas, 1 nay. In Tennessee, the Senate ratified by a majority of 21: 25 yeas, 4 nays, 2 not voting. SUFFRAGE WINS INITIAL FIGHT IN TWO STATES, announced the front-page newspaper headline in Great Falls, Montana.[10] Carrie Chapman Catt wrote to Mary Gray Peck:

> We now have 35 ½ states. We are up to the last half of the last state. . . . The opposition of every sort is here fighting with no scruple, desperately. Women, including Kate Gordon and Laura Clay, are here, appealing to Negrophobia and every other cave man's prejudice. Men, lots of them are here. . . . We believe they are buying votes. We are terribly worried, and so is the other side. . . . It's hot, muggy, nasty, and this last battle is desperate. . . . We are low in our minds. . . . Even if we win, we who have been here will never remember it with anything but a shudder.[11]

Legislators adjourned for the weekend. In Nashville, suffragists kept close watch on the House members who had pledged support, inviting them to movies, rides in the country, dinner. Anti-suffragists published a pamphlet warning legislators: "Beware! Men of the South! Heed not the song of the suffrage siren!"[12] In a room on the eighth floor of the Hermitage Hotel, they plied legislators with liquor. Catt later described the anti-lobbyists in Tennessee as the most "nefarious" she had ever encountered:

> I was more maligned, more lied about, than in the thirty previous years I worked for suffrage. I was flooded with anonymous letters, vulgar, ignorant, insane. Strange men and groups of men sprang up. Men we had never

met before in the battle. Who were they? We were told, this is the railroad lobby, this is the steel lobby, these are the manufacturers' lobbyists, this is the remnant of the old whiskey rig. Even tricksters from the U.S. Revenue Service. . . . They appropriated our telegrams, tapped our telephones, listened outside our windows and transoms. They attacked our private and public lives.[13]

In North Carolina, opponents and supporters were inflamed. On August 17, the day the Senate met to vote, the gallery was divided into two separate sections, the east wing for the "ratificationists," the west wing for the "rejectionists."[14] Fired-up senators debated for more than five hours. Ratification seemed possible, until Senator Lindsay Warren, the floor leader for the opposition, made a deft move and interjected a resolution to defer action until a regular meeting of the legislature in 1921. The resolution passed: 25 yeas, 23 nays, ending any possibility that North Carolina would be the thirty-sixth state. (Ratification was finally approved on May 6, 1971.)

TENNESSEE SLENDER THREAD UPON WHICH SUFFRAGE HOPES HANG, warned a Chattanooga, Tennessee newspaper.[15] That same day, August 17, the Tennessee House Committee on Constitutional Amendments reported in favor of ratification. A heated debate ensued. Seth Walker, the Speaker of the House, had promised to support the measure, but now inexplicably led the opposition. His rip-roaring, anti-ratification speech got shouts and cheers from the red-rose-wearing anti-suffragists in the gallery. C. F. Boyer, another opponent, vehemently proclaimed that his nine daughters would trust their seven "brothers to represent them politically."[16] T. K. Riddick, chairman of the Committee on Constitutional Amendments, bellowed: "If beaten, I will leave this hall a dishonored man, ashamed of the name of Tennessee."

Finally, Walker forced a motion to adjourn until the next day. The tactic—designed to gain time for opponents to work on "wobbling" representatives—passed with 54 yeas, 44 nays. As representatives, one after another, voted for Walker's motion, "tears rolled out of the eyes of suffrage women in the gallery, who seemed to feel their chance slipping vote by vote . . . the cards were stacked against them." The pressure on legislators was enormous. "There was a trouble-hunted look in many eyes particularly of those classified as 'wobbly.'"[17]

The next day, the House would vote on ratification of the federal woman suffrage amendment. That night Carrie Chapman Catt told her co-workers, "There is one more thing we can do—only one. We can pray."[18]

Abby Crawford Milton remembered Wednesday, August 18, 1920, as "the most exciting and dramatic session ever held in the House."[19] The House floor was cleared of lobbyists. At 10:30 a.m., Speaker Seth Walker banged his gavel to open the session. "Every onlooker knew that the fate of the question might depend upon a single vote," recalled Carrie Chapman Catt, who had remained at the Hermitage Hotel, keeping to her vow to never watch a vote again.[19]

The debate began and soon ended when Walker took the floor and moved to table the ratification resolution, a tactic to indefinitely suspend consideration of the resolution to ratify. Harry Burn, who wore a red rose, voted "yea." Banks Turner's vote got lost in the din of exhortations and exclamations, although it appeared to some that he voted "nay." The first roll call was contested. Walker had tallied a victory—49 to 47. The clerk counted 48-48, a tie that would defeat the motion to table.

The clerk began the second roll call. Again Burn voted "yea." As the clerk approached the Ts, Walker sat down beside Banks Turner, forcefully draped his arm over his shoulder, and urgently whispered in his ear. Suddenly, Turner shook off Walker's arm, jumped to his feet, and shouted out his vote— "nay," making the final tally a tie—48 to 48. The motion was defeated. The ratification resolution was alive. Cheers and shouts resounded again and again from the yellow rose side of the gallery.

Walker called for a vote to concur with Senate Joint Resolution #1, ratifying the Nineteenth Amendment. The clerk started the roll call through the As to the Bs to twenty-four-year-old Harry Burn who had recently received a letter from his mother, Febb Ensminger Burn, telling him to "be a good boy" and help Mrs. Catt with her "Rats."[20] Burn, despite the red rose in his lapel, voted "aye." He later explained "I knew that a mother's advice is always safest for a boy to follow."[21] Now, all eyes were on Banks Turner. Twice the clerk called his name. He did not respond. The clerk listed him as not voting. But, then, rising from his chair, Turner said: "Mr. Speaker, I wish to be recorded as voting Aye."[22] The federal woman suffrage amendment was approved by a majority of 2: 49 yeas to 47 noes.

Suffragists erupted—whooping, shouting, cheering, laughing, weeping, clapping, dancing, and wildly waving yellow and purple, white, and gold suffrage flags and banners. The sounds could be heard through the open window of Carrie Chapman Catt's hotel room. Representatives threw their yellow roses in the air, creating a shower of petals.

Alice Paul unfurled the purple, white and gold ratification banner with 36 stars from the balcony of the NWP's headquarters—victory, at last! (Library of Congress)

Photographers recorded the jubilant scene. President Wilson sent a congratulatory telegram to Governor Roberts. Suffrage leaders from France, Sweden, Italy, South Africa, and Great Britain sent messages of great cheer. "Congratulate the American States on the overwhelming victory. . . . The world power women hold will greatly strengthen them internationally," cabled Lady Constance Lytton, who had served a prison sentence disguised as Jane Warton.[23] A Cordova, Alaska newspaper marked the triumph with a banner headline: WOMEN OF AMERICA WIN RIGHT TO VOTE.[24]

Seth Walker changed his "no" vote, a parliamentary maneuver that gave him three days to call up the motion to reconsider. (Changing the final vote to 50 yeas, 46 nays.) During that time, Catherine Kenny reported, the "opponents . . . attempted every unscrupulous scheme known" to overturn the victory.[25] At one point, thirty-six of the losing legislators went to Decatur, Alabama, where they stayed for ten days in an attempt to prevent a quorum, thus delaying action on the motion to reconsider, or perhaps hoping that some of the forty-nine legislators who voted "yea," would change their mind.

The relentless opposition kept up their attacks and attempted to enjoin Governor Roberts from signing the ratification certificate. Finally, on August 24, 1920, Governor Roberts signed the certificate and sent it to Secretary of State Bainbridge Colby in Washington, D.C. The document arrived by train in the early hours of the morning of Thursday, August 26, 1920. A signing ceremony was scheduled at 10 a.m. in Colby's office at the State Department. Instead, at 8 a.m., in his own home, after he drank one and a half cups of coffee, Colby used one of his regular pens to sign the Proclamation of the Nineteenth Amendment, enfranchising more than 26,000,000 women in America.

His momentous act was not witnessed by suffragists, or recorded with photographs and movies. There was no ceremony, no speeches, or the presentation of the pen. His explanation for changing plans was to avoid the "considerable contention as to who shall participate." In particular, "the vehement objections voiced" by Helen Gardener of NAWSA about the participation of Alice Paul and other officers of the NWP.

When officials from NAWSA and the NWP arrived for the signing ceremony, Colby told them that the deed was done. NAWSA's contingent left with "an air of indignant disappointment."[26] Alice Paul said she was "confident" that Colby's signature "completes the suffrage struggle." The NWP "will not relax its vigilance, however, until it is satisfied that no further attempts will be made to wrest from the women of the United States the political equality which they have won."[27] (Opponents' efforts continued until 1922, when the United States Supreme Court handed down its second decision affirming the validity of the Nineteenth Amendment.)

Colby invited the women to return later in the day. Ushering Catt and NAWSA officials into his private office, Colby showed them the proclamation. Although he denied Catt's request to re-create the signing for the movie cameras, he did allow photographs. The arrival of the Spanish Ambassador preempted the time Colby had allotted to Alice Paul and the NWP officials. After a protracted wait outside his office, Alice Paul left, followed in time by the others, until no one was left when Colby finally emerged.

Newspapers across America and abroad announced the epochal news of the Nineteenth Amendment. EQUAL SUFFRAGE IS LAW OF LAND, proclaimed the front-page headline in a Pensacola, Florida newspaper.[28] A photograph of Alice Paul unfurling the ratification flag from the balcony of NWP headquarters to the delight of suffragists standing on the sidewalk appeared in a Mount Sterling, Kentucky newspaper with the headline: THE STAR THAT COMPLETED THE BANNER.[29] In a general store in Arkoe, Missouri, Maye Shipps Corrough, a trombone player who marched in the Missouri Ladies Military Marching Band in the 1913 parade in Washington, D.C. "got up on the counter and danced!"[30]

The next day, August 27, four hundred suffragists and the governor of New York, Alfred E. Smith, welcomed Carrie Chapman Catt when she arrived by train in New York City. Mollie Garrett Hay presented her with a spectacularly large bouquet of yellow chrysanthemums and blue Canterbury bells. A procession led by six mounted policemen, a brass band, an automobile carrying Catt, and a group of suffragists slowly made its way to Catt's hotel.

At a dinner celebration at the Waldorf Astoria Hotel, Carrie Chapman Catt said: "This is a glorious, a wonderful day. For many a year we have marched up the long hill together. . . . Now we will go our separate ways, holding in our hearts tender memories of our comrades in the great war. . . . We are no longer petitioners . . . but free and equal citizens."[31]

The next day, Saturday, August 28, at noon, there was a clamorous nationwide celebration. "Every owner or custodian of a bell, whistle, horn, dishpan, dinner gong, bass drum or other noise-making instrument" was called upon "to go the limit on noise" in celebration of equal suffrage.[32] In Bridgeport, Connecticut, "a tremendous din of factory whistles rent the air intermingled with the ringing of the church bells."[33] More than a thousand people joined a horn-honking automobile parade in Birmingham, Alabama. A Fairmont, West Virginia newspaper celebrated: BELLS PROCLAIM THE TRIUMPH OF SUFFRAGE.[34] (In Baltimore, anti-suffragists tried to get the bell in City Hall "tolled mournfully . . . for the death of chivalry and of womanly womanhood.")[35]

One more bell remained to be rung—the one-ton bronze Justice Bell. On September 25, an elaborate ceremony with a community songfest and a pageant of forty-eight girls, each representing a state, was held in Independence Square in Philadelphia. "To my opinion," said Governor William Sproul, "this is one of the four greatest occasions in American history. The first was the Declaration of Independence; the second, the adoption of our Constitution; the third, the wiping out of slavery; and fourth, the accomplishment of equal rights for women."[36]

The bell's clapper that had been chained until women were free to vote was unchained by a woman wearing a white satin gown draped in gold, representing justice. Catherine Wentworth, the young niece of Katherine Wentworth Ruschenberger, who had commissioned the Justice Bell, pulled the rope to ring it forty-eight times, once for each state. Earlier in September, Carrie Chapman Catt had written an article addressed to the new women voters: "The vote is the emblem of your equality, women of America, the guaranty of your liberty. . . . *Prize it!*"[37]

Epilogue

We must not rest . . . —Mary White Ovington

WOMEN VOTERS OUTNUMBER MEN, was the front-page headline in a Chattanooga, Tennessee newspaper on Election Day, November 2, 1920. A sub-headline read: FEMININE FOLK OUT 90 PER CENT, STRONG—NEGRO WOMEN IN MAJORITY AT NEW ORLEANS.[1] A Fairmont, West Virginia newspaper reported: WOMEN VOTERS HEAVY IN STATE.[2] In Seattle, a headline announced: WOMEN OF U.S. ARE ENJOYING NEW DUTY.[3] A Philadelphia newspaper published a photograph of a woman voter at a polling place with her son 'Billy' in his baby carriage, with the caption "Even Baby Goes to the Polls."[4]

Out of more than twenty-six million women of legal voting age (twenty-one years and over), just over a third voted, about ten million women. They came on foot, carriage, wagon, horseback, and in cars, including the popular Ford Model T. Olympia Brown voted at the age of ninety-one. Judith Winsor Smith voted at the age of ninety-nine. Although Sarah Penrose was "strongly opposed to suffrage," she felt it was her "duty nevertheless to vote."[5] Josephine Pearson, leader of the anti-suffragists in Tennessee, enlisted a compliant man to vote in her stead, according to her instructions. In Ocala, Florida, where there were segregated lines to the voting booths, a reporter wrote: "On the colored side this morning early there was a crush, lasting about three hours. . . . A majority of the colored voters are women." On the white side, in the mid-afternoon, "most of the voters at that time were women."[6]

Across the country, however, there were women who were not able to vote. Women (and men) who were denied citizenship, such as Native Americans and immigrants of Asian descent, were prohibited from voting. (In 1924, the Indian Citizenship Act granted Native Americans the right to citizenship. In 1943, the 1882 Chinese Exclusion Act was repealed, allowing Chinese people to be naturalized. In 1946, Filipinos and Asian Indians became eligible for naturalization. In 1952, the McCarran-Walter Act granted citizenship to first-generation Japanese Americans.)

Women were blocked from voting in two Southern states, where election judges refused to waive the requirement that voters register months before an election: four months in Mississippi and six months in Georgia. A Richmond, Kentucky newspaper reported that in Savannah, Georgia: "Negro women were refused ballots at voting places here."[7] In South Carolina, registrars forced "colored women" to stand and wait for hours while they registered "every white person in sight, man or woman, even late-comers." Unlike white people, black women were required to answer arcane questions, a tactic used to disqualify them. Despite "every means of trickery and brutality," black women continued to try to register: "No discouragement, or 'test,' no petty insult stopped them," wrote William Pickens, an official of the National Association for the Advancement of Colored People (NAACP).[8]

Efforts to curtail many citizens' right to vote in America continue to this day, including impeding registration, passing stringent voter ID laws, purging voters from the rolls, and limiting voting hours. In words that resonate today, Mary White Ovington, a stalwart suffragist, journalist, and cofounder of the NAACP, wrote that in the fight to protect the right to vote—"We must not rest."[9]

An enduring question about women's fierce fight for the vote is—why did it take so long? "Why the delay?" asked Carrie Chapman Catt and Nettie Rogers Shuler in their post-victory book, *Woman Suffrage and Politics: The Inner Story of the Suffrage Movement.* Their answer was "the trading and trickery, the buying and the selling of American politics . . . [by] certain combinations of interests" that included the liquor industry, manufacturers, and political bosses.[10]

Certainly that was a key dynamic. But the delay was clearly exacerbated by deep-seated, circumscribed cultural conceptions of women that most women and men unquestionably accepted. Over and over women fighters for the vote had to overcome entrenched preconceived beliefs and strictures, and, to act persistently and boldly—speaking in public, petitioning, organizing, canvassing, campaigning, recruiting, fund raising, drafting legislation, lobbying, marching, picketing, and enduring mob violence, jail and forced-feeding. The fight continues to this day as women seek to share equally in the local, state, and national governance of the United States.

Another intriguing question is: How was the fierce fight for the vote won? Alice Paul acknowledged "all the efforts that had been made" up to when she joined the fight. But, picketing and going to jail, she said, focused "all the political leaders in the country from the President down . . . on the desire and demand of women for political equality." Holding the party in power responsible and mobilizing women voters, Paul believed, had the biggest impact by demonstrating women's political power.[11] Indeed it did. But, that strategy was dependent on increasing the number of women voters through NAWSA's grueling state-by-state suffrage referenda campaigns. Given the extraordinarily multifaceted, powerful, and heavily financed opposition, victory had doubtlessly required the strategies and tactics of both NAWSA and the NWP, and the relentless resourcefulness and perseverance of generations of a diverse cadre of women and men.

The year—1920— that victory was won was arguably due to Alice Paul and the NWP. As one Southern congressman told Dora Lewis—by the NWP "being so annoying and persistent and troublesome and being just like that sand that gets into your eyes when the wind blows . . . like a cinder in your eyes, you have to get rid of" the federal woman suffrage amendment passed "ten years sooner than it ever would have."[12]

There was still much work to be done. Just two weeks after the Nineteenth Amendment was added to the United States

Constitution, Alice Paul advised that no "woman should consider the fight for full equality won. It has just begun."[13]

In 1920, Carrie Chapman Catt turned her attention to international suffrage and the peace movement.[14] NAWSA was reorganized into the National League of Women Voters with Maud Wood Park as the president. Once the League was solidly established, Park resigned, moved to Maine, and wrote a well-received play, *Lucy Stone: A Chronicle Play in Nine Episodes.* She donated her considerable collection of books, papers, and memorabilia to Radcliffe College, founding what became known as the "Woman's Rights Collection" (now The Arthur and Elizabeth Schlesinger Library on the History of Women in America).

Lucy Burns, considered the bravest of the brave, retired, returning to Brooklyn, where her life revolved around the Catholic Church and raising an orphaned niece. Exhausted and fed up with women who had not joined the fight, she said, "We have sacrificed everything we possessed for them, and now let them fight for it. I am not going to fight any more."[15] Alice Paul continued with the NWP focused on passage of an Equal Rights Amendment (ERA) that reads, "Equality of rights under the law shall not be denied or abridged by the United States or by any state on account of sex." Maud Younger continued as the NWP's lobbyist, setting up a new card index for the ERA.

Congress passed the ERA in 1972. In 1982, a time limit for ratification expired with the ERA three states short of ratification. Efforts continue today to win ratification. "I would like my granddaughters," said Supreme Court Justice Ruth Bader Ginsburg, "when they pick up the Constitution, to see that notion—that women and men are persons of equal stature—I'd like them to see that is a basic principle of society."[16]

After the fight was won, the NWP lobbyist, Maud Younger, known for her speech-making and card index replete with information about politicians, with her dog Sandy, drove her new convertible across the country. (Library of Congress)

The post-fight lives of suffragists were varied. Some were sad. Annie Arniel was physically debilitated and committed suicide. MILITANT SUFFRAGE WORKER SUICIDE, announced the banner headline in a Wilmington, Delaware newspaper. "Good-bye, daughter," she signed a note instructing the bank to give her money to her daughter.[17] Jessie Hardy Stubbs also committed suicide. (Seeking solace, her bereft husband, Benton MacKaye, formulated his idea for what became the Appalachian Trail.) Kate Heffelfinger, a survivor of repeated solitary confinements, the Night of Terror, and force-feeding became a recluse in her hometown, Shamokin, Pennsylvania, engaging in bizarre behavior that got her labeled "Crazy Katie," and eventually committed to Danville State Hospital, where she spent the rest of her life, unable to vote.[18]

Other women thrived. Mabel Vernon worked for the ERA, disarmament, and peace, living in Washington, D.C. with her life companion, Consuelo Reyes-Calderon. Doris Stevens focused on international law and foreign policy regarding women's rights. Louisine Havemeyer, brought back to life by her suffrage work, resumed collecting art and building an extraordinary collection that she willed to the Metropolitan Museum of Art. Betsy Graves Reyneau studied art for thirteen years in Europe, returned, and became a prominent artist who created portraits of illustrious African Americans. Forty-four of her portraits, including of W. E. B. Du Boise and Mary Church Terrell, are in the National Portrait Gallery, Washington, D. C., and can be seen online.

Ida B. Wells-Barnett raised her family and led efforts to improve the lives of black people in Chicago. She attempted to win a seat in the Illinois State Senate, becoming one of the first black women to run for elected office. Adelina Otero-Warren also jumped into politics and ran for Congress as the representative from New Mexico, losing by less than nine percent. An educator and writer, she worked to preserve the record of Spanish culture. As a businesswoman, she ran a real estate agency with her companion Mamie Meadors. They lived on a ranch called, *Las Dos.*

Helena Hill Weed became a writer and crusader for people fighting for freedom in Haiti and Latin America. Maud Malone devoted herself to improving the low status and paltry wages of public librarians. A founder of the first union of public library workers in United States, Maud Malone was its main spokesperson. Dora Lewis, Alice Paul's "tower of strength," resumed her work for prison reform and headed the NWP's efforts to build an international relations network.[19]

To be near her daughter, Alva Belmont moved to France, where she organized an International Advisory Council of the NWP. Jeannette Rankin served one more term in Congress, where she was the only member to vote against entering World War II. At the age of eighty-eight, she led a coalition of women's peace groups, the Jeannette Rankin Brigade, in an anti-war march. Mary Church Terrell organized campaigns against lynching and racial and gender discrimination. In her 80s, she joined pickets, boycotts, and sit-ins that resulted in desegregating restaurants and department stores in Washington, D.C.

Hazel Hunkins (later Hunkins Hallinan) moved to England, became a socially active journalist, married a financial editor for the United Press International, and had three children. Betty Gram married Raymond Gram Swing, went to Europe, and had three children. (She took his last name and insisted he take hers.) Gram Swing and Hunkins Hallinan joined a feminist group working for women's rights, including passage of the Representation of the People (Equal Suffrage) Act 1928 that enfranchised women in the United Kingdom over the age of twenty-one. (In 1918, only women over thirty were enfranchised. Emmeline Pankhurst's decision to suspend militancy during World War I perhaps contributed to the delay.) Gram Swing returned to the United States in 1934, and worked with the NWP for international women's rights.

In 1972, eighty-two-year old Hazel Hunkins Hallinan traveled to Washington, D.C., on "a sentimental journey to revisit the scene of my crimes." She stayed at the NWP headquarters, where she was interviewed for an article in a Washington, D. C. newspaper headlined: HALF A CENTURY OF FEMINISM. She recalled President Wilson, with his top hat and "granite face" driving by the pickets, and police brutality. She could not remember how many times or how long she had been in jail: "We were living day-to-day, a vivid hectic life, and the times weren't very important in relation to the intensity of our lives."[20]

In 1977, Hunkins Hallinan returned to visit relatives and Alice Paul on her ninetieth birthday on January 14. "She was the dominating character of our movement. . . . Now that doesn't mean I'm taking anything away from those suffragettes who worked state by state, stubborn man by stubborn man," she told a reporter.

350

Alice Paul died that July. On August 26, Hunkins Hallinan came back to Washington, D. C., to march in the Women's Equality Day parade, dedicated to honoring Alice Paul and to show support for the E.R.A. (In 1973, Congress designated August 26, the day the Nineteenth Amendment was adopted in 1920, as Women's Equality Day.) Offered a ride in a car, she declined, and, "blithely swinging her cane" walked the nearly mile-long route down Pennsylvania Avenue to Lafayette Park, where years ago she was once pelted with eggs while giving a suffrage speech. "My coat was dripping when I finished," she recalled.[21]

Hazel Hunkins Hallinan died in 1982, two years after the 1980 presidential election when the final vote count revealed for the first time a gender gap, or a difference between the proportion of women and men who supported a particular candidate. (Eight percent more women than men supported Democrat Jimmy Carter for president.)[22] Every subsequent presidential election has revealed a gender gap. In addition, more women than men register to vote—83.8 million women to 73.8 million men in 2016. And more women go to the polls. Since 1964, the number of female voters has exceeded the number of male voters in every presidential election.[23] In typically low-turnout midterm elections, women voters also outnumber men. Clearly, women armed with the vote are a force to be reckoned with in American politics!

The tumultuous time in America—the 2016 presidential campaign and the aftermath that I found unnerving while writing *The Vote: Women's Fierce Fight*—was leavened by the historic victories of women candidates for state and national offices in the 2018 midterm election. Three of the record number of women newly elected to Congress—Democratic Representatives Alexandria Ocasio-Cortez, Ilhan Omar, and Madeleine Dean—explicitly wore suffragist-inspired all-white outfits to the official swearing-in ceremony in the House of Representatives. "I wore all-white today to honor the women who paved the path before me. . . . I wouldn't be here if it wasn't for the mothers of the movement," tweeted Representative AlexandriavOcasio-Cortez.[24]

Many Democratic women members of Congress, including House Speaker Nancy Pelosi, wore suffrage-white to the 2019 State of the Union Address. The first African American congresswoman, Shirley Chisholm, wore white when she was elected in 1969. As did Geraldine Ferraro in 1984, when she accepted the Democratic Party's nomination as its vice presidential candidate, and Hillary Clinton in 2016 when she accepted the Democratic Party's nomination as its presidential candidate.

Here and there across America, women's fierce fight for the vote is remembered in landmarks—historic markers, memorials, signs, and statues. A highway sign in Uxbridge, Massachusetts, marks the section of Route 146 named for Lydia Taft who voted in the 1700s. A statue in Cheyenne, Wyoming, titled "The Franchise," represents Louisa Swain, the first woman to vote on September 6, 1870. Statues, markers, and a national historic site honor Harriet Tubman who promoted woman suffrage, because, she said, "I suffered enough to believe [in] it." In Saint Paul, Minnesota, the names of twenty-five suffragists are listed on the Minnesota Woman Suffrage Memorial, located on the grounds of the Minnesota State Capitol.

The centennial celebration of the Nineteenth Amendment has spurred efforts to honor suffragists with a record number of landmarks, including the Turning Point Suffragist Memorial, located near the site of the Occoquan Workhouse, Fairfax County, Virginia, and statues of Sojourner Truth, Rosalie Jones, Elizabeth Cady Stanton and Susan B. Anthony in New York. A bill is pending in the Montana Legislature to name a stretch of Interstate 90 the Jeannette Rankin Memorial Highway. See my website (www.pennycolman.com) for information about woman suffrage landmarks, aligned with the chapters in *The Vote: Women's Fierce Fight*.

There is much to learn from women's fight for the vote, the monumental nonviolent civil rights struggle in America that achieved passage of the Nineteenth Amendment to the United States Constitution. Lessons about strategy and tactics. Examples of commitment and courage. Warnings about choosing expediency over principle and schisms over unity. Words of inspiration and empowerment. It is our obligation to permanently weave the names and deeds and lessons of suffragists into the national narrative of America so that this transformative fight remains a lodestar for present and future activists.

In 2012, Harriet "Hattie" Redmond's organizing efforts that helped secure equal suffrage in Oregon in 1912 were rediscovered, and this headstone was dedicated in Lone Fir Cemetery, Portland, Oregon. A recent visitor put an "I Voted" sticker on the marker. Headstones were also placed on the graves of suffragists Esther Pohl Lovejoy, Harry Land, and Martha Cardwell Dalton. (Friends of Lone Fir Cemetery)

Acknowledgments

The Vote: Women's Fierce Fight has consumed my life for some time. First and foremost, I am grateful to the generations of women and men of goodwill who fiercely fought the fight for woman suffrage. My life has been greatly enriched by immersing myself in the lives and work of these historic fighters for justice. I owe many thanks to so many people for their support and good cheer, including Julie Chita, Susan Kirch, Charlotte Bennett Schoen, Annie Unverzagt, and so many others.

When I finished my term as a distinguished lecturer at Queens College, the City University of New York, several special colleagues, Myra Zarnowski, Eileen Bowen, Raeann Farrell, Daisy Sanchez, and Susan Turkel, presented me with the perfect gift—a framed photograph of a tugboat with New York suffragists on board who were embarking for a rendezvous in the Hudson River with a tugboat bearing New Jersey suffragists.

Throughout the process of doing research and writing *The Vote: Women's Fierce Fight,* I was profoundly grateful to all the creators and keepers of primary and secondary material: activists, historians, archivists, and librarians. There is a treasure trove of written and visual suffrage material online. To the people and organizations that create and maintain such sites, I extend a heartfelt thank you. (An extensive list is on my website, www.pennycolman.com.)

I also must express my deep appreciation to Molly Murphy MacGregor, cofounder of the National Women's History Alliance, for enriching my life with her ceaseless commitment to and passion for multicultural women's history; Kenneth Florey, who graciously showed me his extensive collection of suffrage memorabilia; Jennifer Krafchik, Acting Executive Director, Belmont-Paul Women's Equality National Monument, who answered my question about the dimensions of the picket's banners and offered additional assistance; and Coline Jenkins, the great-great-granddaughter of Elizabeth Cady Stanton, and a passionate keeper of Stanton's legacy, who showed me suffrage items in the comprehensive collection in the Elizabeth Cady Stanton Trust.

Janet Joslin read *The Vote: Women's Fierce Fight* and provided invaluable insights and comments, as did Molly Murphy MacGregor, Robert P. J. Cooney, Jr., Jonathan Colman, and Stephen Colman, who alerted me to the story about Eugene Debs and Susan B. Anthony. David Morgan Colman provided insightful comments about race relations. As always my life-partner, Linda Hickson, who over and over read every word, provided indispensable feedback, suggestions, and sustenance. There are not enough words to express my gratitude for her love and involvement.

Selected Bibliography

(See www.pennycolman.com for an extensive bibliography.)

Books:

Abbott, Chris. *21 Speeches that Shaped Our World: The People and Ideas that Changed the Way We Think*. London: Rider, 2010.

Adams, Katherine H. and Michael L. Keene. *Alice Paul and the American Suffrage Campaign*. Urbana, IL: University of Illinois Press, 2008. *After the Vote Was Won: The Later Achievements of Fifteen Suffragists*. Jefferson, NC: McFarland & Companies, Inc., 2010.

Anderson, Bonnie S. *Joyous Greetings: The First International Women's Movement, 1830-1860*. New York: Oxford University Press, 2000. *The Rabbi's Daughter: Ernestine Rose International Feminist Pioneer*. New York: Oxford University Press, 2017.

Anthony, Susan B. & Ida Husted Harper. *History of Woman Suffrage (1883-1900),* Vol. 4. Indianapolis: The Hollenbeck Press, 1902.

Aptheker, Bettina. *Woman's Legacy: Essays on Race, Sex, and Class in American History*. Amherst, MA: The University of Massachusetts Press, 1982.

Bailyn, Bernard. *Barbarous Years: The Peopling of British North America*. New York: Vintage Books, 2012.

Baker, Jean H. *Sisters: The Lives of American Suffragists*. New York: Hill and Wang, 2005. *Women and the U.S. Constitution, 1776-1920*. Washington, D.C.: American Historical Society, 2003.

Banaszak, Lee Ann. *Why Movements Succeed or Fail: Opportunity, Culture, and the Struggle for Woman Suffrage*. Princeton: Princeton University Press, 1996.

Bay, Mia. *To Tell the Truth Freely: The Life of Ida B. Wells*. Hill and Wang, 2009.

Behn, Beth A. "Woodrow Wilson's Conversion Experience: The President and the Federal Woman Suffrage Amendment," 2012. University of Massachusetts —Amherst. https://scholarworks.umass.edu/cgi/viewcontent.cgi?article=2447&context=theses.

Berg, A. Scott. *Wilson*. New York: G.P. Putnam, 2013.

Bijon, Beatrice and Claire Delahaye. "'Forward, Sisters, Forward!'": Community As Family in the British and American Suffrage Movements." In *Exchanges and Correspondence: The Construction of Feminism,* eds. Claudette Fillard and Francoise Orazi. Newcastle upon Tyne: Cambridge Scholars Publishing, 2010.

Blight, David W. *Frederick Douglass: Prophet of Freedom.* New York: Simon & Schuster, 2018.

Brown, Gertrude Foster. "The Opposition Breaks." In *Victory: How Women Won It.* New York: The H. W. Wilson Co, 1940.

Cahill, Bernadette. *Alice Paul, the National Woman's Party and the Vote: The First Civil Rights Struggle of the 20th Century.* Jefferson, NC: McFarland & Company, Inc., 2015.
Arkansas Women and the Right to Vote: The Little Rock Campaigns, 1868-1920. Little Rock, AK: Butler Center Books, 2015.

Caraway, Nanci. *Segregated Sisterhood: Racism and the Politics of American Feminism.* Knoxville: The University of Tennessee Press, 1991.

Catt, Carrie Chapman and Nettie Rogers Shuler. *Woman Suffrage and Politics: The Inner Story of the Struggle of the Suffrage Movement.* New York: Charles Scribner's Sons, 1926.

College Equal Suffrage of Northern California. *Winning Equal Suffrage in California.* San Francisco: Press of the James H. Barry, Co., 1913.

Colman, Penny. *Elizabeth Cady Stanton and Susan B. Anthony: A Friendship That Changed the World.* New York: Macmillan, 2011.

Cooney, Robert P. J. *Remembering the Last Campaign of Inez Milholland, Suffrage Martyr.* Santa Cruz: American Graphic Press, 2015.
Winning the Vote: The Triumph of the American Woman Suffrage Movement. Santa Cruz: American Graphic Press, 2005.

Davis, Angela. *Women Race and Class.* New York: Random House, 1981.

Dodyk, Delight W. "Education and Agitation: The Woman Suffrage Movement in New Jersey," PhD diss., Rutgers, The State University of New Jersey, 1997.

Dorr, Rheta Childe. *Susan B. Anthony: The Woman Who Changed the Mind of a Nation.* New York: Frederick A. Stokes, 1928.

Douglass, Frederick. "The Rights of Women." In *Frederick Douglass: Selected Speeches and Writings,* edited by Philip S. Foner. Chicago: Lawrence Hill Books, 1999.

DuBois, Ellen Carol. *Harriot Stanton Blatch and the Winning of Woman Suffrage.* New Haven: Yale University Press, 1997.

Eckhardt, Celia Morris. *Fanny Wright: Rebel in America.* Cambridge: Harvard University Press, 1984.

Ellis, Joseph J. *American Sphinx: The Character of Thomas Jefferson.* New York: Vintage, 1998. *First Family: Abigail & John Adams.* New York: Alfred A Knopf, 2002.

Epps, Garrett. *American Epic: Reading the U.S. Constitution.* New York: Oxford University Press. 2013.

Faulkner, Carole. *Lucretia Mott's Heresy: Abolition and Women's Right's in Nineteenth- Century America.* Philadelphia: University of Pennsylvania Press, 2011.

Finnegan, Margaret. *Selling Suffrage: Consumer Culture & Votes for Women.* New York, Columbia University Press, 1999.

Flexner, Eleanor and Ellen Fitzpatrick. *Century of Struggle: The Women's Rights Movement in the United States.* rev. ed. Cambridge: The Belknap Press of Harvard University Press, 1975.

Florey, Kenneth. *American Woman Suffrage Postcards.* Jefferson, NC: McFarland Books, 2015.

Women's Suffrage Memorabilia. Jefferson, NC: McFarland Books, 2013.

Ford, Linda G. *Iron-Jawed Angels: The Suffrage Militancy of the National Women's Party.* New York: Da Capo Press, 1992.

Fought, Leigh. *Women in the World of Frederick Douglass.* New York: Oxford University Press, 2017.

Franzen, Trisha. *Anna Howard Shaw: The Work of Woman Suffrage.* Urbana: IL: University of Illinois Press, 2014.

Freeman, Jo. *We Will Be Heard: Women's Struggle for Political Power in the United States.* Lanham, MD: Rowman & Littlefield, 2008.

Friedl, Bettina, ed. *On To Victory: Propaganda Plays of the Woman Suffrage Movement* Boston: Northeastern University Press, 1987.

Frost, Elizabeth and Kathryn Cullen-DuPont. *Women's Suffrage in America: An Eyewitness History.* New York: Facts On File, 1992.

Giddings, Paula. *When and Where I Enter: The Impact of Black Women on Race and Sex in America.* New York: Amistad, 2006.

Gilman, Charlotte Perkins. *Suffrage Songs and Verses.* New York: The Charlton Co., 1911.

Ginzberg, Lori D. *Elizabeth Cady Stanton: An American Life.* New York: Hill and Wang, 2009.

Gluck, Sherna, ed. *From Parlor to Prison: Five American Suffragists Talk about Their Lives.* New York: Vintage Books, 1976.

Goldsmith, Barbara. *Other Powers: The Age of Suffrage, Spiritualism, and the Scandalous Victoria Woodhull.* New York: Alfred A. Knopf, 1998.

Gordon, Ann D. ed. *The Selected Papers of Elizabeth Cady Stanton & Susan B. Anthony,* 6 Vols. New Brunswick, NJ: Rutgers University Press, 1997-2013.

Gordon, Ann D., with Bettye Collier-Thomas. *African American Women and The Vote, 1837-1965.* Amherst, MA: University of Massachusetts Press, 1997.

Graham, Sarah Hunter. *Woman Suffrage and the New Democracy.* New Haven: Yale University Press, 1996.

Green, Elna C. *Southern Strategies: Southern Women and the Woman Suffrage Question.* Chapel Hill: The University of North Carolina, 1997.

Griffith, Elisabeth. *In Her Own Right: The Life of Elizabeth Cady Stanton.* New York: Oxford University Press, 1984.

Hamlin, Kimberly A. "Bathing Suits and Backlash: The First Miss America Pageants." In *There She Is: Miss America: The Politics of Sex, Gender, and Race in America's Most Famous Pageant.* eds. Elwood Watson and Darcy Martin. New York; Palgrave/St. Martin's, 2004.

Harper, Ida Husted. *History of Woman Suffrage.* Vols. 5-6. New York: National American Woman Suffrage Association, 1922.

The Life and Work of Susan B. Anthony. Indianapolis and Kansas City: Bowen- Merrill Company, 1898.

Harrison, Patricia Greenwood. *Connecting Links: The British and American Woman Suffrage Movement, 1900-1914.* Westport, CT: Greenwood Press, 2000.

Hoffert, Sylvia. *Alva Vanderbilt Belmont: Unlikely Champion of Women's Rights.* Bloomington: Indiana University Press, 2012.

Hull, N. E. *The Woman Who Dared to Vote: The Trial of Susan B. Anthony.* Lawrence, KS: University Press of Kansas, 2012.

Irwin, Inez Hayes. *The Story of Alice Paul and the National Woman's Party.* Fairfax, VA: Denlinger's Publishers, 1977.

Katzenstein, Caroline. *Lifting the Curtain: The State and National Woman Suffrage Campaigns in Pennsylvania as I Saw Them.* Philadelphia: Dorrance, 1955.

Kerber, Linda K. and Jane Sherron De Hart. *Women's America: Refocusing the Past, 5th* ed. New York: Oxford University Press, 2000.

Kerr, Andrea Moore. *Lucy Stone: Speaking Out for Equality.* New Brunswick: Rutgers University Press, 1992.

Keyssar, Alexander. *The Right to Vote: The Contested History of Democracy in the United States.* New York: Basic Books, 2000.

Kraditor, Aileen S. *The Ideas of the Woman Suffrage Movement, 1890-1920.* New York: W.W. Norton, 1981.

Kroeger, Brooks. *The Suffragents: How Women Used Men to Get the Vote.* Albany: State University of New York Press, 2017.

Kukla, Jon. Mr. Jefferson's Women. New York: Alfred A. Knopf, 2007.

Lerner, Gerda. *The Grimké Sisters From South Carolina: Pioneers for Woman's Rights and Abolition.* New York: Schocken Books, 1967.

Levin, Phyllis Lee. *Abigail Adams: A Biography.* New York: St. Martin's Griffin, 2001.

Lloyd, Trevor. *Suffragettes International: The World-wide Campaign for Women's Rights.* London: Macdonald Unit and New York: American Heritage Press, 1971.

Lunardini, Christine. *From Equal Suffrage to Equal Rights: Alice Paul and the National Woman's Party, 1910-1928.* New York: New York University Press, 1986.

Macdonald, Charlotte, ed. *The Vote the Pill and the Demon Drink: A History of Feminist Writing in New Zealand, 1869-1993.* Wellington, New Zealand: Bridget Williams Books, 1993.

MacKenzie, Midge. *Shoulder to Shoulder: A Documentary.* New York: Alfred A. Knopf, 1975.

Marlow, Joyce, ed. *Votes for Women: The Virago Book of Suffragettes.* London: Virago Press, 2000.

Marilley, Suzanne M. *Woman Suffrage and the Origins of Liberal Feminism in the United States, 1820-1920.* Cambridge: Harvard University Press, 1997.

McBridge, Genevieve. *On Wisconsin Women: Working for Their Rights from Settlement to Suffrage.* Madison: The University of Wisconsin Press, 1993.

McCammon, Holly J. & Lee Ann Banaszak. *100 Years of the Nineteenth Amendment: An Appraisal of Women's Political Activism.* Oxford University Press, 2018.

McConnaughy, Corrine M. *The Woman Suffrage Movement in America: A Reassessment.* New York: Cambridge University Press, 2013.

McGoldrick, Neale & Margaret Crocco. *Reclaiming Lost Ground: The Struggle for Woman Suffrage in New Jersey.* Trenton: New Jersey Council for the Humanities, 1994.

Mead, Rebecca. *How the Vote Was Won: Woman Suffrage in the Western United States, 1868-1914.* New York: New York University Press, 2004.

Merrick, Caroline E. *Old Times in Dixie Land: A Southern Matron's Memories.* New York: The Grafton Press, 1901.

Miller, John Chester. *The Wolf by the Ears: Thomas Jefferson and Slavery.* Charlottesville: University Press of Virginia, 1991.

Million, Joelle. *Woman's Voice, Woman's Place: Lucy Stone and the Birth of the Woman's Rights Movement.* Westport, CT: Praeger Publishers, 2003.

Moynihan, Ruth Barnes. *Rebel for Rights: Abigail Scott Duniway.* New Haven: Yale University Press, 1983.

National American Woman Suffrage Association. *Victory: How Women Won It: A Centennial Symposium 1840-1940.* New York: The H.W. Wilson Company, 1940.

Noun, Louise R. *Strong-Minded Women: The Emergence of the Woman-Suffrage Movement in Iowa.* Ames: IA: Iowa State University Press, 1969.

O'Brien, Mary Barmeyer. *Bright Star in the Big Sky: Jeannette Rankin, 1880-1973.* Helena: Falcon, Press, 1995.

Orleck, Annelise. "From the Russian Pale to Labor Organizing in New York City," in *Women's American: Refocusing the Past,* eds. Linda K. Kerber and Jane Sherron De Hart. New York: Oxford University Press, 2000.

Painter, Nell. *Sojourner Truth: A Life, A Symbol.* New York: W.W. Norton, 1996.

Palmer, Beverly Wilson, ed. *Selected Letters of Lucretia Coffin Mott.* Urbana and Chicago, Illinois: University of Illinois Press, 2002.

Pankhurst, Emmeline. *My Own Story: The Autobiography of Emmeline Pankhurst* London: Virago, 1979.

Pankhurst, E. Sylvia. *The Suffragette Movement: An Intimate Account of Persons and Ideals.* London: Longmans, Green and Co., 1931.

Park, Maud Wood. *Front Door Lobby: An Account of the Achievement of Woman Suffrage in the United States.* 1960. Reprint, Minneapolis: Filiquarian Publishing, 2017.

Peck, Mary Gray. *Carrie Chapman Catt: A Biography.* New York: The H. W. Wilson Company, 1944.

Petrash, Antonia. *Long Island and the Woman Suffrage Movement.* Charleston, SC: The History Press, 2013.

Preskill, Stephen and Stephen D. Brookfield. *Learning as a Way of Leading: Lessons from the Struggle for Social Justice.* New York, John Wiley & Sons: 2008.

Richardson, Marilyn. *Maria W. Stewart, America's First Black Woman Political Writer: Essays and Speeches.* Bloomington: IN: Indiana University Press, 1987.

Schwarz, Judith. *Radical Feminism of Heterodoxy: Greenwich Village 1912-1940.* Norwich, VT: New Victoria Publishers, 1986.

Scott, Anne Firor and Andrew M, eds. *One Half the People: The Fight for Woman Suffrage.* Philadelphia: Lippincott, 1975.

Shaw, Anna Howard. *The Story of a Pioneer.* New York: Harper and Brothers, 1915.

Sheppard, Alice. *Cartooning for Suffrage.* Albuquerque, NM: University of New Mexico Press, 1994

Shirley, Gayle C. *More Than Petticoats: Remarkable Montana Women.* Helena, MT: Twodot Book, 1996.

Solomons, Selina. *How We Won the Vote in California: A True Story of the Campaign of 1911.* 1912. Reprint, London: Forgotten Books, 2015.

Stanton, Elizabeth Cady. *Eighty Years and More: Reminiscences 1815-1897.* 1898. Reprint, New York: Schocken Books, 1971.

Stanton, Elizabeth Cady, Susan B. Anthony, and Matilda Joslyn Gage, eds. *History of Woman Suffrage.* Vols. 1-3. Rochester: Susan B. Anthony, 1887.

Stanton, Theodore and Harriot Stanton Blatch, eds. Vol. 2, *Elizabeth Cady Stanton as Revealed in Her Letters, Diary and Reminiscences.* New York: Harper & Brothers, 1922.

Stevens, Doris. *Jailed for Freedom.* Carol O'Hare, ed. Trout, OR: NewSage Press, 1995. Original edition published in 1920, Createspace Independent Publishing, 2014.

Strom, Sharon Hartman. *Politico Woman: Florence Luscomb and the Legacy of Radical Reform.* Philadelphia: Temple University Press, 2001.

Stuart, Amanda MacKenzie. *Consuelo & Alva Vanderbilt: The Story of a Daughter and Mother in the Gilded Age.* New York: HarperCollins, 2005.

Stuhler, Barbara. *Gentle Warriors: Clara Ueland and the Minnesota Struggle for Woman Suffrage.* St. Paul: Minnesota Historical Society, 1995.

Terborg-Penn, Rosalyn. *African American Women in the Struggle for the Vote, 1850- 1920.* Bloomington, IN: Indiana University Press, 1998.

Terrell Mary Church. *A Colored Woman in a White World.* 1940. Reprint, Amherst, NY: Humanity Books, 2005.

Van Voris, Jacqueline. *Carrie Chapman Catt: A Public Life.* New York: The Feminist Press at the City University of New York, 1987.

Wagner, Sally Roesch. *A Time of Protest: Suffragists Challenge the Republic: 1870-1887.* Aberdeen, SD: Sky Carrier Press, 1992.

Walton, Mary. *A Woman's Crusade: Alice Paul and the Battle for the Ballot.* 2010. Reprint, New York: St. Martin's Griffin, 2016.

Weatherford, Doris. *A History of the American Suffragist Movement.* Santa Barbara: ABC-CLIO, 1998.

Weiss, Elaine. *The Woman's Hour: The Great Fight to Win the Vote.* New York: Viking, 2018.

Wellman, Judith. *The Road to Seneca Falls: Elizabeth Cady Stanton and the First Woman's Rights Conventions.* Urbana: University of Illinois Press, 2004.

Wheeler, Marjorie Spruill. *New Women of the New South: The Leaders of the Woman Suffrage Movement in the Southern States.* New York: Oxford University Press, 1993.

One Woman One Vote: Rediscovering the Woman Suffrage Movement. Troutdale: OR: NewSage Press, 1995.

Votes for Women! The Woman Suffrage Movement in Tennessee, the South, and the Nation. Knoxville: The University of Tennessee Press, 1995.

Wolff, Francie. *Give the Ballot to the Mothers: Songs of the Suffragists.* Springfield, MO: Denlinger's Publishers, 1998.

Yellin, Carol Lynn and Janann Sherman. *The Perfect 36: Tennessee Delivers Woman Suffrage.* Memphis: Serviceberry Press, 1998.

Zahniser, J.D. and Amelia Fry. *Alice Paul: Claiming Power.* New York: Oxford University Press, 2014.

Articles and Blogs:

Adickes, Sandra. "Sisters, not demons: the influence of British suffragists on the American movement." *Women's History Review* 11, no. 4 (2002): 675-690, http://dx.doi.org/10.1080/09612020200200336.

Borda, Jennifer L. "The Woman Suffrage Parades of 1910-1913: Possibilities and Limitations of an Early Feminist Rhetorical Strategy." *Western Journal of Communication* 66, no. 1 (2002), 25-52.

Brown, Diane. *How Women Got the Vote in Oklahoma,*" League of Women Voters of Oklahoma, 1978, 1990. http://norman.ok.lwvnet.org/files/HowWomenGotVote.pdf

Caldwell, Martha B. "The Woman Suffrage Campaign of 1912." *The Kansas Historical Quarterly* 12, no. 3 (1943): 300-326, www.kshs.org/p/the-womansuffrage-campaign-of- 1912/12944.

Clifford, Deborah P. "The Drive for Women's Municipal Suffrage in Vermont 1883- 1917." *Vermont History* 47 (1979): 173-190, http://www.worldcat.org/title/drive-for- womensmunicipal-suffrage-in-vermont-1883-1917/ocle/527808328.

Edwards, G. Thomas. "Susan B. Anthony and the Struggle for Woman Suffrage in Oregon." Century of Action: Oregon Women Vote Dexchutes County Historical Society, http://centuryofaction.org/index.php/main_site/Essays/susan_b._anthony_and_the_struggle_for_woman_suffrage_in_oregon_18711906.

Ford, Sabrina. "How Racism Split the Suffrage Movement." *Bust Magazine*

Gallagher, Robert S., "I Was Arrested, Of Course." *American Heritage* 25, no. 2 (1974): http://www.americanheritage.com/content/%E2%80%9Ci-was-arrested- course%E2%80%A6%E2%80%9D.

Gillis, Emalee Gruss. "May Arkwright Hutton and the Battle for Women's Suffrage." *Pacific Northwest Inlander* (2008), http://www.washingtonhistory.org/research/whc/milestones/suffrage/hutton.

Havemeyer, Lousine, "Memories of a Militant: The Suffrage Torch." *Scribner's* 71, no. 5 (1922): 528-538, http://www.unz.com/print/Scribners-1922may-00528. "Memories of a Militant The Prison Special." *Scribner's* 72, no. 6 (1922): 661- 675, http://www.unz.com/print/Scribners-1922jun-00661.

Klinghoffer, Judith Apte and Lois Elkis. "The Petticoat Electors': Women's Suffrage in New Jersey, 1776-1807." *Journal of the Early Republic* 12, no. 2 (1992): 159-193, http://www.jstor.org/stable/3124150.

Lanctot, Catherine J. "We Are at War and You Should Not Bother the President: The Suffrage Pickets and Freedom of Speech During World War I." Villanova University School of Law (2008): 1-62, https://papers.ssrn.com/sol3/ papers.cfm?abstract_id=1126806.

Osselaer, Heidi. "From the Sidelines to Center Stage: Women and Arizona's Quest for Statehood," *Territorial Times* (2011), https://www.womensheritagetrail.org/resources/WomenAndStatehood.pdf

Pauley, Garth E. " W.E.B. Du Bois on Woman Suffrage: A Critical Analysis of His *Crisis* Writings." *Journal of Black Studies* 30, no. 3 (2000): 383-410. https://journals.sagepub.com/doi/abs/10.1177/002193470003000306

Rea, Tom. "Right Choice, Wrong Reasons: Wyoming Women Win the Right to Vote." WyoHistory.org. http://www.wyohisotry.org/essays/right-choice-wrong-reasons- wyoming-women-win-right-vote.

Sanford, J.B. "Argument Against Women's Suffrage, 1911." http://sfpl.org/pdf/libraries/main/sfhistory/suffrageagainst.pdf.

Slanley, Catherine. "The Library Employees' Union of Greater New York, 1917-1929, *Libraries & Culture* 30, no. 3, (1995): 235-264.

Sloan, Kay. "Sexual Warfare in the Silent Cinema: Comedies and Melodramas of Woman Suffragism," *American Quarterly* 33 (1981): 412-36.

Smith, Armantine M. "The History of the Woman's Suffrage Movement in Louisiana." *Louisiana Law Review.* 62, no. 2 (2002): 514-519, http://digitalcommons.law.lsu.edu/cgi/viewcontent.cgi?article=5926&context=lalrev.

Trout, Grace Wilbur. "Side Light on Illinois Suffrage History." *Journal of the Illinois State Historical Society* 13, no. 2 (1920): 145-179, https://archive.org/details/jstor-40194491/page/n1.

Yellin, Carol Lynn. "Countdown in Tennessee, 1920." *American Heritage Magazine* 30, no. 1, (1978), http://www.americanheritage.com/content/countdown-tennessee- 1920.

Notes

Abbreviations:

APNWP—Inez Haynes Irwin, *The Story of Alice Paul and the National Women's Party* (Fairfax, VA: Denlinger's Publishers, 1964, 1977).

CA—Chronicling America, Library of Congress https://chroniclingamerica.loc.gov.

HWS—Elizabeth Cady Stanton, Susan B. Anthony and Matilda Joslyn Gage, eds. *History of Woman Suffrage. Volumes 1-3* (Rochester: 1887); *Volume 4* by Susan B. Anthony & Ida Husted Harper, eds. (Rochester: 1902) *Volumes 5-6* by Ida Husted Harper, ed. (New York: 1922).

FDL—Maud Wood Park. *Front Door Lobby* (1960; rept., Minneapolis: Filiquarian Publishing, 2017).

JFF—Doris Stevens, *Jailed for Freedom: American Women Win the Vote*, Edited by Carol O'Hare from original edition published in 1920 (Troutdale, Oregon: NewSage Press, 1995).

NYT—*The New York Times*

PQ—ProQuest Historical Newspapers https://www.proquest.com/products-services/pq-hist-news.html

TPG—The Project Gutenberg www.gutenberg.com

Epigraph

1. Carrie Chapman Catt and Nellie Rogers Shuler, *Woman Suffrage and Politics: The Inner Story of the Suffrage Movement* (New York: Charles Scribner's Sons, 1926), 107-108, https://www.loc.gov/resource/rbnawsa.n6874/?sp=115.
2. The White House, "National Monument for Women's Equality," *The United States of Women* (blog), April 2, 2016, https://www.theunitedstateofwomen.org/blog/national-monument-womens-equality.
3. Mary Church Terrell, *A Colored Woman in a White World* (1940; rept., Amherst, NY: Humanity Books, 2005), 349.

Author's Note

1. Catt and Shuler, *Woman Suffrage and Politics,* 107-108.
2. Elizabeth Frost and Kathryn Cullen-DuPont, *Women's Suffrage in America: An Eyewitness History* (New York: Facts on File, 1992), 360.
3. Jacqueline Van Voris, *Carrie Chapman Catt: A Public Life* (New York: The Feminist Press at The City University of New York, 1987), 129.

Chapter 1

1. Frost and Cullen-DuPont, *Women's Suffrage in America,* 359-361.
2. Ibid., 407.

364

3. Lois Green Carr, "Margaret Brent—A Brief History," Archives of Maryland, last updated February 2, 2002. https://msa.maryland.gov/msa/speccol/sc3500/sc3520/002100/002177/html/mbrent2.htm, https://msa.maryland.gov/msa/speccol/sc3500/sc3520/002100/002177/html/mbrent2.html

4. Bernard Bailyn, *Barbarous Years: The Peopling of British North America* (New York: Vintage Books, 2012), 116.

5. Carr, "Margaret Brent."

6. Linda K. Kerber and Jane Sherron De Hart, *Women's America: Refocusing the Past,* 5th ed. (New York: Oxford University Press, 2000), 15.

7. Joseph J. Ellis, *American Sphinx: The Character of Thomas Jefferson* (New York: Alfred A. Knopf), 90-91.

8. John Chester Miller, *The Wolf by the Ears: Thomas Jefferson and Slavery* (Charlottesville: University Press of Virginia, 1991), 184.

9. Phyllis Lee Levin, *Abigail Adams: A Biography* (New York: St. Martin's Griffin, 1987, 2001), 82-83.

10. "From John Adams to James Sullivan, 26 May 1776," Founders Online National Archives, https://founders.archives.gov/documents/Adams/06-04-02-0091.

11. "Abigail Adams to Mercy Otis Warren, 27 April 1776," Founders Online, National Archives, https://founders.archives.gov/documents/Adams/04-01-02-0257.

12. Neale McGoldrick and Margaret Crocco, *Reclaiming Lost Ground: The Struggle for Woman Suffrage in New Jersey* (Trenton: New Jersey Historical Commission, 1994), 2.

13. Ibid., 5.

14. Joseph Bloomfield, *Laws of the State of New Jersey* (Trenton: James J. Wilson, 1811), The New Jersey Digital Legal Library, 33, http://njlegallib.rutgers.edu/statutes/1811.php.

15. Delight W. Dodyk, "Education and Agitation: The Woman Suffrage Movement in New Jersey" (Ph.D. diss., Rutgers, The State University of New Jersey, 1997), 249.

16. " U.S. Constitution — Preamble," U.S. Constitution, https://www.usconstitution.net/xconst_preamble.html.

17. Jean H. Baker, *Women and the U.S. Constitution, 1776-1920* (Washington, D.C.: American Historical Association and the Institute for Constitutional Studies, 2009), 1.

18. Linda K. Kerber, *Toward an Intellectual History of Women* (Chapel Hill: The University of North Carolina Press, 1997), 247.

19. John Inazu and Burt Neuborne, "Interactive Constitution: Right to Assembly and Petition," Constitution Daily (blog), National Constitution Center, August 14, 2017, https://constitutioncenter.org/blog/interactive-constitution-right-to-assemble-and-petition

20. "Judith Sargent Murray Society Quotes," Judith Sargent Murray Society, http://www.jsmsociety.com/Quotes.html.

21. Bee Rowlatt, "The Original Suffragette; the Extraordinary Mary Wollstonecraft," *The Women's Blog, The Guardian*, October. 5, 2015, https://www.theguardian.com/lifeandstyle/womens-blog/2015/oct/05/original-suffragette-mary-wollstonecraft.

22. Celia Morris Eckhardt, *Fanny Wright: Rebel in America* (Cambridge: Harvard University Press, 1984), 172.

23. Stanton et al., *HWS*, 1:35, http://www.gutenberg.org/files/28020/28020-h/28020-h.htm#CHAPTER_I.

24. Eckhardt, *Fanny Wright*, 217.

25. J. Akins, "A Downright Gabbler," Library of Congress, https://www.loc.gov/item/2002708975.

26. Eckhardt, *Fanny Wright*, 249.

27. Stanton et al., *HWS*, 1:35, http://www.gutenberg.org/files/28020/28020-h/28020-h.htm#CHAPTER_I.

28. Bonnie S. Anderson, *The Rabbi's Atheist Daughter: Ernestine Rose International Feminist Pioneer* (New York: Oxford University Press, 2017), 78.

29. Gerda Lerner, *The Grimké Sisters From South Carolina: Pioneers for Woman's Rights and Abolition* (New York: Schocken Books, 1967), 189.

30. Catherine Beecher, "Essay on Slavery and Abolitionism Addressed to Miss A. D. Grimké," Uncle Tom's Cabin & American Culture, A Multi-Media Archive, University of Virginia, 101-105, http://utc.iath.virginia.edu/abolitn/abesaegb5t.html.

31. Angelina E. Grimké, "Letters to Catherine Beecher, Letter XII. Human Rights Not Founded on Sex," Uncle Tom's Cabin & American Culture, A Multi-Media Archive, University of Virginia, 116, http://utc.iath.virginia.edu/abolitn/abesaegb5t.html.

32. Lerner, *The Grimké*, 192.

33. Judith Wellman, *The Road to Seneca Falls: Elizabeth Cady Stanton and the First Woman's Rights Convention* (Urbana: University of Illinois Press, 2004), 58.

34. Elizabeth Cady Stanton, *Eighty Years and More: Reminiscences 1815-1897* (1898, 1881, New York: Shocken Books, 1971), 82-83.

35. Wellman, *The Road to Seneca Falls*, 189.

36. Frost and Cullen-DuPont, *Women's Suffrage in America*, 359-360.

37. Wellman, *Road to Seneca Falls*, 203.

38. Ibid., 161.

39. Frost and Cullen-DuPoint, *Women's Suffrage in America*, 360.

40. Wellman, *Road to Seneca Falls*, 209.

41. Stacey M. Robertson, *Hearts Beating for Liberty: Abolitionists in the Old Northwest* (Chapel Hill: University of North Carolina Press, 2010), 138.

42. Robert W. Audretsch, ed., "The Salem, Ohio 1850 Women's Rights Convention Proceedings (Salem, Ohio: Salem Area Bicentennial Committee and Salem Public Library, 1976), 24-25,

    http://www.salem.lib.oh.us/wp-
content/uploads/2015/11/WellDoneSister.pdf.

43. Andrea Moore Kerr, *Lucy Stone Speaking Out for Equality* (New Brunswick: Rutgers University Press, 1995), 60.

44. Ibid., 51-52.

45. Ibid., 50.

46. Joelle Million, *Woman's Voice, Woman's Place: Lucy Stone and the Birth of the Woman's Rights Movement* (Westport: Connecticut: Praeger, 2003), 108.

47. Kerr, *Lucy Stone Speaking Out for Equality,* 60.

48. Sally Roesch Wagner, "Native American Women Inspired Women's Suffrage Movement," *Bust Magazine in Feminism,* https://bust.com/feminism/14922-how-native-american-women-inspired-the-feminist-movement.html.

49. "More Women's Rights Conventions," Women's Rights National Historical Park, National Park Service, https://www.nps.gov/wori/learn/historyculture/more-womens-rights-conventions.htm.

50. Ivins, Sam P., "Woman's Rights," *The Athens Post* (Athens, OH), October 20, 1854, CA.

51. "Women on the Rampage," *Staunton Spectator* (Staunton VA), January 1, 9, 1866. CA.

Chapter 2:

1. "Woman's Rights," *New York Herald,* May 11, 1866, 4, CA.

2. Stanton et al., *HWS*, 2:172, http://www.gutenberg.org/files/28039/28039-h/28039-h.htm.

3. Lori D. Ginzberg, *Elizabeth Cady Stanton: An American Life* (New York: Hill and Wang, 2009), 119.

4. Frost and Cullen-DuPont, *Women's Suffrage in America*, 381.

5. Ida Husted Harper, *The Life and Work of Susan B. Anthony, Including Public Addresses, Her Own Letters, and Many from her Contemporaries During Fifty Years*, TPG, 1:284, https://www.gutenberg.org/files/15220/15220-h/15220-h.htm.

6. Ibid.,1:291.

7. Alan Lewis, "Kansas Suffrage Song," Oocites.com 2009, (archived www.OoCities.org).

8. Alma Lutz, *Created Equal: A Biography of Elizabeth Cady Stanton* (New York: The John Day Company, 1940), 141.

9. Elisabeth Griffith, *In Her Own Right: The Life of Elizabeth Cady Stanton* (New York: Oxford University Press, 1984), 127.

10. Bernadette Cahill, *Arkansas Women and the Right to Vote: The Little Rock Campaigns, 1868-1920* (Little Rock, AK: Butler Center Books, 2015), 34.

11. Dodyk, *Education and Agitation*, 101.

12. Frost and Cullen-DuPont, *Women's Suffrage in America*, 384.

13. Ginzberg, *Elizabeth Cady Stanton,* 117.

14. Rosalyn Terborg-Penn, *African American Women in the Struggle for the Vote, 1850-1920* (Bloomington: Indiana University Press, 1998), 33.

15. Kerr, *Lucy Stone Speaking Out for Equality,* 140.

16. Paula Giddings, *When and Where I Enter: The Impact of Black Women on Race and Sex in America* (New York: Bantam Books, 1984), 65.

17. Stanton et al., *HWS,* 2:392, TPG, http://www.gutenberg.org/files/28039/28039-h/28039-h.htm#CHAPTER_XXIII.

18. Leigh Fought, *Women in the World of Frederick Douglass* (New York: Oxford University Press, 2017), 199.

19. Ibid., 201.

20. Kerr, *Lucy Stone Speaking Out for Equality,* 129.

21. Stanton, *Eighty Years and More,* 256.

22. Beverly Wilson Palmer, ed., *Selected Letters of Lucretia Coffin Mott* (Urbana: University of Illinois Press, 2002), 437.

23. Fought, *Women in the World of Frederick Douglass,* 201.

24. Giddings *When and Where I Enter,* 80.

25. "Virginia Minor and Women's Right to Vote," *Gateway Arch National Park Missouri,* https://www.nps.gov/jeff/learn/historyculture/the-virginia-minor-case.htm.

26. Stanton et al., *HWS,* 2:408, TPG, http://www.gutenberg.org/files/28039/28039-h/28039-h.htm#CHAPTER_XXIII.

27. "John Campbell and Women's Right to Vote" Wyoming State Museum Traveling History Bug, Wyoming State Museum, http://wyomuseum.state.wy.us/Geocache/index.aspx?ID=5.

28. Guy Hamilton, "Letter to the Editor," *Tiffin Tribune* (Tiffin, OH), February 18, 1970, CA.

29. "The Combat Deepens!" *Bellows Falls Times* (Bellows Falls, VT), February 25, 1870, CA.

30. "Mary Olney Brown," Obituary, Find-a-Grave, https://www.findagrave.com/memorial/63326813/mary-brown.

31. Stanton et al., *HWS,* 3:781-784, http://gutenberg.readingroo.ms/2/8/5/5/28556/28556-h/28556-h.htm#CHAPTER_LIV.

32. "Mary Olney Brown," Obituary.

33. Doris Weatherford, *Women in American Politics: History and Milestones* (Thousand Oaks, California: CQP Press, 2012,) 270.

34. Barbara Goldsmith, *Other Powers: The Age of Suffrage, Spiritualism, and the Scandalous Victoria Woodhull* (New York: Alfred A. Knopf, 1998), 303.

35. Ibid., 274.

36. Frost and Cullen-DuPont, *Women's Suffrage in America,* 228.

37. Ann Gordon, *The Selected Papers of Elizabeth Cady Stanton and Susan B. Anthony* (New Brunswick: Rutgers University Press, 1997), 2: 407.

38. N.E. Hull, *The Woman Who Dared to Vote: The Trial of Susan B.* Anthony (Lawrence: University Press of Kansas, 2012), 65.

39. Ibid., 102.

40. Ibid., 157.

41. Ibid., 149.

42. Gordon: *The Selected Papers of Elizabeth Cady Stanton and Susan B. Anthony,* 2:xxii.

43. Stanton et al., *HWS,* 2:742, http://www.gutenberg.org/files/28039/28039-h/28039-h.htm#CHAPTER_XXV.

44. Anthony & Harper, *HWS,* 4:40, http://www.gutenberg.org/files/29870/29870-h/29870.

45. Stanton et al., *HWS,* 3:2, http://gutenberg.readingroo.ms/2/8/5/5/28556/28556-h/28556-h.htm.

46. Ibid.,3:507, http://www.gutenberg.org/files/28556/28556-h/28556-h.htm#CHAPTER_XL.

47. "The Baxter Steam Engine with Flowers," The Life and Adventures of Emma Allison (blog), May 20, 2013, www.emmaallison.me.

48. Frost and Cullen-DuPont, *Women's Suffrage in America,* 398.

49. Eleanor Flexner and Ellen Fitzpatrick, *Century of Struggle* (Cambridge: The Belknap Press of Harvard University Press: 1959, 1975), 164.

Chapter 3

1. Stanton et al., *HWS,* 3:76, http://gutenberg.readingroo.ms/2/8/5/5/28556/28556-h/28556-h.htm#CHAPTER_XXVIII.

2. Ibid., 3:93.

3. Ibid., 3:102.

4. Anthony & Harper, *HWS,* 4:xxxvii, http://www.gutenberg.org/files/29870/29870-h/29870-h.htm.

5. Ibid., 4:86, http://www.gutenberg.org/files/29870/29870-h/29870-h.htm#CHAPTER_VI.

6. Ibid., 4:101. TPG, http://www.gutenberg.org/files/29870/29870-h/29870-h.htm#CHAPTER_VI

7. Stanton et al., *HWS,* 3:122, http://gutenberg.readingroo.ms/2/8/5/5/28556/28556-h/28556-h.htm#CHAPTER_XXVIII.

8. Gordon, *The Selected Papers of Elizabeth Cady Stanton and Susan B. Anthony:* 5:25.

9. Theodore Stanton and Harriot Stanton Blatch, *Elizabeth Cady Stanton: As Revealed in Her Letters, Diary, and Reminiscences,* (New York: Harper & Brothers, 1922), 2: 501.

10. Anthony & Harper, *HWS,* 4:134, http://www.gutenberg.org/files/29870/29870-h/29870-h.htm#CHAPTER_VIII.

11. Carole Faulkner, *Lucretia Mott's Heresy: Abolition and Women's Rights in Nineteenth-Century America,* (Philadelphia: University of Pennsylvania Press, 2011), 57.

12. Bonnie S. Anderson, *Joyous Greetings: The First International Women's Movement, 1830-1860* (New York: Oxford University Press, 2000), 9.

13. Anthony & Harper, *HWS,* 4:1041, http://www.gutenberg.org/files/29870/29870-h/29870-h.htm#CHAPTER_LXXIV.

14. Charlotte Macdonald, ed., *The Vote the Pill and the Demon Drink: A History of Feminist Writing in New Zealand, 1869-1993* (Wellington, New Zealand: Bridget Williams Books, 1993), https://books.google.com/books?isbn=0908912404.

15. Stanton et al., *HWS,* TPG, 1:234-235, https://www.gutenberg.org/files/28020/28020-h/28020-h.htm#CHAPTER_I.

16. "Susan B. Anthony Day," *The Evening Star,"* (Philadelphia, PA) February 19, 1890, CA.

17. "Women Associations Consolidate," *The Evening Bulletin* (Maysville, KY), February 18, 1890, CA.

18. "United Suffragists," *The Los Angeles Daily Herald,* February 19, 1890, 3, CA.

19. "Mrs. Stanton's Prediction," *The Rock Island Argus* (Rock Island, IL), February 19, 1890, CA.

20. Anthony & Harper, *HWS,* 4:999, http://www.gutenberg.org/files/29870/29870-h/29870-h.htm#CHAPTER_LXXII.

21. Ibid., 4:1001.

22. Ibid., 4:999-1000.

23. Stanton and Blatch, *Elizabeth Cady Stanton,* 2:265.

24. Harper, *The Life and Work of Susan B. Anthony,* 2:691, http://gutenberg.readingroo.ms/3/1/1/2/31125/31125-h/31125-h.htm#CHAPTER_XXXVIII.

25. Van Voris, *Carrie Chapman Catt,* 35.

26. Ibid., 6.

27. Ibid., 12.

28. Harper *The Life and Work of Susan B. Anthony,* 2:691, TPG, http://gutenberg.readingroo.ms/3/1/1/2/31125/31125-h/31125-h.htm#CHAPTER_XXXVIII.

29. Van Voris, *Carrie Chapman Catt,* 24-25.

30. "South Dakota Woman's suffrage (1890)," Ballotpedia, https://ballotpedia.org/South_Dakota_Woman%27s_Suffrage_(1890).

31. Stanton, et.al, *HWS,* 1:234-235, https://www.gutenberg.org/files/28020/28020-h/28020-h.htm#CHAPTER_VIII.

32. Anthony & Harper, *HWS*, 4:1001, http://www.gutenberg.org/files/29870/29870-h/29870-h.htm#CHAPTER_LXXII.

33. Stanton and Blatch, *Elizabeth Cady Stanton*, 2:265.

34. Anthony & Harper, *HWS*, 4:647, http://www.gutenberg.org/files/29870/29870-h/29870-h.htm#CHAPTER_XL.

35. Sabrina Ford, "How Racism Split the Suffrage Movement," Bust Magazine in Feminism (blog), https://bust.com/feminism/19147-equal-means-equal.html.

36. Terborg-Penn, *African American Women in the Struggle for the Vote*, 110.

37. Anthony & Harper, *HWS*, 4:246, https://www.gutenberg.org/files/29870/29870-h/29870-h.htm#CHAPTER_XV.

38. Van Voris, *Carrie Chapman Catt*, 45.

39. Anthony & Harper, *HWS*, 4:252, https://www.gutenberg.org/files/29870/29870-h/29870-h.htm#CHAPTER_XVI.

40. "Emmeline B. Wells," The Church of Jesus Christ of Latter-day Saints Church History, https://history.ids.org/event/emmeline-b-wells.

41. Anthony & Harper, *HWS*, 4:589, https://www.gutenberg.org/files/29870/29870-h/29870-h.htm#CHAPTER_XXXVI.

42. Randall A. Lake, "About Scott Duniway," She Flies with Her Own Wing: The Collected Speeches of Abigail Scott Duniway, last updated August 3, 2017. www.asduniway.org.

43. Anthony & Harper, *HWS*, 4:592-593, https://www.gutenberg.org/files/29870/29870-h/29870-h.htm#CHAPTER_XXXVI.

44. "Our Women Can Vote," *Lewiston Teller* (Lewiston, ID), December, 17, 1896, CA.

45. *Woman's Journal*, November 14, 1896.

46. Anthony & Harper, *HWS*, 4: 498, https://www.gutenberg.org/files/29870/29870-h/29870-h.htm#CHAPTER_XXVIII.

47. Van Voris, *Carrie Chapman Catt*, 48.

48. Anthony & Harper, *HWS*, 4:492, https://www.gutenberg.org/files/29870/29870-h/29870-h.htm#CHAPTER_XXVIII.

49. Ibid., 4:27, https://www.gutenberg.org/files/29870/29870-h/29870-h.htm#CHAPTER_II.

50. Caroline E. Merrick, *Old Times in Dixie Land: A Southern Matron's Memories* (New York: The Grafton Press, 1901) 224, http://www2.latech.edu/~bmagee/louisiana_anthology/texts/merrick/merrick--old_times.html.

51. Ibid.,125-126.

52. Ibid., 226.

53. Flexner and Fitzpatrick, *Century of Struggle*, 241.

54. Sara Hunter Graham, "The Suffrage Renaissance: A New Image for a New Century," in Marjorie Spruill Wheeler, ed., *One Woman One Vote: Rediscovering the Woman Suffrage Movement* (Troutdale, OR: NewSage Press: 1995), 161.

55. Van Voris, *Carrie Chapman Catt*, 49.

56. Anna Howard Shaw, "The Fate of Republics," in Mary Kavanaugh Oldham, ed., *The Congress of Women: Held in the Woman's Building, World's Columbian Exposition,*152, (Philadelphia: International Publishing, CO: 1895): A Celebration of Women Writers, www.digital.library.upenn.edu/women/eagle/congress/congress.html.

57. Elna C. Green, *Southern Strategies: Southern Women and the Woman Suffrage Question* (Chapel Hill: The University of North Carolina Press, 1997), 23.

58. "Early History," *National Woman's Christian Temperance Union*, www.wctu.org..

59. W.E.B. Dubois, "Mary Ann Shadd Cary House," National Park Service Quick Facts, https://www.nps.gov/places/the-mary-ann-shadd-cary-house.htm.

60. Patricia Hill Collins, "Black Feminist Thought," in *Theories on Race and Racism: A Reader,* Les Black and John Solomon, eds., (London: Routledge, 2000), 414.

61. Flexner, *Century of Struggle,* 182.

62. Stanton and Blatch, *Elizabeth Cady Stanton*, 4:288.

63. Anthony & Harper, *HWS*, 4:292, https://www.gutenberg.org/files/29870/29870-h/29870-h.htm#CHAPTER_XVIII.

64. Maude T. Jenkins, *The History of the Black Women's Club Movement in America* (New York: Teachers College, 1984), 79.

65. Terrell, *A Colored Woman in a White World*, 180.

66. Anthony & Harper, *HWS*, 4: 351, http://www.gutenberg.org/files/29870/29870-h/29870-h.htm#CHAPTER_XX.

67. Harper, *The Life and Work of Susan B. Anthony*, 3:1170, The Internet Archive, https://archive.org/details/lifeandworksusa02harpgoog/page/n89.

Chapter 4

1. Wikipedia contributors, "College Equal Suffrage League," Wikipedia, The Free Encyclopedia, https://en.wikipedia.org/w/index.php?title=College_Equal_Suffrage_League&oldid=848089845.

2. Harper, *HWS*, 5:32, http://www.gutenberg.org/files/29878/29878-h/29878-h.htm#CHAPTER_II.

3. Gordon, *Selected Papers of Elizabeth Cady Stanton and Susan B. Anthony*, 6:494.

4. Harper, *HWS*, 5:78, http://www.gutenberg.org/files/29878/29878-h/29878-h.htm#CHAPTER_III.

5. Maud Wood Park, "Campaigning State by State," in *Victory: How Women Won it*, (Washington: National American Woman Suffrage Association,),74.

6. Lee Ann Banaszak, *Why Movements Succeed or Fail: Opportunity, Culture, and the Struggle for Woman Suffrage*, (Princeton: Princeton University Press: 1996), 21.

7. Louise R. Noun, *Strong-Minded Women: The Emergence of the Woman-Suffrage Movement in Iowa* (Iowa City: The Iowa State University Press, 1969), 244.

8. "A Pioneer Gone: Mrs. Laura E. Peters Passes Away Saturday," *Clallam County Courier*, January 17, 1902, Washington State Historical Society, http://hometownchronicles.com/wa/clallam/obits/petersle.html.

9. Rebecca J. Mead, *How the Vote Was Won: Woman Suffrage in the Western United States, 1868-1914* (New York: New York University Press, 2004), 49.

10. *HWS*, 4:972, http://www.gutenberg.org/files/29870/29870-h/29870-h.htm#CHAPTER_LXIX.

11. "A Pioneer Gone: Mrs. Laura E. Peters Passes Away Saturday."

12. Ellen Carol DuBois, *Harriot Stanton Blatch and the Winning of Woman Suffrage* (New Haven: Yale University Press,1997), 40.

13. Jane Adams, "Why Women Should Vote," in *One Woman, One Vote, in* Wheeler, 201.

14. Victoria Bissell Brown, *Introduction to "Why Women Should Vote,"* in *One Woman, One Vote, in* Wheeler, 180.

15. Stephan Preskill and Stephen D. Brookfield, *Learning as a Way of Leading: Lessons from the Struggle for Social Justice* (New York, John Wiley & Sons: 2008) 38.

16. Harper, *HWS*, 5:189, http://www.gutenberg.org/files/29878/29878-h/29878-h.htm#CHAPTER_VI.

17. Eugene V. Debs, *Susan B. Anthony: A Reminiscence*, www.marxists.org/archive/debs/works/1909/1909-anthony.htm.

18. "Debs and Women's Rights —A Lifetime Commitment," *Eugene V. Debs Foundation*, www.debsfundation.org/index.php/landing/debs-biography/womens-rights.

19. Charlotte Perkins Gilman, *Suffrage Songs and Verses* (New York: The Charlton Co., 1911), https://archive.org/details/GilmanSuffrageSongs.

20. "Mrs. C. C. Catt For the Women," *The Times* (Richmond, VA), 5 October, 1901, CA.

21. Van Voris, *Carrie Chapman Catt*, 58.

22. Harper, *HWS*, 5:xviii, http://www.gutenberg.org/files/29878/29878-h/29878-h.htm

23. Susan Lyman Whitney, *"LDS Were Pioneers in Women's Suffrage" Deseret News,* March 13, 1992, ttps://www.deseretnews.com/article/215103/LDS-WERE-PIONEERS-IN-WOMENS-SUFFRAGE.html.

24. Marjorie Spruill Wheeler, *New Women of the New South: The Leaders of the Woman Suffrage Movement in the Southern States* (New York: Oxford University Press, 1993), 121.

25. Anna Howard Shaw, *The Story of a Pioneer,* 118.

26. Harper, *HWS,* 5:122, http://www.gutenberg.org/files/29878/29878-h/29878-h.htm#CHAPTER_V.

27. Ibid. 5:184-185, http://www.gutenberg.org/files/29878/29878-h/29878-h.htm#CHAPTER_VI.

28. Geoffrey C. Ward and Ken Burns, *Not For Ourselves Alone: The Story of Elizabeth Cady Stanton and Susan B. Anthony,* (New York: Alfred A. Knopf: 1999), 212.

29. "Susan B. Anthony, Dies Peacefully" *Los Angeles Herald,* March 13, 1906, CA.

30. Sara Hunter Graham, "The Suffrage Renaissance," in Marjorie Spruill Wheeler *One Woman, One Vote,* 174.

31. Harper, *HWS,* 5:202-203, http://www.gutenberg.org/files/29878/29878-h/29878-h.htm#CHAPTER_VII.

32. Ibid., 6:544, http://www.gutenberg.org/files/29878/29878-h/29878-h.htm#CHAPTER_XX.

33. Harper, *The Life and Work of Susan B. Anthony,* 3:1441, The Internet Archive, https://archive.org/details/lifeandworksusa02harpgoog/page/n391.

34. Harper, *HWS,* 5:211, http://www.gutenberg.org/files/29878/29878-h/29878-h.htm#CHAPTER_XVII

35. Ibid., 5:200.

Chapter 5

1. "Women's League Formed," *Lincoln County Leader,* August 23, 1907, CA.

2. DuBois, *Harriot Stanton Blatch,* 94.

3. Ibid., 91.

4. Ibid., 99.

5. E. Sylvia Pankhurst, *The Suffragette Movement: An Intimate Account of Persons and Ideals* (1931; London: Longmans, Green Co, rept. Milton Keynes, UK: Lightning Source, 2010), 185-186.

6. John Simkin, "Anne Cobden Sanderson," *Spartacus Educational* (2015), www.spartacus-educational.com/Wsanderson.htm.

7. George Bernard Shaw, "Shaw on Woman's Rights," *NYT,* November 15, 1906, PQ.

8. "English Suffragette Hits American Suffragists," *Evening Star,* January 11, 1908, PQ.

10. Izola Forrester, "Maud Malone: Always the Unafraid," *The World Magazine,* November 17, 1912, 11.

9. "Suffragettes Open Their Campaign Here," *NYT*, January 1, 1908, PQ.

10. Letter to the Editor, *NYT*, December 28, 1907, PQ.

11. "Suffragettes Protest," *NYT*, April 30, 190, PQ.

12. Emmeline Pankhurst, *My Own Story: The Autobiography of Emmeline Pankhurst* (London: Virago, 1914, 1979), 88. Ghostwritten by Rheta Childe Dorr, for a series in *Good Housekeeping*. Dorr had access to notes and documents, interviewed her during their voyage from England to America, and accompanied her on her speaking tour. It is a vivid compelling account but requires double-checking because of various errors.

13. "Arrest Maud Malone Again," *NYT*, June 27, 1909, PQ.

14. Catherine Shanley, "Maud Malone Arrested, Arrest Maud Malone Again, Maud Malone Martyr, Sad for Suffragette: Maud Malone Warned, Blackwell's Island for Her if She Keeps Talking," "The Library Employees' Union of Greater New York, 1917-1929." *Libraries and Culture*, 30 no. 3 (1995): 235-264.

15. Jennifer Davis McDaid, "Equal Suffrage League of Virginia (1909-1920)," *Encyclopedia   of   Virginia*, http://www.EncyclopediaVirginia.org/Equal_Suffrage_League_of_Virginia_1909-1920.

16. Gabrielle Steward Mulliner, "Woman's Suffrage as a By-Product," *NYT*, January 5, 1908, 10, PQ.

17. "Women Are Divided on Outdoor Talks," *NYT*, January 3, 1908, PQ.

18. "To The Editor," *NYT*, December 28, 1908, PQ.

19. "Suffragist Parade Despite the Police," *NYT*, February 17, 1908, PQ.

20. Harper, *HWS*, 5:242, http://www.gutenberg.org/files/29878/29878-h/29878-h.htm#CHAPTER_VIII.

21. Ibid. 5:317, http://www.gutenberg.org/files/29878/29878-h/29878-h.htm#CHAPTER_XI.

22. "Prominent Ladies Who Were in Parade of Agitators for Equal Suffrage," *The Hawaiian Star*, March 25, 1908, CA.

23. "Vassar Meets in Graveyard," *The Sun*, June 9, 1908, CA.

24. Annelise Orleck, "From the Russian Pale to Labor Organizing In New York City," in *Women's America*, 5th ed., eds. Linda K. Kerber and Jane Sherron De Hart, 299.

25. "Women Who Want the Ballot Give Their Reasons," *NYT*, November 8, 1908, PQ.

26. "Women Had An Election," *NYT*, November 4, 1905, PQ.

27. "Oh The Women!: They are Coming to Seattle by the Train Load this Week," *The Seattle Times*, June 27, 1909, CA.

28. "Cupid to Travel with Suffragettes," *The Evening Statesman* (Walla Walls, WA), May 9 1909, CA.

29. Beatrice Bijon and Claire Delahaye, "'Forward, Sisters, Forward!': Community As Family in the British and American Suffrage Movements," in *Exchanges and Correspondence: The Construction of Feminism*, eds. Claudette Fillard and Francoise Orazi, (Newcastle upon

Tyne: Cambridge Scholars Publishing, 2010), 97, https://books.google.com/books?isbn=1443824429.

30. "The Suffrage Song Book-14," Kansas Memory, https://www.kansasmemory.org/item/204064/page/16.

31. Paula Becker, "Prominent Suffragists Arrive in Spokane on June 28, 1909," The Free Online Encyclopedia of Washington State History (March 20, 2008), www. Historylink.org/File/8522.

32. "Tall Timber: Bunnard [sic] Has No Chance in His Campaign with a Suffragette," *The Marion Daily Mirror*, (Marion, OH), October 9, 1909, CA.

33. "Suffragette is Headed This Way," *The Evening Statesman*, August 4, 1909, CA.

Chapter 6

1. "Hail Mrs. Pankhurst As Their Champion," *NYT*, October 25, 1909, PQ.

2. "Great Throng Hears Mrs. Pankhurst," *NYT*, October 26, 1909, PQ.

3. Van Voris, *Carrie Chapman Catt*, 109.

4. Amanda MacKenzie Stuart, *Consuelo & Alva Vanderbilt: The Story of a Daughter and Mother in the Gilded Age* (New York: HarperCollins, 2005), 310.

5. "Suffrage Breaks Out at Newport," *Daily Capital Journal* (Salem, OR), August 24, 1909, CA.

6. Stuart, *Consuelo & Alva Vanderbilt*, 313.

7. Flexner and Fitzpatrick, *Century of Struggle*, 234.

8. Annelise Orleck, *Common Sense and a Little Fire: Women and Working-Class Politics in the United States, 1900-1965* (Chapel Hill: University of North Carolina Press: 1995), 61.

9. Stuart, *Consuelo & Alva Vanderbilt*, 320.

10. "Invites Negroes to Join," *The Topeka Daily State Journal*, February 7, 1910, CA.

11. Stuart. *Consuelo & Alva Belmont*, 317.

12. Irwin, *APNWP*, 14.

13. Katherine H. Adams and Michael L. Keene, *Alice Paul and the American Suffrage Campaign* (Urbana: University of Illinois Press, 2008), 9.

14. "Alice Paul Talks," *Philadelphia Tribune*, January 1, 1910, Library of Congress, https://www.loc.gov/item/rbcmiller003903.

15. "Won't Try to Start Suffrage War Here," *NYT*, January 2, 1910, PQ.

16. Pankhurst, *My Own Story*, 116.

17. Pankhurst, *The Suffragette Movement*, 332.

18. Midge MacKenzie, *Shoulder to Shoulder: A Documentary* (New York: Knopf, 1975), 96.

19. Ibid., 150-151.

20. Harper, *HWS*, 5:281, http://www.gutenberg.org/files/29878/29878-h/29878-h.htm#CHAPTER_X.

21. Ibid., 5:270-273.

22. 6:342-43, http://www.gutenberg.org/files/30051/30051-h/30051-h.htm#CHAPTER_I.

23. Ibid., 6: 434.

24. Frost and Cullen-DuPont, *Women's Suffrage in America*, 302.

25. Anthony & Harper, *HWS*, 4:889, http://www.gutenberg.org/files/29870/29870-h/29870-h.htm#CHAPTER_LIX.

26. Ibid., 6:527, http://www.gutenberg.org/files/30051/30051-h/30051-h.htm#CHAPTER_I.

27. Ibid., *HWS*, 6:587, http://www.gutenberg.org/files/30051/30051-h/30051-h.htm#CHAPTER_I.

28. Mead, *How the Vote Was Won*, 102-03.

29. Ibid., 108.

30. Laura Arksey, "Hutton, May Arkwright (1860-1915), The Free Online Encyclopedia of Washington State History, http://www.historylink.org/File/7547.

31. Mead, *How the Vote Was Won*, 99.

32. "Woman Suffrage Sweeps the State," *The Wenatchee Daily World* (Wenatchee, WA), November 9, 1910, CA.

33. Van Voris, *Carrie Chapman Catt*, 81.

34. Harper, *HWS*, 6:439, http://www.gutenberg.org/files/30051/30051-h/30051-h.htm#CHAPTER_I.

35. Midge MacKenzie, *Shoulder to Shoulder*, 167.

36. "Suffragette Dies on Leaving Prison," *Bridgeport Evening Farmer* (Bridgeport, CT), December 28, 1910, CA.

Chapter 7

1. Pankhurst, *The Suffragette Movement*, 347.

2. "Miss Pankhurst Arrives Like a Lamb, Not Like Lion," *St. Louis Post-Dispatch,*

March 17, 1911, CA.

3. Pankhurst, *The Suffragette Movement*, 347.

4. "Hits at British Jails," *The Sun* (New York, NY), February 18, 1911, CA.

5. "Reason Why Told By Suffragette," *The Washington Times*, February 22, 1911, CA.

6. American Women Timid Says British Heroine," *The San Francisco Call*, March 12, 1911, CA.

7. "Bridge, Balls and Dinner Women—Soundly Scored," *Chickasha Daily Express* (Chickasha Indian Territory, OK), February 2, 1911, CA.

8. Frost and Cullen-DuPont, *Women's Suffrage in America*, 303.

9. "3,000 Women in March for Votes," *The Sun*, May 7, 1911, CA.

10. "Parade of Women," *NYT,* May 6, 1911, PQ.

11. Anthony & Harper, *HWS*, 4:40, http://www.gutenberg.org/files/29870/29870-h/29870-h.htm#CHAPTER_III.

12. Selina Solomons, *How We Won the Vote in California: A True Story of the Campaign of 1911* (1912; San Francisco: The New Woman Publishing Co., rept London, ForgottenBooks, 1915), 52.

13. Ibid., 47-48.

14. J. B. Sanford, "Argument Against Women's Suffrage, 1911," San Francisco Public Library, https://sfpl.org/pdf/libraries/main/sfhistory/suffrageagainst.pdf.

15. "'The Times' and Suffrage, *Los Angeles Times,* September 22, 1911, CA.

16. Robert P. J. Cooney, Jr., *Winning the Vote: The Triumph of the American Woman Suffrage Movement* (Santa Cruz: American Graphic Press, 2005), 145.

17. Margaret Finnegan, *Selling Suffrage: Consumer Culture & Votes for Women* (New York: Columbia University Press, 1999), 2.

18. "Auto Parties Will Whoop Up Votes for Women," *The San Francisco Call,* August 5, 1911, CA.

19. Julia Hochheimer, "Mrs. Hochheimer Says Vote Will Not Unsex Women," *The San Francisco Call,* September 24, 1911, CA.

20. "Diva Sings for Suffrage," *The San Francisco Call,* October 10, 1911, CA.

21. Mead, *How the Vote was Won,* 145.

22. *Winning Equal Suffrage in California: Reports of Committees of the College Equal Suffrage League of Northern California in the Campaign of 1911* (San Francisco: National College Equal Suffrage League, 1911), 72, https://archive.org/details/winningequalsuf00caligoog.

23. Solomons, *How We Won the Vote in California,* 61.

24. "Hopes of California Women Mount with the Rising Tide of Suffragette Votes, *Arizona Republican,* October, 11, 1911, CA.

25. Solomons, *How We Won the Vote in California,* 64.

26. Park, "Campaigning State by State," in The National American Woman Suffrage Association, *Victory,* 77.

27. Harper, *HWS,* 5:330, http://www.gutenberg.org/files/29878/29878-h/29878-h.htm#CHAPTER_XI.

28. "Wall Street Howls at Suffragettes," *The World,* November 27, 1911, CA.

29. "Vote NO on Woman Suffrage," *Jewish Women's Archive,* www.sblc.registereastconn.org.

Chapter 8

1. "Colonel Target of Suffragist," *The Salt Lake Tribune,* March 26, 1912, CA.

2. "Militant Woman Bests Roosevelt," *The Palatka News and Advertiser* (Palatka, FL), March 26, 1912, CA.

3. A. Scott Berg, *Wilson* (New York: G. P. Putnam's Son, 2013), 488.

4. DuBois, *Harriot Stanton Blatch,* 141-42.

5. "Johanna Neuman, "The 'Mere" Men Who Helped Win the Vote for Women," From the Square (blog)*,* August 25, 2017, https://www.fromthesquare.org/mere-men-helped-win-vote-women/#.XDvwtPx7nn4.

6. "The Uprising of the Women, *NYT,* May 5, 1912, PQ.

7. "For and Against Equal Suffrage," *NYT*, May 11, 1912, PQ.

8. "Maud Malone Halts Wilson," *NYT*, October 20, 1912, PQ.

9. "Maud Malone Held; Court Rebukes Her, *NYT*, October 24, 1912, PQ.

10. "Maud Malone Asks in Vain to be Fined, *NYT*, November 13, 1912, PQ.

11. "Miss Maud Malone Convicted for Her Heckling of Wilson," *Bismarck Daily Tribune* (Bismarck, ND), November 18, 1912, CA.

12. "How Lawless Suffragettes Would Soon Be Suppressed in America," *The Washington Post*, April 27, 1913, CA.

13. Harper, *HWS*, 6:510, http://www.gutenberg.org/files/30051/30051-h/30051-h.htm#CHAPTER_I.

14. Antonia Petrash, *Long Island and the Woman Suffrage Movement* (Charleston, SC: The History Press, 2013), Nook edition, chap. 6.

15. Marion Morton, "How Cleveland Women Got the Vote," *Teaching Cleveland Digital* (June 18, 2016), www.teachingcleveland.org/category/progressive_/how-cleveland-women-got-the-vote.

16. "Woman's Suffrage Only Amendment Lost by Ohio Vote," *The Washington Times*, September 4, 1912, CA.

17. Claudette Simpson, "Frances Munds and Arizona's History of Suffrage," Sharlot Hall Museum, 1998, www.sharlot.org.

18. Heidi Osselaer "From the Sidelines to Center Stage: Women and Arizona's Quest for Statehood," *Territorial Times*, November 2011, https://www.womensheritagetrail.org/resources/WomenAndStatehood.pdf.

19. Simpson, "Frances Munds."

20. Genevieve G. McBride, *On Wisconsin Women: Working for Their Rights from Settlement to Suffrage* (Madison: The University of Wisconsin Press, 1993), 213.

21. Ibid., 117.

22. Ibid., 213.

23. Harper, *HWS*, 6:201, http://www.gutenberg.org/files/30051/30051-h/30051-h.htm#CHAPTER_I.

24. Ibid., 6:197.

25. "Lucy Browne Johnson Papers," Kansas Historical Society, July 1978, https://www.kshs.org/p//lucy-browne-johnston-papers/14052.

26. Harper, *HWS*, 6:545, http://www.gutenberg.org/files/30051/30051-h/30051-h.htm#CHAPTER_I.

27. Diedra Cates, "Chinese American Woman Suffrage in 1912 Portland," *Century of Action: Oregon Women Vote 1912-2012*, http://centuryofaction.org/index.php/main_site/document_project/chinese_american_woman_suffrage_in_1912_portland.

28. Ruth Barnes Moynihan, *Rebel for Rights: Abigail Scott Duniway* (New Haven: Yale University Press, 1983), 216.

29. "400,000 Cheer Suffrage March," *NYT*, November 10, 1912, PQ.

30. "Women will Hail Ten-Starred Flag," *NYT*, November 12, 1912, PQ,

31. "Jubilee for Mrs. Catt," *NYT*, November 20, 1912, PQ.

32. "Anti-Suffrage Cry is to 'Bore the Men,'" *NYT*, November 20, 1912, PQ.

33. Harper, *HWS*, 5:337, http://www.gutenberg.org/files/29878/29878-h/29878-h.htm#CHAPTER_XII.

34. Irwin, *APNWP*, 4.

35. "General Jones and Army Reach Capital," *Evening Capital News*, December 29, 1912.

36. "Suffragettes at End of Their Hike," *The Times-Dispatch*, December 29, 1912, CA.

Chapter 9

1. Harper, *HWS*, 6:149, http://www.gutenberg.org/files/30051/30051-h/30051-h.htm#CHAPTER_I.

2. Grace Wilbur Trout, "Side Lights on Illinois Suffrage History" in *Transactions of the Illinois State Historical Society for the Year 1920* by Oliver Albert Harker, no. 27 (Springfield: Phillips Bros., 1921), 95-96, https://archive.org/details/jstor-40194491.

3. "Husband and Wife Partners in Business and Housework," *The Tacoma Times* (Tacoma, WA), June 21, 1910, CA.

4. "Woman Justice" *The Morning Astorian* (Astoria, WA), April 7, 1907, CA.

5. Anthony & Harper, *HWS*, 4:602, http://www.gutenberg.org/files/29870/29870-h/29870-h.htm#CHAPTER_XXXVII.

6. Trout, *Side Lights*, 96.

7. Gertrude Foster Brown, "The Opposition Breaks," in The National American Woman Suffrage Association, *Victory*, 86.

8. Ibid., 88-89.

9. Trout, *Side Lights*, 108.

10. Brown, 90-91.

11. Trout, *Side Lights*, 164

12. "Partial Suffrage for Illinois Women,: *The Salt Lake Tribune*, June 12, 1913, CA.

13. Harper, *HWS*, 5:370, http://www.gutenberg.org/files/29878/29878-h/29878-h.htm#CHAPTER_XIII.

14. Irwin, *APNWP*, 18.

15. "Most Beautiful Suffragist to be Pageant Herald," *The Washington Times*, January 20, 1913, CA.

16. "Suffragettes Plan Big Unique Parade," *The Tulsa Daily World* (Tulsa, OK), January 4, 1913, CA.

17. Wanda A. Hendricks, *Gender, Race, and Politics in the Midwest: Black Club Women in Illinois* (Bloomington: Indiana University Press, 1998), 91-93.

18. "Cool Greetings in South," *The Chicago Daily Tribune*, February 27, 1913, CA.

19. "Gen. Jones Dodges the Color Question," *NYT*, February 20, 1913, PQ.

20. "Gloom for Suffrage Army," *The Chicago Daily Tribune*, February 27, 1913, CA.

21. "Hoots, Insults, Clubs and Rocks for Hiking Army," *The Times Dispatch* (Richmond, VA), February 28, 1912, CA.

22. "Color Line in 'Army,' *The Baltimore Sun,* February 27, 1913, CA.

23. "Jones Army Makes Goals; Folks Shout," *The Rock Island Argus,* February 28, 1913, CA.

24. "5,000 Women March, Beset by Crowds," *NYT,* March 4, 1913, PQ.

25. Mary Walton, *A Woman's Crusade: Alice Paul and the Battle for the Ballot* (New York: St. Martin's Griffin, 2010, 2016), 76.

26. "Women Battle Hostile Mobs in Capital Parade," *New-York Tribune,* March 4, 1913, CA.

27. Trout, *Side Lights,* 99.

28. Harper, *HWS,* 6:713, http://www.gutenberg.org/files/30051/30051-h/30051-h.htm#CHAPTER_L.

29. "Alaska Gets a Legislature," *Alaska Humanities Forum History & Cultural Studies,* www.akhistorycourse.org.

30. Pankhurst, *The Suffragette Movement,* 493.

31. Pankhurst, *My Own Story,* 326.

32. "Mrs. Pankhurst Enters N.Y. in Triumph," *The San Francisco Call,* October 20, 1913, CA.

33. Chris Abbott, *21 Speeches That Shaped Our World: The People and Ideas That* Changed the Way We Think (London: Rider, 2010), 23.

34. Harper, *HWS,* 5:365, http://www.gutenberg.org/files/29878/29878-h/29878-h.htm#CHAPTER_XIII.

35. Irwin, APNWP, 48.

36. "What Will New York Do With Mrs. Pankhurst," *NYT,* September 14, 1913, PQ.

37. Pankhurst, *My Own Story,* 327.

38. Ibid., 330.

39. "Militant Burn Mansion to Avenge Mrs. Pankhurst Who Collapses in Prison," *The Evening World* (New York, NY), December 5, 1913, CA.

40. "Militant Methods Not For Americans, Says, Dr. Anna Shaw," *The Evening World,* December 5, 1913, CA.

Chapter 10

1. "Whole Nation Observes Woman's Day," *The Daily Missoula* (Missoula, MT), May 3, 1914, CA.

2. "Maypole Dance Feature of Suffragist Rally," *Louisville Journal* (Louisville, KY), May 3, 1914, CA.

3. "Belleville Men Keep Wives Out of Suffrage Parade," *St. Louis Post-Dispatch,* May 1, 1914, CA.

4. Irwin, *APNWP,* 53.

5. Ibid., 56.

6. "Militants End Hostilities in Great Britain," *The Christian Science Monitor,* August 28, 1914, PQ.

7. John Simkin, "Maud Arnclife Sennett," *Spartacus Educational*, February 2015, http://spartacus-educational.com/Wsennett.htm.

8. Millicent Garrett Fawcett, "Progress of the Women's Movement in the United Kingdom," *HWS*, 6:741, http://www.gutenberg.org/files/30051/30051-h/30051-h.htm#CHAPTER_LI.

9. Marlow, *Votes for Women*, 234.

10. Sylvia D. Hoffert, *Alva Vanderbilt Belmont: Unlikely Champion of Women's Rights* (Bloomington: Indiana University Press, 2012), 89.

11. Irwin, *APNWP*, 76-77.

12. "War on Congressmen," *The Washington Post*, August 23, 1914, CA.

13. "Attacks Belmont Meeting," *NYT*, August 24, 1914, PQ.

14. Adams and Keene, *Alice Paul and the American Suffrage Campaign*, 32.

15. "Suffragists Who Have Invaded the Western States," *The Lehi Banner*, September 26, 1914, CA.

16. Irwin, *APNWP*, 80-83.

17. Harper, *HWS*, 6: 512-513, TPG, http://www.gutenberg.org/files/30051/30051-h/30051-h.htm#CHAPTER_I.

18. "Wields Trenchant Pen," *The Greenville Journal*, October 1, 1914, CA.

19. "Challenge Accepted by Anti-Suffragists," *The Greenville Journal*, October 8, 1914, CA.

20. Harper, *HWS*, 6:342-344, TPG, http://www.gutenberg.org/files/30051/30051-h/30051-h.htm#CHAPTER_I.

21. Tim O'Neil, "Look Back 250: Missouri Suffragists Make Final Push for Right to Vote," Political Fix (blog), *St. Louis Post-Dispatch*, September 13, 2014, http://www.stltoday.com/news/local/govt-and-politics/look-back-missouri-suffragists-make-final-push-for-right-to/article_flabd693-5eb0-5869-9f91-6c488d30454a.html.

22. Harper, *HWS*, 6:420, http://www.gutenberg.org/files/30051/30051-h/30051-h.htm#CHAPTER_I.

23. Ibid., 6:78.

24. Harper, *HWS*, 6: 873-875, http://www.gutenberg.org/files/30051/30051-h/30051-h.htm#CHAPTER_LIV.

25. "Facts Which Nebraska Women Must Face," *Omaha Daily Bee*, November 2, 1914, CA.

26. Harper, *HWS*, 6:421, http://www.gutenberg.org/files/30051/30051-h/30051-h.htm#CHAPTER_I.

27. Ibid., 6:590.

28. Ibid., 6:421.

29. Ibid., 6:502.

30. "40,000 North Dakota Women Ask for the Ballot, "*Bismarck Daily Tribune*, November 1, 1914, CA.

31. Harper *HWS*, TPG, 5: 421, http://www.gutenberg.org/files/29878/29878-h/29878-h.htm#CHAPTER_XV.

32. Belle Fligelman Winestine, "Mother was Shocked," *Montana: The Magazine of Western History,* vol. 24, no. 3 (Summer 1974), 71, http://www.jstor.org/stable/4517906.

33. Ibid., 73.

34. Gayle C. Shirley, *More Than Petticoats: Remarkable Montana Women* (Helena: Twodot Books, 1995), 123.

35. Winestine, "Mother Was Shocked," 73.

36. *Sara Bard Field: Poet and Suffragist,* An Interview Conducted by Amelia R. Fry, "Suffragist Oral History Project," The Bancroft Library, University of California at Berkeley, 1979, 255, http://content.cdlib.org/view?docId=kt1p3001n1&brand=calisphere&doc.view=entiretext.

37. DuBois, *Harriot Stanton Blatch,* 184.

38. Harper, *HWS,* TPG, 6:400-401, http://www.gutenberg.org/files/30051/30051-h/30051-h.htm#CHAPTER_I.

Chapter 11

1. Katherine H. Adams and Michael L. Keene, *After the Vote Was Won: The Later Achievements of Fifteen Suffragists* (Jefferson, NC: McFarland & Companies, Inc., 2010), 39.

2. Louisine Havemeyer, "The Suffrage Torch Memories of a Militant," *Scribner's Magazine,* May 1922: 528, http://www.unz.com/print/Scribners-1922may-00528.

3. "Suffragist Sailors Meet Perils of Hudson and Deliver Torch of Liberty to Jersey Sisters," *The Sun,* August 8, 1915, CA.

4. Havemeyer, "The Suffrage Torch," 535.

5. "Suffrage Orator Tells of Campaign," *NYT,* August 8, 1915, PQ.

6. Havemeyer, "The Suffrage Torch," 536.

7. Ibid., 530.

8. "Westerners To Aid Suffragists Here," *NYT,* July 23, 1915, PQ.

9. "Women Open 'Hopperie,'" *NYT,* June 27, 1915, PQ.

10. "Match Boxes to Throw 'Light' on Suffrage," *Evening Public Ledger,* (Philadelphia, PA), October 27, 1915, CA.

11. "Hitchcock for Suffrage," *Evening Public Ledger,* October 22, 1915, CA.

12. Havemeyer, "The Suffrage Torch," 538-539.

13. "Suffrage Resolution Voted Down in the House Yesterday," *Tulsa World,* January 13, 1915, 1, CA.

14. "Votes for Women Defeated in the House," *The Omaha Daily Bee,* January 13, 1915, CA.

15. Irwin, *APNWP,* 102.

16. "First Convention of Women Voters Has 3,000 Delegates," *The Evening World,* September 14, 1915, CA.

17. "Suffrage War," *The Washington Post,* June 8, 1915, CA.

18. Irwin, *APNWP,* 102.

19. "Suffrage Petition 18,333 Feet Long," *The Washington Times,* September 17, 1915, CA.

20. "Suffrage Car Racing From Pacific Coast to White House with Long Petition," *The Day Book,* (Chicago, IL), November 20, 1915, CA.

21. Amelia Fry, *Sara Bard Field,* 249.

22. Ibid., 308.

23. "Away! Mere Man!" *The Topeka State Journal,* September 14, 1915, CA.

24. Irwin, *APNWP* 107.

25. Ibid., 109.

26. "On to Washington Suffrage War Cry," *Bismarck Daily Tribune,* September 17, 1915, CA.

27. Amelia Fry, *Sara Bard Field,* 309.

28. Ibid., 321.

29. "Suffs Envoy Ends Cross-Country Run," *The Sun,* (New York, NY) November 27, 1915, CA.

30. Dodyk, *Education and Agitation,* 392.

31. Ibid., 421.

32. Flexner and Fitzpatrick, *Century of Struggle,* 263.

33. Rebecca Beatrice Brooks, "Louisa May Alcott: the First Woman Registered to Vote in Concord," History of Massachusetts (blog), September 19, 2011, http://historyofmassachusetts.org/louisa-may-alcott-the-first-woman-registered-to-vote-in-concord.

34. "The Anti-Suffrage Rose," *NYT,* August 28, 1915, PQ.

35. Sharon Hartman Strom, *Politico Woman: Florence Luscomb and the Legacy of Radical Reform* (Philadelphia: Temple University Press, 2001), 87.

36. "45,000 March for Suffrage Braving Wind and Darkness in Greatest Woman's Parade," *New-York Tribune,* October 24, 1915, CA.

37. Van Voris, *Carrie Chapman Catt,* 129.

38. Irwin, *APNWP,* 118.

39. Kimberly A. Hamlin, "Bathing Suits and Backlash: The First Miss America Pageants" in *There She is, Miss America: The Politics of Sex, Gender, and Race in America's Most Famous Pageant,* eds. Elwood Watson and Darcy Martin (New York: Palgrave/St. Martin's, 2004), 28.

40. Harper, *HWS,* 5:441, http://www.gutenberg.org/files/29878/29878-h/29878-h.htm#CHAPTER_XIV.

41. Walton, *A Woman's Crusade,* 112.

42. Ibid., 5:453.

43. Van Voris, *Carrie Chapman Catt,* 130.

44. Mary Gray Peck, *Carrie Chapman Catt* (New York: The H. W. Wilson Company, 1944), 237-238.

45. Harper, *HWS,* 5:454, http://www.gutenberg.org/files/29878/29878-h/29878-h.htm#CHAPTER_XIV.

Chapter 12

1. Irwin, *APNWP,* 129-130.

2. Ibid., 153.

3. Frost and Cullen-DuPost, *Women's Suffrage in America*, 310.

4. Peck, *Carrie Chapman Catt*, 243.

5. Irwin, *APNWP*, 152-153.

6. "Suffrage Autoists Motor 10,700 Miles," *NYT*, October 1, 1916, PQ.

7. Irwin, *APNWP*, 159.

8. Adams and Keene, *Alice Paul and the American Suffrage Campaign*, 149-150.

9. "Rival Suffrage Workers Busy," *Courier Journal*, June 7, 1916, CA.

10. Peck, *Carrie Chapman Catt*, 244-246.

11. Ibid., 247.

12. "Women Move On St. Louis To Demand Equal Rights," *New York Tribune*, June 12, 1916, CA.

13. "Delegates Walk Suffrage Lane," *New York Tribune*, June 13, 1916, CA.

14. "Convention Ends; Platform Voted Raps Hyphenism," *NYT*, June 17, 1916, PQ.

15. Peck, *Carrie Chapman Catt*, 250.

16. Van Voris, *Carrie Chapman Catt*, 132.

17. Irwin, *APNWP*, 169-170.

18. Peck, *Carrie Chapman Catt*, 258.

19. Park, FDL, 7.

20. Harper, *HWS*, 5:446, http://www.gutenberg.org/files/29878/29878-h/29878-h.htm#CHAPTER_XIV.

21. Flexner and Fitzpatrick, *Century of Struggle*, 273-274.

22. Van Voris, *Carrie Chapman Catt*, 136.

23. William Keylor, "The Long-Forgotten Facial Attitudes and Policies of Woodrow Wilson" Professor Voices Boston University (March 4, 2013), http://www.bu.edu/professorvoices/2013/03/04/the-long-forgotten-racal-attitudesand-policies-of-woodrow-wilson.

24. "Miss Elisabeth Freeman," *The Kansas City Sun*, Kansas City, MO), August 19, 1916, CA.

22. Irwin, *APNWP*, 178.

23. Van Voris, *Carrie Chapman Catt*, 150.

24. "Congressional Union Notes," *Washington Times*, October 21, 1916, CA.

25. Van Voris, *Carrie Chapman Catt*, 150.

26. Frost and Cullen-DuPont, *Women's Suffrage in America*, 311.

27. "Rose Winslow Will Speak at Central Theatre Wednesday," *The Bisbee Daily Review* (Bisbee, AZ), October 31, 1916, CA.

28. Cooney, *Winning the Vote*, 314.

29. "Mrs. Boissevain Dies in Hospital," *New York Tribune*, November 27, 1916, CA.

30. "She Comes Here," *The Topeka Daily State Journal*, October 2, 1916, CA.

31. "Many Turn Out to Hear the Beauty," *The Cut Bank Pioneer Press* (Cut Bank, MT), October 20, 1916, CA.

32. Robert P.J. Cooney, Jr., *Remembering Inez: The Last Campaign of Inez Milholland, Suffrage Martyr* (Santa Cruz: American Graphic Press, 2015), 27-29.

33. Cooney, *Winning the Vote*, 315.

34. "Inez Boissevain," *The Tacoma Times*, November 28, 1916, CA.

35. Irwin, *APNWP*, 191.

36. Noun, *Strong-Minded Women*, 256.

37. Harper, *HWS*, 6:190, http://www.gutenberg.org/files/30051/30051-h/30051-h.htm#CHAPTER_I.

38. Ibid., 6:691.

39. Ibid., 6:693.

40. Ibid, 6:590-591.

41. Gayle Shirley, *More Than Petticoats*, 124.

42. "The 'Suff Bird Women' and Woodrow Wilson," From the Stack (blog), New York Historical Society, March 26, 2014, http://blog.nyhistory.org/the-suff-bird-women-and-woodrow-wilson.

43. Irwin, *APNWP*, 186.

44. "Mrs. Catt on Suffrage Methods," *NYT*, December 9, 1916, PQ.

Chapter 13

1. Ford, *Iron-Jawed Angels*, 76-77.

2. Stevens, JFF, 56.

3. Irwin, *APNWP*, 192-195

4. "Women Begin Silent Picket," *Ogden Standard*, (Ogden, UT), January 10, 1916, CA.

5. Stevens, JFF, 57-58.

6. Ford, *Iron-Jawed Angels*, 3.

7. Fry, *Conversation with Sara Bard Field*, 286.

8. "Women Begin Silent Picket, *Ogden Standard*, January 10, 1916, CA.

9. "'Suffs' Picket White House," *Evening Times-Republican* (Marshalltown, IA), January 10, 1916, CA.

10. Cooney, *Winning the Vote*, 323.

11. Ford, *Iron-Jawed Angels*, 125.

12. Terrell, *A Colored Woman in a White World*, 355.

13. Ford, *Iron-Jawed Angels*, 97.

14. Ibid., 127.

15. Stevens, *JFF*, 99.

16. Ford, *Iron-Jawed Angels*, 129.

17. Van Voris, *Carrie Chapman Catt*, 145.

18. "House Moves for Woman Suffrage," *NYT*, September 9, 1917, PQ.

19. Stevens, *JFF*, 61.

20. "Book Advertising Wins Wilson Smile," *The Washington Times*, January 28, 1917, CA.

21. "Nation on Verge of War," *The Bismarck Daily Tribune*, February 3, 1917, CA.

22. Park, *FDL*, 60.

23. Peck, *Carrie Chapman Catt*, 267.

24. Van Voris, *Carrie Chapman Catt*, 138.

25. Park, *FDL*, 60.

26. Irwin, *APNWP*, 206-207.

27. Stevens, *JFF*, 64.

28. "Suffragists Girdle White House in Rain," *NYT*, 5 May 1917, PQ.

29. Stevens, *JFF*, 65.

30. Irwin, *APNWP*, 210.

31. "Rain Soaked, 500 Suffragists Parade Four Times Around White House as 5,000 Cheer," The Washington Post, March 5, 1917, CA.

32. Stevens, *JFF*, 66.

33. Woodrow Wilson, "War Message to Congress, 1917," http://wps.prenhall.com/wps/media/objects/107/110495/ch22_a2_dl-pdf.

34. "Jeannette Rankin Pledges Her Best to Women's Cause," *The Daily Missoulian*, April 7, 1917, CA.

35. Shirley, *More Than Petticoats*, 119.

36. "Women of Russia to Vote for Assembly," *NYT*, March 23, 1917.

37. Pankhurst, *The Suffragette Movement*, 603.

38. "Suffragists in U.S. Buoyed by British Action," *The Washington Times,* March 29, 1917, 4, CA.

39. "Lloyd George is Lauded by New York Suffragists," *New-York Tribune*, 29 March 1917, CA.

40. Park, *FDL*, 76-77.

41. *Conversations with Alice Paul*, An Interview Conducted by Amelia R. Fry, "Suffragist Oral History Project," The Bancroft Library, University of California at Berkeley, 1979, 175.

42. Park, *FDL*, 76-77.

43. Shirley, *More Than Petticoat*, 121.

44. Park, *FDL*, 78, 109.

Chapter 14

1. D. Jerome Tweton, "The Crusading Elizabeth Preston Anderson," *North Dakota Studies,* www.ndstudies.org/articles/the_crusading_elizabeth_preston_anderson.

2. "Section 3: Woman Suffrage 1912 to 1920," *North Dakota Studies,* www.ndstudies.gov.

3. "Tennessee Suffrage Leaders: The Meriwethers," Tennessee4me, www.tnme.org.

4. Wikisource contributors, "The New Woman of the New South," *Wikisource,* https://en.wikisource.org/w/index.php?title=The_New_Woman_of_the_New_South&oldid=5225104.

5. Harper, *HWS*, 6: 601, http://www.gutenberg.org/files/30051/30051-h/30051-h.htm#CHAPTER_I.

6. Marjorie Spruill Wheeler, ed., *Votes for Women!: The Woman Suffrage Movement in Tennessee, the South, and the Nation* (Knoxville: The University of Tennessee Press, 1995), 165.

8. Ibid.,163.

9. Ibid., 57.

10. Harper, *HWS,* 6:514, http://www.gutenberg.org/files/30051/30051-h/30051-h.htm#CHAPTER_I.

11. "Suffrage," The Suffrage Movement and the WCTU, ,www.wwctu.org/resources_pdff/convention_2013/20130507_suffrage.pdf.

12. Cahill, *Arkansas Women and the Right to Vote,* 47.

13. "Woman Suffrage in Arkansas," *St. Louis Post-Dispatch,* May 11, 1917, CA.

14. *A Brief History of the New Hampshire Women Suffrage Association and Report of the Annual Meeting* (Concord: Rumford Printing Company, 1907), 19, https://books.google.com/books?id=nylNAAAAlAAJ.

15. Deborah P. Clifford, "The Drive for Women's Municipal Suffrage in Vermont 1883-1917," *Vermont History, Vermont Historical Society* 183-184 (1979): 174-177, http://vermonthistory.org/journal/misc/DriveForWomensSuffrage.pdf.

16. Harper, *HWS,* 6:663, http://www.gutenberg.org/files/30051/30051-h/30051-h.htm#CHAPTER_I.

17. "Suffrage Breaks Through," *New-York Tribune,* April 19, 1917, CA.

18. Park, *FDL,* 70.

19. "Emily Pierson To Move Out of State to Vote," *The Hartford Courant,* (Hartford, CT), April 24, 1917, CA.

20. Harper, *HWS,* 6:874, http://www.gutenberg.org/files/30051/30051-h/30051-h.htm#CHAPTER_LIV.

21. Harper, *HWS.,* 6:382, http://www.gutenberg.org/files/30051/30051-h/30051-h.htm#CHAPTER_I.

22. Ibid., 6:255.

23. "Another Inning for Women: Mrs. W.M. Ellicott Says Suffragists Ought to Feel Encouraged," *The Baltimore Sun,* February 5, 1914.

24. "Elizabeth King Ellicott (1858-1914)," *Archives of Maryland* (Biographical Series) MSA SC 3520-13588, http://msa.maryland.gov/megafile/msa/speccol/sc3500/sc3520/013500/013588/html/13588bio.html.

25. "Question of Color with the Suffragettes," *The Pascagoula Democrat-Star* (Pascagoula, MI), June 12, 1914, CA.

26. "House Passes Part Suffrage," *Detroit Free Press,* April 19, 1917, CA.

27. "Suffrage Worker Elated by News," *Los Angeles Times,* April 20, 1917, CA.

28. Charlotte Perkins Gilman, *Suffrage Songs and Verses,* 21, http://www.digital.library.upenn.edu/women/gilman/suffrage/suffrage.html#anti.

Chapter 15

1. Ruth Ferris, "Hazel Hunkins Billings Suffragist," Montana Historical Society, https:///mhs.mt.gov/education/women/HazelHunkins/.

2. Katherine Conger Kane, "Hazel Hunkins Hallinan," *The Washington Post,* August, 21, 1977, CA.

3. Park, *FDL,* 80.

4. Ibid., 83.

5. Ibid., 69

6. Ibid., 91-92.

7. "White House Picketing Has Few Sympathizers in South," *Nashville Tennessean and the Nashville American,* June 3, 1917, CA.

8. Park, *FDL,* 90.

9. "Woodrow Wilson, The White House, Washington, May 14, 1917, to Edward W. Pou, House of Representatives, Washington," *North Carolina Digital Collections, State Library of North Carolina,* www.digital.ncdcr.gov/cdm/ref/collection/p15012coll11/id/322/.

10. Irwin, *APNWP,* 312-13.

11. Park, *FDL,* 97.

12. Griffith, *In Her Own Right,* 110.

13. Irwin, APNWP, 213.

14. "Mob Attacks Suffragists in Streets of Washington," *Evening Public Ledger,* June 22, 1917, CA.

15. "Enraged Mob in Front of White House Tears Down Suffragists' Banner Which Attacked the President," *The Washington Times,* June 20, 1917, CA.

16. Susan Olp, "Montana Woman Fought on the Front Lives of Women's Suffrage in 1910s," *Missoulian,* July 3, 2017, https://billingsgazette.com/news/local/billings-woman-fought-on-the-front-lines-for-women-s/article_f0d30606-8ac4-55ec-99b9-ec6aee59c02c.html.

17. "Persistent Suffragists Appear With New Banners," *Carson City Daily Appeal,* Carson, NV), June 21, 1917, CA.

18. "Suff Banners Ripped Again," *Daily Ardmoreite,* (Ardmore, OK),June 21, 1917, CA.

19. "Capital Police Stop Picketing, *Evening Public Ledger,* June 22, 1917, CA.

20. "Crowd Destroys Suffrage Banner at White House," *NYT,* June 20, 1917, PQ.

21. Stevens, *JFF,* 74.

22. Irwin, APNWP, 217.

23. "Capital Police End Suffrage Picketing," *Daily Missourian,* June 22, 1917, CA.

24. "White House Picketing Stopped by Police," *Evening Public Ledger,* June 22, 1917, CA.

25. Ford, *Iron-Jawed Angeles,* 155.

26. *Mabel Vernon: Speaker for Suffrage and Petitioner for Peace,* An Interview Conducted by Amelia R. Fry, Suffragists Oral History Project, The Bancroft Library, University of California, Berkeley, 75, https://archive.org/details/suffragepeace00vernrich.

27. Irwin, *APNWP,* 271.

28. Dora Kelly Lewis to Mrs. Henry K. Kelley, postcard, 4 July1917, Dora Kelly Lewis Correspondence, Historical Society of Pennsylvania,

http://digitalhistory.hsp.org/pafrm/doc/selected-dora-kelly-lewis-correspondence-july-4-1917-april-14-1920.

29. Irwin, *APNWP*, 231-232.

30. Stevens, *JFF*, 79.

31. "Woman Picket From Omaha Says Arrest Came During Lawful Protest," *The Omaha Bee*, July 14, 1917, CA.

32. Stevens, *JFF*, 80-82.

33. Ford, *Iron-Jawed Angels*, 205.

34. Stevens, *JFF*, 83.

35. "Suffragists Are in Jail Dress," *The Ogden Standard*, July 18, 1917, 4, CA.

36. Irwin, *APNWP*, 234.

37. Stevens, *JFF*, 85-86.

38. "Hartford Irishwoman Was Heroine of Suffrage Drive," *The Shanachie* XVIII (Winter 2006), http://digitalcommons.sacredheart.edu/cgi/viewcontent.cgi?article=1011&context=shanachie.

39. Irwin, *APNWP*, 237-238.

40. Stevens, *JFF*, 90.

41. Ford, *Iron-Jawed Angels*, 160.

42. "Flanagan Described Her 1917 'Vacation' in Bridgeport Newspaper," *The Shanachie* XVIII (Winter 2006), 5.

43. "Suffs Go to Hospital," *Washington Herald*, August 31, 1917, CA.

44. Irwin, *APNWP*, 276.

45. "Pickets Bring Charges," *Washington Post*, August 30, 1917, CA.

46. Harper, *HWS*, 6:241, http://www.gutenberg.org/files/30051/30051-h/30051-h.htm#CHAPTER_LI.

47. Ford, *Iron-Jawed Angeles*, 104.

48. Marguerite E. Harrison, "Suffragists' Fight A Three-Cornered One," *The Sun*, July 4, 1917, CA.

49. "12 Pickets Get 60-Day Sentence; One is Released," *The Washington Times*, September 5, 1917, CA.

50. David Dismore, "Banquet Honors Jailed 'Silent Sentinels," Founding Feminists (blog), Feminist Majority Foundation, September 11, 2014, https://feminist.org/blog/index.php/2014/09/11/september-11-1917-banquet-honors-jailed-silent-sentinel-suffragists.

51. "Malone Quits Rich Office as Rebuke to the President," *The Arizona Republican* (Phoenix, AZ), September 8, 1917, CA.

52. Catherine J. Lanctot, "We Are At War and You Should Not Bother the President': The Suffrage Pickets and Freedom of Speech During World War I," *Villanova University School of Law* (April 2008), 42, PQ.

53. Ford, *Iron-Jawed Angeles*, 172.

54. Ibid., 174.

55. Irwin, *APNWP*, 250.

56. "House Votes for Woman Suffrage," *NYT*, September 25, 1917, PQ.

57. Park, *FDL*, 122.

58. Ford, *Iron-Jawed Angeles*, 189.

Chapter 16

1. Sherna Berger Gluck, *From Parlor to Prison: Five American Suffragists Talk About their Lives* (New York: Monthly Review Press, 1985), 251, 253.

2. Ford, Ironed-Jawed Angels, 109.

3. Gluck, *From Parlor to Prison*, 256-257.

4. "Pickets on Strike; Decline to Work," *The Evening Star*, October 19, 1917, CA. The document is also in Frost and Cullen-DuPont, *Women's Suffrage in America*, 405; Stevens, *Jailed for Freedom*, 107-108.

5. "Letter of the Board of Charities to the Commissioners of the District of Columbia," *Annual Report of the Commissioners of the District of Columbia Year Ended June 30, 1917*, 1, 452-454, https://books.google.com/books?id=ESA_AQAAMAAJ.

6. Gluck, *From Parlor to Prison*, 261-262.

7. Ford, *Iron-Jawed Angels* 208-209.

8. "White House Picket Broken in Health," *The Delmarvia Star* (Wilmington, DE), November 11, 1917. http://www.angelfire.com/space/kingstonroots/Menard/AnnieArniel.html.

9. Ford, *Iron-Jawed Angels*, 276-277.

10. Stevens, *JFF*, 99.

11. "Occoquan 'Suff' Riot," *The Washington Post*, October 4, 1917, CA.

12. Ford, *Iron-Jawed Angels*, 206.

13. Gluck, *From Parlor to Prison*, 259.

14. Ford, *Iron-Jawed Angels*, 216.

15. "'Solitary' Threat for Militants at Workhouse," *The Washington Times*, October 11, 1917, CA.

16. Irwin, *APNWP*, 252-254.

17. Ibid., 255

18. Ford, *Iron-Jawed Angels*, 176.

19. Stevens, *JFF*, 114-115.

20. Mary Law, "'Suff' Forcibly Fed," *The Washington Herald*, November 9, 1917, CA.

21. "Charge Hunger Striker is to be Railroaded," *Richmond Times-Dispatch* (Richmond, VA), November 10, 1917, CA.

22. Stevens, *JFF*, 118-119.

23. "Suffragettes Forcibly Fed Take It Like Little Lambs," *The Daily Gate City*, (Keokuk, IA), November 9, 1917, CA.

24. "Tube Employed for Feeding Two Suffragists in Hunger Strike," *Albuquerque Morning Journal*, November 9, 1917, CA.

25. "Pickets to be Fed Today By Force," *The Washington Times*, November 8, 1917, CA.

26. "Forcible Feedings to Hunger Strikers," *Evening Capital News*, (Boise, ID), November 9, 1917, CA.

27. "Messages Protest Forcible Feeding," *Evening Ledger*, November 9, 1917, CA.

28. Adams and Keene, *Alice Paul and the American Suffrage Campaign,* 191.

29. Ford, *Iron-Jawed Angels,* 176.

30. Van Voris, *Carrie Chapman Catt,* 147.

31. Alice Paul, "The Lady of My Dream: Ada Davenport Kendall," Winslow Eliot (blog), October 16, 191, www.winsloweliot.com/2012/04/the-lady-of-my-dreams-ada-davenport-kendall.

32. "Force Yard of Jail to Cheer Miss Paul," *NYT,* November 12, 1917, PQ.

33. "Arrest 41 Pickets for Suffrage at the White House," *NYT,* November 11, 1917, PQ.

34. "Pickets Resume Their 'Reign of Terror,'" *NYT,* November 18, 1917, PQ.

35. Ford, *Iron-Jawed Angels,* 178.

36. Ibid., 179.

37. "Kathryn Lincoln (August 25, 1895-January 1974), Turning Point Suffragist Memorial, http://suffragistmemorial.org/kathryn-lincoln-august-25-1895-january-1974.

38. Irwin, *APNWP,* 279.

39. Walton, *A Woman's Crusade,* 197.

40. Steven, *JFF,* 122-123.

41. Irwin, *APNWP,* 282.

42. Stevens, *JFF,* 123-124.

43. Irwin, *APNWP,* 283.

44. Walton, *A Woman's Crusade,* 199.

45. Irwin, *The Story of Alice Paul,* 282-283.

46. Ibid., 284.

47. "Accuse Jailers of Suffragists," *NYT,* November 17, 1917, PQ.

48. Ford, *Iron-Jawed Angels,* 181-82.

49. Irwin, *APNWP,* 288.

50. Ford, *Iron-Jawed Angels,* 183.

51. "'Pickets' Jail Given Clean Bill of Health," *New York Tribune,* November 22, 1917, PQ.

52. John Arthur Seavey, "White House Pickets Well Treated in Jail," *New York Tribune,* November 22, 1917, PQ.

53. Ford, *Iron-Jawed Angels,* 188.

54. Stevens, *JFF,* 129.

55. "Move Militants From Workhouse," *NYT,* November 25, 1917, PQ.

56. "Militants Win Out for Hunger Strike," *The Rock Island Argus,* November 27, 1917, CA.

57. "Suffrage Pickets Freed from Prison," *NYT,* November 28, 1917, PQ.

58. "Suffs Raise $86,000 For Vote Drive," *The Washington Herald,* December 10, 1917, CA.

59. "Suffragist Army Invades Capitol," *The Evening Star,* December 12, 1917, CA..

60. Harper, *HWS,* 5: 514.

61. Pankhurst, *The Suffragette Movement,* 607.

Chapter 17

1. Park, Front Door Lobby, 143-145.

2. Ibid., 164.

3. Irwin, *APNWP*, 346-347.

4. "Wilson Backs Amendment for Woman Suffrage," *NYT*, January 10, 1918, PQ.

5. "Votes-for-Women Amendment is Expected to Win in Lower House Today," "President Throws Full Weight of Influence in Favor of Amendment for Nation-Wide Suffrage," *Albuquerque Morning Journal*, January 10, 1918, CA.

6. Park, *FDL*, 145.

7. Irwin, *APNWP*, 346.

8. Ibid., 347.

9. Park, *FDL*, 147.

10. Stevens, *JFF*, 135-136.

11. Park, *FDL*, 149.

12. Ibid.152-153.

13. Irwin, *APNWP*, 347.

14. Park, *FDL*, 159-160.

15. Trisha Franzen, *Anna Howard Shaw: The Work of Woman Suffrage* (Bloomington: University of Illinois Press, 2014), 176.

16. "Arrest of Pickets at the White House Illegal, Says Court," *New York Tribune*, March 5, 1918, CA.

17. "Right To Picket Established in Capital of U.S.," *The Labor World*, (Duluth, MN), March 30, 1918, CA.

18. Ralph Block, "Anne Martin, First Woman Candidate for U.S. Senate, Has Fighting Record," *New York Tribune*, March 5, 1918, CA.

19. Belle Fligelman, "She Whom the Antis Call 'Nevada Anne,'" *New York Tribune*, August 25, 1918, CA.

20. Adams and Keene, *Alice Paul*, 247.

21. Park, *FDL*, 170.

22. Irwin, *APNWP*, 355-356.

23. Ibid., 350.

24. Irwin, *APNWP*, 357-358.

25. Park, *FDL*, 199.

26. Van Voris, *Carrie Chapman Catt*, 149.

27. Stevens, *JFF*, 142.

28. "Picket Suffs Arrested by Park Police," *The Washington Herald*, August 7, 1918, CA.

29. "N.Y. Suffragists Term Militants 'Foolish and Futile,'" *New York Tribune*, August 8, 1918, CA.

30. Stevens, *JFF*, 143.

31. "Woman Suffragists Are Sent to Jail," *Arizona Republican*, August 16, 1918, CA.

32. Stevens, *JFF*, 144.

33. Ibid., 146.

34. Irwin, *APNWP*, 373.

35. Park, *FDL*, 212.

36. Irwin, *APNWP*, 376.

37. Park, *FDL*, 214, 220.

38. Ibid., 229.

39. Stevens, *JFF*, 152.

40. Park, *FDL*, 230-231.

41. Irwin, *APNWP*, 380-381.

42. Park, *FDL*, 232.

44. Irwin, *APNWP*, 381.

Chapter 18

1. Green, *Southern Strategies,* 128.

2. Ibid., 131.

3. Tyler, Pamela "Kate and Jean Gordon," In *knowlouisiana.org Encyclopedia of Louisiana,* edited by David Johnson. Louisiana Endowment for the Humanities, 2010–. Article published March 29, 2011, http://www.knowlouisiana.org/entry/kate-and-jean-gordon.

4. Green, *Southern Strategies,* 135.

5. Harper, *HWS,* 6:593, http://www.gutenberg.org/files/30051/30051-h/30051-h.htm#CHAPTER_I.

6. Park, *FDL,* 235.

7. "Suffragette Invasion of the Senate Foiled," *The North Platte Semi-Weekly Tribune,* (North Platte, NE), November 1, 1918, CA.

8. Irwin, *APNWP*, 388-389.

9. Ford, *Iron-Jawed Angels,* 235.

10. Stevens, *JFF,* 156.

11. Adams and Keene, *Alice Paul,* 233.

12. Park, *FDL,* 244.

13. "Suffs All Peeved at Wilson; Will Burn His Books," *The Topeka State Journal,* December 16, 1918, CA.

14. Stevens, *JFF,* 158-160.

Chapter 19

1. Irwin, *APNWP*, 402.

2. "Crowd Charges Women Pickets," *San Francisco Chronicle,* January 2, 1919, CA.

3. "Pavements Explode As Suff Fire Burns," *The Washington Herald,* January 4, 1919, CA.

4. Ford, *Iron-Jawed Angels,* 238.

5. Irwin, *APNWP*, 404.

6. "Suffragists Go On Hunger Strike," *The Washington Times,* January 7, 1919, CA.

7. Ford, *Iron-Jawed Angels,* 205.

8. M. Toscan Bennett, "May It Please Your Honor: A True Story," *The Suffragist,* January 18, 1919.

9. Ford, *Iron-Jawed Angels,* 239.

10. Irwin, *APNWP,* 408.

11. "Suffragists Who Burned Speeches All Go To Jail," *New York Tribune,* January 15, 1919, CA.

12. "Dutch Cabinet Supports Woman Suffrage Bill," *New York Tribune,* January 15, 1919, CA.

13. Irwin, *APNWP,* 412-413.

14. Louisine Havemeyer, "The Prison Special," *Scribner's,* 663-664, http://www.unz.org/Pub/Scribners-1922jun-00661.

15. Ibid., 665-666.

16. "Suffragists Burn Wilson in Effigy: Many Locked Up," *NYT,* February 10, 1919, PQ.

17. Havemeyer, *The Prison Special,* 670-671.

18. "Suffragists Burn Wilson in Effigy: Many Locked Up."

19. Fry, *Conversation with Alice Paul,* 122.

20. Park, *FDL,* 258.

21. "Senate Rejects Suffrage for Fourth Time," *South Bend News,* (South Bend, IN), February 10, 1919, CA.

22. "Woman Suffrage Loses By One Vote," *Boston Daily Globe,* February 11, 1919, PQ.

23. Havemeyer, "The Prison Special," 669-671.

24. "The Suffrage Prison Special Comes to Louisiana," *Morgan City Daily Review,* Morgan City, LA), February 18, 1919, CA.

25. Havemeyer, "The Prison Special," 675.

26. Adams and Keene, *Alice Paul,* 199.

27. Maude Martin Evers, "'Must Be Free' Suffs Tell Why and Also What," *Chicago Daily Tribune,* March 7, 1919, CA.

28. "Militants Demand a Special Session," *NYT,* March 11, 1919, PQ.

29. Ford, *Iron-Jawed Angels,* 241.

30. Stevens, *JFF,* 173.

31. "Women Jailed in Boston," *NYT,* February 25, 1919, PQ.

32. "Fine Paid They Refuse to Quit Jail — Ejected!!" *The Arizona Republican,* February 27, 1919, CA.

33. Mary Gray Peck, *Carrie Chapman Catt,* 307.

34. Stevens, *JFF,* 177.

35. "Suffs Fight in Street To Burn Wilson Speech," *The Sun,* March 5, 1919, CA.

36. Stevens, *JFF,* 177.

37. "Suffs Fight in Street to Burn Wilson Speech," *The Sun,* March 5, 1919, CA.

38. "Says Suffs Hit By Police and Soldiers," *Boston Daily Globe,* March 7, 1919, PQ.

39. Stevens, *JFF,* 179.

40. "Suffs Charge the Police in New York," *The Boston Daily Globe,* March 5, 1919, PQ.

41. Stevens, *JFF,* 180.

42. Doris Stevens, *Jailed For Freedom* (New York: Boni Liveright, 1920), Full Text Archive, viii, http://www.fullbooks.com/Jailed-for-Freedom1.html.

Chapter 20

1. Harper, *HWS,* TPG, 6:351, http://www.gutenberg.org/files/30051/30051-h/30051-h.htm#CHAPTER_I.

2. Marie B. Ames, "History of the Presidential Suffrage Bill in Missouri," *Missouri Historical Review,* XIV (2003), 338-343, http://www.law.wustl.edu/Staff/Taylor/women/v6n2/suffrage.htm.

3. Harper, *HWS,* 6:245, http://www.gutenberg.org/files/30051/30051-h/30051-h.htm#CHAPTER_I.

4. Park, *FDL,* 265.

5. Irwin, *APNWP,* 428.

6. Park, *FDL,* 269-270.

7. Ibid., 271.

8. Ibid., 280.

9. Ibid., 282-83.

10. McBride, *On Wisconsin Women,* 290.

11. "House Adopts Suffrage Amendment," *El Paso Herald,* May 21, 1919, CA.

12. Park, *FDL,* 284.

13. Park, *FDL,* 287.

14. Irwin, *APNWP,* 429.

15. Park, *FDL,* 292.

16. Frost and Cullen-DuPont, *Women's Suffrage in America,* 407.

17. Park, *FDL,* 294.

18. "Ballot in 1920 Says Miss. Paul," *The Washington Herald,* June 5, 1919, CA.

19. Irwin, *APNWP,* 429.

20. Walton, *A Woman's Crusade,* 235.

21. "Woman Suffrage Victorious in Senate," *The Washington Herald,* June 5, 1919, CA.

22. "Suffrage is Winner," *The Los Angeles Times,* June 4, 1919.

23. "Suffrage Strengthens South's White Vote: Number of White Women in South Far Exceeds Number of Negroes of Both Sexes," *The Independent,* (Elizabeth City, NC), June 4, 1920, CA.

24. "Antis Lining Up New Fight," *The Seattle Star,* June 4, 1919, CA.

25. "The Race for Suffrage is Now On," *The Logan Republican,* (Logan, UT), July 31, 1919, CA.

Chapter 21

1. "Women's Suffrage Now Up To the States," *Boston Daily Globe,* June 5, 1919.

2. McBridge, *On Wisconsin Women,* 290.

3. "Illinois by Approval is First to Act," *The Rock Island Argus,* June 10, 1919, CA.

4. "Miss Alice Paul: 'Joan of Arc,'" *The North Platte Semi-Weekly Tribune,* June 20, 1919, CA.

5. "Women Are Sure of Victory," *The Sunday Star* (Washington, D. C.), June 20, 1919, CA.

6. Irwin, *APNWP*, 436, 439.

7. Harper, *HWS*, 6:518, TPG, http://www.gutenberg.org/files/30051/30051-h/30051-h.htm#CHAPTER_I.

8. "Great Suffrage Worker Dies on Eve of Fruition of Her Life's Endeavor," *Great Falls Daily Tribune*, (Great Falls, MT), July 3, 1919, CA.

9. Franzen, *Anna Howard Shaw*, 179.

10. Ibid.,182.

11. Harper, *HWS*, TPG, 6:7, http://www.gutenberg.org/files/30051/30051-h/30051-h.htm#CHAPTER_I.

12. Ibid., 6:142.

13. Carrie Chapman Catt and Nettie Rogers Shuler, *Woman Suffrage and Politics*, www.loc.gov/resource/rbnawsa.n6874.

14. Harper, *HWS*, 6:22, TPG, http://www.gutenberg.org/files/30051/30051-h/30051-h.htm#CHAPTER_I.

15. Catt and Shuler, *Woman Suffrage and Politics*, 354.

16. Harper, *HWS*, TPG, 6:22, http://www.gutenberg.org/files/30051/30051-h/30051-h.htm#CHAPTER_I.

17. "Battle Line of Suffrage Moved to West Coast," *Nashville Tennessean and the Nashville American*, July 24, 1919, CA.

18. "Ratification of the Suffrage Amendment at a Standstill," *New York Tribune*, July 27, 1919, CA.

19. "Emma S. Ingalls (1860-Unknown), National Women's History Museum, https://www.nwhm.org/education-resources/biography/biographies/emma-ingalls.

20. Harper, *HWS*, 6:383, http://www.gutenberg.org/files/30051/30051-h/30051-h.htm#CHAPTER_I.

21. Park, *FDL*, 172.

22. Peck, *Carrie Chapman Catt*, 317-318.

23. Harper: *HWS*, TPG, 6:246, http://www.gutenberg.org/files/30051/30051-h/30051-h.htm#CHAPTER_I.

24. Ibid., 6:595.

25. Park, *FDL*, 303.

26. "Two Dakotas Added to List of Ratifiers, *New York Tribune*, December 7, 1919, CA.

Chapter 22

1. "Madeline McDowell Breckinridge," Wikipedia contributors, "Madeline McDowell Breckinridge," *Wikipedia, The Free Encyclopedia*, https://en.wikipedia.org/w/index.php?title=Madeline_McDowell_Breckinridge&oldid=872312711.

2. Harper, *HWS*, 6:577, http://www.gutenberg.org/files/30051/30051-h/30051- h.htm#CHAPTER_I.

3. Ibid., 6: 180.

4. Ibid., 6: 710.

5. Irwin, *APNWP*, 445.

6. Ibid., 447.

7. Ibid., 450-451.

8. Harper, *HWS*, 6:15, http://www.gutenberg.org/files/30051/30051-h/30051-h.htm#CHAPTER_I.

9. Ibid., 5:594.

10. Ibid., 5:599.

11. McBride, *On Wisconsin Women*, 294.

12. Harper, *HWS*, 5:610-611.

13. Ibid., 5:617.

14. Irwin, *APNWP*, 452.

15. Suffragists Say No Need Here For Maryland Advice," *The West Virginian* (Fairmont, WVA), February 25, 1920, CA.

16. "Wife Won't Let Legislator Fly to Save Suffrage," *The Evening World*, March 9, 1920, CA.

17. Irwin, APNWP, 453-454.

18. "Charges Corrupt Tactics, *NYT*, March 9, 1920, PQ

19. "They Saved Suffrage in West Virginia," *The Washington Times*, March 12, 1920, CA.

20. Harper, *HWS*, 6:685-686, http://www.gutenberg.org/files/30051/30051-h/30051-h.htm#CHAPTER_I.

21. "Woman Suffrage But One Notch Away," *Norwich Bulletin* (Norwich, VT), March 23, 1920, CA.

22. Harper, *HWS*, 6:97, http://www.gutenberg.org/files/30051/30051-h/30051-h.htm#CHAPTER_I.

23. Marjorie Julian Spruill and Jesse Spruill Wheeler, "Mississippi Women and the Woman Suffrage Amendment," Mississippi HistoryNow, Mississippi Historical Society, http://www.mshistorynow.mdah.ms.gov/articles/245/mississippi-women-and-the-woman-suffrage-amendment.

24. "Fate of Suffrage Rests with Two States Today," *The Bismarck Tribune*, March 31, 1920, CA.

25. "The States That Did Not Ratify" in Catt and Shuler, *Woman Suffrage and Politics*, 462-489, https://cdn.loc.gov/service/rbc.rbnawsa/n6874xml.

26. Harper, *HWS*, 6:341, http://www.gutenberg.org/files/30051/30051-h/30051-h.htm#CHAPTER_I.

27. Ibid., 6:657.

28. "Suffragists Fail to Swerve Holcomb," *Norwich Bulletin*, May 11, 1920, CA.

29. Kenyon Hayden Rector, "Women Awake," Ann Lewis Women's Suffrage Collection, https://lewissuffragecollection.omeka.net/items/show/954.

30. "Ohio Referendum Law Knocked Out By Supreme Court," *Evening Times-Republican*, June 1, 1920, CA.

31. A. Elizabeth Taylor, "The Woman Suffrage Movement in Florida," *The Florida Historical Quarterly*, 36, (1957), 1, 59, http://www.jstor.org/stable/30138972.

32. Harper, *HWS*, 6:233, 235.

33. "Women Slapped in Face by G.O.P. Governor," *The Atlanta Constitution,* July 13, 1920, PQ.

Chapter 23

1. "Suffs' Eyes on Race to Ratify Act," *The Rock Island Argus and Daily Union,* August
1920, CA.

2. "Urges North Carolina To Ratify Suffrage," *NYT,* June 26, 1920, PQ.

3. Carol Lynn Yellin and Janann Sherman, *The Perfect 36: Tennessee Delivers Woman Suffrage* (Oak Ridge, TN: The Iris Publication Group, 1998), 72.

4. Carol Lynn Yellin, "Countdown in Tennessee, 1920." *American Heritage,* 30 (1978), paragraph 34, https://www.americanheritage.com/content/countdown-tennessee-1920.

5. Carrie Chapman Catt and Nettie Rogers Shuler, "Tennessee," in Wheeler, *Votes for Women!,* 256.

6. "'Don't forget to be a good Boy': Harry T. Burn's letter from Mom and the Ratification of the 19th Amendment in Tennessee," Teach Tennessee History, East Tennessee Historical Society, http://www.teachtnhistory.org/File/Harry_T._Burn.pdf

7. Carol Lynn Yellin, "Countdown in Tennessee, 1920." Paragraphs 43-44.

8. Harper, *HWS,* 6:622, http://www.gutenberg.org/files/30051/30051-h/30051-h.htm#CHAPTER_I.

9. Ibid., 6:498.

10. "Suffrage Wins Initial Fight in Two States," *Great Falls Daily Tribute,* August 14, 1920, CA.

11. Flexner and Fitzpatrick, *Century of Struggle,* 315-316.

12. Catt and Shuler "Tennessee," in Wheeler, 305.

13. Harper, *HWS,* 6:621, http://www.gutenberg.org/files/30051/30051-h/30051-h.htm#CHAPTER_I.

14. Ibid., 6:499.

15. G. F. Milton, Jr., "Tennessee Slender Thread Upon Which Suffrage Hopes Hang," *The Chattanooga News,* August 18, 1920, CA.

16. "Do Not Reach Vote in House," *The Chattanooga News,* August 17, 1920, CA.

17. "Suffrage Hangs on Votes of 5 Tennessee Men," *New York Tribune,* August 18, 1920, CA.

18. Catt and Shuler "Tennessee," in Wheeler, 263.

19. Harper, *HWS,* 6:623, http://www.gutenberg.org/files/30051/30051-h/30051-h.htm#CHAPTER_I.

20. "Letter Harry Burn from Mother" Knox County Public Library Calvin M. McClung Historical Collection. www.cmdc.knoxlib.org Banks Turner should also receive equal credit because his "aye" vote prevented the motion from being tabled.

21. Elaine Weiss, *The Woman's Hour: The Great Fight to Win the Vote* (New York: Viking, 2018), 315.

22. Ibid., 307.

23. "Suffragists Abroad Cable Congratulations to Leaders," *Richmond Times-Dispatch,* August 20, 1920.

24. "Women of America Win Right To Vote," *The Cordova Daily Times,* (Cordova, AK) August 18, 1920, CA.

25. Harper, *HWS,* 6:624, http://www.gutenberg.org/files/30051/30051-h/30051-h.htm#CHAPTER_I.

26. "Colby Avoids Film in Final Suffrage Act," *Chicago Daily Tribune,* August 27, 1920, PQ.

27. "Colby Signs Official Proclamation Giving Vote to Women of U.S.," *St. Louis Post-Dispatch,* August 26, 1920, PQ.

28. "Equal Suffrage is Law of Land," *The Pensacola Journal* (Pensacola, FL), August 27, 1920, CA.

29. "The Star That Completed The Banner," *The Mt. Sterling Advocate* (Mt. Sterling, KY), August 26, 1920 CA.

30. "Alma Nash & Her Band," Missouri Women: Women of the Past, Inspiring Women Today," https://missouriwomen.org/2010/11/16/alma-nash-her-maryville-ladies-marching-band.

31. Peck, Carrie Chapman Catt, 340.

32. "Suffragists To Hold Noisy Jubilee Today," *The Sun,* August 28, 1920, CA.

33. "Whistles Blow for Suffrage, *The Bridgeport Times and Evening Farmer,* (Bridgeport, CT), August 28, 1920, CA.

34. "Bells Proclaim the Triumph of Suffrage," *The West Virginian*, August 28, 1920, CA.

35. "Suffragists To Hold Noisy Jubilee Today,"

36. "'Justice Bell' Rings in Honor of New Citizens," *The Evening Star,* September 27, 1920, CA.

37. Peck, *Carrie Chapman Catt,* 342.

Epilogue

1. "Women Voters Outnumber Men, *The Chattanooga News,* November 2, 1920, CA.

2. "Women Vote Heavy in State," *The West Virginian,* November 2, 1920, CA.

3. "Women of U.S. Are Enjoying New Duty," *The Seattle Star,* November 2, 1920, CA.

4. "Even Baby Goes to the Polls," *Evening Public Ledger,* November 2, 1920, CA.

5. "Women on Hand Early to Vote," *Evening Public Ledger,* November 2, 1920, CA.

6. "Election Day in Marion County," *The Ocala Evening Star,* November 2, 1920, CA.

7. "Negro Women Refused Ballots at the Polls," *The Richmond Daily Register,* November 2, 1920, 1, CA.

8. Pickens, William. "The Woman Voter Hits the Color Line." *The Nation,* October 6, 1920, 372-73.

9. Mary White Ovington, "Free Black as Well as White Women," *The Suffragist,* November 1920.

10. Carrie Chapman Catt and Nettie Rogers Shuler, *Woman Suffrage and Politics.* viii, https://www.loc.gov/resource/rbnawsa.n6874/?sp=6.

11. *Conversations with Alice Paul,* "Suffragist Oral History Project," 399.

12. Bernadette Cahill, *Alice Paul, the National Woman's Party and the Vote: The First Civil Rights Struggle of the 20th Century* (Jefferson, NC: McFarland & Company, 2005), 215.

13. "Women Pickets Will Continue War for Rights," *NYT,* September 11, 1920, PQ.

14. Van Voris, *Carrie Chapman Catt,* 172.

15. Biography.com Editors. "Lucy Burns Biography, *Biography.com,* June 30, 2016, https://www.biography.com/people/lucy-burns-063016.

16. Nikki Schwab. "Ginsburg: Make ERA Part of the Constitution," The Civic Report (blog), U.S. News, April 18, 2014, https://www.usnews.com/news/blogs/washington-whispers/2014/04/18/justice-ginsburg-make-equal-rights-amendment-part-of-the-constitution√ https://www.usnews.com/news/blogs/washington-whispers/2014/04/18/justice-ginsburg-make-equal-rights-amendment-part-of-the-constitution.

17. "Militant Suffrage Worker Suicide," *The Star,* (Wilmington, DE), February 10, 1924, CA.

18. Aaron Bellve, "Kate Heffelfinger: From the Workhouse to the State Hospital," Spit, Bristle and Fury (blog), March 13, 2010, www.spitbristleandfury.wordpress.com.

19. Fry, *Conversation with Alice Paul,* 354, http://bancroft.berkeley.edu/ROHO/projects/suffragist.

20. Jeannette Smyth, "Half a Century of Feminism," *The Washington Post,* July 2, 1972, PQ.

21. Katherine Conger Kane, "Hazel Hunkins Hallinan: A Suffrage Survivor Stands Ready for Battle," *The Washington Post,* August 21, 1977, PQ.

22. "The Gender Gap: Voting Choices in Presidential Elections." CAWP Fact Sheet, Rutgers, the State University of New Jersey. Eagleton Institute of Politics. Center for American Women and Politics Center for the American Woman and Politics, http://cawp.rutgers.edu/sites/default/files/resources/ggpresvote.pdf.

23. Kelly Dittmar. "The Gender Gap in Voting: Setting the Record Straight," Footnotes: A blog of the Center for American Women and Politics, Rutgers Eagleton Institute of Politics, July 3, 2018, http://www.cawp.rutgers.edu/footnotes/gender-gap-voting-setting-record-straight.

24, Ocasio-Cortez, Alexandra. Twitter Post. January 3, 2019, 7:39 PM. https://twitter.com/AOC.

Index

abolitionists, 8, 10–11, 12, 13, 15, 16, 18, 20

activism and protest: effect of conservative traditions on, 217; embrace of in Progressive Era, 57; Malone's tactics, 68–69; militancy in, 79; open air meetings, 68–71; Prison Special, 294; protests to centennial year celebrations, 30–32; Suffrage Day, 144–145; Susan B. Anthony's trial, 29; withholding taxes, 33; women voting, 24–25. *See also* "Army of the Hudson"; *A.W. Smith* (tugboat); demonstrations; Lafayette Monument; militant tactics, use of; open-air meetings; picketing the White House; songs of suffrage movement; suffrage parades; suffrage pilgrimage; Suffrage Special; transcontinental suffrage tours; Valentine's Day barrage to congressmen; Watchfires of Freedom; *W.S. Holbrook* (tugboat)

Adams, Abigail, 5, 6

Adams, John, 5–6

Adams, Katherine H., 254

Adams, Pauline Fortall, 243, 247, *248*

Addams, Jane, 57, 107, 117, 130, 153, 208–209

Ainge, Edith "Aingy," 242–243, 247, *248, 249,* 275, 285, 291, 293

Alabama: partial ratification of the Nineteenth Amendment, 315; ratification of the Nineteenth Amendment, 318

Alaska, vote to enfranchise women, 138

Alaska-Yukon-Pacific Exposition (AYP), events at, 75, 76

Alcott, Louisa May, 173

Allen, Genevieve, 319

Allen, Henry J., 313

Allender, Nina, 141

Allison, Emma, 31

Alma Nash and her Missouri Ladies Marching Band, 137, 341

Alpha Suffrage Club, 131

American Anti-Slavery Society, 10

American Association of University Women, 38

American Equal Rights Association (AERA), 17, 20, 22

American Woman Suffrage Association (AWSA), 21. *See also* National American Woman Suffrage Association (NAWSA)

Ames, Marie B., 303

Amidon, Beulah, 210, 239, 273

Anderson, Elizabeth Preston, 216

Anderson, Naomi Bowman Talbert, 45

Andrews, Harriet, 291

Anna Howard Shaw Memorial Park, *61*

Anneke, Mathilde Fransziska: *Deutsche Frauen-Zeitung,* 114

Anthony, Susan B.: arrest of, 28–29; call to arms, 64; death of, 64–65; "Declaration of Rights for Women of the United States," 31; eulogy for Douglass, 43; exchange with Debs, 59; extolling foremothers, 64; fight against Fifteenth Amendment, 21; Frederick Douglass at NAWSA, 42–43; at German suffrage conference, 61–62; International Council of Women meeting, 34–35; joining women's rights movement, 15; at NAWSA conventions, 43–44, 46, 51; organizations founded, 21, 62; role in NAWSA, 36; sixty-year struggle, 66; state suffrage campaigns, 19, 37, 39, 44, 45, 63, 94; statue of, x, 352; on success in Wyoming, 37; suspension of efforts, 16; tribute to, 61–62; use of martial language, 72; view on Fourteenth Amendment, 18; on women's literacy, 53

anti-ratification efforts: tactics to delay and defeat ratification, 313–314, 319–320, 321, 327–328, 329, 336, 337, 338, 340

The Anti-Slavery Society Convention (painting, Haydon, 1841), 10–11

anti-suffrage campaigns: continued opposition after ratification, 341; national campaign, 242; novelties and ephemera, 164. *See also* individual states

anti-suffrage editorial, 98, 108

"The Anti-Suffrage Rose" (song), 174

anti-suffrage tactics: claims that women did not want the vote, 100, 113, 153; court challenges, 7, 115–116, 220; delays, 128, 282, 307–308; distribution of paper roses, 173–174; election fraud, 198, 222; false claims, 100, 336–337; interference with parades, 137; lawsuits, 45; legislative chicanery, 7, 55; liquor dealers' tactics, 39, 65, 113, 151, 267; manufacturers' and businessmen's tactics, 152, 155, 199, 337; organizing groups, 99; petitions, 33–34, 219, 224; picture show and speech, 157; referenda, 219, 224; silent films, 117–118; summary of, ix; tours, advertisements, and literature, 100, 151, 218; typical tactics, 41; using race-based fears, 198–199 (*See also* Dodge, Josephine Jewell). *See also* assaults on suffragists; harassment

anti-suffrage views: in colonial times, 6; in editorials, 98, 108; reasons woman suffrage efforts should fail, 105; suffragists as menace to civilization, 15, 36–37, 97, 244; that Grimkés encountered, 10; vote is privilege for those who are "fit," 152–153; woman's place is in the home, 107, 172, 224, 305. *See also* women did not want the vote

anti-suffragists: on black women voting, 53, 198–199, 207, 279, 309, 315, 335; fears of, 99, 105, 153; in Georgia legislature, 315; in Maryland House of Delegates, 224; planning ratification failure, 309; types of, 225; on unsexed women and men, 15, 36–37, 97; woman voters among, 344. *See also* Dodge, Josephine Jewell; National Association Opposed to Woman Suffrage (NAOWS)

The *Anti-Suffragists* (poem, Gilman), 225

"Arguments Against Women's Suffrage, 1911" (speech, Sanford), 99–100

Arizona: ratification of the Nineteenth Amendment, 317, 323, 324–325; suffrage referendum and campaign in, 111, 113

Arkansas: constitutional convention, 19; ratification of the Nineteenth Amendment, 316; suffrage campaign in, 219, 225

"Army of the Hudson," 121–122, *134,* 134–136, 137

Arniel, Anna [Annie] M.: after the fight, 348; arrests of, 242–243, 290–291, 293; banner criticizing Wilson, 289; imprisonment and release, 247, *248,* 249; picketing, 232–233, 285

Arnold, Berthe, 293

Arnold, Ethel, 87

Arnold, Virginia, 149, 239–240

arrests and imprisonment: activities to keep up the spirits, 249; after burning effigy of Wilson, 295–297; confronting Wilson, 109; crossing police line, 301; for demonstrating at Wilson speech, 299; demonstration at Lafayette Monument, 274–275; distribution of literature, 194; in England, 84, 85–86, 93, 142, 157; forgotten story of, vii; illegality of, 271; of picketers, 232, *234,* 235–244, *241,* 246–247, 252–253, 257–258; prison experiences, 232–233, 236–237, 241–242, 245, 248–249, 258–261, 275, 296–297, 299; psychopathic ward imprisonment, 253–254; role in winning the fight, 346; solitary confinement, 247, 250–251; for watchfires, 290–293. *See also* District Jail (Washington, D.C.); jail, condemned; "Night of Terror"; Occoquan workhouse; prison experiences of suffragists

Asquith, Henry, 83–84, 92

assaults on suffragists: at demonstrations, 194, 289; by husbands, 145; at Metropolitan Opera House to protest Wilson, 300–301; on parade, 135, 137–138; picketing with Kaiser Wilson banner, 238–239; at picket line, 257; in prison, 250–251; Russian banner incident, 229–231. *See also* force-feeding; harassment; "Night of Terror"; police assault on picketers

Athens, Tennessee, newspaper article, 15

"The Australian Boys," 101

automobile tours, 123, 153. *See also* "Blue Liner" as suffrage vehicle

automobile trips to deliver petitions, 87, 139, 168–171, *170*

A.W. Smith (tugboat), 160

Bailyn, Bernard, 3

Baker, Abby Scott, 243, *263,* 298, 319

Baker, Jean H., 8

Baker, Mabel Ruth, 321

Baltimore, Lord. *See* Calvert, Cecil

Bamberger, Simon, 318

Banaszak, Lee Ann, 54

Barber, Mary, 89

Barkley, Edna M., 222–223
Barkley v. Pool, 223
Barnhart, Henry, 268–269
Bartlett, Dorothy Jones, 247, *248,* 250
Barton, Clara, 52
Bates, Katharine Lee, 185
Beachey, Lincoln, 115
Beard, Charles, 193–194
Beard, Mary Ritter, 130, 262
Beecher, Catharine, 9, 10
Beecher, Henry, 27
Beecher-Tilton Affair, 27
Beeckman, Robert Livingston, 322
Belmont, Alva: after the fight, 349; characteristics of, 79; and conservatism, 147; on force feeding, 254; fund-raising events, 79–81; funeral and mausoleum, xi; harassment of, 105; inclusion of black women, 81–82; at IWSA's London meeting, 79; in NWP, 209; professions of suffragists, 78, 139, 169; relocation of NAWSA headquarters, 81; warning to Wilson, 243–244
Belmont mausoleum, xi
Belmont-Paul Women's Equality National Monument, ix
Benbridge, Helen, 323
Bennett, Josephine Day, 291, 292
Bennett, M. Toscan, 291
Bickett, Thomas, 333, 335
Bigelow, May, 321
Bill of Rights, 8. *See also* United States Constitution
Black, Alda Robins, 145
Blackwell, Henry B., 18, 21, 27, 43, 221–222
black women: advocating for suffrage, 22, 40; alienation of, 21; attempt to bar from suffrage parade, 132–133; campaign to register and vote, 333, 345; Delta Sigma Theta, xi, 137; equal rights for, 6, 9, 20, 135; Hattie Redmond headstone, *353;* newspaper for, 49; organizations aligning with, 65, 81–82; organizing efforts of, 49–50, 131–132; prison experiences, 232–233, 237, 249–251; running for office, 349; used by anti-suffragists, 237, 250; voting while dressed as men, 28. *See also* Anderson, Elizabeth Preston; Cary, Mary Ann Shadd; Cooper, Anna Julia; Ensley, Elizabeth Piper; Garnet, Sarah J. S.; Harper, Frances Ellen Watkins; Meredith, Ellis; Pierce, Juno Frankie; racial discrimination; Randolph, Florence Spearing; Ruffin, Josephine St. Pierre; Talbert, Mary Burnett; Terrell, Mary Church; Truth, Sojourner; Tubman, Harriet; Wells-Barnett, Ida B.; Williams, Frances "Fannie" Barrier
Blair, Emily Newell, 187
Blair, Henry A., 34
Blair, Ida, 200

Blanton, Thomas L., 305

Blatch, Harriot Stanton: assault on, 69; and English suffrage movement, 56–57, 94; Equality League of Self-Supporting Women, 67; film appearance, 117; harassment of, 105; influence on Havemeyer, 160; picketing the White House, 204; polling event in New York, 74; presentation with copy of 1869 Wyoming act, 184; suffrage parades, 88, 96–98, 107–108; on Suffrage Special, 183–184; torch as emblem of woman suffrage, 159; tour of open air meetings, 72–73

Bloch, Jesse A., 327–328

"Blue Liner" as suffrage vehicle, 101, 102–103

Blumberg, Hilda, 246, 247, 257

Booth, Elizabeth K., 125–128, 141

Bovee, Virginia H., 241

Bower, Rose, 162

Brackenridge, Mary Eleanor, 283

Brandt, Schuyler Coe, 132–133

Branham, Lucy, 242–243, 247, *248, 274,* 276, 293

Brannan, Eunice Dana, 202, *234,* 235–237, 256–258, 259, 288

Brannan, John Winters, 264

Breckinridge, Madeline McDowell, 322

Bremer, Frederika, 35

Brent, Margaret, 1, 2–4, 223, 224

Bright, William, 23–24

Bristow, Frank, 144

Bristow-Mondell Resolution, 144

Bronson, Minnie, 153, 158

Brooke, Minnie, 194

Brooks, Virginia, 131, 133

Brough, Charles Hillman, 219, 316

Brown, Amelia, 83–84

Brown, Gertrude Foster, 126, 175, 179, 207

Brown, Joseph E., 34

Brown, Mary Olney, 24, 25

Brown, Olympia, 114, 202, 205, 223, 288, 344

Brown, Victoria Bissell, 57

Brunner, Elwood, 138

Bugbee, Emma, 121

Burke, Alice Snitje, 183, 185

Burn, Harry, 338–339

Burn, Phoebe "Febb" Ensminger, 334–335, 338

Burnquist, Joseph A. A., 317

Burns, John, 67

Burns, Lucy: after the fight for the vote, 347; arrests and imprisonment, 233–234, 242–243, 245, *248,* 257–258, 275, 293; assault on, 230, 238–240; burning effigy of Wilson, 294–295; campaigning against Democratic candidates, 148, 194; command of Prison Special, 298;

editorial writer, 141; federal woman suffrage campaign, 129–131, 143; hunger strikes, 260–261, 291; Kaiser Wilson banner, 238; media campaign, *184*; most time in jail, 249; and Pankhurst, 140; as picketer, 232, 285; role in NWP, 209; in Scotland, 84; speech condemning Wilson, 148; on Suffrage Special, 184; train tour to West, *149, 150*

Burr, Hattie A., 91

A Busy Day (film), 118

Butterworth, Emily DuBois, 258, 260

California: ratification of the Nineteenth Amendment, 319; suffrage campaigns, 45–46, 98–104

Calvert, Cecil, 3–4

Calvert, Leonard, 3

Campbell, John A., 23

Cantrill, James Campbell, 270

Carnegie Hall celebration, 120, 135

Cary, Mary Ann Shadd, 49

Casey, Josephine, 149

Cassatt, Mary, 159–160

Catt, Carrie Chapman (née Lane): after the fight for the vote, 247; celebrations, 92, 120, 211, 342; defeats as victories deferred, 48; on Democratic convention platform, 189; differences with Paul, NWP, and CU, 79, 141, 200–201, 207, 257; on Douglass's funeral, 43; flag stand prop, 227; formation of ESCC, 175; Great Petition, 74, 87; international efforts for suffrage and peace, 347; length of fight for vote, ix; national strategy, 190–192; NAWSA activities, 63, 104–105, 208–209; passage of Nineteenth Amendment, 270, 272, 273, 277, 278; photograph, *182*; policy of nonpartisanship, 180, 193; presidency of NAWSA, 51, 60, 178–179; pressure on politicians, 190, 214, 228, 313; ratification campaign, 312, 316–317, 325, 336, 338; respectful description of, 60; role in IWSA, 61–62; rousing the suffragists, 182–183; sick with flu, but voted anyway, 283–284; start of activism, 37–38; state suffrage campaigns, 39, 40–41, 44–45, 63, 197–198, 255–256, 280–281, 334, 336–337; staying away from vote, 307; on suffrage fight, 326; suffrage parade, 186; use of martial language, 72; the vote as emblem of equality, 333, 343; voting at women's polling place, 74; "Wake Up, America!" tour, 318–319; Woman's Peace Party, 208–209; *Woman Suffrage and Politics: The Inner Story of the Suffrage Movement,* 345; in Woman Suffrage Procession, 137

Catt, George, 38

centennial year celebrations, 29–30

CESL. *See* College Equal Suffrage League (CESL)

Chace, Elizabeth Buffum, 221

Chamberlain, George, 158

Chan, Bertie, 119

Chan, S. K., 119

Chapman, Leo, 38
Charles Street Jail, 299
Chisholm, Shirley, 352
Churchill, Caroline Nichols, *Queen Bee,* 40
citizenship: Native American women and immigrants, 119; women married
    to foreign men, 195; women not citizens, 28
Civil War, suspended suffrage campaigns during, 16, 229
Clark, Adele, 70–71
Clark, Pansy, 117
Clarke, Grace Julian, 219
Clarke, Mary Jane, 93
Clarkson, Thomas, 11
class prejudice, 85, 86
Clay, Laura, 191
Clinton, Hillary, 352
Cobden-Sanderson, Anne, 67–68
Coe, Viola, 118
Colby, Bainbridge, 340, 341
Colby, Clara Bewick, 53
College Equal Suffrage League (CESL), 52, 100
Colman, Eleanor A. (Calnan), 247, *248*
colonies, American: patriarchal system in, 4–6; voting rights in, 6
Colorado: ratification of the Nineteenth Amendment, 320–321; recognition
    for equal suffrage, 44; suffrage campaign in, 40
Colored Women Equal Suffrage League, 118
Colored Women's Clubs, 46, 49, 172, 324, 333
Colored Women's League of Washington, 50
Colored Women's Suffrage League, 103
Colvin, Sarah Tarleton, 298
Conciliation Committee for Woman's Suffrage, 84
Condict, John, 6
Congressional Committee: Executive Committee, 130–131, 139; Paul
    resigns, 141
Congressional Union (CU): Advisory Committee, 147, 148; Cameron
    House headquarters "Little White House," 177; exhibit and petition at
    National Convention of Woman Voters, 168; federal woman suffrage
    campaign, 143; formation of, 139; merger with Woman's Party, 209;
    as national organization and challenge to NAWSA, 167; in
    nonsuffrage states, 183; official newspaper, 141; party-in-power
    campaigns to defeat Democratic candidates, *149,* 149–150, 158, 193;
    presentation of resolutions to congressmen, 184–185; pressure on
    Congress, 146; relationship with NAWSA, 141, 146, 158, 179–180;
    on Wilson, 193
Connecticut: ratification of the Nineteenth Amendment, 330; suffrage
    campaigns, 140, 222, 238
Connecticut Woman Suffrage Association (CWSA), 238

Coolidge, Mary, 103
Cooper, Anna Julia, 33, 49
Cosu, Alice, 258, 259–260
Cotnam, Florence, 162–163, 283
coverture, 4, 8
Cowles, Betsy Mix, 12
Craft, Ida, 121, 198
The Crisis on lynching of Jesse Washington, 193
Crocker, Gertrude, 253, *263,* 293
Crocker, Ruth, 244
Croly, Jane Cunningham, 48
Cross, Grace, 301
CU. *See* Congressional Union (CU)
Cunningham, Minnie Fisher, 283

Dalton, Martha Cardwell, *353*
Daniel, Josephus, 315
Darrow, Clara L., 154
Davis, Paulina Wright, 14, 221
Day, Dorothy, 258, 260
Dayton, Anna, 171
Dean, Madeleine, 351
Debs, Eugene V., 59
Declaration of Independence: centennial year celebrations, 29–30; inclusion of women in, 15, 233; main author of, 4; model for Declaration of Sentiments, 11
"Declaration of Rights for Women of the United States," 31
Declaration of Sentiments and Resolutions, 11–12, 20, 32
De Hart, Jane Sherron, 4
Delaware: ratification of the Nineteenth Amendment, 329, 330–331
Delta Sigma Theta, xi, 137
Democratic Party: blockage of progress on suffrage measure, 148; campaigns against Democratic candidates, 148–150, 158, 193–194; credit for suffrage, 305; national convention, 187–189; statement on woman suffrage, 146
demonstrations: at Democratic National Convention, 188–189; at Metropolitan Opera House, 300–302; on Milholland's birthday, 273, *274;* by NWP, 209–210; against Wilson, 194, *195,* 299. *See also* activism and protest; picketing of Congress; picketing the White House
Dennett, Mary Ware, 96, 104
Deroin, Jeanne, 35
DeVoe, Emma Smith, 75, 91–92, 117, 223, 328
Diggs, Annie, 42
Diserenz, Ida, 102
District Jail (Washington, D.C.), 247–248, 253, 291, 292

Dixon, Edna, 241, 243

Dobyne, Margaret, 127

Dock, Lavinia, 121–122, 148, 232–233, 241, 243, 248–249, 257, 275

Dodge, Josephine Jewell, 105, 148, 153, 166

Dodyk, Delight, 7

Dolph, Joseph N., 34

Dorr, Rheta Childe, 141; 7, 375n12

Douglass, Frederick: Anthony's eulogy for, 43; description of, 12; relationship with Anthony and Stanton, 12, 17, 20, 21, 22, 42–43; statue with Anthony, x; support for woman suffrage, 12, 14

Drake, Emma F. A., 324

Du Bois, W.E.B., 193, 208

Dubrow, Mary, 289, 290–291, 327–328, *331*

Dudley, Anne Dallas, 217, 334

Duniway, Abigail Scott, x, 44, 90, 118, 119

Eastman, Crystal, 130

education as focus of suffrage campaign, 53–54, 223

Eighteenth Amendment, 265

elections: attempts to vote in 1800s, 19–20, 25, 28; refusal of women's ballots, 24–25

Ellicott, Elisabeth King, 224

Ellington, Alice, 162–163

Emerson, Henry, 207

Emory, Julia, 243, 258, 260, *263*, 276, 285, 290–291, 312–313

Empire State Campaign Coordinating Committee (ESCC), 175

England, fight for woman suffrage in: arrests and imprisonment, 67–68, 83–84; attack on women, 92–93; enfranchisement for women over thirty, 213, 266, 270; hunger strikes in, 140; militant tactics, 95. *See also* Blatch, Harriot Stanton; Lytton, Constance; Pankhurst, Christabel; Pankhurst, Emmeline; Pankhurst, Sylvia

English Common Law, coverture under, 4

Ensley, Elizabeth Piper, 40

Equality League of Self-Supporting Women, 67, 107. *See also* Women's Political Union (WPU)

equal pay, 59, 81

Equal Rights Amendment, 347, 351

Equi, Marie, 118

Evans, Rebecca Winsor, 291

Ewing, Lucy, 241, 243

Fawcett, Millicent Garrett, 147, 270

federal woman suffrage amendment: 1917 activities, 227 (*See also* House of Representatives; Senate); Bristow-Mondell Resolution, 144; campaigns against Democrats, 193–194; Democratic National Convention, 187–189; hope for vote in 1918, 267–268; House debate and vote, 166; indefinite postponement, 182; march on Washington, D.C., 145, *145*; as Nineteenth Amendment, 143; pressure on presidential nominees, 190–191, 192–193; reintroduction in Congress, 212, 215; Republican National Convention, 186–187; revitalization of, 129–130; Sixty-Sixth Congress, 304–309; transcontinental publicity tours, 182–185; valentine campaign, 181–182; Winning Strategy, 190–192; Woman's Party convention, 185–186. *See also* ratification of Nineteenth Amendment; Susan B. Anthony Amendment

Feickert, Lillian, 324

feme covert and *feme sole,* 4, 54

feminine behavior, norms of, 33, 33, 54, 71, 153, 155–156. *See also* women's roles in society

feminist movement, 153, 204

Fendall, Mary Gertrude, 273–274, 293

Ferguson, James E., 188–189, 283

Ferraro, Geraldine, 352

Field, Sara Bard, 168, 169–171, *170,* 176, 194, 202–203, 204

field organizers, 88, 173

Fifteenth Amendment, 20–21, 329

Finnegan, Margaret, 100

Finnigan, Annette, Elizabeth and Katharine, 283

First Amendment, use in seeking the right to vote, 8

Fisher, Katharine Rolston, 244, 249, *263*

Flanagan, Catherine, 238–239, 240–241, *241,* 243, 256, 324, 335

Fletcher, Mary, 219

Fligelman, Belle, 155, 156

Florey, Kenneth, 164

Florida, ratification of the Nineteenth Amendment, 332

Flynn, W. G., 262

Follette, Robert La, 106

Foltz, Clara Shortridge, 45

force-feeding: Burns and Lewis, 261; in England, 84, 86, 93; forgotten story, vii; at Occoquan workhouse, 260–261; Paul and Winslow, 253, 254; public pressure and, 297

Ford, Linda, 204

Fotheringham, Janet, 235–237, 248

Fotheringham, Margaret M., 247, *248*

Fought, Leigh, 21

Fourteenth Amendment, 17–18, 329

Freeman, Elisabeth, 112, 135, 192–193

French, Charlotte Olney, 25

French women, 4

Funk, Antoinette, 126–128, 141, 152, 153, 154, 155

Gage, Matilda Joslyn, 14–15, 31

Gage, Portia, 17, 19

Gale, Zona, 178

Gannon, A. J., 253, 254, 261

Gardener, Helen Hamilton (née Alice Chenoweth), 131, 228, 278, 341

Gardner, Gilson, 210, 232

Garnet, Sarah J. S., 81

Garrison, William Lloyd, 9–10

Gellhorn, Edna Fischel, 151, 303

gender gap in voting, 351

General Federation of Women's Clubs, 48

George, David Lloyd, 213

Georgia: ratification of the Nineteenth Amendment, 315–316; women blocked from voting, 345

Gillespie, Elizabeth Duane, 30–31

Gilman, Charlotte Perkins: "The Anti-Suffragists," 225; on Congressional Union (CU) Advisory Committee, 147; epigraph, 52; "The Socialist and the Suffragist," 59–60; *Women and Economics,* 63

Ginsburg, Ruth Bader, 347

"The Golden Age of Suffrage Memorabilia," 164

"Golden Lane" strategy, 187–188

Gordon, Jean, 332

Gordon, Kate, 191, 279–280, 332

Gordon, Laura de Force, 45

Graham, Sara Hunter, 48

Gram, Alice, 249, 258

Gram, Betty: after the fight for the vote, 350; arrests, 249, 258; as organizer, 315, 324, 327–328, 335

Gray, Howard, 303

Gray, Natalie, 239–240, 241, 243

The Greek Slave (statue, Powers), 13

Greeley, Horace, 19, 27

Green, Elna C., 48, 280

Green, Frances, 234

Gregg, Laura, 88, 113

Gregori, Elsa, 97

Greiner, Gladys, 234, 253

Grimké, Sarah and Angelina, 9–10, 28

Gwinter, Anna, 244

habeas corpus, hearing on, 263–264

Hamilton, Cicely, 145

Hamilton, Elizabeth, 258

Hara, Ernestine (later Ketter), 246, 247–248, 250, 251

harassment: by the police, 80; by the public, 69, 71, 83, 105

Harlem Equal Rights League, *110*

Harper, Frances Ellen Watkins, 20

Harper's Weekly cartoon of Fanny Wright, 9

Harrington, Emerson, 312

Harris, William J., 304

Havemeyer, Louisine: about, 159; after the fight, 349; burning effigy of Wilson, 293–297; campaigning against Democratic candidates, 194; epigraph, 289; holding Torch of Liberty crossing the Hudson, *161*, 161–162; on Prison Special, 298; "Ship of State," 165–166; "The Truth About Occoquan" lecture tour, 243

Hay, Mollie Garrett, 275, 278, 284, 295–296, 308, 342

Hayden, Carl, 177

Hayward, Elizabeth, 318

Heffelfinger, Kate, 250–251, 252, 253, 348

Heflin, James, 231

Henkle, Alice, 273

Hennesy, Minnie, 252, 253

Hepburn, Katharine "Kit" Houghton, 140, 238, 265

Herndon, Minnie, 263; arrests and imprisonment, 257

Hicks, Frederick, 268–269

Hill, Alberta, 96–97

Hill, Carrie, 328

Hill, Elsie, 137, 194, 301

Hilles, Florence Bayard, 235–237, 236

Hinchey, Margaret, 140

Hipple, Ruth B., 310, 320

hiss incident, 86–87

History of Woman Suffrage (Stanton, Anthony, and Gage), 15, 72, 198, 223

Hitler, Adolph, the vote and his rise to power, viii

Hochheimer, Julia, 101–102

Hodges, Katherine, 246

Holloway Prison, 68, 79, 84, 142

Holloway Prison Medal, 79

Holman, Lydia Wickliffe, 332

Hopkins, Alison Turnbull, *234*

House of Representatives: creation of Woman Suffrage Committee, 244–245, 267; debate and vote on woman suffrage amendment resolution, 166; passage of amendment, 304–307; suffragists strategies in, 227–228; vote on woman suffrage amendment, 267–270

Howe, Julia Ward, 53, 80

Howey, Elsie, 86

How the Vote Was Won (one-act comedy), 152

Hughes, Charles Evans, 189–190, 192, 321

Hull House, 57

human rights, women's rights as, 22

hunger strikes: after burning effigy of Wilson, 297; after Lafayette statue demonstration, 275; after watchfire arrests, 291; Burns and Lewis, 260–261; in England, 84, 85–86, 142; forgotten story, vii; Lewis, *263*; Paul and Winslow, 253

Hunkins, Hazel (later Hunkins Hallinan): about, 214; after imprisonment, *263*; after the fight, 350; on Alice Paul, 350; arrest and imprisonment, 274, 275; assault on, 230–231; brother's claim she was deluded, 248; death of, 351; in Equality Day parade, 351; meeting Alice Paul, 226–227; picketing at Lafayette Monument, 273; watchfires, 290
Hunt, Jane, 11
Hunt, Rhoda, 298
Hunter, Gertrude, 149, 150
Hurst, Sadie Dotson, 323
Hutchinson, John, 18, 53
Hutchinson Family Singers, 18, 32
Hutton, May Arkwright, 75, 90–92, 184
Hyde, Clara, 273

Idaho: ratification of the Nineteenth Amendment, 323, 324; suffrage campaign, 44–45
Illinois: first to ratify Nineteenth Amendment, 310; suffrage campaign in, 124–129
Illinois Equal Suffrage Association (IESA) CK, 128
Illinois Supreme Court decisions, 125
Indiana: presidential suffrage, 303–304; ratification of the Nineteenth Amendment, 323; suffrage campaign in, 218–219, 225
Ingalls, Emma, 317
initiative and referendum process, 89, 90, 151, 152
International Council of Women (ICW), 34–35, 62
international efforts for woman suffrage, 35–36, 61–62, 66, 118, 119, 227, 292, 347. *See also* England; Russia's enfranchisement of women
international suffrage battle hymn, 76
International Woman Suffrage Alliance (IWSA) formerly the International Woman Suffrage Conference, 61–62, 76
Iowa: presidential suffrage, 303; ratification of the Nineteenth Amendment, 314; suffrage campaigns, 94–95, 143, 197–198
Ireland, Clifford, 268
Irish, John, 197–198
Irwin, Inez Haynes, 52, 82, 121

Jacobs, Aletta, 292
Jacobs, Patti Ruffner, 315
Jacobson, Pauline, 251–252
jail, condemned, 275, 296–297
"Jail Door Pin," 264–265
Jakobi, Paula, 258
James, Ada L., 114–115
James, David, 310
Jamison, Maud, 232–233, 252, 253
Jeannette Rankin Memorial Highway, 352

Jefferson, Thomas, 4–5

Jenkins, Theresa, 323

Jersey State Federation of Colored Women's Clubs, 172

Johanssen, Anina, 220

Johns, Laura M., 42

Johns, Peggy Baird, 246, 250, 258

Johnston, Lucy Browne, 116

Joliffe, Frances, 168, 170, 176

Jones, Andrieus Aristieus, 227, 244, 273, 275, 276, 278, 296

Jones, Rosalie Gardiner: about, 112; "Army of the Hudson," 121, 122, *134, 134–136*; in Nebraska, 153; statue of, 352

Julian, George Washington, 33, 219

Justice Bell (Women's Liberty Bell), x, 10, *165,* 172–173, 176, 186, 342–343

Kalb, Benigna Green, *331*

Kalb, Elizabeth Green, 286, 292, *331*

Kansas: countertactics to Tibbles, 116; ratification of Nineteenth Amendment, 313; suffrage referendum and campaign, 18, 41, 42, 111, 116–117

Kearney, Belle, 53–54

Keene, Michael L., 254

Kelley, Florence, 58, 147

Kempner, Otto, 108–109

Kendall, Ada Davenport, 205, 244, 245, 250, 251, 262

Kendrick, Senator, 278

Kenney, Annie, 85

Kenney, Mary, 58

Kenny, Catherine Talty, 333–334, 340

Kent, Elizabeth Thacher, 131, 194, 197, 265

Kentucky: partial suffrage to women, 7; ratification of the Nineteenth Amendment, 322

Kerber, Linda, 4, 8

Kessler, Margaret Wood, 246–247

Kindberg, Maria, 169–171, *170*

Kindstedt, Ingeborg, *170*

King, William H., 273, 277

Kinkead, Beatrice Reynolds, 235–237

Kinstedt, Ingeborg, 169–171

Kitchin, Claude, 305

Kohler, James P., *110*

Lafayette Monument, 273–275, *274,* 276, 288, 289

Lafayette Park, 294

Lafferty, Alma, 100

La Follette, Lola, 152

Lancaster, Elsie, 149

landmarks and monuments to suffrage fight: Abigail Scott Duniway historic marker, x; Belmont-Paul Women's Equality National Monument, ix; Hattie Redmond headstone, 352, *353*; Justice Bell, x; Margaret Brent Garden, 2, *2*; markers and plaques, x, 352; Occoquan Workhouse, x; statues and sculpture, x, 23, *61,* 352; Turning Point Suffragist Memorial, 352; Women's Rights National Historical Park, ix

Langley, Miles L., 19

Larch-Miller, Aloysius, 325

Larch-Miller Park (Shawnee, Oklahoma), 325

Latimer, Edna Story, 149

Law, Mary, 253

Lawrence, David, 262

League of Women Voters (LWV), 326, 347

Lee, Mabel Ping-Hua, 107

Lemlich, Clara, 80, 81

Lenroot, Irvine L., 272

Leslie, Miriam Folline, 255

Lewis, Dora Kelly: about, 130–131; after the fight for the vote, 349; arrests and imprisonment, 233, 257–258, 274–275; assault on, 230; burning Wilson's words, 289; hunger strike, 260–261, *263*; legality of suffragists' activities, 226; on Night of Terror, 258, 259–260; ratification campaigns, 313, 315; role in NWP, 209; "The Truth About Occoquan" lecture tour, 243; watchfires, 291

Lewis, Shippen, 321

Lincoln, Kathryn, 258, 260

liquor interests: evaporation of anti-suffrage argument, 265–266; fears that women would vote to prohibit alcohol, 39, 153; groups, 46, 65, 115, 153, 199; influence on politicians, 116, 172; influence on ratification, 315; opposition to woman suffrage, 46, 65, 115, 151, 152–153, 155, 174; role in length of suffrage fight, 345

Livingston, Deborah Knox, 242

Lockwood, Belva, 68

Lodge, Henry Cabot, 186, 278

Longley, Mary T., 46

Louisiana: ratification of the Nineteenth Amendment, 332; suffrage campaign in, 279

Louisiana Constitutional Convention, 46–47

Lovejoy, Esther Pohl, 118, *353*

Ludington, Katharine, 330

Luscomb, Florence, 174

lynching, 50, 193, 314

Lytton, Constance, 84, 340

Main, Effie Boutwell, 248

Maine: ratification of the Nineteenth Amendment, 319–320; suffrage campaign in, 242, 303, 304

Malone, Dudley Field, 237, 244, 264, 265

Malone, Maud: after the fight for the vote, 349; arrest for picketing, 242–243; assistance to prisoner, 68–70, 250; challenging Roosevelt, 106; confrontation with Wilson, 108; conviction, 110, 111; demands during mayoral campaign, 77; new tactics initiated, 68; open-air meetings, *70, 72–73*; as political prisoner, 247; poll watcher, 176; suffrage parade, 71–72; women's polling places, 68, 73–74

Mann, James Robert, 268–269, 305

Mann, S. A., 24

manufacturers' and businessmen's opposition to woman suffrage, 152, 155, 199

Margaret Brent Garden (Maryland), 2, *2*

Maroney, Terah "Tom," *184*

martial language, use of, 72, 191–192

Martin, Anne: campaigning against Democratic candidates, 194; at Milholland memorial, 197; in NWP, 209; ratification campaigns, 315; Senate run, 271, 284; suffrage activities, 157, 162; at White House, 176, 235–237

Martineau, Harriet, 35

Martz, William "Bill," 216, 224–225

Maryland: Brent saves colony in crisis, 2–4; ratification of the Nineteenth Amendment, 312–313, 328–329; suffrage campaign in, 223–224

Massachusetts: ratification of the Nineteenth Amendment, 313–314; suffrage campaigns, 158, 162–163, 164, 171, 173–174

Massachusetts Association Opposed to the Further Extension of Suffrage to Women (MAOFESW), 173–174

Masto, Catherine Cortez, 284

"Maud Maloners," 78

Mays, James H., 269

McCormick, Ruth Hanna, 126–128, 141, 267

McCoy, Mary, 49

McCue, Anne, 149, *149,* 150

McCulloch, Catharine Waugh, 123, 124, 125, 219

McCumber, Porter, 272, 277

McKelvie, Samuel R., 317

McKinley, William, 90, 127

M'Clintock, Mary Ann, 11

McPike, Sarah, 96–97

McShane, Elizabeth, 294

Mead, Rebecca, 90

media campaigns by suffragists, 100, 101–102, 127, 184, *184, 220*

Meehan, Sake, 280

Men's Anti-Suffrage League, 172

Men's League for Woman Suffrage, 59, 108

Men's Ratification Committee, 334

Meredith, Ellis, 40

Meredith, Emily R., 40

Meriwether, Elizabeth Avery, 216–217

Meriwether, Lide Smith, 217

Merrick, Caroline Elizabeth, 46–47

Meyer, Conrad, 332

Michigan: election trickery, 120–121; history of suffrage bill defeats, 115–116; partial suffrage, 115; ratification of Nineteenth Amendment, 310; suffrage referendum and campaigns in, 111, 116, 224–225, 279, 280; victory in, 119

Michigan State Association of Colored Women's Clubs, 49

Michigan Woman Suffrage Amendment, 115, 121

Milholland, Inez (later, Boissevain): on Congressional Union (CU) Advisory Committee, 147; death and memorial service, 196–197; description of, 72–73, 131; film appearance, 117; fortitude in cause, 106; her last words and her banner, 210, 274; memorial resolutions, 202–203; speaking tour, 195–196; in suffrage parades, 96–97, 107–108, 120, *136,* 136–137; targeted as feminist, 153

Milholland, Vida, 195, 196, 210, 233, 256, 288, 298

militant tactics, use of, 79, 83–84, 95, 96, 111, 129, 141

Miller, Lucy Kennedy, 313

Miller, Thomas, 55

Milliken, Carl, 319

Million, Joelle, 14

Mills, J. Warner, 40

Milton, Abby Crawford, 334, 338

Minnesota: presidential suffrage, 303, 304; ratification of the Nineteenth Amendment, 317

Minnesota Woman Suffrage Memorial, 352

Minor, Francis, 22–23, 27–28

Minor, Virginia, 22, 27–28

Minor v. Happersett, 28, 29

Mississippi: ratification of the Nineteenth Amendment, 329; women blocked from voting, 345

Missouri: ratification of the Nineteenth Amendment, 314; suffrage campaign in, 87, 150, 151–152, 303

Mist, Dawn, 137

Mondell, George, 144

Montana: first woman elected to Congress, 199; ratification of the Nineteenth Amendment, 317; suffrage campaign in, 150, 155, 156

monuments: dedicated to Margaret Brent, 2, *2;* statue of Esther Morris, 23; Turning Point Suffragist Memorial, 352. *See also* landmarks and monuments to suffrage fight

Moorman, Irene L., 81

Morey, Agnes, 253, 256, 257, 288, 298–299

Morey, Katharine, 230–231, 232–233, 238–239, 261, 298–299

Morgan, Maritza Leskovar, viii

Morris, Esther, 23–24

Morris, Mildred, 290

motion pictures, 117, 118, 159, 307

Mott, Lucretia Coffin, 11, 12, 14, 20, 22, 31, 35

Muller, Mary (pseud. Femmina): *An Appeal to the Men of New Zealand,* 35

Muller, Phyllis, 107

Mulliner, Gabrielle Steward, 71

Mullowney, Alexander, 232, 233–235, 236, 244, 252, 257, 264

Munds, Frances "Fannie" Willard, 113–114

Munnecke, Phoebe, 290–291, 293

Murray, Judith Sargent, 8

music at events, 18, 32, 53, 76, 137, 169, 185, 197. *See also* songs of suffrage movement

NAOWS. *See* National Association Opposed to Woman Suffrage (NAOWS)

National American Woman Suffrage Association (NAWSA): alliances with organizations, 48–49; Congressional Committee, 130–131, 139, 141, 146; convention in Southern states, 42–43; conventions, 43–44, 52–53, 63–64, 75, 76, 104, 140–142; Emergency Convention, 190–191; films produced, 117; Golden Jubilee Convention, 303; hiss incident at 1910 convention, 86; intensified efforts to pass federal amendment, 287; lack of protest regarding arrests, 237; merging of NWSA and AWSA, 36; National Press Bureau, 78; new presidency, 178–179; nonpartisan policy, 107, 265; petitioning Congress, 265; policy on state affiliates, 191; pressure on Wilson, 190; Rankin at headquarters, *212*; ratification campaigns, 311–312; relationship with Congressional Union (CU), 167, 179–180; relationship with NWP, 341; relocation of headquarters, 81; resolution to seek federal amendment, 74; state-by-state strategy, 281, 283–284, 346; suffrage parade in the rain, 186; targeting of Democratic candidates, 177–178; Victory Convention, 325–326. *See also* Anthony, Susan B.; Catt, Carrie Chapman (née Lane); Shaw, Anna Howard; Stanton, Elizabeth Cady

National Association for the Advancement of Colored People (NAACP), *132,* 193, 208, 345

National Association Opposed to Woman Suffrage (NAOWS), 105, 148, 174, 242, 332. *See also* Dodge, Josephine Jewell

National Constitution Center, 7–8

National Convention of Woman Voters, 167–168, 169, 177

National Federation of Afro-American Women, 49

National Union of Women's Suffrage Societies (NUWSS), 147

National Woman's Party (NWP): banner at Republican National Convention, *331*; complaint filed by, 251; criticized by NAWSA, 295–296; on false claim of universal suffrage in America, 230;

formation of, 209; head of, *82*; headquarters attacked, 292; persistence of, 271–272; pressure on Wilson for Senate passage, 304; ratification campaigns, 311–312, 335; role in winning the fight, 346; view of Wilson's speech to Congress, 287. *See also* Belmont, Alva; Burns, Lucy; Havemeyer, Louisine; Lewis, Dora Kelly; Malone, Maud; Martin, Anne; Paul, Alice; Stevens, Doris; Vernon, Mabel; Younger, Maud

National Woman's Party of Western Women Voters (Woman's Party), 183

National Woman Suffrage Association (NWSA), 21, 27, 31–32, 34. *See also* National American Woman Suffrage Association (NAWSA)

National Women's Rights Conventions, 1, 14, 15, 16, 17

Native Americans, 15, 39, 119, 154, 344–345

NAWSA. *See* National American Woman Suffrage Association (NAWSA)

Nebraska: ratification of the Nineteenth Amendment, 317; suffrage campaigns, 150, 152–153, 222–223, 225

Nebraska Men's Association Opposed to Woman Suffrage, 152

Nelson, Alice Dunbar, 173

Nelson, Julie B., 88

Netherlands, woman suffrage bill in, 292

Nevada: ratification of the Nineteenth Amendment, 323; suffrage campaign in, 150, 157

Nevison, Henry, 92–93

New Departure strategy, 27–28, 29

New England Woman Suffrage Association, 14

New Hampshire: ratification of the Nineteenth Amendment, 317–318; suffrage campaign in, 60, 220–221

New Jersey: ratification of the Nineteenth Amendment, 323, 324; suffrage campaigns, 158, 160–163, 171–172; voting rights in the colony, 6–7; women's voting rights in, 171

New Jersey Association Opposed to Woman Suffrage, 171

New Mexico: clause in state constitution, 92; ratification of the Nineteenth Amendment, 323, 325; suffrage campaign in, 87

New York (state): constitutional convention, 18–19; ratification of Nineteenth Amendment, 313; suffrage campaigns, 41–42, 143, 158, 159, 162–163, 166, 171, 174–175, 255–256

New York Times anti-suffrage editorials, 98, 108

Nicholes, S. Grace, 123

"Night of Terror," 258–260; forgotten story, vii; publicity and aftermath, 262–263

Nineteenth Amendment. *See* federal woman suffrage amendment; ratification of Nineteenth Amendment

Nolan, Mary, 257, 259, 262, 265, 293

Nonpartisan League (NPL), 216

Norbeck, Peter, 320

Nordica, Lillian (Madame), 93, 94, 102–103

North Carolina: ratification of the Nineteenth Amendment, 333, 335–336, 337

North Dakota: ratification of the Nineteenth Amendment, 320; resolution urging Senate 'yes' vote, 273; suffrage campaign in, 150, 154–155, 216, 225

North Dakota Association Opposed to Woman Suffrage, 155

Noyes, Ruth Astor, 148, *149,* 150

NUWSS. *See* National Union of Women's Suffrage Societies (NUWSS)

NWP. *See* National Woman's Party (NWP)

NWSA. *See* National Woman Suffrage Association (NWSA)

Oates, William C., 36

O'Brien, Matthew, 261, 264

Ocasio-Cortez, Alexandria, 351–352

Occoquan workhouse: harsh treatment and abuse at, 245; historic marker at, x; increased sentences at, 243; Night of Terror, 258–260; November 14th prisoners, 258–259; picketers demand treatment as political prisoners, 246–247; picketers' imprisonment at, 235, 236–237, 241; riot in, 249–251; senator's visit to, 244; "The Truth About Occoquan" lecture tour, 243; unsanitary conditions at, 241–242

Ohio: debate on women's voting rights, 12–13; history of legislative consideration of woman suffrage, 111; presidential suffrage, 303–304; ratification of the Nineteenth Amendment, 313, 321, 332; suffrage campaigns, 112, 150–151, 218, 225

Ohio Supreme Court ruling on Prohibition Amendment, 321, 331–332

Oklahoma: initiative and referendum vote in, 88–89; ratification of the Nineteenth Amendment, 323, 325; removal of term *male* from voter qualifications, 282; suffrage campaign in, 279, 281

Oklahoma Anti-Suffrage Association, 282

Oklahoma Woman's Suffrage Association, 281

Older, Cora Miranda Baggerly, 169

Olzendam, Lillian, 330

The Omaha Bee on Doris Stevens's arrest, 235–236

Omar, Ilhan, 351

The Suffragists on Night of Terror, 262

open-air meetings, 69–71, *70,* 72–73

Oregon: ratification of the Nineteenth Amendment, 323; referendum and suffrage campaigns, 63, 65, 111, 118–119

Oregon Equal Suffrage Association, 63

Oregon Equal Suffrage Association (OESA), 118

Orleck, Annelise, 80

Osborn, Chase, 116, 121

Osselaer, Heidi, 113

O'Sullivan, Mary Kenney, 58

Otero-Warren, Adelina "Nina": after the fight for the vote, 349; organizer, 87

"Our Right is Might" (song, Walsh), 120
Ovington, Mary White, 344, 345
Owen, Marie Bankhead, 315

Palmer, Alexander M., 146
Pankhurst, Christabel, 56, 83, 85, 97, 146–147
Pankhurst, Emmeline: arrest of, 142; assault on, 69, 92–93; film appearance, 117; founder of Women's Franchise League with husband Richard, 56; founding of Women's Social and Political Union (WSPU), 56, 69; Freedom or Death speech, 140; her own story, 375n12; Holloway Prison Medal, 79; in Missouri, 151; New York attempt to refuse entry to, 139; presentation of medal to Paul and Brown, 84; speaking tour in New York City, 77–79; on tour in America, 104–105; war work, 146–147
Pankhurst, Sylvia: American lecture tour, 94–95, 96; break with mother and sister, 147; design of brooch, 79; mentioned, 56; in Missouri, 151; objection to age limit for woman suffrage, 213; partial victory, 266; second American tour, 154, 216
Park, Alice, 113
Park, Maud Wood: after the fight for the vote, 347; on Anne Dallas Dudley, 217; on anti-suffragist tactics, 54; astonished at lack of interest in woman suffrage, 52; on the brink of success, 267, 268; on Catt's convictions, 209; at congressional debates and votes, 245, 269–270, 273, 278, 299, 305, 306, 307–308; federal campaign, 304; handshake with Mann, 307; letter writing campaign, 287; at NAWSA's Emergency Convention, 191; on Rankin's "no" vote for war, 214–215; on ratification opposition, 321; on Rhode Island victory, 222; role in federal woman suffrage passage, *306*; on Senator Smoot, 284–285; teasing of Catt, 227
partial suffrage, 114; campaigns in 1917, 216; Illinois, 125; Louisiana, 46–47; mixed value of, 54
patriarchal systems, 4
Patterson, Frances Baker, 100
Patterson, Hannah, 189
Paul, Alice: about, *82,* 82–83; after Night of Terror, 264–265; arrests and imprisonment, 251–252, 301; assault on, 239; with banner displayed at RNC, *331*; banner stunt at Wilson speech, 200; campaign for federal woman suffrage, 143; campaign to burn Wilson's words, 287–288, 289–292, *290*; Congressional Union (CU) as national organization, 167; death of, 351; on delay tactics, 328; and Democratic Party, 148; encouragement of suffragists, 226; on England's example, 213; Equal Rights Amendment, 347; formation of Woman's Party, 183; on harsh treatment, 255; hunger strike in jail, 253, 291; inviting picketers, 256; at NAWSA, 86; new publicity campaign, 243–244; persistence of, 166, 202, 246, 271–272, 278; picketing activities, 204, 206, 229, 231, 271, 284–285, 286, 300–301; planning ratification campaign, 307,

308; pressure on politicians, 138–139, 190, 214, 304; pressure on states, 318; principle of nonpartisanship, 180; Prison Special, 294; in psychopathic ward, 253–254; ratification campaigns, 311–312, 319, 320, 324, *339*; report to NAWSA, 140–141; role in winning the fight, 346; scheduling of Woman's Party convention, 185; silent tribute to, 211; suffrage activities in England, 83–84; unity in suffrage movement, 209; Woman Suffrage Procession, 129–131

Paul, Helen, 253, 254

Pearson, Josephine Anderson, 335, 344

Peck, Annie Smith, 108

Peck, Mary Gray, 208, 318–319

Pelosi, Nancy, 352

Pennsylvania: ratification of the Nineteenth Amendment, 313; suffrage campaigns, 143, 158, 162–163, 164–165, 171, 172–173

Pennsylvania Association Opposed to Woman Suffrage, 305–306

Penrose, Sarah, 344

Peters, Laura E., 55–56

Pethick-Lawrence, Emmeline, 208–209

Pethick-Lawrence, Frederick, 147

Petition for Universal Suffrage, 16

petitions, 8, 16, 74, 87, 139, 168–169, 176, 218, 324

Phillips, Wendell, 17

Pickens, William, 345

picketing, legality of, 271

picketing of Congress, 284–285, *285*

picketing the White House: Bastille Day demonstration and arrests, 235–237; Catt's request to Paul, 228; continued picketing despite risks, 248–249; as forgotten story, vii; Independence Day arrests, 233–235; Kaiser Wilson banner riot and arrests, 238–242; November 2017, 256–257; Russian banner incident, 229–231; vigilance of women, 204–208, *206,* 212; during war, 229

Pierce, Juno Frankie, 333–334

Pierce, Vivian, 316, 319

Pierson, Emily, 140, 222

Pincus, Jane, 149, *149,* 150

Pittman, Key, 189, 277

police assault on picketers, 239–240, 285, 286, 300–301

political buying and trading: role in length of suffrage fight, 345

Political Equality Association (PEA), 81

Political Equality League (PEL), 219

political parties, responsibility for federal suffrage, 130

political power of women, vii–viii, 167, 346, 351

political prisoner status, demand for, 246–247, *248,* 258, 260

politics as male domain, 4–5

Pollitzer, Anita, 318, 320

Pollock, Robert M., 216

Ponder, Henry, 316
Postcard Day, 102
Pou, Edward, 228–229, 244
Pratt, Nelson S., 76
Presidential and Municipal Suffrage Bill (Illinois), 126–128
presidential suffrage, 129, 216, 219, 222, 303–304
prison brutality, 253–254, 275
Prisoner's Temporary Discharge of Ill Health Act, dubbed the "Cat and Mouse Act, 140
prison experiences of suffragists, 232–233, 236–237, 241–242, 245, 248–249, 258–261, 275, 296–297, 299
prison reform, 85, 86
Prison Special (train, "The Democracy Limited"), 294, 297–298
Progressive Party, 106
Progressivism, 57
Prohibition Amendment, 321
prohibition and states' argument against suffrage, 265–266
Pryor, Margaret, 19
public attention, garnering, 67–78; banner and press releases at Wilson speech, 200–201; biplane stunt, 200. *See also* "Golden Lane" strategy; Suffrage Special (train); transcontinental suffrage tours
public outcry against arrests, prison conditions, and force feeding, 237, 241–242, 254, 275, 297
Pugh, Sara, 58
Pullman, Raymond W., 231–232, 240
Purvis, Harriet Forten and Margarette, 15
Pyle, Mary Shields, 153–154, 320

Quakers, 83
Quay, Mary "Minnie," 258
Queen Bee (newspaper), 40

racial discrimination, 132–133, 134, 135, 191–192, 198–199, 335. *See also* abolitionists; class prejudice; segregation; white supremacy
racism: factor in ratification fights, 315; tactics appealing to, 42–43; in touting passage of federal suffrage amendment, 309
radicalization of suffragists, 251
Raker, John E., 267, 268
Randolph, Florence Spearing, 172
Rankin, Jeannette: candidate for House of Representatives, 197; candidate for Senate, 284; as congresswoman, 199, 211–212, 269–270, 349; leader of anti-war march, 349–350; at NAWSA headquarters, *212*; in New Hampshire, 220; suffragist work in Washington and Montana, 156, 162; war vote, 214–215; women as a force, 144
Ratavitch, Marya, 301
ratification banner, *339*

ratification certificates, 310, 340

ratification flag, 341

ratification of the Nineteenth Amendment: date ratified, 1; initial votes, 310–316; last state to ratify, 333–340; newspaper publicity and national celebration, 341–342; signing ceremony, 340–341; suffragists begin fight for, 309; votes from August to December 1919, 316–321; votes in January and February, 1920, 322–325; votes in March 1920, 327–329; Western states and special sessions, 316; won by two votes, vii

Reagon, John, 37

Rector, Kenyon Hayden, 322, 331, *331*

Redmond, Harriet "Hattie," 118, *353*

Remond, Charles, 20

Representation of the People Act (England), 270

Representation of the People (Equal Suffrage) Act 1928, 350

Republican Party: credit for suffrage, 305; national convention, 186–187, *331*; presidential primary, 106

Reuter, Josephine, 71

The Revolution, 21, 22

Reyneau, Betsy Graves, 235–237, 349

Reynolds, James, 218

Reynolds, Minnie, 172

Rhode Island: ratification of the Nineteenth Amendment, 322; suffrage campaign in, 221–222, 225

Rhode Island Woman Suffrage Association, 221–222

Richardson, Dee, 230, 231

Richardson, Grace, 223

Richardson, Nell, 183, 185

Richberg-Hornsby, Leda, 200, 258, 260

Ricker, Marilla, 28

Riddick, T. K., 337

Riddle, Agnes, 321

Riggs, John Andrew, 219

"river of fire," 119–120

Roberts, Albert, 335, 340

Robinson, Helen Ring, 147

Roby, Henry W., 76

Roessing, Jennie Bradley, 172–173, 189, 190

Rogers, Elizabeth Selden, 207, 279, 288, 309

Rogers, John R., 56

Roland, Pauline, 35

Rollin, Charlotte "Lottie," 22

Rollin, Louisa, 22

Roosevelt, Theodore, 106

Rose, Ernestine (née Ernestine Louise Potowska), 9, 14, 15

Rowe, Clara Louis, *263*

Ruffin, Josephine St. Pierre, 49

Ruschenberger, Katherine Wentworth, x, 164–165, *165,* 343

Russian banner, 229–230

Russia's enfranchisement of women, 212–213

Sacajawea, dedication of statue, 63

Samarodin, Nina, 244

Sams, Murray, 332

The San Francisco Call prediction of victory, 104

Sargent, Aaron Augustus, 33

Sargent, Ellen Clark, 45

Saxon, Elizabeth Lyle, 47

Schneiderman, Rose, 67, 73

Schuler, Marjorie, 282

Schuler, Nettie Rogers: *Woman Suffrage and Politics: The Inner Story of the Suffrage Movement,* 345

Schuyler, Margaretta, 300–301

Schwarz, Florence Goff, 151

Schwimmer, Rosika, 208–209

Scott, Charles L., 126

segregation, 192–193. *See also* racial discrimination

Senate: campaigns for passage of amendment, 33–34, 272–278, 304; revised suffrage amendment blocked, 299–300; votes on suffrage amendments, 34, 146, 273, 277–278, 296, 307–309

Senate Woman Suffrage Committee, 227

Seneca Falls, New York, ix, 11–12, 72

Seneca Falls Women's Rights Convention, 11–12

settlement houses, 57

Seventeenth Amendment, 143

Shafroth, John F., 146

Shafroth-Palmer Amendment, 158

Shafroth-Palmer Resolution, 146

Sharp, Evelyn, 147

Shaw, Anna Howard: after House passage of amendment, 270; after Night of Terror, 262–263; criticism of OESA, 118; death of, 314–315; epigraph, 181; eulogy for Susan B. Anthony, 65; film appearance, 117; honorary gavel to, 76; on House debate of suffrage, 166; letter to Taft, 87; NAWSA convention, 177; on Oregon vote, 66; on picketing the White House, 207; pressure on Wilson, 192; role in NAWSA, 51, 60–61, 158, 178–179; on Russian banner, 231; state campaigning, 63, 153, 156; statue of, *61;* thanking Wilson, 255; on tribute to Susan B. Anthony, 62; use of martial language, 72; view of militant tactics, 141; young women at NAWSA convention, 177

Shaw, George Bernard, 68

Sherman, Ellen Ewing, 33

Sherwood, Grace, 221

Shields, Lucille, 234, 293
"Ship of State," 165–166
Shout the Revolution of Women (song), 249
Shuler, Marjorie, 317–318, 333
Shuler, Nettie Rogers, 281, 282, 283, 287
Silent Sentinels, 204–208, *206*
Silver, Clara, 67
Sims, Thetus, 268–269, 270
Sixteenth Amendment, 33–34, 42, 46, 129, 143
slavery, speeches against, 8–9, 13. *See also* Thirteenth Amendment
Smith, Alfred E., 341–342
Smith, Judith Winsor, 344
Smith, Julia and Abby, 24, 33
Smyth, Ethel, 145
Socialist Party of America, 59
socialist support, 89
society plan, 40, 48
Solomons, Selina, 99, 104
songs of suffrage movement, 53; collection of, 76; composed, 32, 97, 120, 145, 169, 174, 249, 258; new lyrics to familiar tune, 18; patriotic songs, 103, 185; prisoners' songs, 249; Woman's Marseillaise, 288, 298
South Carolina: black woman registration, 345; ratification of the Nineteenth Amendment, 323
South Carolina Woman's Suffrage Association (SCWSA), 22
South Dakota: ratification of the Nineteenth Amendment, 320; suffrage campaigns, 39, 89, 150, 153–154, 197, 199, 279, 283
Southern States Woman Suffrage Conference (SSWSC), 280
Spanish flu, effect on American society, 279, 280, 281–282
Spencer, Paul and Caroline, 252
Spokane, Washington, festivities at, 75–76
Sproul, William, 313, 342
Spruill, Marjorie Julian, 329
Squire, Belle, 131, 133
Stafford, Kate, 258, 282
Stanton, Elizabeth Cady: campaigning in New York, 17–19; commemoration of Seneca Falls conference, 35; death of, 54; Declaration of Sentiments and Resolutions, 11–12, 32; "Educated Suffrage," 53; fight against Fifteenth Amendment, 21; fight against Fourteenth Amendment, 18; first meeting with Mott and first women's rights convention, 11; first meeting with Susan B. Anthony, 15, 16; founding of ICW, 62; founding of NWSA, 21; on Grimké sisters and Theodore Weld, 10; merging of NWSA and AWSA, 22; at National Woman's Rights Convention, 14; at NAWSA convention, 36, 49; on New York failure, 41–42; pin with her image, 110, *110*; plaque honoring resolution, ix–x; racist and xenophobic diatribes, 21;

relationship with Victoria Woodhull, 26–27; resolution presented at convention, 1; role in Beecher-Tilton Affair, 27; speaking in support of Senate committee, 33; statue of, 352; suspension of efforts during war, 16, 229; tribute to Douglass, 43; use of martial language, 72; on Wyoming's equal suffrage, 37

Stanton, Henry, 10, 11, 12

state-by-state strategy, 129, 187, 188, 189, 346

states' rights, 280, 299–300, 329, 332, 335

state suffrage campaigns. *See* individual states

state suffrage map, *220,* 221

Stephens, Adelia, 89

Stevens, Doris: after the fight, 349; arrests and imprisonment, *234,* 235–237, 251, 256, 301; banners' messages, 231; campaigning against Democratic candidates, 148; display of new woman feminism, 204; at Lafayette Monument, 288; picketing Wilson at Metropolitan Opera House, 300–301; police assault on suffragists, 239; role in NWP, 209; on suffragists after Night of Terror, 263; train tour, *149,* 150; on Wilson's appeal to Senate, 277; on women ignored by Wilson, 211; writ of habeas corpus, 261

Stevens, William B., 319

Stewart, Ella S., 123

Stewart, Maria, 9

Stoddard, Helen M., 283

Stone, Lucy, 13, 16, 18, 20, 21, 36, 38

strikes, 80–81. *See also* hunger strikes

Strong, J. F. A., 138

Stubbs, Jessie Hardy, 121, 144, 149, *149,* 150, 348

Stuyvesant, Elizabeth, 233, 238–240

suffrage colors and ribbons, 18, 147, 160

Suffrage Day, 144–145

Suffrage Emergency Corps, 330, 332

suffrage flag, 43–44, 53

suffrage novelties and ephemera, 164, 172–173

suffrage parades: Boone, IA, 71; Boston, 173; first large scale parade, 88; New York City, 71–72, 96–98, *98,* 107–108, 119–120, 143, 171, 175–176; Oakland, CA, 71; Republican National Convention, 186; Washington, D.C., xi, 129, 130, 131–132

suffrage pilgrimage, 121–122, *134,* 134–136

suffrage renaissance, 48

suffrage schools, 175, 283

The Suffrage Song Book: Original Songs, Parodies and Paraphrases (Roby, 1909), 76

Suffrage Special (train), 183–184

suffragette, coining and use of term, 56, 131

Suffragist: about, 141; describing Emory meeting Maryland governor, 312 suffragists: characteristics of, ix, 47, 121, 126, 171, 185, 205, 209, 346; defenses against assault, 138; modern tribute to, 351–352; projection of respectability, 14; redefining feminine behavior, 54, 97; tactics and strategies, ix, 68, 77, 130, 140–141, 163–164, 346–347. *See also* activism and protest; Anthony, Susan B.; Belmont, Alva; Blatch, Harriot Stanton; Burns, Lucy; Catt, Carrie Chapman (née Lane); Chan, S. K.; Cooper, Anna Julia; Havemeyer, Louisine; Hunkins, Hazel (later Hunkins Hallinan); Jones, Rosalie Gardiner; Lee, Mabel Ping-Hua; Lewis, Dora Kelly; Malone, Maud; Martin, Anne; Meredith, Ellis; Milholland, Inez (later, Boissevain); Otero-Warren, Adelina "Nina"; Pankhurst, Emmeline; Pankhurst, Sylvia; Park, Maud Wood; Paul, Alice; Rankin, Jeannette; Ruffin, Josephine St. Pierre; Shaw, Anna Howard; Stanton, Elizabeth Cady; Stevens, Doris; Talbert, Mary Burnett; Terrell, Mary Church; Truth, Sojourner; Vernon, Mabel; Wells-Barnett, Ida B.; Williams, Frances "Fannie" Barrier; Younger, Maud

Sullivan, James, 5

Sumney, Katherine, 223

Supreme Court Appellate Division, New York, 111

Susan B. Anthony Amendment, 74

Susan B. Anthony Museum and House, x

Susan B. Anthony pageant, 177

Swain, Louisa, 352

Swing, Raymond Gram, 350

Taft, Lydia, 5, 352

Taft, William Howard, 86–87, 106

Talbert, Mary Burnett, *311*

Tarbell, Ida, 185–186

tax matters, voting on, 47

Taylor, Belle Grey, 71

telephone brigade, 127

temperance movement, 15, 48, 89, 218

Tennessee: presidential suffrage, 303, 304; ratification of the Nineteenth Amendment, 333, 336, 337–339; suffrage campaign in, 216–217

Tennessee Association Opposed to Woman Suffrage, 335

Tennessee League of Women Voters (TLWV) convention, 333–334

Terrell, Mary Church: about, 49–51, *50*; after the fight for the vote, 350; German Suffrage Conference, 62–63; marching, 137, 208; picketing, 208

territories. *See* individual state names

Texas: ratification of the Nineteenth Amendment, 313, 314; suffrage campaign in, 279, 283

theatrical shows in support of woman suffrage, 101

Thirteenth Amendment, 16

Thompson, Grace, 238

Thompson, Lily Wilkinson, 329

Thurman, Lucinda, 49

Tibbles, C. F., *Business Versus Woman Suffrage,* 116

Toledo Woman Suffrage Association, 30

Topping, Lucille, 156

Torch of Liberty, 159, *161,* 161–162

trade unionism, 73

Train, George Francis, 21

transcontinental suffrage tours, 176, 183, 185

Trax, Lola Carson, 149, 150

Treadwell, Harriette Taylor, 127

Triangle Shirtwaist Factory fire, 95–96

Trout, Grace Wilbur, 123–124, 125–128, 131, 132–133, 138

Truth, Sojourner: attempt to vote, 28; on fight for women's rights, 20; memorabilia, 195; statue of, 352

Tubman, Harriet, 352

tugboat publicity in Hudson River, 160–161

Turner, Banks, 338–339

Turning Point Suffragist Memorial, 352

Underwood, Oscar, 278, 307

United Liquor Dealers Association head, 127

United States Constitution: First Amendment, use in seeking the right to vote, 8; Thirteenth Amendment, 16; Fourteenth Amendment, 17–18, 329; Fifteenth Amendment, 20; Sixteenth Amendment, 33–34, 42, 46, 129, 143; Seventeenth Amendment, 143; Eighteenth Amendment (Prohibition), 265, 321; Nineteenth Amendment (*See* ratification of Nineteenth Amendment); Bill of Rights, 8; Equal Rights Amendment, 347, 351; insertion of *male,* 17–19; writing and ratification of, 7–8

United States Federal Appeals Court, 271

United States Senate Committee on Privileges and Elections, 33

United States Supreme Court: on appeal of Ohio court ruling, 331–332; *Minor v. Happersett,* 28, 29; on Nineteenth Amendment, 341

Uprising of 20,000, 80–81

Upton, Harriet Taylor, 112, 151, 321, 326–327

Utah: ratification of the Nineteenth Amendment, 318; recognition for equal suffrage, 44; woman suffrage before statehood, 24

Valentine, Lila Meade, 325

Valentine's Day barrage to congressmen, 181

Vanderbilt, Cornelius, 26

Van Winkle, Mina A., 160–162, 172

Vassar College, 72–73

Vermont: delay of special session, 330; ratification of the Nineteenth Amendment, 332; suffrage campaign in, 221, 225

Vernon, Mabel: after the fight, 349; arrest and imprisonment, 232–233; asking for contributions, 298; banner stunt at Wilson speech, 200; challenge to Wilson, 190; description of, 171; description of Alice Paul, 168; in NWP, 209; picketing the White House, 232; ratification campaigns, 315; response to attacks on picketers, 231; welcoming events, 171

Vervane, Elsie, 292

Vest, George G., 34, 37

Villard, Fanny Garrison, 208

Virginia: ratification of the Nineteenth Amendment, 325; suffrage campaign, 60

voter registration denied, 28, 29, 345

Votes for Women Club, 99

Votes for Women League, 154

"Votes for Women," origin of slogan, 56

voting rights: in the American colonies, 5; based on citizenship, 53, 283, 344–345; efforts to curtail, 345; enfranchisement and disenfranchisement of women, 6–7; fight not over, 346–347; first demand by Margaret Brent, 3; how woman suffrage fight was won, 346; importance of, viii; as tool of self-government, 57. *See also* woman suffrage movement

Waddill, Edmund, Jr., 263–264

Wage Earners' Suffrage League (WESL), 81, 101

Wagner, Sally Roesch, 15

Wainwright, Evelyn Wotherspoon, 276

Waldo, George, 115–116

Walker, Seth, 337, 338–339, 340

Wall, Louise Herrick, 103

Wallace, Zerelda G., 218

Walsh, Joseph, 244

Walsh, Minnie C. E., 120

Walton Gaol, 85–86

Warren, Lindsay, 337

Warren, Mercy Otis, 6

Washington (state): ratification of the Nineteenth Amendment, 328; suffrage campaigns, 55, 75, 90–92; woman suffrage before statehood, 7

Washington, Jesse, lynching of, 193

Washington, Joseph E., 36

Washington Women's Cook Book (DeVoe and Hutton, 1906), 90

Washington Women's Right to Vote Amendment, 56, 92

Watchfires of Freedom, 289–292

Watkins, Gertrude, 158, 162

Watson, Elizabeth Lowe, 98–99

Watson, James Eli, 307

Watson, Madeleine, 239, 240–241, *241*, 243

Watts, R. H., 329

Way, Amanda, 218

Weaver, Carrie and Eva, 292

Webb, Edwin Y., 182, 227–228

Weed, Helena Hill: after the fight for the vote, 349; arrest, 234; organizer, 149; watchfire, 289

Weeks, Cora, 258

Weible, Mary Darrow, 216

Weil, Mathilde C., 28–29

Weld, Theodore, 10

Welling, Milton, 318

Wells, Bettina Borrmann, 69, 71–72

Wells, Emmeline B., 44

Wells-Barnett, Ida B.: about, 131; after the fight for the vote, 349; discrimination, 132–133; issue with Anthony, 42–43, *132*

Wentworth, Catherine, 343

WESL. *See* Wage Earners' Suffrage League (WESL)

West, Oswald, 119

"Western invasion," 194

West Virginia: ratification of the Nineteenth Amendment, 327–328; suffrage campaign in, 197, 198–199

What 80 Million Women Want (film), 117

Wheeler, Jesse Spruill, 329

White, Armenia and Nathaniel, 220

White, Ruth, 213

White, Sarah C., 282, 313

White, Sue Shelton, 294, 315, *331*, 335

white clothing: as symbol of suffrage fight, 76, 79, 96, 120; worn by recent female politicians, 351–352

Whitehouse, Florence Brooks, 319

Whitehouse, Vira Boarman, 163

white outfits as tribute, 351–352

white supremacy, 53–54, 207, 280, 309

Whittaker, Raymond, 237, 242, 245, 251, 258–260, 261, 263–264

Whittemore, Margaret Fay, 149, 224–225, 233

Wiley, Anna Kelton, 258, 288

Willard, Frances, 48

Williams, Frances "Fannie" Barrier, 65

Williams, John Sharp, 277, 296

Willis, Portia, 186

Wilson, Bird May, 156

Wilson, Edith, 192

Wilson, Woodrow: about, 107; actions after Night of Terror, 262; congratulations to Roberts, 340; eschews party leadership role, 109, 190, 203; events to get Wilson's attention and action, 130, 199–200,

207–208, 300–301; headed to Paris Peace Conference, 286; at NAWSA's Emergency Convention, 192; nominated for reelection, 189; NWP's disdain for, 249; presentation of petition to, 176–177; pressure on, 190, 194; response to imprisonment of suffragists, 139, 237; response to suffragists' deputations, demonstrations, and petitions, 138–139, 202–203, 210–211, 275–277; secures a senator's vote, 109, 304–305; support for creation of House Woman Suffrage Committee, 228; support for federal suffrage amendment, 217, 268, 277, 287, 304; supports ratification of the Nineteenth Amendment, 315, 333; supports segregation, 192–193; witnesses attacks on picketers, 239

"The Winning Plan," 191–192

Winslow, Rose, 148, *149*, 150, 194, 252, 253, 254

Winsor, Mary, 242–243, 247, *248*, 249, 251, 275

Winston, Kate, 291

Wisconsin: first certified ratification of Nineteenth Amendment, 310; presidential suffrage, 303–304; suffrage referendum, 111

Wisconsin Women's Suffrage Referendum, 115

Wise, Stephen S., 108

Wold, Clara, 286

Wollstonecraft, Mary: *A Vindication of the Rights of Woman*, 8, 35

The Woman Citizen (formerly the *Woman's Journal*), 276–277

Woman's Era, 49

Woman's Journal: on Catt's rallying of suffragists, 182; founders of, 22; on Idaho victory, 45

Woman's Party of Western Women Voters (Woman's Party), 183, 185–186, 188, 193, 194, 209

Woman's Peace Party, 209

Woman Suffrage and Politics: The Inner Story of the Suffrage Movement (Catt and Schuler), 345

Woman Suffrage Association of Missouri, 22–23

The Woman Suffrage Cook Book (Burr, 1886), 90

woman suffrage movement: emblem of, 159, *161*; establishment of suffrage organizations, 21–22; first federal and state campaigns, 17–21; the first two hundred years, 1–16; as forgotten story, vii; garnering public attention 1907–1909, 67–77; lessons from, 353; literature about, vii; literature and memorabilia, ix; nineteenth century victories and disappointments, 33–51; perseverance in the fight 1900–1906, 52–66; strikes, militancy, and continued fight 1909–1910, 78–93; whirlwind events of 1911, 94–105. *See also* activism and protest; anti-suffrage campaign; arrests and imprisonment; class prejudice; Congressional Union (CU); federal woman suffrage amendment; international efforts for woman suffrage; landmarks and monuments to; National American Woman Suffrage Association (NAWSA); National Woman's Party (NWP); racism; suffragists; women's rights; individual states

Woman Suffrage Procession (March 3, 1913), 129, 130, 131–132, *136,* 136–137
women did not want the vote: claims of, 33, 41, 54, 100, 153, 186, 225, 225; Greeley's belief, 19; repudiation of claim, 63, 255
women in government, 41, 148, 316, 319, 351–352
Women's Association Opposed to Woman Suffrage, 99
"Women's Campaign Train," 192–193
women's clubs, 48
women's equality, 8–10, 9, 10
Women's Equality Day parade, 351
Women's Franchise League, 56
Women's Freedom League and the United Suffragists, 147
Women's Liberty Bell. *See* Justice Bell
Women's Loyal National League, 16
Women's Political Union (WPU), 107, 159–160, 184
women's polling places, 68, 73–74
women's rights: based on citizenship, 22–23; under colonial law, 4; conventions, 11–15; criticism of poking fun, 15; other than voting rights, 124; property rights, 9; right to speak in public, 8–10; Wollstonecraft's writing, 8. *See also* voting rights; woman suffrage movement
Women's Rights National Historical Park, ix
women's roles in society, ix; role in length of suffrage fight, 346
Women's Social and Political Union (WSPU), 56, 84, 129, 130, 146–147
Women's Trade Union League (WTUL), 58
women's victories in 2018 midterm elections, 351–352
women voters, a power, 121, 129, 158, 183, 344, 351
Woodhull, Victoria Claflin, 25–28, *26;* "Free Lover," 27
Woodhull & Claflin Weekly: Beecher-Tilton Affair, 27; financing of, 26
Woolley, Mary E., 147
working women and the vote, 57–58, 67, 73, 80–81, 96, 118, 184. *See also* Uprising of 20,000
World Anti-Slavery Convention, 10, 58
World War I, effect on suffrage movement, 146–147, 208–209, 215
Wright, Frances "Fanny," 8–9
Wright, Martha Coffin, 11
W.S. Holbrook (tugboat), 159, 160, *161*
WSPU. *See* Women's Social and Political Union (WSPU)
WTUL. *See* Women's Trade Union League (WTUL)
Wyoming: ratification of the Nineteenth Amendment, 323; recognition for equal suffrage, 43–44; woman suffrage before statehood, 24, 36–37
xenophobia, 53
Yost, Lenna Lowe, 198
Youmans, Theodora Winton, 115, 306, 310, 326
Young, Joy, 234, 297–298
Young, Matilda, 257, 291, 293

Young, Rose, 276–277

Younger, Maud: after congressional passage of amendment, 308–309; after the fight, 347, *348*; applauding Paul, 265; campaigning against Democratic candidates, 194; campaign to win Senate vote, 272; card index of state information, 311–312; description of, 101; eulogy at Milholland memorial, 197; excitement of women at Senate vote, 308; handed Wilson resolutions, 202–203; keynote speech, 185; role in NWP, 209, 268; on Senate deliberation of amendment, 277, 278; in suffrage parade, 101; testifying before Rules Committee, 228–229; took Jones to view prison conditions, 275; women's political power, 303

Zinkhan, Louis, 254, 263

Made in the USA
Middletown, DE
20 January 2020

83471986R00249